Violence on Television

Television is often accused of showing too much violence. However, it is rare that anyone stops to ask what this statement means. *Violence on Television* provides an objective analysis of the violence on television, how much there is and what form it takes.

It presents findings from the largest ever study of the depiction of violence on television carried out in Britain, funded by the British Broadcasting Corporation and the Independent Television Commission. As well as presenting a quantitative analysis of the amount of violence on television, this research places great emphasis on investigating the character of violent portrayals and the contexts in which they occur.

Barrie Gunter and Jackie Harrison present a detailed literature review, which examines previous research from around the world. They then explain the methodology and look at the problems of measuring and quantifying violence on television. They examine the specific attributes of violence, including the form it takes, its physical setting, its motives and consequences, and the nature of the characters involved as either aggressors or victims. They also examine the amount and nature of violent portrayals in different programme genres, such as films and drama, entertainment programming, news and factual programmes, and children's programmes.

The book will be of interest to students and researchers in psychology, communication studies and media studies.

Barrie Gunter is Professor of Journalism Studies at the University of Sheffield and has previously worked as head of research at both the Independent Television Commission and the Independent Broadcasting Authority. His previous publications include *Children and Television* (1990, 2nd edition 1997, with Jill McAleer) and *The Anatomy of Adolescence* (1989, with Adrian Furnham). **Jackie Harrison** is Lecturer in Journalism Studies at the University of Sheffield.

Routledge Progress in Psychology

Violence on Television

An analysis of amount, nature, location and origin of violence in British programmes

Barrie Gunter and Jackie Harrison

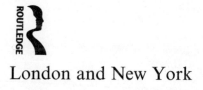

London and New York

First published 1998
by Routledge
11 New Fetter Lane, London EC4P 4EE

Simultaneously published in the USA and Canada
by Routledge
29 West 35th Street, New York, NY 10001

Typeset in Times by Pure Tech India Ltd, Pondicherry
Printed and bound in Great Britain by TJ International Ltd, Padstow, Cornwall

British Library Cataloguing in Publication Data
A catalogue record for this book is available from the British Library

Library of Congress cataloguing in Publication Data
Gunter, Barrie.
    Violence on television: an analysis of amount, nature, location,
and origin of violence in British programmes/Barrie Gunter and
Jackie Harrison.
        p.   cm.
    Includes bibliographical references and index.
    1. Violence in television–Great Britain.   I. Harrison, Jackie,
1961–   . II. Title.
PN1992.8.V55G86   1998
303.6'0941–dc21   97–23330

ISBN 0-415-17260-8

Contents

Tables

1 Introduction

Concern about violence on television can be traced back to the earliest days of the medium. In fact, this concern has its roots in the unease that is expressed about any new entertainment medium which appeals to the masses. Such reactions were reported with the appearance of popular romantic and adventure novels in the nineteenth century and were present again in response to the growing popularity of motion pictures in the early part of the twentieth century.

In tracing the history of research into questions about violence in the media, a number of historical milestones can be identified over a period spanning more than sixty years. These were related to concerns about violence in the cinema, violence or horror on the radio, violence in comics and finally, violence on television. Much of the early research was conducted in the United States where particular theoretical approaches within the social sciences have dominated the major mass media research initiatives and traditions.

With the arrival of motion pictures in the United States in the 1920s as the first of the mass popular media, there began an almost ritual-like invoking of experimental, quantitative social science to investigate what powers such mass entertainment forms held over the public at large, which was to be repeated in the 1950s, 1960s, 1970s and 1980s. This pattern of concern, with special interest groups representing parents, educators and the church at the forefront of highly public debates lobbying their governments and political representatives about media influences, emerged during this period in other countries, the United Kingdom included. At different times, public anxieties centred on the potentially harmful effects of a particular mass medium, with television being the focal point of the public's attention since the 1950s. The most frequent source of concern was the portrayal of violence in programmes which, according to television's critics, could undermine the moral values of young people, teach lessons which encouraged delinquent behaviour, and play a significant part in contributing towards rising levels of crime in society. Meanwhile, those involved with the media, together with more liberal minded members of the public, countered that television could enhance a young viewer's life in so many ways, provide a source of education and information, and offer varied forms of high-brow as well as low-brow entertainment in a convenient and cheap fashion. Given this rhetorical stalemate, the industry and politicians turned to social scientists as impartial arbiters whose independent and objective data could be invoked to give a dispassionate account of what influences television did indeed have (see Rowland, 1983).

The scientists failed to resolve this dispute, in spite of the expectations that had been placed upon them. Arguments frequently occurred among social scientists about the quality and validity of data derived from different research methodologies, while on a more profound level, there have been debates about the efficacy of particular scientific paradigms to provide an appropriate form of analysis of the way in which the mass media can shape the public consciousness, whether for good or ill (see Gauntlett, 1995; Rowland, 1983). Mass communications research developed initially out of a research tradition in the social sciences which derived from the pure sciences. In the United States, scientists were sponsored by and worked in the service of industrial corporations which expected results with economic and wealth-creating consequences. The physical sciences were preoccupied with dis-covering the deterministic, universal, predictable 'laws of nature' in order to control them for technical purposes. This pragmatic spirit of the technical and engineering sciences was to suffuse the developing social sciences. Even by the 1950s, questions were being raised about the effectiveness of this approach to the analysis of cultural phenomena. The focus was placed on the effects of media output rather than upon the economics and value systems underpinning media productions themselves.

VIOLENCE IN THE MOVIES

The earliest coordinated social scientific research effort connected with the depiction of violence in the mass media, occurred in the 1920s in the United States. This was the decade when the motion picture industry became the major source of mass entertainment. By 1922, for example, the year when cinema audience measurement was first properly carried out, 40 million cinema tickets were sold in the United States every week. By the end of the decade, this figure had risen to 90 million, including 17 million children aged under 14 years. During this period American films took over the world market. Hollywood became the centre of the movie industry – the glamour capital of the world. Obscure people were discovered by the studios and propelled into overnight stardom, earning vast sums of money and becoming the idols of many millions of ordinary people. One interesting observation is that the content of motion pictures made in the 1920s was actually not much different from the content of movies today. One study of movies' themes at this time found that film stories could be grouped into just ten categories. Three quarters of all movies fell into just three categories, however – love, sex and crime.

In a society that had barely emerged from the Victorian age, the themes that dominated films seemed to many to pose troublesome challenges to established moral standards. By the mid–1920s pressure began to mount on the motion picture industry. Numerous editorials, sermons, magazine articles and other forms of public criticism raised questions and made charges that movies were a negative influence on children.

During the same period, important developments were taking place in the social sciences. Increased attention was being paid to quantitative research techniques and new methods were developed, which meant that researchers were able to get answers to questions they had previously not had the tools and techniques properly to investigate. For one thing, statistics were introduced to social science research, which facilitated a more scientific approach to opinion research. Armed with these few techniques and a growing confidence in how to use them, social scientists began to seek opportunities to undertake research into the existence, nature and extent of mass media effects on their audiences.

In 1928 William H. Short, Executive Director of the Motion Picture Research Council, invited a group of university psychologists, sociologists and educators to design a series of studies to assess the influence of the movies on children. The research was funded by a private philanthropic foundation called the Payne Fund.

The research findings were published in the early 1930s in ten volumes and represent classic works. Among the questions they tackled were whether the movies eroded moral standards and had an influence on conduct. Findings indicated that many scenes of crime and sex could be found in the movies that were contrary to moral standards of the day, but no conclusive evidence emerged that the movies actually had degenerating effects on their audiences.

Dale (1935) reported an analysis of the major themes of 1,500 films as part of the Payne Fund research and found that about one in four films had a major theme of crime and, in an in-depth analysis of 115 films, found an average of 3.9 crimes per film. His conclusions, like so many later studies of television violence, were suffused with assumptions about the harmful effects 'due to this excessive and dramatic way of presenting crime' (Dale, 1935, p. 140).

The study reported evidence of media effects. Research into movies' influences on delinquency suggested that there might be a link. One study of delinquency-prone youngsters reported that motion pictures played a direct role in shaping delinquent and criminal careers. The methods and strategies of some of this work were highly criticized at the time by criminologists and specialists in the study of deviant behaviour; nevertheless the findings caused a considerable stir. Unfortunately, like many subsequent major research programmes on the mass media, the Payne Fund project was uncertain how to separate out the precise effects of media from the complex influences of family, school, church and teenage peer groups.

VIOLENCE ON THE RADIO

A few years after the Payne Fund studies had reported their findings about the movies, another stir was caused by an incident that occurred on radio. On 30 October 1938, *Mercury Theatre on the Air*, starring among others Orson Welles and John Houseman, broadcast a radio adaptation of H.G. Wells' science fiction masterpiece *War of the Worlds*. Because the dramatization was presented in a clever newscast style, many listeners believed that the Martians really had landed. What happened that October night was one of the most remarkable media events of all time. If nothing else, the incident demonstrated that radio drama could have a powerful impact on its audience.

At the time, radio in the United States had become the primary source of information and home entertainment for the masses. The popularity of newspapers had begun to fade. It was estimated that of 32 million families in the United States in 1938, 27 million had radio. The crucial broadcast was aired one Sunday evening between 8.00 and 9.00 pm. The introduction by Welles was very realistic in regard to the time frame and events. After Welles' introduction, an anonymous announcer read what was apparently a routine news bulletin. Twelve minutes into the show there was a newsflash announcing that a mysterious flaming object had been sighted over New Jersey. Further flashes revealed, in realistic fashion, an apparent alien invasion.

As newspaper headlines over the next day or two revealed, there were many people who believed they were listening to real events rather than a fictional dramatization. Many people panicked, leaving their homes, and even their towns or cities, in order to escape what they believed was a real invasion from Mars.

Subsequent research showed that many listeners joined the programme part of the way through, having listened through to the end of a popular radio music and variety show on a different station. They had missed Welles' explanation at the very beginning of the programme that the events they were about to hear were fictional. Many people, missing this information and the context it provided, thought they were listening to an authentic news bulletin.

HORROR COMICS

During the 1950s in the United States, there was renewed concern about the role of mass media in juvenile delinquency. Senate hearings insisted on getting from behavioural scientists conclusive evidence of long-term harmful effects of media. Unfortunately, psychologists and representatives of the new field of communications could only give conflicting theories of media and delinquency, which made reference to such mechanisms as catharsis, arousal and social learning (imitation). Politicians were further dismayed by social scientists who argued their cases on the basis of significant correlations between media and behaviour, which did not offer the direct proof of causality needed for legislation.

Attention switched, at one point, to a popular printed entertainment medium of that time – horror comics. This attention was triggered by the appearance of a book called *Seduction of the Innocent* by a psychiatrist, Dr Frederick Wertham. He argued that comic books were, contrary to what their name suggested, not in the least bit funny. Instead, at their worst, they were turning children into dangerous juvenile delinquents; at best, they were giving children who read them a distorted view of the world. They were also blamed by Wertham for contributing to reading problems.

Throughout his book Wertham catalogued instances where children supposedly initiated violent acts found in crime comics. He claimed that 'there is a significant correlation between crime comics reading and the more serious forms of juvenile delinquency'. Reduced to its simplest terms, Wertham's argument was that

1 comic books were read by a large number of children;
2 a large component of the comic diet consisted of crime, violence, horror and sex; and therefore
3 children who read the comics were necessarily stimulated to the performance of delinquent acts, cruelty, violence and undesirable social behaviour.

Perhaps the most significant impact of Wertham's work was to nearly destroy the comic book industry. Theoretically, however, there were inconsistencies in his analysis. His evidence for comic book effects on delinquent tendencies in youngsters, based as it was on interviews with children in clinical settings, was often unsystematic and ambiguous in its potential interpretations, creating more questions than answers. Even media researchers who did utilize systematic modes of investigation were unable to produce results which offered conclusive evidence of media effects.

VIOLENCE ON TELEVISION

Since the 1950s when television broadcasting became widespread in the United States and the United Kingdom, the attention of social science researchers has been predominantly drawn to this medium, particularly with reference to the possible impact its depictions of violence might have upon viewers. Although much of this research has been focused upon the potential impact of violent television on children (e.g., Himmelweit *et al.*, 1958), who are regarded as especially susceptible to media effects, there has been wider public concern about television violence and its influences on the audience as a whole.

During the 1960s, as television became increasingly well established, competing channels and stations engaged in a fierce race for audiences and advertising revenues. One aspect of this changing environment was the introduction of more and more attention-gripping programmes featuring fast-paced action and simple storylines – with themes commonly centred around westerns, crime, and espionage – many with the stock feature of violent resolutions to problems. Even then, despite calls for a tightening of regulations (the need for greater self-regulation in the United States, and the need for a more active external regulator and greater emphasis on research establishing viewers' needs and interests in the United Kingdom), there was no call for an analysis of the relationship between the medium's economic foundations and its programme content (Rowland, 1983). Instead, researchers offered more and more complex forms of analysis based on the increasingly fashionable multi-variate computational techniques that were becoming available. These often gave the appearance of having greater scientific weight and credibility, but came little closer to establishing the kind of causal evidence governments needed to support new legislation.

The debate about the effects of television violence has frequently been accompanied by calls for tighter controls over television content and the way it is regulated. These demands have emphasized the need to establish the extent of violence on television as a basis for developing public policy in the area. It has become clear, however, that the measurement of television violence is a complex problem to which there are no ready or clear cut solutions. One complication is the fact that the meaning of violence can vary widely from one individual to another. A portrayal that is perceived as extremely violent by one viewer may be seen as relatively innocuous by another. Attempts by professional researchers to make statements about the violence profile of television on the basis of quantitative data derived from simplistic definitions of 'violence', without any recourse to public values, attitudes and perceptions, are fraught with conceptual difficulties because the television violence ratings of professional researchers may differ in significant respects from those which would be applied by ordinary viewers. The perception of television violence can vary according to the kind of violence, the context in which it occurs, the nature of the perpetrator and victim, the consequences which follow from it, the types of weapons employed, and the reasons why it occurred (see Gunter, 1985). These are matters which need to be borne in mind by those who attempt to develop procedures for measuring the amount of violence on television, since they may largely determine the meaning that the subsequent results might have (Watson *et al.* 1991):

Television came under particularly close scrutiny at the beginning of the 1970s. In the United States, fear about rising crime, concern about inner city riots and college campus rebellions against the Vietnam war, together with other forms of civil unrest, gave many the impression that the fabric of American society was being ripped apart. These anxieties were brought into sudden and dramatic focus by the assassinations of four prominent public figures: John F. Kennedy, Malcolm X, Martin Luther King and

Robert Kennedy. In response to public concern surrounding these incidents, in 1968 President Johnson set up a National Commission on the Causes and Prevention of Violence. Among the possible causal agents investigated was television. The report by the Commission's Media Action Group did not find television to be a substantial cause of social violence.

Following soon after this report came another large US investigation which, on this occasion, focused specifically on television's alleged effects upon social behaviour. The Surgeon General's Scientific Advisory Committee on Television and Social Behaviour was set up in 1969 to investigate the effects of television violence on children's attitudes and behaviour. Controversy surrounded this research programme before it got under way, however, because TV network representatives on the Committee blackballed seven leading social scientists distinguished for their past research and expertise on the subject of television violence. Further arguments followed the publication of the five-volume report and summary document published in 1972 mainly because according to some analysts, the summary played down the negative findings of some of the studies. The main conclusions were that:

1 television content is heavily saturated with violence;
2 children and adults are spending more and more time watching this content;
3 there is some evidence that on balance viewing violent television entertainment increases the likelihood of aggressive behaviour among viewers.

The studies commissioned under the US Surgeon General's research programme examined the extent to which violence occurred on television output; noted different kinds of effects television violence might have upon viewers, with special reference to children; and introduced some new methodologies designed to shed light on how people used and responded to television. Content analysis studies, which attempted to quantify violence on television, were commissioned from researchers outside the United States as well as from American researchers. Thus, an attempt was made to produce comparative international data about violence on television, with studies carried out in Britain (Halloran and Croll, 1972) and Israel (Shinar *et al.*, 1972). In addition to assessing the amount of violence on television, this research programme also addressed the issue of how violence on television is perceived by viewers. Findings emerged which indicated that viewers did attach different weight or degrees of seriousness to different types of violent behaviour (Greenberg and Gordon, 1972b, c). These perceptual distinctions provided indications that not all forms of televised violence are judged in the same way by even young viewers.

One of the major recommendations of the US Surgeon General's report was for an ongoing index of violence levels in television programming. The most important of these indices was developed by Professor George Gerbner and his colleagues at the Annenberg School of Communication, University of Pennsylvania. This system mechanically recorded all apparent violent actions – regardless of meaning or context – in order to provide an objective and quantitative measurement of incidence of violence. This analysis discounted any subjective variances in reactions to violence one might find among different members of the mass audience. A more detailed look at this research will be taken later in this chapter.

Major issues

There are several major issues relating to the depiction of violence on television. These typically relate to accusations levelled against television about its alleged enthusiasm for featuring violence in programmes as an apparently essential ingredient of entertainment, and the impact that such material can have on viewers, especially upon children. A number of common assumptions are made in the recurrent public debate about television violence. First, it is frequently argued that television contains a great deal of violence. Second, there is a common belief that regular viewers are therefore exposed to large quantities of violence during the course of their everyday television watching. Third, it is assumed that constant exposure to violent content in programmes must have a deleterious effect upon viewers and contributes, as a causal factor, to the enactment of antisocial behaviour in society.

This volume will not examine all of these issues, but the research on which it reports does have an important bearing on a number of statements critics have made about television, particularly those which refer to the *amount* of violence on television. This work and its findings, in turn, have implications for the amount of violence on the small screen to which viewers can be exposed.

MEASURING VIOLENCE ON TELEVISION

The focus of this book is upon an objective, quantitative analysis of the amount of violence on British television. Traditionally, the most commonly used method for assessing how much violence television programmes contain is known as *content analysis*. When measuring violence on television, researchers using content analysis begin by setting up an 'objective' statement of what they mean by violence. Violence is defined in broad terms. Accompanying this definition will be a frame of reference which specifies how and where that definition should be applied in the assessment of programmes. This instructional frame of reference is given to teams of trained coders who watch samples of programmes recorded from television and count up incidents which match the definition of violence drawn up for the purposes of the analysis. This enables researchers to produce a quantitative assessment of the 'amount' of violence on television in terms of the numbers of violent incidents or events catalogued by coders.

Content analysis does not provide a measure of the effects of television violence, nor does it provide any sort of indication of public opinion about violence on television. Its aim is purely to yield an indication of the extent and location of particular classes of incident or event in television programmes. This research methodology attempts, as far as possible, to exclude any element of subjective judgement about violent television portrayals. All violence tends to be treated in the same way by a content analysis, regardless of the type of programme or dramatic context or setting in which it occurs. Thus, cartoon violence, for example, is treated no differently than violence occurring in a contemporary drama series. Traditionally, content analysis researchers define the intensity of violence in a programme in terms of the numbers of certain kinds of incidents it contains, rather than in terms of the nature of those incidents. This type of measurement does not, of course, reflect the way in which viewers might respond to violence on television. Research on viewers' perceptions of television violence has shown that viewers differentiate between violent portrayals on the basis of the context in which they occur, the form of violence displayed, and the types of characters involved as perpetrators or victims of violence (Gunter, 1985). The important objective in content analysis, however, is consistency and reliability of assessment across different coders (see Krippendorf, 1980; Wimmer and Dominick, 1994). It is essential that different coders should use the coding frame in the same way and produce the same or very similar incident counts, otherwise it would be impossible to obtain accurate measures of what has happened on television.

Even within the content analysis perspective, it is possible to utilize different definitional terms of reference. Content analysis methodologies can vary in terms of the definitions of violence they use, the way in which they sample programmes and the degree of detail they obtain about violence on television. Most content analysis, however, places emphasis on the specification of profiles and structures of programme content. With regard to the measurement of television violence, the commonality in the application of this technique lies in the objective counting of incidents which match a single normative definition of violence.

Early content research

The earliest content analysis studies of violence on television occurred in the early 1950s in the United States. Smythe (1954) reported evidence from several studies sponsored in 1952 and 1953 by the National Association of Educational Broadcasters. In one week of content analysis of prime-time output on seven New York City channels, any acts or threats of violence that occurred in all programmes except news, current affairs and sports shows were recorded. Altogether 3,421 acts and threats were observed, averaging 6.2 violent incidents per hour. Serious drama shows accounted for 87% of all violent portrayals, an average of about ten incidents per hour. Crime-drama contributed 28% of all violent incidents and western drama a further 23%.

Turning his attention next to violence in children's programmes, Smythe found a much higher incidence of aggressive acts than in adult programming, although perhaps more important than the actual volume of violent episodes here is the way they were distributed throughout different categories of programmes. Children's fictional entertainment programmes had three times the frequency of violent acts or threats recorded in adult programmes, but this was largely a reflection of the very high incidence of violence in children's comedy and cartoon programmes, which averaged nearly 37 incidents per hour. In fact, about one-quarter of all violence observed in adult and children's programmes monitored by Smythe occurred in a humorous context.

Remmers (1954) reported an increase in television violence from 1952 to 1954 based on single week samples. Acts of violence (including physical or psychological injury) nearly doubled from 1953 to 1954 from 6.2 violent acts per hour to 11 acts per hour. Testimony presented to the US Senate Subcommittee to Investigate Juvenile Delinquency hearing in 1962 indicated that action/adventure programmes increased between two- and threefold in four cities between 1954 and 1961 and yet an analysis of 80 programmes in this category in 1961 found only 319 episodes of violent assaultive behaviour – a rate of four episodes per programme (around six acts per hour), below that reported for 1953.

Schramm *et al.* (1961) coded the number of violent incidents occurring in 100 hours of weekday programming broadcast between 4.00 pm and 9.00 pm during one week in October 1960 on four television channels in the San Francisco area. Schramm *et al.* observed that violence was a prevalent feature of children's programming put out by these television stations, with shootings and fist-fights occurring frequently. Once again, though, much of this violence was found in comedy programmes.

Unlike many researchers using content analysis, Schramm *et al.* made a clear distinction between incidents occurring in humorous and serious contexts and based their measures of the volume of television violence exclusively on the content of non-humorous programmes. While providing some early insights into the amount of violence on television, these various American studies from the 1950s and 1960s are difficult to compare because they used different definitions of violence, different television programme samples and different coding frames. The US government-sponsored research programme on violence at the end of the 1960s saw the birth of an annual content analysis project which would run for many years and, for the first time, yield trend data based on a common analytical framework.

Cultural Indicators project

The most extensive quantitative content analysis of television violence was carried out by Gerbner and his colleagues of the Annenberg School of Communications, University of Pennsylvania. This group analysed violence on network television in the United States over a period spanning nearly 20 years. Their primary focus was on prime-time evening television (7.30 pm to 11.00 pm) and Saturday and Sunday daytime television (8.00 am to 2.30 pm). The analysis was limited to dramatic entertainment programmes. News, documentaries, variety and quiz shows, and sports programmes were excluded. The samples taken annually for Gerbner's content analyses were typically single weeks of all dramatic fiction, including cartoons. In response to criticisms that one week was too small a sample, seven weeks were taken in 1976, yielding 409 programmes (Signorielli *et al.*, 1982). By the mid–1980s, the data base apparently covered 2,105 programmes (Gerbner *et al.*, 1986). After 1980, however, published analyses of the Violence Profile became more sporadic.

A single normative definition of violence was used: 'the overt expression of physical force (with or without a weapon) against self or other, compelling action against one's will on pain of being hurt or killed, or actually hurting or killing' (Gerbner, 1972, p. 31). Further specifications were made that the incidents must be plausible and credible; but that no idle threats should be included. However, violent accidents or natural catastrophes, whose inclusion in dramatic plots was reasoned by Gerbner to be technically non-accidental, were included (Gerbner and Gross, 1976). The violence definition emphasized incidents resulting in the infliction of injury or suffering, but largely ignored the context in which incidents occurred. Any events likely to cause or actually causing injury to a character on screen were catalogued and given equivalent weightings of intensity or seriousness whether they occurred in contemporary drama or animated cartoons.

Using the above scheme to guide them, a team of trained coders was employed to record such features as the frequency and nature of violent acts, the perpetrators and victims of violence, and the temporal and spatial settings in which the acts occurred. From certain combinations of these measures, Gerbner derived the 'Violence Profile' which purported to represent an objective and meaningful indicator of the amount of violence portrayed in television drama.

The Violence Profile itself comprised two sets of indicators: the Violence Index and the Risk Ratios. The amount of violence occurring on television was represented by the Violence Index. Essentially this index represented the percentage of programmes containing any violence at all, the frequency and rate of violent episodes per programme and per hour, and the number of leading characters involved in violence either as aggressors or as victims.

The Risk Ratios signified a character's chances of involvement in violence in television drama programmes and, once involved, the likelihood of positive or negative consequences for them. The Risk Ratios also represented a composite of more than one measure: the violence–victim ratio, which denoted the chances of being an aggressor or a victim, while the killer–killed ratio denoted the risk of killing or being killed. Both ratios were catalogued within each dramatic and demographic category for a wide spectrum of character types.

The Violence Index

This index is comprised of three types of direct observational data called *prevalence, rate* and *role*. They showed the extent to which violence occurred at all in the programmes monitored and were combined according to a formula as shown in Table 1.1. Prevalence represented the percentage of programmes containing any violence in a particular programme sample. Rate expressed frequency of these acts in units of programming and in units of time and each of these frequencies was entered into the Index. Role was defined as the portrayal of characters as perpetrators of violence, or *'violents'*, and as those who were subordinated to violence or *victims*. This category yielded several measures: % of 'violents' out of all characters in a sample; % of victims out of all characters in a sample; % of all characters who featured as violents or as victims (%V); % of killers out of all characters in a sample; % of killed out of all characters in a sample; and % of all those involved in killing either as killers or killed (%k). Only %V and %k measures were entered into the index.

Table 1.1 Computation of Gerbner Violence Index

Violence Index = %p + 2(R/P) = 2(R/H) + %V + %k		
Where		
%p	=	percentage of programmes studied in which there is violence
R/P	=	number (or rate) of violent episodes per programme
R/H	=	number (or rate) of violent episodes per hour
%V	=	percentage of leading characters involved in violence – either as violent or victim
%k	=	percentage of leading characters involved in killing – either as killer or killed

Source: Gerbner, 1972

Throughout the 1970s, Gerbner *et al.* (1986) monitored levels of violence in prime-time television drama programming in the USA. This work began in the 1967–68 television season. During the next ten years, an average of 80% of programmes contained violence and 60% of major characters were involved in violence. The average rate of violent episodes was seven and a half per hour, and in weekend, daytime children's programmes, violent episodes averaged almost 18 per hour. Indeed, programmes directed at children typically scored high on most measures of violence except for killing; cartoons in particular consistently exceeded all other categories of programmes, including adult action-adventure and crime-detective shows.

The overall rates of violence found by Gerbner *et al.* remained very consistent over the years, averaging five or six acts of overt physical violence per hour on prime-time television (Gerbner *et al.*, 1986). The rates of violence per programme averaged 4.81 acts for prime-time television and 5.77 per programme for weekend daytime television.

Risk Ratios

The Risk Ratios component of the Violence Profile was designed to analyse patterns of portrayals among certain groups of the television population and thus to represent in an objectively quantifiable way the intrinsic power structure of the violent fictional society which is brought by television into the homes of viewers. This phase of Gerbner's analysis began by coding the involvement of different character-types in violent episodes. An 'involved' character was defined as one who takes part in a scene of overt physical force and who either committed or suffered violence, or both.

According to Gerbner *et al.* the portrayal of violence on television drama programming demonstrated a pattern of unequal relative risks among characters of different sex, age, socio-economic and ethnic groups, in which certain character types were victimized consistently more often than others. Victimization risk data reported for prime-time television samples between 1969 and 1978 have indicated that victims are generally more prevalent than perpetrators of aggression but that the ratio of attackers to victims was greater for some character types than others. Whilst men were much more likely than women overall to become involved in violence of some kind, once involved they were much less likely than their female counterparts to be victimized.

Risks of victimization were high among children and adolescents and unmarried women, and were especially high for elderly women who were more than three times as likely to be victims as aggressors when involved in violence. Further analyses indicated that 'good' male characters were more likely to be killers than killed. Good female characters were much more likely to be fatally victimized than 'bad' female characters, even though they were less often involved in violent episodes.

The Cultural Indicators project continued into the 1980s and revealed that the world of American network television was characterized more by stability than change. Despite year-on-year fluctuations in levels of violence, the general patterns of involvement in violence among different social groups were very consistent across a 20-year period (Gerbner *et al.*, 1986). The index of violence reached its highest level since 1967, when the study began, in the 1984/85 television season. Eight out of every ten prime-time programmes contained violence at that time, and the rate of violence was nearly eight incidents per hour. The 19-year average was six per hour. Children's programmes were customarily found to be saturated with violence on American television. During the 1984/85 season, the average rate of occurrence was 27 violent acts per hour, compared with the 19-year average of 21 acts per hour for children's programmes.

According to Gerbner (1988), the mid-1980s report brought up to date the cumulative results of the analysis of violence as a demonstration of power. For every ten male characters on prime-time network television who committed violence, there were 11 who fell victim to it. But for every ten female perpetrators of violence, there were 16 female victims. 'As television drama goes down the social pecking order, it raises the price to be paid for getting involved in violence. Foreign women and women from ethnic minority groups pay the highest price. For every ten perpetrators from these groups there are 21 and 22 victims respectively' (p. 17).

Cnions 7,92. 16-18, 286

Other American research

Early American studies of television in which occurrences of violence on the small screen were monitored have already been mentioned earlier in this chapter (e.g., Smythe, 1954; Schramm *et al.*, 1961). Further content analysis studies were conducted during the 1970s and 1980s by researchers working independently of the Gerbner group.

Clark and Blankenberg (1972) analysed the synopses of programmes offered in October weeks on *TV Guide* from 1953 to 1969, coding all 'prime-time' programmes that appeared to contain violence. They reported reasonable agreement between synopses coding and direct coding of programmes in a reliability study where 78 programmes were coded using both methods.

The synopsis coding led to an underestimate of violent programmes compared with direct coding (35% by synopsis coding; 43% by direct coding). Clark and Blankenberg found that overall, 27% of programmes could be described as violent but their data did not suggest increases over the sample period. Thus, the overall proportion of violent programmes from 1953 to 1959 was 29% compared with 27% from 1963 to 1969.

The authors pointed out that considerable variation took place from year to year, apparently following a four-year cycle with peaks in 1955 (27% of programmes violent), 1959 (41% violent), 1963 (29% violent) and 1967 (38% violent). However, as with almost all content analyses, some caution must be urged given the small samples. For example, the peak of 1967 is provided by only 20 violent programmes while the trough of 1961 is given by 13 programmes. Larger samples might smooth out these cyclical trends.

CBS (Columbia Broadcasting System, 1980) carried out its own monitoring from 1973/74 to 1978/79. This study may be compared with that of Gerbner and his colleagues for similar samples of prime-time television only for their rates of violent acts per hour (see Table 1.2).

Table 1.2 Violent acts per hour for US prime-time TV

	1973/74	1974/75	1975/76	1976/77	1977/78	1978/79
Gerbner	4.9	5.4	6.0	6.1	5.5	4.5
CBS	2.3	2.5	1.9	2.3	1.9	1.6

Source: Comstock (1982)

There was little agreement between the two studies except that 1978/79 displayed the lowest violence score in both samples. The Gerbner study suggested rates of violence some two and a half times greater than those reported by CBS. This discrepancy is partly explained by the more generous definition of violence given by Gerbner, which included natural disasters exhibited by CBS, and by the programme types included (CBS would have excluded cartoon comic violence) and by differences in the sampling unit taken.

Even the Gerbner definition has been challenged, however, for being too narrow. Being restricted as it was to acts of physical aggression, it omitted to take into account other forms of violent activity which commonly occur in everyday life and on television. As Stein and Friedrich (1975, p. 190) pointed out, 'Virtually all of the research on television content and behaviour limits the definition of violence to physical injury or damage. The verbal abuse, aggressive humour and control over other people by threat or imperative that are so prevalent on television are not included in most investigations.' Another problem was that it failed to distinguish between cartoons, comedy and action adventure drama, treating incidents of violence throughout as being exactly the same in terms of the seriousness and meaning (Gunter, 1985).

Another research group did, however, take this point into account in a content analysis study of US television conducted over a three-year period in the late 1970s (Greenberg *et al.*, 1980). This analysis was based on an expanded range of antisocial behaviour that included verbal aggression, deception and theft. Verbal aggression was the single largest category of antisocial acts in all three seasons and constituted a majority in two of the three seasons. Like Gerbner, Greenberg *et al.* focused on dramatic fiction presented in prime-time and Saturday morning television, so the extent of portrayals of aggression in other types of programming and at other times of the day was not established.

Using their broader definition of aggression to include verbally aggressive behaviour, Greenberg and his colleagues observed averages of 14.5, 15.2 and 23.2 acts of physical aggression and 23.8, 18.9 and 23.2 acts of verbal aggression per programme hour for the 1975–76, 1976–77 and 1977–78 seasons, respectively. The Annenberg group focused on physical violence and reported a mean of 5.21 incidents per programme hour across the years 1967–79 (Signorielli *et al.*, 1982). Greenberg *et al.* (1980) found fairly equal amounts of prosocial and antisocial behaviours on screen. They counted a total of 42.7 prosocial acts per hour against 35 antisocial acts in 1975–76, and averages of 47 and 43 in the two subsequent television seasons. The high levels of verbal aggression noted by Greenberg on prime-time television in North America were corroborated by Williams *et al.* (1982).

Taylor and Dozier (1983) and Boemer (1984) studied violence in television series from 1950 to 1976 and in radio 'thriller drama'. Crime programmes generally were found to sanction the use of deadly force to enforce the law and protect the *status quo*. Interestingly, black television characters in violent television programmes were usually found to be portrayed as policemen or collaborators with law enforcement.

The National Television Violence Study

The latest and most substantial American study of violence on television is the National Television Violence Study funded over three years (1994–97) by the national Cable Television Association in the United States. This study developed an elaborate methodology which assessed not just the quantity of violence depicted on American television, but also the nature of violent portrayals and context within which violence occurred (Potter *et al.*, 1996; Wilson *et al.*, 1996a).

The National Television Violence Study developed a definition of violence which embodied three concepts: the notion of credible threat of violence, the overt occurrence of violent behaviour, and the harmful consequences of unseen violence. The idea of credible threat covered situations where an individual threatened another in such a way that there was a realistic likelihood that violence would follow, with the perpetrator having the clear means to carry out such action. The harmful consequences of unseen violence covered scenes where someone is depicted suffering some kind of pain or discomfort, and indeed actual physical damage may be shown, and where other clues from the storyline establish that they were a victim of violence.

Much emphasis was placed on the context in which violence occurred and an elaborate framework of analysis was created to enable a comprehensive classification of violence in terms of a range of attributes: its dramatic setting, motivational context, graphicness, rewards and punishments, severity of consequences for victims, physical form, and the nature of the perpetrators and victims. All these factors were rationalized in terms of their significance as possible mediators of audience response to media depictions of violence as signalled by the published research literature on media violence effects (Wilson *et al.*, 1996a).

To underpin the emphasis on context the units of analysis adopted by this study were not restricted to the simple counting of individual acts of violence, as in previous studies of this sort. Three levels of measurement were devised: (1) the PAT; (2) the scene; and (3) the programme. A PAT represented an interaction between a perpetrator (P), an act (A), and a target (T). A sequence of PATs, either continuous and uninterrupted or separated by brief cutaways or scene changes, might comprise a violent scene and afforded an opportunity to examine relationships between discrete acts. Finally, the researchers here argued that larger meanings could be conveyed by the pattern of violence considered as a whole within a programme, which could only be effectively interpreted when analysed along with the context in which it was presented in the programme.

This study analysed a far larger sample of programme output than any previous American content analysis of televised violence. In total, the project sampled nearly 2,500 hours of material. The sample was not restricted to peak-time, unlike most earlier work. Furthermore, it used a random sampling frame to select programmes for analysis over a period of 20 weeks on 23 separate television channels. This provided for a more representative sampling of television output than the convenience sampling methods used by earlier published studies.

The first year of this study found a total of more than 18,000 violent interactions in the sample of programming monitored. Violence occurred in a majority (57%) of these programmes. Two-thirds of these incidents (66%) involved a perpetrator committing an actual behavioural act of violence. Far fewer interactions involved credible threats (29%) where the perpetrator demonstrated a clear intent to physically harm the target with the means to do so, and a small proportion of incidents (3%) involved depictions of the harmful consequences of unseen violence.

Violent programmes were found to vary quite a bit in terms of the number of violent interactions they contained. The frequency of violent interactions per programme ranged from one to 88. Most of the programmes, however, clustered at the lower end of the frequency distribution, with 15% of programmes containing only one violent interaction, 12% containing two, and 10% containing three. This meant that slightly more than one-third of all violent programmes contained between one and three violent interactions. Another one-third contained between five and eight violent interactions, and the remaining one-third featured nine or more violent interactions.

The prevalence of violence varied significantly by programme genre. A higher percentage of movies and drama series contained violence compared to the overall average of television, whereas fewer comedy series, reality-based shows, and music videos contained violence. Perpetrators of violence were far more likely to be male than female, and in the majority of cases were individuals working on their own rather than in a group. Most violent characters were human, although over one in five were anthropomorphized animals or supernatural creatures. Perpetrators were mostly young to middle-aged adults; very few perpetrators of violence on television were children, teenagers or elderly people. Most perpetrators were white, with relatively few being members of any other particular ethnic group. The victim profile was very similar to the perpetrator profile.

In the case of four out of ten violent incidents, perpetrators used parts of their own body to hit, punch or kick their target. When weapons were used, hand held firearms were the most common. The next most common weapon type involved the use of unconventional instruments of aggression such as ropes or chairs. Violence was extremely graphic in its portrayal on relatively rare occasions. Nearly half of all incidents of violence were classified as occurring in purely fantasy settings, while more than four in ten were classed as fictional. Few incidents were regarded as real. Violent incidents were slightly more likely to be punished than rewarded. In about three in ten cases, violence was accompanied by self-condemnation by the perpetrator, or was criticized or punished by another person or by some form of authority, while self or other punishment followed in around four in ten cases. Immediate punishment for violence, however, was not common. In well over four in ten cases, no physical injury followed violence, and more than one in three incidents depicted unrealistic harm. On balance, violence on American television in 1994–95 was found to be largely sanitized. It was rarely punished immediately and rarely caused observable harm to victims.

VIOLENCE ON TELEVISION IN OTHER COUNTRIES

Studies of the depiction of violence on the small screen have been carried out in countries beyond the United States. Before turning to results for Britain, it might be worth reviewing the evidence from a number of other countries. Some of these national studies adopted the content analysis framework and violence definition of Gerbner. At the time of Gerbner's early work for the Surgeon General's inquiry into television and social behaviour at the beginning of the 1970s, there were attempts in other countries to use the same approach to provide comparative evidence from beyond the United States. These other efforts, however, were not entirely successful. Researchers in Sweden gave up on the idea almost before they started. They felt, after viewing material from their own television services, that there was so little violence (and sex) that an elaborate analysis schedule was rendered meaningless (Gurevitch, 1972). An Israeli study fared only slightly better, producing just ten dramatic fiction programmes from its sample of television output, with violent acts running at an average 3.8 per programme.

Violence on Canadian TV

In recent years, the US government has been feeling pressure to bring violence on television under control not only from its own citizenry but also from those of foreign countries, especially where the latter are importers of substantial amounts of American productions. This point applies with particular acuity in the case of the United States' closest neighbour, Canada, where so many American programmes are routinely broadcast (Brown, 1994).

Canadian studies found that, in general, editorial and programme mix determined not only the amount but in some cases the nature of violence in the media. Linton and Jowett (1977) studied feature films and concluded that of all incidents involving conflict, 50% depicted violence, with an average of 13.5 violent incidents per film. Non-Canadian films contained about twice as many violent incidents as those produced in Canada. These incidents occurred most frequently in action films, including crime drama.

Comparative analyses of violence in newspapers, radio and television in Canada and the United States were conducted by Gordon and Ibson (1977) and Gordon and Singer (1977) for the Royal Commission on Violence in the Communication Industry. Of the 8,000 news items analysed, 45% related to conflict and violence. Of 2,400 news items broadcast on 15 Canadian and American television stations, 48% were related to conflict and violence. However, almost 60% of lead items in both media were related to violence and conflict.

The American media were found to place greater emphasis on homicide and other physical violence than the Canadian, while the latter showed more of other types of conflict and property damage. Direct, physical violence (including natural and man-made disasters) was about 10% more common in television news than in newspapers. Television was more likely to personalize violence in terms of private gain or deviance.

Differences between French and English language television in Canada were found by Caron and Couture (1977) to relate again to the programme mix: English-speaking markets received more American crime drama. Content analyses of seven French-language serials popular in Quebec indicated that the majority of conflicts presented in the serials were nonviolent and mostly verbal. In the 27% of conflict scenes that did involve physical violence, the violence was usually humorous and off-screen.

Williams *et al.* (1982) carried out content analysis research as part of work commissioned by the Ontario Royal Commission on Violence in the Communication Industry (1977). Programmes were selected for analysis on the basis of audience viewing figures. Canadian Bureau of Broadcast Measurement (BBM) data for the Toronto area for January 1976 were used to select the top 100 programmes (excluding news, sport and public affairs) for each of the adult (19+), teenage (12–18) and child (11 and under) viewing populations.

In all, 109 programmes were used, covering 81 hours of television output. Twenty-two per cent of these programmes were produced in Canada; 76% were from the United States. Williams *et al.* chose to examine different types of aggression, including, but not only, physical violence, along with milder forms of conflict.

Conflict, aggression and violence were considered to differ in degree and to form a hierarchy. Each programme segment was first coded as containing no conflict or some degree of conflict. Conflict was then designated as argument, as non-aggressive conflict or as aggressive conflict. Aggressive conflict was designated as aggression or violence according to the following definitions: Aggression is behaviour that inflicts harm, either physically, including explicit or implicit threats and nonverbal behaviours. Violence was physically aggressive behaviours that do, or potentially could, cause injury or death. Lower levels of conflict were superseded by more severe forms. For example, if an argument led to aggression (within the same programme segment), the segment was coded as aggressive, and the context as argument.

Williams *et al.* catalogued an average of 18.5 acts of aggression per programme hour. A total of 594 acts of physical aggression involving the body (assault or battery) or a weapon (typically a gun or object not intended for aggression) were observed. These broke down into 254 acts which involved the use of a body part (which occurred at a rate of 3.1 per programme hour) and 340 acts involving the use of a weapon (4.2 per programme hour). In addition, there were 135 acts involving physical threat (1.7 acts per programme hour) and 274 acts involving the use of verbal threat (3.4 per programme hour). Altogether there were 632 acts of verbal aggression (verbal threat, verbal abuse and sarcasm), representing 42.1% of all aggressive acts and a mean rate of 7.8 acts per programme hour.

Different levels of aggression were found in different programme categories. Relatively few segments of instruction/religion (7.7%), game shows (10.2%) and non-animated children's shows (12.2%) depicted aggression. There was a low level of aggression in drama/medical programmes (6.9%). Higher levels of aggression occurred in animated programmes (27.8%), crime shows (27%) and situation comedies (40%).

If all forms of conflict were combined, situation comedies ranked highest (58%), followed by crime (40%) and animated shows (32.9%), with adventure (23%) and drama/medical programmes (21.6%) portraying lesser amounts of conflict. Most (59%) of the aggression in situation comedies was verbal, whereas most of the aggression in adventure programmes (79%), animated programmes (72%), children's non-animated programmes (61%), crime drama (72%) and documentary (88%) was physical. Less than 2% of aggression observed was accidental and most (69%) was incidental to the plot. Aggression, especially verbal abuse, was often portrayed as humorous, and there was little evidence of consequences. For more than 81% of recipients of aggression (i.e., victims) no visible injury occurred. Neither was much pain (3.1%) or blood (1.2%) depicted.

Violence on TV in the Netherlands

Research into the cultivation effects of television was carried out during the late 1970s in the Netherlands, part of which involved an analysis of television content (Bouwman and Stappers, 1984). A Dutch Violence Profile, modelled on the American system developed by George Gerbner and his colleagues, was derived from an analysis of four weeks of programming across ten broadcasting organizations in the Netherlands. This content analysis concentrated on prime-time broadcasts (8.30–10.00 pm) and pre-prime-time broadcasts comprising family and children's programmes.

Bouwman and Stappers reported less violence on Dutch television on the whole than had been reported earlier for American television. Using the Gerbner model of analysis, the Violence Index for Dutch crime programmes during prime-time, however, was comparable with that for prime-time programmes in the United States. Crime programmes on Dutch television at this time were mainly imported from Britain and Germany, with just a handful originating from the United States.

Looking further at the relative degrees of risk of being a victim of violence on Dutch television among particular social groups, Bouwman and Stappers found that females were more vulnerable than males in line with the findings from the United States. Unmarried men were more likely to commit violence, while married men were more likely to be killed. The elderly were the most vulnerable group on Dutch television, while young adults were most likely to be killers.

Violence on TV in Israel

A small-scale study of violence on Israeli television was carried out as part of the Surgeon General's investigation of Television and Social Behaviour launched in 1970. The aim was to obtain comparative data with the United States. A content analysis of programmes transmitted over a one-week period in May 1971 covered a sample of just 65 broadcasts, which included fictional drama, entertainment and news and information programmes (Shinar *et al.*, 1972). Some of these programmes were broadcast in Hebrew and others in Arabic. Only a small number of violent incidents was catalogued, totalling 52 separate violent episodes in all. Most of these incidents (38) occurred in fictional drama programmes.

For the purposes of this analysis, a violent incident was defined as 'a continuous action involving the same set of characters in which any act(s) that may cause physical and/or psychological injury, hurt or death to persons, animals and property, whether intentional or accidental, actually shown on the screen, suggested or verbal, take place' (Shinar *et al.*, 1972, p. 521). The researchers reported the percentages of programmes in different programme categories which contained any violence and the rate of violence in terms of numbers of incidents per programme. Violent incidents were also classified in terms of a variety of features including motivational context, types of injuries caused, and demography of perpetrators and victims of violence.

Adults' programmes were more likely to contain violence than were children's programmes. Nearly half (48.4%) of all adult-oriented programmes in Hebrew and nearly one in three (30.4%) in Arabic contained at least one violent incident. Just over one in five children's programmes (21.1%) contained violence. Television series dealing with such themes as crime, detective stories or espionage were the most violent programmes, while long-running serials, especially historical drama, were the least violent programmes.

The majority of violent incidents were judged to have been presented in a fairly realistic style and were more likely to occur in serious than in humorous contexts. Over half the violence (55.2% of incidents) was physical and intentional, while around one in five incidents (21.1%) comprised verbal violence. One in seven incidents (15.4%) comprised threatened physical violence. The remaining incidents (8.3%) were accidental incidents. Of the physical and intentional acts of violence, most involved the use of a part of the aggressor's body. There were few instances of violence involving guns or other instruments of aggression. The majority of violent incidents resulted in no observable harm to victims or targets (52.7%), and most of the remainder (36.3%) produced only minor pain or suffering. Just two incidents resulted in death and two further incidents caused significant pain and suffering. For the most part (83.3% of incidents) violence produced no blood or wounds. Just two incidents (5.5%) produced a large amount of blood.

Violence was most likely to occur within the context of criminal activity (23.2%) or law enforcement activity (12.6%) underlining the earlier observation that violence on Israeli television at the time of this study occurred most often in crime drama programmes. Other 'personal' violence, however, was the single largest category of contexts for violence (29.2% of incidents). Small numbers of incidents occurred in war situations, in the context of civil strife or rioting, or within domestic, family contexts.

The perpetrators or instigators of violence were overwhelmingly found to be male (90.7% of incidents), while female perpetrators were found in just two incidents (9.3%). Victims of violence were also most likely to be male (69.2%), although females were clearly more likely to be victims (30.8%) than aggressors. The instigators of violence were usually 'bad'. Among both heroes and villains, though, the perpetrators were nearly always male.

Violence on TV in Japan

Iwao *et al.* (1981) conducted a study of violence on Japanese television and compared it with violence on American television. They used the categories and procedures developed by Gerbner and his colleagues. The Japanese sample consisted of one week of entertainment programming from 1977 broadcast between 5.00 and 11.00 pm on five Tokyo television stations, one carrying public broadcasting and the others being commercial stations. Half of the programmes (69) were children's programmes, of which 51 or 37% of the total were cartoons. Twenty-four programmes were foreign imports, mainly from the United States.

Iwao *et al.* (1981, pp. 30–31) distinguished three types of violence on Japanese television: random, purposive and suffering:

Random violence, so named because it tends to occur in frequent short bursts without much reference to a plot, is typically seen in cartoons and programs for children. The victim may be run over by a car and flattened like a pancake, only to rise a moment later as if nothing had happened. Violence of this type lacks realism. In many cases, the characters are not human but personified animals or objects and the violence is rarely acute.

A second type of violence, often seen in police dramas is portrayed as a means to achieving some end. Often, this purposive violence furthers the plot but need not arouse the emotions of the audience. The robber who overcomes a guard in order to steal money from a bank is a typical example. Here, although the violence may be realistic, the suffering of the victim is generally not portrayed in detail. Scenes of purposive violence tend to be unsentimental, with more importance given to the means–end relation than to the feelings associated with the violence.

Finally, there are portrayals of violence which arouse viewers' compassion toward the victim, rather than primarily developing the plots. Such violence, which often includes detailed revelation of suffering, is most common in Samurai dramas, in which a 'good guy' is generally tormented by a 'bad guy', but by virtue of his stoical courage wins in the end. In a majority of cases, the victim of the violence is the good guy rather than the bad guy, and the portrayals are sentimental.

Iwao *et al.* found that the number of violent incidents per programme was slightly lower in Japan than in the United States, but this was fully accounted for by the fact that the average Japanese programme was slightly shorter and the average violent episode was slightly longer than their American counterparts. The minutes of violence per hour were virtually identical in the two countries.

The proportion of all programmes containing some violence was virtually identical – 81% in the Japanese sample and 80% over the nine years of the Gerbner American samples (ranging from 73% to 89%). The proportions of leading characters committing some violence or experiencing some violence were also very similar.

Table 1.3 Quantity of violence on Japanese and US television

	Violent incidents per programme (n)	*Violent incidents per hour* (n)	*Violent minutes per hour* (n)
Japanese TV			
Japanese produced	4.4	6.8	2.3
Imported	5.2	8.1	2.4
Total	4.5	7.0	2.3
American TV			
1977	5.0	6.7	2.3
1978	5.8	8.3	2.2
1967–78	5.2	7.5	2.4
Range	4.8 to 6.2	6.7 to 9.5	2.2 to 3.7

Source: Iwao *et al.* (1981)
Data on American TV taken from Gerbner *et al.* (1979)

While there were overall similarities between the two countries, there were also some marked differences in the kinds of action in which the violence was embedded. Violent scenes mainly occurred in police dramas, cartoons and Samurai dramas. There were differences in the patterns of violence in various dramatic forms. In all, 7.8% of total time in Samurai dramas was devoted to violent action, compared to 6.2% of the time in cartoons. But there were 14.3 violent incidents per hour in cartoons and 8.7 per hour in Samurai stories. This was because the violent incidents were frequent but short in cartoons (average 15.6 seconds) and more than twice as long in the Samurai dramas (average 32.3 seconds). Police dramas fell between the two in terms of average duration of incidents and somewhat below them in number of violent incidents per hour.

While the amount of violence on Japanese television did not differ noticeably from that on American television, the nature of Japanese violence differed markedly with a much greater emphasis on suffering. In 54% of violent incidents in the Japanese-produced non-cartoon programmes, the actual wounding or killing was portrayed, while this happened in only 24% of the incidents in the equivalent imported programmes shown on Japanese television. Further, the good guys in major roles are three times as likely to be wounded or killed as the bad guys. In imported programmes (mainly American) bad guys were far more likely to be wounded or killed.

The violence that was shown in Japanese dramatic programmes was no bloodier than that on imported programmes. This similarity, however, masked a more interesting difference. In Japanese programmes blood appeared often in the case of wounding as well as in the case of deaths. In imported programmes, blood appeared far more frequently in instances of death; in Japanese programmes it was more likely to appear on the face or body of a surviving character, not just on those characters who were phased out of the action.

In any dramatic confrontation between a good and bad character, either may assault the other, and either (or neither) may be wounded or killed. On the imported programmes there were almost equal numbers of 'bad' assaulters and 'good' assaulters; on the Japanese programmes there were over twice as many bad assaulters as good assaulters. Thus, on the imported programmes, good and bad characters were about equally likely to initiate violence, and the villains were most likely to suffer its consequences. On Japanese-produced television, the villains tended to initiate violence and the heroes tended to suffer.

According to Iwao *et al.* (1981, p. 36), 'the net tone of Japanese programs is more that of a morality story than is the American. Bad assaulters initiate violence against good characters; good assaulters (though less often) initiate violence against bad characters. The most important violence that is experienced by major characters is something that arouses distress and sympathy, not something to be cheered.'

Violence on TV across the Far East

More recently, research has been carried out in a number of Far Eastern countries comparing levels of violence on television in different national markets (Menon, 1993). In 1988, the Asian Mass Communication Research and Information Centre launched a study of violence on television in Asia which covered eight countries: Bangladesh, India, Indonesia, Japan, Malaysia, Pakistan, Philippines and Thailand. The monitoring work was carried out in 1989. The main objectives of the study were to:

- determine the frequency and the level of violence on TV in Asia;
- identify the types of violent programme;
- determine the countries of origin of violent programmes;
- explore the sources of locally produced violent programmes;
- describe the dramatic contexts and the nature of violence;
- analyse the trends in the depiction of violence, in order to assess if levels of violence on television are increasing or decreasing;
- examine the cross-cultural similarities and differences in the depiction of violence on television.

Four main categories of programming were selected for analysis: social dramas, action adventures, cartoons and comedies. Violence was defined as 'the use of physical force or verbal abuse which is psychologically or physically injurious to a person or persons, including the destruction of property and animals'. A total of 256 programmes were analysed ranging from 15 in Indonesia to 65 in Malaysia. The average number per country was 32. More than half the programmes (56%) were local in origin. The biggest foreign supplier of programmes was the United States, with Japan the next most popular source of material. Nearly six in ten (59%) of the programmes monitored were classified as violent. The percentage ranged from around 18% in Bangladesh and 20% in Malaysia to 94% in Thailand and 100% in the Philippines. In India, which screened only locally produced programmes, 72% of programmes were violent. In the Philippines, around one in four programmes were local.

Foreign programmes were reported to contain more violent incidents per hour than locally produced programmes, reaching a high of 23 per hour in the Philippines and a low of 3.2 in Indonesia. While foreign programmes had more violent incidents, little or no blood was generally shown. In these programmes the villains were drawn from upper and lower classes and violence usually related to social and institutional conflicts. Local productions featured fewer violent incidents, but these tended to be more bloody. Villains were mainly drawn from the upper classes and violence was chiefly due to personal vendettas and inter-familial conflicts.

A Violence Index was computed as a quantitative, descriptive summary of the prevalence of violence on television. This was based on the percentage of programmes containing any violence, the average number of incidents per hour of broadcasting and the percentage of major characters involved in violence and in killings. Bangladesh and Malaysia ranked the lowest while Pakistan and the Philippines were the highest.

Violence on TV in New Zealand

Three major content analyses of violence on television have been conducted in New Zealand in the past 20 years. Since methodologies have remained the same in respect of most of the key measures, comparisons over time have been facilitated. The first study in the mid-1970s measured the amount of violence in all programmes with the exception of news, sports, weather, documentaries and commercials that were screened between 4.00 pm and 10.00 pm on weekdays and 12.00 noon and 10.00 pm on weekends. The author of this study used Gerbner's violence definition and methodology. He found that there were 7.3 violent episodes per hour, only slightly less than the eight episodes per hour recorded in the United States (Ginpil, 1976).

In 1982, Hilary Haines of the New Zealand Mental Health Foundation's 'Media Watch' group conducted a survey of television violence also largely based on Gerbner's model (Haines, 1983). The survey showed similar results to those obtained earlier by Ginpil. All dramatic programmes, except news, documentaries, sports and variety shows, were rated for one week on both New Zealand TV channels. The findings showed that there were 6.09 violent episodes per hour on TV1 and 5.30 per hour on TV2. By far the highest incidence of violence occurred in children's 'animated' programmes in which an average of 26.14 episodes occurred each hour. This was only slightly ahead of westerns which scored 24.85 violent episodes each hour. Haines concluded that the level of violence within each programme had not changed much since the earlier Ginpil study. While the total number of violent episodes per hour was slightly less than in 1976, Haines points out this was largely the result of fewer cartoons being shown rather than any change in broadcasting policy.

More recently, a team from Massey University, funded by New Zealand's Broadcasting Standards Authority, analysed violent acts on the three New Zealand television channels during one week in February 1991 (Watson *et al.*, 1991) using a modification of the violence definition developed by Cumberbatch *et al.* (1987): 'Any *violent image* or action of physical force *or threat thereof* with or without a weapon, against oneself or another person, animal or inanimate object, whether carried through or merely attempted, and whether the action caused injury or not' (the Massey team's additions are in italics).

Watson and his colleagues found 3,012 acts or images classified as 'violent' in 336 hours of programming. Eighteen per cent of these episodes were images rather than acts, and half of these images occurred in news programmes. This produced a violence rate of 8.95 incidents per hour including threats and images, and 6.3 per hour focusing on 'acts' only. This finding falls between the levels reported by Ginpil (1976) of 7.3 acts per hour and Haines (1983) of 5.7 acts per hour.

The latest study from New Zealand found that of victims of violence 85% were male, 81% were white, and 91% were adults. These three categories also represented the great majority of perpetrators of violence (84%, 75% and 87% respectively). The main 'weapons' used included guns (33%), the body – fists/feet (31%) – and voice/raised voices (24%). The use of a variety of weapons in cartoons and the military hardware of the Gulf War, which was being covered at the time of the study, contributed to a much longer list of weapon types. The purposes of violence were not always clear, but most commonly the intention was to kill (26%) or to coerce (16%) the victim. The main results of violence, however, were not harmful. If victims were harmed, death (17%) or mild injury or damage (14%) were the most frequently identified outcomes.

In concluding, Watson *et al.* (1991) argued that their use of a broader definition of violence and their more comprehensive programme output sample, which covered all programmes and not just peak-time ones, produced a higher violence incident count than the earlier New Zealand studies. When this analysis was adjusted with reference to different programmes included in the other studies, however, the overall violence count exhibited no significant increase over the prior studies by Ginpil (1976) and Haines (1983).

Violence on TV in Australia

In Australia, much emphasis has been placed on comparing violence on Australian television with that on television in other countries. Initial evidence about the amount of violence on television derived from a study of the portrayal of family life on television (Stewart, 1983). This study included an analysis of violence within family-centred fiction programmes, broadcast on prime-time Australian television. The only type of violence portrayed between family members was verbal abuse, while physical violence occurred only between family members and outsiders and almost exclusively between males. Overall, 20 of the 39 programmes analysed (51.3%) contained scenes of violence, whether verbal or physical.

A more detailed analysis of television violence was conducted by McCann and Sheehan (1985). They sampled programmes over a two-month period during 1981 from four television channels available in the Brisbane area. The total sample comprised 80 programmes, which included fictional and non-fictional broadcasts. This material was recorded from programmes transmitted before 8.30 am and between 3.00 pm and 11.30 pm on weekdays with sampling extended to midnight on Fridays. At the weekend, programmes were recorded between 6.00 am and midnight on Saturdays and 6.00 am and 8.30 pm on Sundays.

The violence profiling procedure was based on that used by Gerbner *et al.* (1980). The Gerbner violence definition was adopted, but the primary unit of violence analysis was the 'violent episode' which was formally defined as a scene depicting violence that was confined to the same participants. Any change in the characters involved in the violent action began another episode.

McCann and Sheehan found that just over half the programmes (51.3%) and programme hours (53%) they monitored contained violence. This compared favourably with available data on other countries at that time, notably a nine-year average for the United States of 80.3% (Gerbner *et al.*, 1980); 81% in Japan (Iwao *et al.*, 1981); and 66.1% in New Zealand (Haines, 1983). Just the United Kingdom exhibited a similar figure of 56% (Halloran and Croll, 1972).

Much of the violence contained in programmes on mainstream Australian television at that time occurred in fictional output, with very little being found in non-fiction programming. Crime drama shows were found to be almost uniformly violent (96.7%), and a clear majority of cartoons (85.7%) and action-adventure series (73.7%) also contained violence. Non-fiction programmes represented 27.5% of the programmes analysed but only 2.4% of the programmes with violence fell into this general category.

The intensity of violence was measured in terms of the rate at which violent episodes occurred in programmes. There was an overall rate of four violent episodes per programme and 5.4 per broadcast hour. When non-fiction programmes were excluded, however, the average rate per hour increased to 7.4. Compared with other countries for which data were available at that time, this result placed Australian television within the mid-range. The rates per hour elsewhere were just over 4.0 in the United Kingdom, 5.7 in New Zealand, 7.0 in Japan, and 8.1 in the United States.

Violence on Australian television was most likely to be perpetrated by males. Nearly nine in ten (89.5%) violent actions and nearly three out of four killings (74.1%) were perpetrated by male characters. Most victims of violence (76.1%) and most of those characters who were killed on screen (90.3%) were male. This pattern of gender involvement in television violence closely mirrored that observed in other countries.

VIOLENCE ON BRITISH TELEVISION

A handful of content analysis studies of violence on television have been carried out in Britain since 1970. Much of this work has been funded by the broadcasting industry. Halloran and Croll (1972) analysed broadcast material on BBC1 and the ITV midlands region during one week of April 1971. They coded violent incidents occurring in fictional drama programmes and news, current affairs and documentary programmes. The coding instruments for violence were based on those used by Gerbner and programmes were coded for the amount and type of violence they contained, the kinds of characters involved in violence and certain themes or contexts in which violent events happened.

At around the same time the BBC's Audience Research Department undertook a more extensive analysis of television over a six-month period and analysed content from dramatic fiction, news and current affairs, documentaries, and light entertainment programmes (Shaw and Newell, 1972). Unlike Halloran and Croll, the BBC researchers did not follow the Gerbner method precisely, although in general terms their analysis was conceptually of the same type. Violence was treated essentially as an explicit form of interaction between human beings. However, because the BBC's study sampled materials from a broader spectrum of programme types than did Gerbner's, it was considered necessary to expand the definition of violence to include unintentional injurious acts and acts of vandalism against property to code incidents of the sort often reported or depicted in non-fictional programmes.

Each of these British studies indicated that although a common feature of programming, violence was not as prevalent on British television as on American television. In fictional drama, the only category of programming in which direct comparisons between American and British findings were possible, Halloran and Croll found that nearly 56% of programmes coded contained violence – compared with a reported 80% of fictional programmes on American television (Gerbner, 1972).

In nearly 48% of fictional programmes, a major character was involved in violence either as aggressor or victim. The rate of violence on British television drama was 2.8 incidents per programme or just over four incidents an hour, again substantially less than an average rate of over seven incidents per hour reported by Gerbner (1972) for American prime-time television drama.

In their more extensive analysis of British television content, Shaw and Newell found a somewhat greater prevalence of violence in fictional drama in terms of the number of programmes containing at least one major violent incident (63%), but somewhat less violence in terms of the rate at which violent incidents occurred; average numbers of just under two violent incidents per programme or just over two per hour were recorded.

The prevalence and rate of violent incidents was also found in both studies to vary considerably across different forms of drama programme. Halloran and Croll noted that the most violent type of programme in the fiction category was the cartoon. All cartoons coded by them contained some violence and the rate of incidents per hour in such shows was nearly 34. None of the cartoon incidents was fatal, however.

Violence was also prevalent in feature films; 80% contained some violence, and incidents averaged over four per hour. This contrasted with plays, of which 50% were violent, but even then, with an average incident rate of less than one per programme, were unlikely to be very violent programme by programme. After cartoons, the most violent programmes coded by Halloran and Croll were crime, western, and action-adventure shows. All programmes in these categories contained violence with an average rate of nearly eight incidents per hour.

Turning to the BBC's analysis of the prevalence of violence for different programme forms or 'themes', once again, agreement with Halloran and Croll was not complete. Feature films contained at least one major violent incident in 86% of cases which compares quite well with Halloran and Croll's 80% figure, whereas the category of programmes labelled as 'TV series' by the BBC's researchers, which consisted largely of crime-detective, western and action dramas, contained violence in only 75% of cases, as contrasted with *all* such programmes monitored by Halloran and Croll.

Inconsistencies across the violence measures produced by these two studies become even more pronounced when consideration is given to mean rates of violent incidents per programme type. The BBC team coded an average of just over three incidents per hour for feature films, one per hour less than Halloran and Croll. Even more significantly, they coded 2.2 incidents per hour for 'TV series', a little over 25% of the average rate of incidents per hour recorded for the crime-drama, western and action-drama categories by Halloran and Croll. Even when examining particular themes or particular series, the BBC's violence rate statistics remained lower than those reported by Halloran and Croll. Thus, the BBC reported that westerns contained a higher rate of violent incidents than any other type of television series, but at 3.9 incidents per programme, this was still only about half the rate reported by Halloran and Croll for crime-drama, western and action-drama categories.

Cumberbatch *et al.* (1987) found an overall rate for dramatic fiction of 3.60 violent acts per hour which reduced to 2.51 in prime time (8.00 pm to 11.00 pm). These findings compared with Shaw and Newell's (1972) result of 2.74 violent acts per hour for dramatic fiction, and the parallel analysis by Halloran and Croll (1972) who found 4.04 acts per hour. Cumberbatch *et al.* (1988) suggested that there may have been a degree of undercoding in the original BBC study.

The Cumberbatch *et al.* (1987) study found a decline in television violence even against the depressed rates of Shaw and Newell. Thus, overall, the proportion of programmes with violence in them declined considerably. The two major channels, BBC1 and ITV, showed decreases from 49% to 28% and from 51% to 32%, respectively, while the minority channel, BBC2, showed a decline from 55% to 26%. The least decline was in dramatic fiction where 63% of programmes contained violence in 1971 compared with 58% in 1986. Other programme genres that could be directly compared showed a consistent pattern of reduction in violence. Light entertainment reduced from 30% to 26%; current affairs (magazine) programmes reduced from 56% to 40%; and cartoons reduced from 89% to 63% in the proportion of programmes within the genre that contained any violence.

During the early 1990s, a series of monitoring studies were published by the Broadcasting Standards Council in Britain. These studies monitored not only how much violence there was on television, but also how much sex and bad language. The first of these studies monitored television output over four separate two- or three-week periods in 1991 and 1992. The second study examined television ouptut over a single two-week period in 1993, and the third study monitored two separate two-week spells in 1994. This exercise involved a survey of panels of respondents who were interviewed about the programmes they watched and kept a viewing diary. In 1992, a content analysis exercise was also run in parallel to the viewer-based monitoring exercise for one of the sampled weeks, which assessed the amount and distribution of violence on the four UK terrestrial channels, BBC1, BBC2, ITV and Channel 4. In 1993 and 1994, the content analysis was repeated and extended to cover two separate weeks each year, one of which also covered output from three satellite movie channels, Sky Movies, The Movie Channel and Sky Movies Gold (see Broadcasting Standards Council, 1994, 1995).

The content analysis conducted in 1994 sampled a total of 648 pro-grammes over two weeks of terrestrial television output, focusing on trans-missions between 5.30 pm and midnight every evening. A further 168 programmes were video-recorded from the three satellite channels during the second of these two weeks.

During the first week of analysis in 1994, a total of 603 violent scenes were found in 165 programmes (51% of all programmes monitored on the four terrestrial channels during that week). These figures compared with 573 violent scenes in 162 programmes (53% of all programmes monitored) for the same week in 1993. The violence in both years covered 3% of broadcast time, with fictional drama programmes and films contributing the greatest amount of any programme genres to overall violence levels.

During the second week analysed in 1994 and 1993, which also coincided with the single week content analysed in 1992, further year-on-year compar-isons were made. It was reported that 165 programmes monitored in 1994 (51% of total) contained 648 violent scenes, compared with 155 programmes (50% of total) in 1993 which contained 666 violent scenes, and 143 pro-grammes in 1992 (43%) which contained 478 violent scenes. The total amount of violence therefore exhibited a steady increase during evening broadcast hours on the four terrestrial channels. This increase was further reflected in changes to the rates of occurrence of violent scenes per hour, recorded as 4.0 per hour in 1994, 4.0 in 1993, and 2.9 in 1992. In 1992, violent scenes occupied 2% of broadcast time monitored, increasing to 3% in 1993 and to 4% in 1994. Certain programme types appeared to contribute disproportionately to this rise in violence on the small screen. Between 1993 and 1994, for this particular week, rates of violent scenes per hour fell for all major categories of programmes (e.g., national news, factual programmes, light entertainment, sport, religion, children's programmes and fictional drama) except one – films. Films exhibited a marked increase, year-on-year, in levels of violence, from 4.0 violent scenes per hour in 1993 to 7.1 in 1994.

Levels of violence on the three satellite movie channels were generally much higher than the level on terrestrial channels. In 1994, nearly nine out of ten (87%) programmes monitored contained some violence. This represented an increase on 1993 (73%). In 1994, however, the numbers of violent incidents (1,107) fell, year-on-year, from the 1993 level (1,139). The rates of occurrence of violent scenes per hour, however, remained fairly stable at 7.8 in 1993 and 7.6 in 1994.

BROADENING THE DEFINITION OF VIOLENCE

The quantitative measurement of violence on television via content analysis has been largely a process of defining the concept of violence clearly and applying the definition in an accurate and consistent manner to television programmes. What the commonly assumed definitions overlook is that there are many forms of violence other than that which involves purely physical injury and harm. There is emotional and psychological violence, verbal violence, institutional and symbolic violence. Of course, these can be as difficult to define and record as a general concept of 'violence' as physical force.

 As Hodge and Tripp (1986) pointed out, violence can be understood as a multi-faceted concept which does not represent a unitary process or a single set of events. Violence can vary in its severity, justification, consequences, and the intentions of the perpetrator. While physical violence may be the most commonly perceived form of violence on television, a more complete measuring procedure also might include other expressions of violence such as verbal violence and violent images.

Whether or not the use of force or infliction of harm or injury is perceived as violent clearly depends on a number of considerations associated with the particular circumstances surrounding the action. The total context in which the action takes place exerts a significant influence as to how the viewer will interpret the episode or image. Violence on television cannot be taken simply at face value. How violent actions are perceived is related to social norms, personal values and the particular form and context of violence itself.

Context is known to be particularly important to viewers' judgements about violence on television. Whether violence occurs in a realistic or fantasy context, or in a serious or humorous context can make a significant difference to the way it is regarded by television audiences. The perceived realism of the situation in which violence on television is depicted tends to be significantly correlated with how violent the behaviour is rated by viewers (Gunter, 1985). Humour can also dilute the degree to which violent behaviour is upsetting to viewers. A recent opinion poll in the United States indicated that 72% of Americans felt that television entertainment contained too much violence and 80% believed that television violence was harmful to society. Most people were not upset, however, about violence that appeared in a humorous context (Galloway, 1993).

Research elsewhere has shown that people may not even see much of the violence when it is presented in a humorous way. Most viewers, for example, do not regard cartoons as violent (Gunter, 1985; Howitt and Cumberbatch, 1974), despite the fact that content analyses have reported far higher rates of violence on cartoons than anywhere else on television (e.g., Halloran and Croll, 1972; Gerbner *et al.*, 1978, 1979). Some researchers have even argued that violence does not exist in humorous contexts such as cartoons, and that content analysis studies which report high levels of violence in cartoons must therefore be employing dubious violence definitions and coding frames of doubtful veracity (Morrisson, 1993a).

Contextual characteristics of violence

With violence, the literature suggests a number of contextual characteristics that provide cues that viewers use in interpreting the meaning of television portrayals. Among these are reward, intention, motive, remorse, consequences and presentation style.

One of the most important contextual characteristics of any portrayal is whether the action is rewarded or punished. Social learning theory predicts that when people watch a behaviour that is rewarded, they are much more likely to learn it than if the behaviour was punished (Bandura, 1977). Reward has featured as a component of analysis in quantitative studies of television violence. In that context, it has been thought by some researchers to exhibit a potential to contribute towards the development of antisocial behaviour among viewers. In a study of violence on Canadian television, Williams *et al.* (1982) found that violence was often portrayed as a successful way to solve conflicts. This observation was reinforced by American research indicating that the great majority of antisocial acts depicted on television was shown as being rewarded (Potter and Ware, 1987).

Much content analysis research in the past has indicated that violence on television is mostly intentional. Williams *et al.* (1982) found that in 81 hours of television output they examined, over 97% of the violent acts were intentional. While violence may be intentional, it is important to know what a character's intentions were. If a character commits a violent act accidentally, viewers interpret this differently from if the character was portrayed carefully planning the act. In general, intentions to commit violence have been found to be divided into three types (Mees, 1990). Using a social norms approach to define aggression, Mees found three modes of intention that underlie conceptions of motivation for aggressive acts: (1) thoughtlessness (the aggressor should have taken possible dangers into consideration but did not); (2) selfishness (the aggressor knows that the action will cause distress or harm, but accepts this and places his/her own interests above those of others); and (3) malice (wickedness is accepted and intended by the aggressor).

Motive is closely linked to intention. A television character's motives are filtered through the viewer's legal or moral context of behaviour (Gunter, 1985). Defensive or altruistic aggression may be interpreted as milder than offensive, intentional, or sadistic aggression. Gunter (1985) argued that unusual forms of aggression in which a strong motive (sadistic or sexual) is apparent are perceived as more serious. Thus, the intention of the character can alter a viewer's interpretation of a violent episode.

In a study of Finnish television, Mustonen and Pulkinen (1993) measured motivation by dividing aggression into defensive and offensive groups. Within offensive aggression there were five values: instrumental, masochistic, reactive-expressive, sadistic and altruistic. They reported finding that spontaneous acts (57%) were more numerous than planned aggression (27%) and that first strike acts (76%) were much higher than retaliatory ones (12%). Aggressors achieved their desired ends fully or almost fully in about 25% of the acts.

Remorse has been linked to reward and punishment of violence, and is conceived as a psychological form of punishment. The greater the displayed remorse over violence that has been committed by a perpetrator, the more one might expect viewers to rate the violent act seriously. The consequences of violence (i.e., the emotional or physical pain or injury) are an important contextual element that is used by viewers to interpret the meaning of those portrayals. Most research indicates that when violence is shown with no consequences (lack of pain, suffering, sorrow or remorse), viewers are not likely to feel inhibited in performing aggressively and their levels of aggressive behaviour usually increase (Baron, 1971a, b, 1979). Audiences' perceptions of televised violence are also affected by any accompanying pain or suffering displayed on the part of victims. Gunter (1983) reported an experiment to determine people's perceptions of the harm of violence after they had viewed one of 18 different violent programme excerpts. He found that when consequences of the violence were shown, viewers thought it was much more serious. However, this finding only held with relatively realistic content and not with fantasy material.

Insights from viewers' perceptions

One assumption of some content analysis researchers has been that 'messages' inferred from programme content profiles concerning various social groups are recognized and encoded by audiences who assimilate them into their existing knowledge structures. It is also assumed that more frequent viewers will be more strongly influenced by television's messages than will less frequent viewers purely as a function of greater volume of exposure to them. However, measures of the *amount* of viewing may not be valid and sufficient indicators of television's effects, because television content and viewers' preferences for that content vary considerably, and two heavy viewers who watch totally different kinds of programmes may hold two quite disparate sets of beliefs as a result.

In comparison with straightforward descriptive content analysis, relatively little research has been done on how viewers perceive television's images of social groups and phenomena. Content analyses, from which inferences about television effects are often made, may actually be poor indicators of audience perceptions (Ceulemans and Fauconnier, 1979; Perl-off *et al.*, 1982). For instance, traditional procedures take into account what viewers themselves perceive to be violent. Typically, the violence of a pro-gramme is assessed in terms of the number of incidents it contains that match what researchers themselves decide is violent.

Although this procedure can produce reliable codings of specific kinds of incidents, these codings may have relevance only for the original coders and may lack any real meaning for the general viewing public untutored in this coding methodology. From those simple frequency counts, Gerbner and his colleagues, for example, have derived more complex assumptions of their results in which units of content occur together on television to form recur-ring profiles that represent messages about the structure and dynamics of contemporary society (Gerbner *et al.*, 1980). No evidence is provided, how-ever, to show whether or not these so-called messages are actually perceived and learned by viewers.

Problems arise when generalizing from statements about or descriptions of television content and the symbolic messages carried by that content to how the content is perceived and understood by the audience. It is necessary to establish the degree of equivalence between the meanings attributed to programmes by trained coders and the meanings attributed to them by ordinary viewers. To what extent do the images and messages defined by content analysis share the same universe of meanings as the perceptions of viewers? With incidents such as shootings or fights, it may be relatively easy to achieve correspondence between programme structures defined *a priori* by a system of content coding and audience perceptions of content. But it may be less easy to accurately infer meaningful messages concerning norms or relationships unless direct information is obtained from the viewers (Gunter, 1981, 1985).

Although it may be impossible to define exactly what the audience in general means by 'violence', there is evidence to suggest that viewers' perceptions do not accord strongly with objective counts of programme incidents. Research has shown that structures such as those monitored in message system analysis are not always perceived by ordinary viewers as salient attributes of programmes. Violent scenes may not appear as impor-tant aspects of content and viewers may fail to mention violence in discussions about films containing violent action shortly after viewing unless speci-fically asked about such content. In a field study conducted by audience researchers at the British Broadcasting Corporation (Shaw and Newell, 1972), viewers were asked to fill out a questionnaire about specific pro-grammes shortly after they had been broadcast, in which reactions to violence and other aspects of programme content were probed. Findings showed that perceptions of programmes as 'violent' did not depend on the actual number of violent incidents. Nor was there any strong relationship between perceiving a programme as violent and verbally reported emotional arousal. Assessment of violence as unjustified, however, was associated with negative evaluations of the programme. Most respondents also claimed that 'realism' was an essential element in their perceptions of televised violence, with violent real-life events reported in news bulletins or shown in documentaries generally rated as more violent than violence portrayed in fictional settings. Although this study can be regarded as little more than exploratory, it nevertheless indicates that viewers' personal assessments of television programmes are determined by many different content factors, of which violence is only one, and by no means the most important.

Research has indicated that adults and children alike are capable of highly refined judgements about television violence. Viewers have their own scales for deciding the seriousness of incidents and their opinions do not always concur with researchers' categorizations of violence (Gunter, 1985; van der Voort, 1986). Researchers who have allowed viewers to decide for themselves about the seriousness of different portrayals of violence have found that viewers' perceptions can vary widely and are influenced by a number of attributes of the portrayals themselves.

Gunter (1985) reported 12 experimental studies in which groups of people were shown scenes taken from British crime series, American crime series, westerns, science fiction series and cartoons. Viewers were invited to make a variety of personal judgements about each scene along a set of qualitative rating scales. Scenes were shown singly or in pairs for comparative judgement. Variations in perceptions of the scenes were examined in relation to a number of things – the types of programmes the scenes came from, the types of weapons or instruments of violence that were used, the physical setting of the action, and the degree of observable harm the violence caused to victims in each scene. The results indicated that viewers may be significantly influenced in their personal opinions about television violence by many of these attributes of television portrayals.

Familiarity of surroundings, for example, is one of the most powerful factors influencing viewers' perceptions of television violence (Gunter, 1985; Gunter and Furnham, 1984). The closer to home the violence is portrayed as being in terms of place and time, the more serious it is judged to be. Thus, it was found that violence in British crime series was generally rated as more violent than similar portrayals on American-made series of the same type. Portrayals of 'violent' behaviour in cartoons or science fiction programmes, however, were seen as essentially nonviolent.

Perceptions of television violence were also found to vary significantly with a number of other characteristics of television portrayals. The kinds of fictional characters who inflict the violence, how the violence is inflicted, and how much harm is done to those on the receiving end all emerged as important mediators of viewers' opinions about television violence.

Some of the results, however, exhibited more complex patterns. One illustration of this was a set of paradoxical opinions about violence perpetrated by law enforcers and by criminals, or by men and by women, which varied with the type of programme from which they came. With extracts from British crime series, for instance, viewers were most concerned about violence inflicted by men upon women; while in scenes from American series, they were concerned more by women being violent to men (Gunter and Furnham, 1985). In an American context, violence performed by criminals was perceived in more serious terms than that used by law enforcers (usually the police); while in British settings, it was law enforcer violence that viewers were more troubled by (Gunter, 1985).

One can only speculate at this stage as to the reasons why these differences in opinion occurred. One answer may lie in the societal norms regarding the use of violence. Traditionally, society approves of some forms of violence under certain circumstances, and disapproves of others. For example, violence used by police officers to uphold the law, or that used by private citizens in self-defence against an attacker are, within certain limits, permissible. Under these circumstances, however, the use of violence must not far outweigh the magnitude of the behaviour of the lawbreaker or attacker. Where the force used to repel an attacker is much greater than that justified by the initial provocation, violent retaliation will not be found so acceptable.

Children can make distinctions between different forms of violence on television as well. While young viewers may not have the maturity of adults, they readily learn to distinguish broad programme genres and the conventions to which they adhere in the kinds of portrayals they contain.

Two American studies conducted as part of the US Surgeon General's research programme on Television and Social Behaviour 25 years ago represented early attempts to assess children's perceptions of television violence. In both cases, young viewers' reactions were obtained to brief extracts taped from prime-time entertainment programmes on the American networks. Groups of boys, aged 11 and 14 years, were individually shown six different scenes of which four were violent and two were not. In all, boys' reactions were obtained to eight different violent scenes. Each set of violent scenes contained an instance of violence against property, non-fatal violence against another person, a killing by gunfire, and a second killing by other means (Greenberg and Gordon, 1972b, c).

Each violent scene was evaluated in terms of amount of perceived violence, liking, realism, and acceptability of observed behaviour. The researchers focused more on differences in ratings between the various socio-economic and ethnic groups who were sampled than upon differences in ratings due to the nature of the violent content. Even so, they did present tables of results showing the average scores per rating scale obtained by each of the eight scenes. These scores indicated that scenes that featured the death of a victim by shooting were perceived as the most violent scenes by both 11-year-old and 14-year-old boys. For the older group the next most violent scene was one which depicted death by a fiery car crash, whereas for the younger group, it was a scene showing killing by suffocation. For both groups, the least violent scenes depicted a stylized fist-fight or showed some-one smashing up furniture.

The fact that children make distinctions between different forms of viol-ence on television was further demonstrated by van der Voort (1976) in a study of Dutch children. In all, 314 children recruited from three different schools were shown full-length episodes of eight television series. The epi-sodes varied from contemporary crime drama (*Starsky and Hutch* and *Charlie's Angels*) to adventure series (*Dick Turpin* and *The Incredible Hulk*) and fantasy cartoons (*Scooby Doo, Tom and Jerry, Popeye* and *Pink Panther*). Immediately after showing each programme, a post-exposure questionnaire was filled in measuring ten perception variables: (1) readiness to see violence, (2) approval of violent actions seen in the programme, (3) enjoyment of the violence seen, (4) evaluation of the programme, (5) emo-tional responsiveness, (6) absorption in the programme, (7) detachment while watching, (8) identification with the programme's chief characters, (9) perceived reality of the programme, and (10) comprehension and reten-tion of programme content.

Van der Voort investigated whether programmes perceived to be realistic were also more absorbing for children who would thereby respond to them with more emotion and less detachment than they showed toward pro-grammes perceived to be more fantastic. Results showed that law enforce-ment programmes as well as children's adventure programmes were rated as realistic. Thus, *Starsky and Hutch* and *Charlie's Angels* were perceived to be realistic, while *The Incredible Hulk, Dick Turpin,* and cartoons were seen as fantastic. Realistic programmes were watched with more involvement, more emotion, and less detachment. The two crime drama series mentioned above were regarded as containing the most violence of any of the programmes the children were shown.

Van der Voort found, in fact, that judgements of the amount of violence programmes contained by 9- to 12-year-olds differed little from those of adults. He made the important point, however, that (p. 329):

> children's violence ratings do differ from those of content analysts who analyze the amount of violence a program contains by means of the systematic observation of programs recorded on videotape. Programs that are extremely violent according to 'objective' content analysis can be seen by children as hardly containing any violence.

Thus, although content analyses have identified cartoons as being among the most violent of television programmes in terms of numbers of objectively identified incidents per hour or per show (Gerbner, 1972; Gerbner and Gross, 1976; Halloran and Croll, 1972), such programmes tend to be seen by children as containing hardly any violence at all.

On the basis of the above findings with adults and children, it is clear that viewers classify programme content differently from the descriptive analysis of research frameworks that employ narrow definitions of violence.

Although objective cataloguing of incidents in programmes has the useful function of providing reliable counts of how often certain categories of items occur, the relevance or meaning of those items for the audience can be properly ascertained only through the perceptions of viewers themselves. There would be some merit in recommending a subjective approach rather than a purely objective one in the analysis at least of televised violence because this perspective enables one to identify the programmes that viewers themselves take most seriously. A subjective audience input to a content analysis can therefore render a useful embellishment to an otherwise dry approach to analyzing the appearance of violence on television.

2   The research

BACKGROUND TO RESEARCH

The research project described in this book was launched in a climate of growing public concern about violence on television in which the major broadcasting organizations in the United Kingdom and their regulators had come under increasing political pressure to tackle what was seen in a number of quarters as being the serious problem of violence on television. Incidents such as the Hungerford massacre in 1988, the more recent murder case of James Bulger in Liverpool, and the Thomas Hamilton mass shooting of small children in Dunblane, Scotland, shocked the nation. In the search for an explanation as to why such horrific incidents could occur, media violence became targeted in all three instances as a possible causal factor. The attention drawn to television, in particular, as an alleged purveyor of violence, led to questions being asked at the highest levels of government about the degree of control over television programme content and the effectiveness with which the medium was regulated.

Many of the accusations levelled against television's depiction of violence have tended to focus upon the quantity rather than the quality of the violence, even though in terms of its possible effects upon the audience, the nature of any violence shown is at least as, if not more, important than how much is shown. Organized lobbies have argued that there is 'too much' violence on television, though often without defining what the acceptable limits might be and invariably without offering an accurate assessment of what is meant by violence and how much of it actually appears on screen.

It is perfectly reasonable to obtain clarification from broadcasters about the rules and procedures they employ to monitor and control violence on television, and for the public to be assured that there is a responsible attitude towards this issue within the television industry, with adequate safeguards being deployed to protect the public interest. Effective control of television content, however, cannot occur without accurate information about the nature of current broadcast output. It makes no sense to accuse television of crimes it did not commit. In the current context, it is essential to know how much violence actually occurs in television programmes, and also whether violence permeates all television or is located predominantly in certain types of programmes, on particular channels and at certain times of the day. It is equally important to realize that violence can come in many different forms and occur in different settings. Since past research has shown that, in terms of the possible impact of media violence upon those who consume it, such features can make an important difference (see Gunter, 1985), it is highly relevant to any analysis of violent content on television to establish a comprehensive classification of the types of violence which actually occur.

As Chapter 1 showed, earlier studies have been carried out on this topic, spanning a period of more than sixty years. Violence levels on British television have been examined periodically over the past twenty-five years. A research methodology known as content analysis has been applied to investigate specifically the question of how much violence is shown on television. This technique involves the elaboration of an *a priori* definition of 'violence' which is combined with a set of instructions, representing a 'coding frame', which can be deployed to quantify and classify particular types of incidents within programmes. It is important to underscore the fact that this research methodology does not set out to measure any possible effects of televised violence upon members of the audience. It is not designed to do so. Thus, it would be wrong to generalize from any findings yielded by a content analysis exercise to draw inferential statements about possible television effects.

ISSUES OF DEFINITION AND METHOD

Content analysis research attempts to provide systematic and objective description and measurement of media phenomena. In the case of television, this means cataloguing on-screen incidents and events, and the types of individual involved in them. Even though this methodology is restricted to the assessment of television programme content rather than audiences and their reactions, it has been employed to define the types of events to which viewers are likely to be exposed. While it cannot demonstrate audience reactions or media effects, whether or not content analysis provides accurate accounts of on-screen phenomena can depend upon the way in which those phenomena are defined by the analytical frame of reference that is used.

Comparisons of different measures of television violence have indicated that estimates of the amount of violence on television can vary considerably, inviting debate about which measures provide the most valid and credible indications about how much violence television displays. Questions have also been asked about particular measurement systems especially where television violence profiles are represented in terms of an 'index' which is itself based on the questionable aggregation of a number of distinct measures which may not belong together (Blank, 1977a, b; Coffin and Tuchman, 1972b). Quite apart from issues of definition, therefore, there are important questions to be addressed about which measures of violence provide the most robust and accurate indicators of how much violence television actually depicts. Most content analysis studies of television violence have adopted as key measures, the percentage of programmes that contain any violence and the numbers of violent acts that occur per programme or per hour of programme output. The violent act measure *per se* may offer a limited and, in some instances, misleading indicator of the quantity of violence on television. Before turning to the methodology used in the current research project, it will be informative to review previous debates about measurement, particularly as they have applied to the most influential programme of research conducted on this subject by the Cultural Indicators group in the United States over a 20-year period spanning the late 1960s to mid-1980s.

One comparison of five different studies of television violence in the United States in which data had been produced from common television seasons showed that variations in the definition of violence could yield widely varying accounts of the amount of violence on television. Coffin and Tuchman (1972a) compared studies which collected violence ratings data across the 1968 and 1969 television seasons: (1) research conducted by George Gerbner for the National Commission on the Causes and Prevention of Violence (the Milton Eisenhower Commission (Baker and Ball, 1969) in 1967 and 1968, then for the Surgeon General in 1969 (Gerbner 1972), and finally for the National Institute of Mental Health in 1970 and 1971 (Gerbner *et al.*, 1972); (2) work carried out by Greenberg and Gordon (1972a) for the Surgeon General in 1969; (3) a further study for the Surgeon General's enquiry by Clark and Blankenburg (1972), covering the period 1953 to 1969; (4) an analysis of programmes broadcast in 1968 by the *Christian Science Monitor* (1968a, b); and (5) an annual monitoring exercise conducted by the National Association for Better Broadcasting covering data obtained by the NABB in 1968.

The Gerbner research was introduced in Chapter 1. His analysis generally focused on one week's programming broadcast in the autumn on the three main US networks (ABC, CBS and NBC) which trained coders who monitored and noted instances of violent acts in accordance with a stated definition. The definition of violence encompassed humorous as well as serious violent incidents, and included accidents and acts of nature. Gerbner excluded for his analysis any programmes which did not have storylines, such as quiz shows and variety shows.

Greenberg and Gordon (1972a) developed violence ratings for programmes in the 1969 season based on the judgement of a sample of professional television critics and a sample of the general public. As an additional refinement, half the general public sample was given a definition of violence to guide them in their ratings ('By violence, I mean how much fighting, shooting, yelling, or killing there usually is in the show.'), while the other half was not given a definition. The results showed a high correlation both within the general public sample (whether or not working with a definition) and between the general public and the critics.

The Clark and Blankenburg study, which was introduced in Chapter 1, examined the prevalence of violence in several American media (network television entertainment, motion pictures, a popular magazine, four leading daily newspapers and network news programmes). Synopses of television programmes, as published in *TV Guide* for the years 1953 to 1969, were used to identify television violence. Pairs of raters coded each synopsis as to whether or not the programme depicted 'physical acts or the threat of physical acts by humans designed to inflict physical injury to persons or damage to property'.

The *Christian Science Monitor* conducted two studies in 1968 in which 31 *Monitor* staff members classified network programmes as nonviolent, moderately violent and violent. At least two and often three monitors kept notes on each show, recording 'all killings, other incidents of violence, and threats of violence'.

Finally, the National Association for Better Broadcasting (NABB) published annual evaluations of television programmes, focusing on their desirable and undesirable features, and overall suitability for viewing by children. This global evaluation was designed to provide a guide to parents and teachers in the selection of programmes for children's viewing. The evaluations were done by an NABB committee consisting of teachers, specialists in child education, parents, students and 'experienced professionals in the fields of psychiatry, mental health, journalism and education'.

Coffin and Tuchman (1972a) made comparisons first between those sources which had produced data for the 1968 television season, and then between those which had studied programmes in the 1969 season. The 1968 season had been covered by Gerbner, the *Christian Science Monitor*, the NABB, and Clark and Blankenburg (1972). Gerbner and the *Monitor* had analysed adjacent weeks of television broadcasts, and both had employed coders to view specific episodes of programmes and to count acts of violence. There were 53 prime-time programmes which both studies had covered in common. Of these, 20 were classified by both studies as 'violent', 14 programmes both agreed were 'nonviolent', but in 19 cases there was disagreement between the two studies. In these cases, Gerbner had coded them as violent, while the *Monitor* had classified them as nonviolent. Thus, around one-half of the programmes that Gerbner had designated as violent were deemed nonviolent by the *Monitor*.

Most of the divergent programmes were situation comedies and network movies. In the case of the situation comedies, the difference emerged as a result of the inclusion of violent acts in humorous contexts on the part of Gerbner, but not on the part of the *Monitor*. The divergence in results for movies could be accounted for by the fact that the nature of network movies could change radically from one week to the next.

When the NABB research findings were compared with Gerbner's, 44 programmes were found to have been mutually studied. Eighteen of these programmes were classified as violent by both studies, while 13 were classed as nonviolent. There were an additional 13 programmes, however, which Gerbner counted as violent but which the NABB did not. The NABB study was found to exhibit a high level of consistency in programme classifications with the *Christian Science Monitor*. Out of the 68 programmes mutually studied here, both agreed in the case of 20 programmes that they were violent, and in the case of 43 programmes that they were nonviolent. There were just five programmes on which the *Monitor* and NABB disagreed. In three instances, they were classed as violent only by the *Monitor*, and in two instances violence classifications were given only by the NABB.

For the 1969 season, Gerbner's results were compared with those produced by Greenberg and Gordon (1972a). In the latter case, an average violence score was computed for each programme based on the 'violence rating' scale. Separate violence scores were obtained from the general public and television critics. Since the violence scores for the various programmes were a continuous variable, it was not readily possible to dichotomize the programmes into violent and nonviolent. Thus the scale scores of Greenberg and Gordon were compared with the total violent acts score for each programme common to both studies. To control for differing programme lengths, Coffin and Tuchman (1972a) created a score of number of violent acts per half hour of programme running time.

Television critics' and the general public's violence ratings for the same programmes were highly correlated. Neither of these groups was found to agree strongly with violence ratings based on Gerbner's content analysis data. Once again, this discrepancy derived mainly from the tendency of ordinary viewers and television critics to discount 'violent' acts occurring in comedy programmes as being essentially 'nonviolent', while such incidents were counted in exactly the same way as any other form of violent behaviour by Gerbner.

Coffin and Tuchman (1972a) identified two major factors underlying the discrepancy between the findings of the standard content analysis design adopted by Gerbner and the alternative studies which had either obtained opinions from viewers or utilized a content analysis-type framework whose definitions of 'violence' were guided by assumptions about audience perceptions. First, Gerbner's analysis tended to omit many network programmes from the violence measurement exercise which were essentially 'nonviolent' programmes. The implication here was that Gerbner's approach gave an inflated impression of the prevalence of violence on television programme output in general. Second, although the core definition of violence across many of the early studies tended to reflect a common set of ingredients ('the overt expression of physical force against others or self, or the compelling of action against one's will on pain of being hurt or killed'), in actual application coders were specifically instructed by Gerbner to include humorous violence, accidents, and acts of nature as falling within the framework of analysis. The other studies reviewed by Coffin and Tuchman clearly indicated that they did not consider such acts as falling within the area of common social concern about the issue of violence on television.

Although recognizing that Gerbner's research represented a painstaking and thorough examination of violence on television, for Coffin and Tuchman (1972a) its shortcomings resided in the selectiveness of the programme samples used and the inclusion in the definition of 'violence' of incidents in contexts which would not be regarded by the public as violent in nature. They argued that a violence *rating* system required more stringent criteria than those adopted by a purely objective and dispassionate count of incidents all weighted in the same way regardless of context. Instead, before a programme could be legitimately classified as 'violent' in an ecologically valid fashion, some consideration of audience opinions and of the potential effects of the violence depicted in the programme should be taken into account. Distinctions needed to be made between potentially harmful and innocuous depictions of violence if the violence ratings were to be meaningful and socially useful.

There is little doubt that in many ways the content analysis research conducted by Gerbner and his colleagues was methodologically tighter than most of the other studies reviewed by Coffin and Tuchman. Indeed, the longitudinal monitoring studies which relied on second-hand sources of information about television content, such as the programme synopses provided in television guides, provided at best only questionable data about violence levels on television. The studies which employed the perceptions of viewers or specialist groups, such as television critics, on the other hand, did point to the distinctions viewers could make about violent portrayals based on their form and the contexts in which they occurred. This finding indicated that audience perceptions might therefore provide an important basis on which to build a system of classification of televised violence. Once established, of course, it would still be necessary to adopt a procedure of monitoring programme output to detect occurrences of different types of portrayal.

The crucial point is that the measurement of violence on television is a difficult problem because violence definitions must be developed as a starting point, and then those definitions must be consistently applied to television content. The more complex the definitions that are deployed, the more difficult it becomes to ensure that they are applied in a similar and consistent fashion by different coders. The significance of such qualitative input to the definition of violence, in which potentially harmful or upsetting violence is distinguished from innocuous content, is that it precludes the adoption of a system which represents little more than a mechanical catalogue with little meaning or social utility. This point is succinctly stated by the US Secretary of Health, Education and Welfare, Elliott Richardson, who was quoted by Coffin and Tuchman (1972a, p. 18):

[A] simple index of the incidence of TV violence is of only limited usefulness. A more constructive profile of TV violence could be developed,
made up of indices of a number of significant dimensions – level, frequency, characteristics of those involved, their motivations, whether the
violence is explained or not, audience perceptions of the violence, and its
short and long-term effects on various kinds of viewers.

This advice was roundly rejected by Gerbner and his colleagues who argued
that their system of violence content analysis had been misunderstood. Input
from media effects or audience perceptions research had no place in their
analysis. Its aim was to articulate the overall structural patterns of content,
some of which might not be consciously apprehended by ordinary viewers or
even by professional television critics (Eleey *et al.*, 1972a). Such patterns
could reveal underlying 'messages' generally concerned with power relations
among different groups within the population, namely those who were
predominantly victimized and those who were the sources of that victimization.

Unlike Coffin and Tuchman (1972a), the Gerbner system of analysis did
not pre-classify programmes either as 'violent' or 'nonviolent'; it simply
counted the extent to which violent acts occurred in different programmes
and who was involved in them. Eleey *et al.* (1972a) further argued that their
analysis did take contextual features into account insofar as examining
whether violence was central or peripheral to the plot and to the characters
in a drama.

The challenge to violent act counting posed by reference to Greenberg and
Gordon's (1972a) analysis of viewers' and television critics' perceptions of
how violent different programmes were judged to be, was brushed aside on
the basis that the perceptual data referred to in this particular study were
derived from viewers' and critics' labelling of programmes, presented as titles
only, as being violent or not. This task was seen as being heavily dependent
on viewers' and critics' abilities to recall former viewing experiences rather
than being based upon actual live viewing experiences with these programmes. Since reportedly heavy viewers of the programmes examined by
Greenberg and Gordon differed consistently from reportedly light viewers,
this study produced evidence which lacked consistency across different
judges in the way particular programmes were rated for violence. (Later
research by Greenberg and Gordon (1972b, c) adopted a different methodology in which viewers rated actual programme excerpts depicting different forms of violence.)

The evaluative analyses reported by the *Christian Science Monitor* and
National Association for Better Broadcasting, both of which purported to
represent quantitative assessments of television violence, were both found
wanting by Eleey *et al.* (1972a) on basic methodological criteria. They lacked
reliability checks across different coders; appeared to provide quantitative
measures of the amount of violence but were unclear about how these

measures were implemented and interpreted to derive the reported violence classifications applied to different programmes; and excluded programmes from their analysis on the basis of an apparent *a priori* and unchecked judgement by the researchers that violence was unlikely to occur in particular programmes. Gerbner and his colleagues accepted that, ideally, the development ratings system for television violence ought to involve research which could distinguish between 'harmful' and 'harmless' depictions of violence, but concern about this point should not be allowed to cloud important distinctions between certain research methodologies and what they are capable of measuring.

> there is a basic confusion running... through much of the current discussion about a rating system [for television violence]. It is the confusion between research on the effects of televised violence and the reliable determination of violent action in television programs. The latter can provide the basis for research about the role of symbolic functions of dramatic violence in real-life conceptions and behaviour, but not the other way around.

> (Eleey *et al.*, 1972a, p. 30)

The argument for scientific rigour in conducting quantitative analyses of television violence is a powerful one. The conceptual distinction between analyzing the characteristics of programme content and measuring the effects of that content is crucial to the establishment of a clearly defined frame of reference designed to yield reliable estimates of the different types of portrayals that programmes contain. Yet, if such a methodology is to produce a system for classifying television programmes in a socially useful and relevant fashion, there is a legitimate question to be asked about the role that may be played in the development of this ratings system of judgements about programmes and their contents as supplied by members of the public and various professional groups such as educationalists, psychologists and television critics. The emphasis upon the need for *reliability* in television violence measurement should not be made at the expense of attaining *validity* in such measurement (see Coffin and Tuchman, 1972b). Validity here centres on the production of data which can effectively assist socially useful decision making about television. At the same time, however, there remains a view that concern about producing 'socially useful and relevant' evidence on television violence should not be based simply on unverified preconceptions about the nature of programmes to the exclusion of independent and objective analysis of the incidents they contain (see Eleey *et al.*, 1972b).

Other measurement issues

Criticisms of the measurement system adopted by Gerbner in the United States also pointed to other shortcomings which further called its validity into question. The first of these centred on whether the programme samples from which violence profiles were derived were sufficiently representative of general programme output on the American television networks. The second problem was associated with the way the Violence Index itself was calculated. Thus, quite apart from whether one accepts or rejects the arguments about the significance of viewers' perceptions and opinions to the framing of a meaningful definition of violence, separate doubts surfaced about other aspects of the content quantification methodology.

The programme sample monitored by Gerbner, for instance, was criticized for its time-span and for what it did not include in its programme analysis. The sample typically comprised one week of prime-time and week-end morning programming selected during the autumn of each year. This sample was designed to reflect the character of each season's television fiction programming for general audiences and for children (Gerbner and Gross, 1976). As one critic observed, however, such is the variation in programming throughout the season it was unlikely that any one week alone could prove to be properly representative of the whole year's output (Blank, 1977a).

Another reason why Gerbner's usual programme samples did not reflect the nature of television programming in general at the time was because they usually excluded news, current affairs, documentaries, 'specials', sports and variety programmes. These programmes tended to occupy large parts of the daily television schedules and took up a large portion of the average viewer's total viewing time.

The Violence Index, which was introduced in Chapter 1, was challenged as being of doubtful validity as a measure of the amount of violence on television because of the arbitrary way in which it combined programme features without justifying the significance of the individual components. The formula through which the Violence Index was obtained consisted of aggregating over five separate features:

1 the percentage of programmes containing an occurrence of violence;
2 double the rate of violent episodes per programme;
3 double the rate of violent episodes per hour of programming;
4 the percentage of leading characters involved in violent acts, either as perpetrators or as victims;
5 the percentage of leading characters involved in killing, either as perpetrators or victims.

The index thus attempted both to quantify and to aggregate a number of disparate and rather unusual observations. The resulting index number was a summary of the frequency with which violence occurred on screen (counted three different ways), of the roles assigned to victims and aggressors, and of the relative frequency with which a violent act resulted in death. The complexity of the process was compounded by the fact that some numbers constituted percentages while others were straightforward numerical sums. The index thus became a composite figure whose validity and usefulness rested on a host of controversial assumptions, which in turn ultimately rested on Gerbner's broad, undiscriminating definition of violence. Shifts in the index were not readily interpretable unless the index was accepted as synonymous with violence. Even if the definition, the time period from which programmes were sampled, and the rules of programme inclusion and exclusion were accepted, any difference of opinion about the kinds of violence that should be emphasized would render the index an imperfect indicator.

Blank (1977a, b) pointed out that it was unlikely that the Violence Index was truly a measure of the amount of television violence in a sample of programmes because among the components which it included were such essentially nonviolent factors as leading characters involved in acts of violence. Thus, while the number of violent scenes on television could decrease over a period of time, an increase in the number of characters involved in violent episodes during the same period could be sufficient to push up the overall Violence Index score, giving an impression that there was more violence on television, when in fact there was less. Gerbner and Gross (1976) argued that indices by definition are arbitrary correlations and that their index served as a heuristic device leading to the analysis of the shifts in components behind the trend in index scores. This statement, however, failed to address the fact that changes in the apparent levels of violence on television as indicated by this figure could be caused by changes in the character of violence rather than any shifts in the frequency with which it occurred.

This review has served to highlight that attempts to quantify violence on television through content analysis can be fraught with difficulties. These problems centre on the validity of the definitional starting point of any such analysis, which may or may not reflect public conceptions of violence. Quite apart from this definitional issue, however, the way it is applied in terms of the programmes that are included for analysis and the nature of the violence counting and reporting procedures, is a matter of crucial importance. Selectivity in the sampling of programmes from the total television output will have a significant bearing on whether content analysis results provide an accurate indication of the extent to which violence permeates the schedules. One week's programming out of 52 in the year is unlikely to represent the full range and variety of television output across the seasons. Taken at the beginning of a new season, however, it may provide a flavour of what television channels regard as the nature of current public tastes and interests, and the extent to which violence features in network planners' thinking about the ingredients likely to prove economically most successful for them in the coming broadcast year.

Recently, researchers in the United States have argued strongly for the adoption of random sampling methods in the selection of programmes for content analysis. Only in this way, it was argued, can programme samples be achieved which are representative of television ouptut more generally. Using this methodology, these researchers constructed a composite week of television output for 20+ television channels based on a random sampling frame which selected time units at random across a time period spanning several months. Once the time units had been selected, programmes which began or ran during these periods were chosen for analysis (Potter *et al.*, 1996).

Putting the core definitional issue aside, the way in which the amount of violence catalogued within a particular coding frame is then expressed in quantitative terms can significantly affect the impression that is created of how much violence is shown on screen. Stating what percentage of programmes contains any violence may create an impression that violence is widespread, but ignores differences which may exist between programmes in their individual violence tally. Expressing the quantity of violence in terms of numbers of violent acts may fail to reveal just how prominent violence was as a feature of programmes. In one programme violence may occur throughout, while in another it might be contained within one short segment of the programme. The prominence of violence may depend upon how much of the programme's total running time it occupies, but this measure is seldom used in content analysis studies. When it has been deployed such a measure gives a completely different impression of how much violence there is on television from violent act counts or measures based on the percentages of programmes that contain any violence (see Cumberbatch *et al.*, 1987). All these various measures need to be explored.

RESEARCH INTO UK TV VIOLENCE IN THE 1990s

Violence on television in the United Kingdom has been measured on only a handful of occasions since television began in this country. While concerns about the impact of television violence, especially upon children, can be traced back to the 1950s (Himmelweit *et al.*, 1958), the first attempts to produce systematic and comprehensive analysis of the amount of violence on television did not occur until the beginning of the 1970s (Halloran and Croll, 1972; Newell and Shaw, 1972). The early 1970s studies were not updated until the mid-1980s (Cumberbatch *et al.*, 1987). During the 1990s, smaller scale content analyses have been commissioned annually by the Broadcasting Standards Council (1994, 1995), which have focused mainly on peak-time programme transmissions. Apart from these few studies, the only other evidence about violence on television has derived from more specialized pieces of research which have focused upon particular episodes, such as the television news coverage given to the miners' strike in the early 1980s (Cumberbatch *et al.*, 1985) and the Gulf War in 1991 (Morrisson, 1992).

The current study represents the latest comprehensive analysis of violence on television which covers all programme output across the day and night.

That it does this not only for the four terrestrial television channels in the United Kingdom but also for four satellite television channels, means that this is the biggest single content analysis study of violence on television ever carried out, in terms of hours of programming analysed. The findings reported in this book focus on:

1 the quantitative assessment of the amount and distribution of violence on UK television;
2 the levels of violence depicted on different channels at different times of the day;
3 the contribution to overall levels of violence made by different types of programmes;
4 the physical attributes of television violence and the settings and contexts in which it occurs; and
5 the types of characters involved as perpetrators and victims of violence and the degree of injury or harm which generally follows from involvement in violence.

The study provides an update on research conducted for the BBC by Aston University's Applied Psychology Division (Cumberbatch *et al.*, 1987) in 1986 which assessed the amount and types of violence on the four terrestrial channels. From time to time, therefore, comparisons are made with the findings of this earlier study, where common measures have been applied.

METHODOLOGY OF CURRENT STUDY

The research methodology involved analysis of selected samples of programme output on eight television channels operating in the United Kingdom. These channels included the four terrestrially transmitted channels – BBC1, BBC2, ITV and Channel 4. In addition, four channels were selected for analysis which were available via satellite transmissions – Sky One, UK Gold, Sky Movies and The Movie Channel. The last four channels were selected on the basis of being among the most watched channels available via satellite transmission. Because they were selected out of a much larger sample of available channels, they cannot be regarded as representative of all satellite television output. It is, nevertheless, of interest to compare the extent to which violence occurs on these channels against its occurrence on the terrestrial channels. In the case of the movie channels, however, it is important to bear in mind that any comparison with terrestrial channels or, indeed, with the non-movie satellite channels examined in this study, does not amount to comparing like with like, given the thematic nature of programming on the movie channels. The complete study covered four weeks of all broadcast programming, together with programme previews and trailers, on all eight channels. Advertisements were not included in the analysis.

Definition of violence

Any content analysis of television violence begins with a definition of violence which stipulates the frame of reference for analysis which coders must follow. For the purposes of the current investigation violence was defined as:

> Any overt depiction of a credible threat of physical force or the actual use of physical force, with or without a weapon, which is intended to harm or intimidate an animate being or a group of animate beings. The violence may be carried out or merely attempted, and may or may not cause injury. Violence also includes any depiction of physically harmful consequences against an animate being (or group of animate beings) that occur as a result of unseen violent means.

Table 2.1 shows how this definition was displayed on the coding schedule as an *aide memoire* to coders. It was divided into a number of separate components with key points emboldened to draw attention to them even more. In addition, coders were provided with a separate information sheet which presented further stipulations and considerations to be borne in mind while coding. In all there were seven such stipulations or considerations.

1 **An overt depiction** means that the violence is occurring on the screen. The threat, the act, or the harmful consequences are shown or heard in the action of the plot. Verbal recounting of previous threats/acts of physical force or talking about violence does not in itself count as violence.
2 **Physical force** refers to action intended to cause physical pain or injury to an animate being, or to the use of physical tactics (such as strong-arming) that are intended to coerce the action of another in a way that threatens harm. Physical force must be enacted by an animate being; physical force or harm that occurs as a result of an act of nature (e.g., earthquake) is **NOT** counted as violence. Physical force can be perpetrated against the self or against another.
3 **A credible threat** means that within the context of the plot the perpetrator must display an intent to harm. Joking threats that have no believable intent to harm are not included (e.g., a character who is embarrassed and says 'I could kill you for saying that').
4 **An animate being** refers to any human, animal or anthropomorphized creature (non-human that possesses human attributes such as the ability to move, talk, think, act against something). A group of animate beings can involve several creatures or more abstract collections of creatures such as institutions or governments.
5 Violence must involve **at least one human or anthropomorphized being**, either as perpetrator or as victim. An act of nature involving two or more animals that threaten or harm each other is not considered violence so long as the animals are not anthropomorphized (i.e., possess human characteristics like talking, thinking).

6 **Accidents** that involve physical harm are considered violence **ONLY** when they occur in the context of an ongoing violent event (e.g., police chase a robber who accidentally falls off a building during the pursuit) or when they involve the use of weapons (e.g., two children are playing with a gun that goes off and hurts one of them).

7 Physical force against **property** (e.g., breaking a window, setting fire to a building) will be considered violence **ONLY** when it is directed at intimidating, punishing, vandalism or seeking revenge against an animate being. Property damage due to accidents, even in the context of an ongoing violent event, will not be considered as violence.

Table 2.1 Definition of violence

- Any overt depiction of a **credible threat of physical force or the actual use of physical force**
- **With or without a weapon**
- Which is intended to **harm or intimidate an animate being or a group of animate beings or inanimate objects** (i.e., property)
- Whether **carried out** or **merely attempted**
- Whether **the action causes injury or not**
- The acts of violence may be **intentional** or **accidental** (in the context of an intentional violent event – e.g., a car crash during a car chase)
- **Violent accidents** and **catastrophes** (if caused by human agents, e.g., a terrorist bomb explodes on a plane causing the plane to crash)

In addition to these stipulations a further set of guidelines was provided in respect of defining a 'violent act'. Thus, a violent act was defined as:

- **same** acts of violence by the **same** perpetrator (i.e., A punches B fives times = one act of violence – A commits the same violent action several times);
- **different** acts of violence by **different** perpetrators (i.e., A hits B and then B hits A back = two acts of violence – A commits a violent act and then B commits a further violent act);
- **different** acts of violence by the **same** perpetrator (i.e., A kicks B and then punches B – two acts of violence – the act of **kicking** and the act of **punching**).

The full details of the coding sheets produced for coders in cataloguing violent acts are presented in the Appendix.

Coding schedule

The coding schedule presented the definition of violence which coders were instructed to use. It contained a series of questions about each programme and about the nature of any violent acts depicted in the programme.

The schedule is broadly divided into two parts. The first part was completed for every programme and obtained general information about the programme itself, such as the channel on which it appeared, its transmission date, start time, length, genre code (31 different programme types were used), and country of origin. General questions were then posed about whether it contained any violence at all, and if so, how much violence it contained in terms of number of violent acts, violent sequences and amount of violence in seconds. A further question asked if there was a warning about violent content before or during the programme. Finally, coders were given the opportunity to add any further comments at the foot of the page concerning difficulties they experienced with coding the programme in question.

The second part of the coding schedule was completed for those programmes that contained any violence. A coding framework was provided to enable coders to supply details about the nature of the violence. Thus, information was provided about the historical setting, environment and country or location where the violence took place. A list of 52 codes for types of violent acts was used to indicate the nature of the violence. A separate list of 47 codes for types of weapons of aggression was also included. Further contextual details included whether the act was 'first strike' or 'retaliatory', the dramatic setting, dramatic outcome (blood, pain and horror), and the types of injuries caused.

The coding schedule for each violent act also probed for details about the status and type of aggressor and victim(s) and, in each case, the aggressor's and victim's gender, ethnic origin, age and, for the aggressor only, their apparent goals or objectives.

Programme samples

The periods recorded were selected at the discretion of the researchers and were not disclosed to the project's sponsors in advance of video-recordings taking place. There were four periods comprising seven consecutive days: 8 to 14 October 1994, 22 to 28 October 1994, 14 to 20 January 1995, and 4 to 10 February 1995. Recordings began at midnight on Friday and finished at midnight on the following Friday each week. The video-recordings covered eight channels, including the four terrestrially transmitted channels – BBC1, BBC2, ITV and Channel 4. In addition, four channels were selected for analysis which were available via satellite transmissions – Sky One, UK Gold, Sky Movies and The Movie Channel.

The programme sample was not constructed via a truly random sampling frame operating at the individual time unit or programme level, as recently recommended by others (Potter *et al.*, 1996). A random selection process was nevertheless applied at the level of weeks selected for analysis. This factor coupled with the overall size of this four-week programme sample contributed towards rendering this analysis one of the most substantial studies of its kind ever undertaken.

Table 2.2 Distribution of coded programmes by channel

	Week 1		Week 2		Week 3		Week 4		All weeks	
	n	*%*	*n*	*%*	*n*	*%*	*n*	*%*	*n*	*%*
BBC1	216	15.6	223	15.6	206	14.6	210	15.0	855	15.2
BBC2	188	13.6	209	14.8	220	15.6	198	14.2	815	14.6
ITV	252	18.2	256	18.0	241	17.1	240	17.2	989	17.6
Channel 4	184	13.3	184	13.0	180	12.7	187	13.4	735	13.1
Terrestrial	*840*	*60.7*	*872*	*61.4*	*847*	*60.0*	*835*	*59.8*	*3,394*	*60.5*
Sky One	170	12.2	168	11.8	200	14.1	192	13.8	730	12.9
UK Gold	187	13.5	191	13.4	189	13.4	187	13.4	754	13.4
Sky Movies	90	6.5	83	6.2	77	5.4	84	6.0	334	6.0
Movie Channel	96	7.0	101	7.1	100	7.1	98	7.0	395	7.1
Satellite	*543*	*39.3*	*543*	*38.5*	*566*	*40.0*	*561*	*40.2*	*2,213*	*39.5*
All channels	*1,383*	*100.0*	*1,415*	*100.0*	*1,413*	*100.0*	*1,396*	*100.0*	*5,607*	*100.0*

All programmes were recorded on Panasonic Nicam video-recorders using four-hour VHS tapes played at normal speed, except for overnight recordings, when they were played at half speed, enabling eight hours of programming to be captured on a single tape. A bank of eight machines was used to carry out the recordings, with one machine being dedicated to each channel. In addition, further machines were used to capture those short periods which might have been lost during tape change-overs.

Table 2.2 shows the number and distribution of coded programmes across the eight channels for weeks one to four. The pattern was fairly constant across all four weeks. The total hours of output across the four weeks amounted to 4,715.34 hours. There were 3,394 programmes coded on terrestrial channels and 2,213 coded on satellite channels. Week by week, the total hours coded amounted to 1185.87 in week one, 1,177.37 in week two, 1161.17 in week three, and 1190.93 in week four.

Coded programmes were classified into 32 different genres which could be clustered into six superordinate genres: drama, entertainment, factual, sport, children's programmes and music/arts/religion. Table 2.3 presents a summary of the distribution of genres across the four terrestrial and two satellite entertainment channels. It should be noted that the movie channels, being thematic, comprised mostly cinema films. The latter represented some 90% of these channels' programming, with the remainder being occupied by animated cartoons, a small amount of documentary material usually about movies and programme-length previews.

Across all channels, over 38% of coded programmes were various forms of drama, including cinema films, made-for-TV films, drama series and serials,

Table 2.3 Distribution of coded programmes per channel by genre

	All %	BBC1 %	BBC2 %	ITV %	Ch.4 %	Sky 1 %	UK Gold %
Drama							
Cinema films	15.8	5.4	4.5	6.0	9.7	1.2	2.6
Non-UK long run series	8.0	6.3	2.1	7.9	2.9	20.8	17.5
UK long run serials	6.0	3.2	0.6	5.8	3.4	0.4	29.0
Other non-UK series/ials	3.9	1.1	1.7	4.0	3.9	14.1	4.4
Other UK series/ials	3.5	2.8	2.0	3.4	3.0	0.5	13.5
Made-for-TV films	0.4	0.5	0.5	0.4	0.4	0.8	0.0
Single plays	0.5	0.1	0.0	0.0	0.3	0.0	0.0
TOTAL	38.1	19.4	11.4	27.5	23.6	37.8	67.0
Children's programmes							
General children's progs	9.2	13.9	15.7	8.1	9.9	13.6	2.1
Children's cartoons	7.2	6.0	10.2	5.9	1.6	6.8	1.9
Pop videos	0.4	0.0	0.2	0.6	0.3	1.2	1.2
TOTAL	16.8	19.9	26.1	14.6	11.8	21.6	5.2
Sport	2.6	3.6	3.6	2.2	6.5	2.3	0.0
Factual							
News – national	8.5	21.9	7.6	16.1	7.3	0.0	0.0
Documentaries	5.4	3.4	14.4	3.7	13.5	2.7	0.0
Hobbies/leisure	1.8	2.0	3.7	1.8	2.7	2.3	0.0
Current affairs (PSE)	2.4	2.0	8.0	1.3	3.1	0.8	0.3
News – regional	1.8	5.3	0.0	11.0	0.0	0.0	0.0
Current affairs (CA)	0.4	1.1	0.7	0.3	2.0	0.0	0.1
Current affairs (SE)	0.1	0.4	0.4	0.0	0.0	0.0	0.0
TOTAL	20.4	36.1	34.8	34.2	28.6	5.8	0.4
Entertainment							
Situation comedy	4.2	2.0	2.5	1.0	7.5	4.8	13.8
Other comedy	1.9	0.8	2.3	0.4	3.7	2.6	4.9
Variety	0.3	0.1	0.0	0.3	0.8	0.1	0.0
Family/people shows	2.3	5.7	0.9	3.5	0.9	4.4	0.0
Cartoon/animation	0.2	0.0	0.9	0.1	0.5	0.5	0.1
Chat shows	2.5	2.2	1.5	2.5	2.4	9.0	0.0
Quiz/games shows	4.6	4.4	3.1	5.8	6.7	7.9	4.0
Special events	0.2	0.8	0.4	0.2	0.0	0.0	0.0
TOTAL	16.2	16.0	11.6	13.8	22.5	29.3	22.8
Music/arts/religion							
Arts programmes	0.8	0.4	3.3	1.2	0.1	0.0	0.1
Music – contemporary	1.9	0.7	1.8	3.5	1.1	1.5	4.4
Music – classical	0.9	0.0	0.4	0.0	0.3	0.0	0.0
Religious programmes	0.5	1.2	0.4	0.9	0.1	0.5	0.0
TOTAL	4.1	2.3	5.9	5.6	1.6	2.0	4.5
Party politicals	0.1	0.1	0.1	0.1	0.0	0.0	0.0
Other	2.0	2.2	4.2	1.8	5.0	0.7	0.1

Note: PSE = political, social and economic affairs; CA = consumer affairs; SE = special events

and single plays. This represented the single biggest genre in terms of numbers of programmes analysed. Over one in five programmes (21.4%) coded were factual programmes. These included national and regional news, current affairs (political, social and economic issues; consumer affairs; and special events), documentaries and programmes about hobbies or leisure activities. Sport was treated as a separate category and accounted for nearly 3% of programmes coded.

The third biggest programme category in this sample was children's programmes (nearly 17% of all programmes analysed) followed closely by entertainment programmes (16%). Children's programmes comprised children's cartoons, other programmes made especially for children, and pop videos. Entertainment programmes included situation comedy, quiz and game shows, chat shows, family/people shows, other comedy shows, and small numbers of variety shows, cartoons for the general audience and special events. A small proportion of the coded output (3%) comprised music, arts and religious programmes.

The programme composition of terrestrial and satellite entertainment channels exhibited some degree of variation. Even though drama was the most represented genre in terms of numbers of coded programmes over all eight channels, it is clear that it was not the most represented genre on the terrestrial channels. Here, the greatest single proportion of programmes coded were factual programmes. There were, however, relatively few factual programmes on the satellite channels. Two out of three programmes on Sky One (67%) and nine out of ten (90%) on UK Gold were in the drama and entertainment categories.

Coding and reliability

The coding of data in this research was performed by a sample of individuals who were resident in the Sheffield area. A pool of 25 coders were recruited (13 males and 12 females), aged between 18 and 60 years. The coders were drawn from a range of occupational backgrounds, though all had carried on their education to university level or equivalent.

The coders were required to master all aspects of the coding frame and the supplementary instructions which accompanied it. Key concepts and terms were described in full and illustrations were provided where necessary to ensure that definitions and their mode of application were understood.

The content analysis focused on pre-defined occurrences of acts of violence. In addition to this basic-level quantification of televised violence, coders were trained to identify and catalogue various attributes of violence which provided some detail about the nature of the violence being depicted. The coders participated in a series of training sessions before the coding exercise began. These sessions were designed to familiarize coders with the details of the coding schedule and to ensure they understood the definition of violence, the instructions for distinguishing individual violent acts, and the general procedures under which the content analysis was to be conducted. Feedback was provided about performance in these pilot exercises and any ambiguities which arose concerning any aspects of the coding frame and procedure were discussed in full in settings where all coders were present. There were opportunities provided for coders to express any concerns they had and to obtain clarification on any points of apparent ambiguity. In total, coders were engaged in around 20 hours of instruction and practice before the study proper began.

It is important in any content analysis research that coders utilize the coding frame in a consistent manner. Coders must be prepared to adopt key definitional terms in the same way. The coding procedure and training of coders should be designed to minimize, as far as possible, the application of subjective judgements by coders. While coders may, subjectively, hold widely varying opinions about particular portrayals of violence, they must not allow their personal views to contaminate the objective assessments of on-screen activity they are required to describe.

Inter-coder consistency was checked both qualitatively and quantitatively. Qualitative checks comprised continuous monitoring of the judgements made by coders at key decision points in the application of the coding frame. The coding procedure involved the compilation of two datasets. The first dataset contained general information about each separate programme such as its time of transmission, length (in minutes), channel, country of origin and aggregate measures of violent content (total number of violent acts and sequences, and length of time occupied by violence). The second dataset concerned violent acts and contained codes relating to 23 different attributes, such as setting (historical, geographical, environmental), form (type of violence, weapons used), motives for violence, consequences of violence, demography and role-type of aggressors and victims. Each violent act also had codes for channel programme, programme genre and programme length.

Checks of returned coding sheets were made to ensure that correct codes had been applied for programmes and violent acts. Coders' aggregate violence scores in the programme dataset were checked against the separate violent act coding sheets they had returned for that programme to make sure that they matched. Consistent errors, either of arithmetic or the application of codes, on the part of coders triggered further one-on-one training and instructional sessions with the researchers.

Quantitative checks on reliability of coding focused on two aspects of the coding process: (1) level of agreement between coders in general violence counts for programmes; and (2) level of consistency in the application of attribute codes and assignment of code values to violent acts.

Reliability checks at the programme level involved double coding of selections of monitored programmes from across the four weeks for which video-recordings were made. There were 254 cases of double coding in total, covering all the major programme genres. In respect of violent acts, violent sequences and violence minutage measures, reliability coefficients were calculated using Scott's *pi* (Scott, 1955; Krippendorf, 1980). There is no simple solution to the problem of deciding the proper level of reliability. It is important to ensure not only that key measures of content achieve reliability, but do so while still remaining relevant and meaningful in the context of the investigation (Holsti, 1969). Reliability coefficients achieved respectable levels for violent acts (0.74), violent sequences (0.82) and violence minutage (0.78) based on data for which the great majority of coder pairings achieved perfect agreement or exhibited only marginal levels of disagreement.

Attribute coding reliability for individual violent acts was checked for each attribute on the violent act coding frame. A sample of 12 violent acts, taken from a number of different programme genres and depicting a variety of forms of violence, were coded by 23 coders. Consistency across coders was assessed across 23 separate attribute measures for each violent act: length (in seconds), historical setting, environmental setting, geographical location, type of action, form of violence, type of weapon, motivational context, injury consequences, dramatic detail (blood, pain, horror), aggressor status, aggressor role-type, aggressor demography (gender, age and ethnicity), aggressor goal, victim status, victim role-type, and victim demography (gender, age and ethnicity).

Each attribute could be judged in terms of a designated number of values. For example, for historical setting there were six values: distant past, recent past, present, near future, distant future, uncodable. In the reliability analysis a 12 (acts) by 23 (coders) matrix was constructed for each attribute. The attribute values allocated by each coder to each of the 12 violent acts were entered into this matrix. The modal value was then identified for each attribute, and occurrences of this value were then aggregated to produce a single score. This score was divided by the total number of cells (276) in the matrix and multiplied by 100 to produce a percentage agreement score. The target score of acceptability was 70% agreement. Across all 23 violent act attributes, the average agreement score among coders was 70% (with a range of 51% to 89%). Although agreement percentage levels for some attributes were below 60%, these relatively low levels of consistency stemmed very often from understandable ambiguities between values which were semantically fairly similar.

The lowest scoring attributes, in terms of reliability of coding, were environmental setting (51%), victim role-type (52%), aggressor role-type (55%), aggressor goal (56%) and injury type (58%). With environmental setting, the major difficulty seemed to occur in distinguishing effectively between suburban and small town locations and between 'rural' and 'uninhabited' codes. With victim role-type, value attribution consistency level was reduced by confusion over armed forces versus inanimate objects codes. Coders were sometimes uncertain about whether heavy armoured vehicles qualified strictly as inanimate objects, whilst the code 'armed forces' was taken to refer more specifically to armed forces personnel.

With aggressor role-type, some confusion existed between the allocation of codes for legitimate and non-legitimate law enforcers, and petty versus serious criminal types. In the latter case, 'serious' generally meant crimes of a serious nature, such as armed robbery, assault and battery, and other incidents where the stakes were high. With law enforcers, in the absence of cues that clearly identified law enforcers as legitimate upholders of the law (i.e., police officers), even though characters might be acting on behalf of the legal system, there were occasions when insufficient additional information was present to enable coders to allocate values more accurately.

With aggressor goals, the key problem concerned distinctions between violence in the service of evil or ambition, and between ambition, evil and desire for money. There were portrayals in which these motives were not mutually exclusive. Finally, confusion over injury values stemmed predominantly from the allocation of codes for various forms of minor injury, such as 'minor injury', 'stunned' and 'bruised'.

Presentation of results

The results are presented in relation to several core measures of violence which identify the total amounts of violence, the rate at which violence occurs, and the extent to which it is distributed across programme output on each channel. The amount of violence is expressed in terms of numbers of discrete incidents and by the amount of programme running time this material occupied.

Chapter 3 presents results relating to these general measures of violence and indicates the extent to which violence in general occurred on the eight channels monitored in this exercise. Chapters 4 to 7 examine the characteristics of violence on television in terms of its physical form, setting, motives and consequences, and participants (aggressors and victims). Chapters 8 to 12 present findings which concern the occurrence of violence in different types of programme. Chapter 8 makes some general comparisons across the major programme genres, while the following chapters examine respectively the nature of violence in dramatic fiction, light entertainment, news and factual programmes, and children's programmes. Chapter 13 turns to the distribution of violence across different day parts, examining in particular the occurrence of violence in daytime television and pre-peak, peak and post-peak evening television. The time-bands examined were also defined by the regulatory watersheds which mark the boundaries before and after which certain categories of programme content may or may not be shown.

3   Amount of violence on television

Concern about violence on television frequently centres on a premise that television programme output is saturated with violence. There is a prevailing 'common sense' view that violence is a prominent ingredient which is almost inescapable for anyone who consumes an average daily diet of television. To what extent does this common sense perception reflect what actually happens on screen?

Surveys of public opinion in which substantial percentages of respondents agree with the sentiment that 'there is too much violence on television' (e.g., Gunter and Wober, 1988) cannot shed light on what actually occurs on screen. Indeed such evidence is of little use to regulators or policy-makers charged with drawing up and implementing codes of practice for broadcasters and programme-makers in relation to the depiction of violence on television. What is needed in this context is research evidence derived directly from the measurement of what happens on screen. This is not to say that public perceptions of television content are not relevant. Viewers can make refined distinctions between different forms of television violence demonstrating a sensitivity to numerous attributes of violent portrayals (Gunter, 1985; van der Voort, 1986). Such perceptions can be most helpful if they refer to actual incidents in programmes. The first step in any analysis of television violence must therefore be to assess programme output and to compile a detailed catalogue of visually displayed events.

To achieve this end, research methodologies such as content analysis are required which attempt to provide an objective assessment of programme contents. This quantitative perspective of addressing violence on television is particularly important in the context of determining the amount of violence shown in programmes. Viewers' subjective impressions may be more significant in relation to ascertaining the strength of television's cognitive or emotional impact upon audiences. In order to establish the likelihood with which viewers might be exposed to violent material though, it is essential to monitor programme output and identify where and how much violence occurs.

The significance of content analysis research lies in its capacity to establish what proportion of programmes contain any violent scenes, how many violent scenes occur in particular programmes, and how much transmission time is occupied by violence. In this way, it becomes possible to find out the extent to which violence permeates television. Does television offer the potential for viewers being exposed to large numbers of violent acts? Can violence be said to represent a significant aspect of television output in terms of the proportion of total programme transmission time it fills?

In this chapter, results are presented which examine the prevalence and quantity of violence on British television. These results focus on the basic measures of violence employed in this study. There were three principal measures of quantity or amount of violence on television:

1 the total number of violent acts;
2 the total number of violent sequences;
3 the total amount of transmission time occupied by violent material.

There were, in addition, four principal measures of prevalence of violence:

1 the proportion of programmes that contained any violence at all;
2 the average number of violent acts per violence-containing programme;
3 the average number of violent sequences per violence-containing programme;
4 the proportion of programme time occupied by violence.

In addition to the above measures of prevalence of violence, a further measure of rates of violent acts per hour was also used. This measure was referred to in the 1986 study (Cumberbatch *et al.*, 1987). It is used again here in order to facilitate comparisons with the results of ten years earlier. The rate-per-hour measure can give a misleading impression about the prevalence of violence on television because it implies that in any hour of television a viewer could expect to witness a certain number of violent acts. This, however, may be far from true. For example, in five hours of viewing, no violent acts at all may occur during the first four hours, while in the fifth a programme might be shown which contains 20 violent acts. Expressed in terms of the average rate of violent acts per hour, the violence score over this five-hour period would come to four acts per hour. The fact is though that the rate is really 20 acts per hour in violence-containing programming and zero acts per hour across four hours of nonviolence-containing programming.

As well as examining the quantity and prevalence of violence over television as a whole, comparisons are made, on these measures, between different television channels. Is there any evidence that televised violence is greater in amount or more frequently occurring on some channels than on others? In making such comparisons, any conclusions reached about specific channels must take into consideration the nature and remit of that channel in terms of the kind of service it is expected to provide. In particular, the programme composition of channels can vary and, as later chapters will show, this can make a considerable difference to the quantity and quality of violence shown on different channels.

Finally, this chapter will examine the extent to which the quantity of violence on television in general and on different channels remains consistent or varies from week to week. Week-on-week fluctuations in the level of violence on television may be aligned with shifts in the programme composition of television schedules. The association of higher violence levels, for instance, with particular patterns of programming may go a long way towards revealing major sources of violence on television.

PREVIOUS RESEARCH

Chapter 1 reported several earlier British studies of television violence. Benchmark studies were conducted by researchers at the British Broadcasting Corporation (Newell and Shaw, 1972) and the Mass Communication Research Centre, University of Leicester (Halloran and Croll, 1972). More recent work was completed by Cumberbatch *et al.* (1987) for the BBC and subsequently for the Broadcasting Standards Council (BSC) (1994, 1995). The latter's work, which forms part of an annual monitoring exercise which includes audience research, was carried out on a relatively small scale compared with the other studies, and focused on peak-time programmes only. The BSC's research does, however, represent the first British content analysis study to provide data about levels of violence on satellite television channels.

In the nearest comparable study to the one presented in this report, Cumberbatch *et al.* (1987) counted a total of 2,375 violent acts in 2,078 programmes or 1,412 hours of television output on BBC1, BBC2, ITV and Channel 4. This yielded a reported overall frequency of just over one (1.14) violent act per programme, or 1.68 acts per hour.

The average duration of violent events was 25 seconds and therefore violence occupied just over 1% of television time (1.10%). If boxing and wrestling were excluded the average duration of violence was around 13 seconds. Under a third of programmes (30.1%) contained some violence. The acts per hour and proportion of time taken up by violence in programmes which portrayed it was correspondingly higher (just over three times the incidence averaged over all – violent and nonviolent – programmes in fact). Individual violent actions added up to 3,872, giving an average of 1.63 per violent act which according to Cumberbatch *et al.* (1987, p. 5) was 'an underestimate of the frequency per violent act since it was not possible to code reliably all repeated actions'.

VIOLENCE ON BRITISH TV IN THE MID-1990s

Ten years on from the last major television violence measurement exercise, this latest study provides an up-to-date assessment of current levels of violence on British television. To facilitate comparisons, many features of the earlier research were preserved, although some of the finer details of the definitional frame of reference were modified. The current analysis also included a selection of new television channels. This latest quantification of violence on television examined the extent to which programmes contain any violence and then, among those which did contain any violence, it measured how much violence they contained in terms of numbers of violent acts or sequences and duration or minutage of violence.

As explained earlier, in the current research the amount of violence on television was expressed in a number of different ways: (1) the proportion of programmes that contained any violence at all; (2) the total number of violent acts; (3) the total number of violent sequences; (4) the amount of time occupied by violent activity; and (5) the average number of violent acts and sequences in programmes containing any violence. The remainder of this chapter will present results derived from these basic measures of televised violence.

Programmes containing violence

A total of 4,715 hours of programme output were recorded over four weeks which was made up of 3,394 programmes on the terrestrial channels (BBC1, BBC2, ITV, Channel 4) and 2,213 programmes on four satellite channels (Sky One, UK Gold, Sky Movies, The Movie Channel). Of those programmes, 2,085 (37.1%) were found to contain violence of some kind, although there were wide differences between channels (see Table 3.1).

It is clear that a considerably greater proportion of programmes on average were found to contain violence on the satellite channels which were

Table 3.1 Number of programmes containing violence by channel

Channel	Number of programmes	%
BBC1	234	27
BBC2	189	23
ITV	299	29
Channel 4	223	30
All terrestrial	*945*	*28*
Sky One	273	37
UK Gold	285	38
Sky Movies	263	79
Movie Channel	319	81
All satellite	*1140*	*52*
All channels	*2085*	*37*

Note: Aggregated data over four weeks

monitored than on terrestrial channels. The satellite channel average was significantly inflated, however, by the contribution of the two movie channels.

DURATION OF THE PORTRAYAL OF VIOLENCE

Of the 4,715 hours of programme output, the overall amount of time occupied by portrayals of violence on the screen was 51.25 hours (3,075.1 minutes), of which 14.9 hours (894.4 minutes) occurred on the four terrestrial channels and 36.3 hours (2180.2 minutes) on the four satellite channels. The nearly 15 hours of violence on the terrestrial channels amounted to 0.61% of the transmission time, which, on the surface, compares favourably with the 1.1% found by Cumberbatch *et al.* (1987) for an equivalent amount of terrestrial output in 1986. This comparison, as will be shown below, needs to be qualified. Controls for the contribution made by certain categories of violence need to be introduced before precise comparisons are possible between 1986 and 1994/95. In particular, violence involving verbal threats and violence which occurred in boxing or wrestling matches needs to be excluded.

Table 3.2 shows the duration of violence on each of the eight channels separately, and the percentage of each channel's output which it constituted. On this criterion, there were large differences between the terrestrial channels, with ITV appearing to contain the highest proportion of violence, and Channel 4 the lowest.

Levels of violence on the four satellite channels were, once again, clearly higher than those observed on terrestrial channels, averaging 1.53% of programme output time over the four weeks analysed. The greatest amount of violence, in terms of duration, occurred on Sky Movies (1.99% of coded output) followed by Sky One (1.74%).

Table 3.2 Duration of violence by channel

Channel	Duration of violence in minutes	Violence as percentage of channel output
BBC1	167.7	0.51
BBC2	142.4	0.46
ITV	442.8	1.11
Channel 4	141.5	0.37
All terrestrial	*894.4*	*0.61*
Sky One	618.9	1.74
UK Gold	243.4	0.75
Sky Movies	728.4	1.99
Movie Channel	590.0	1.62
All satellite	*2180.7*	*1.53*
All channels	*3075.1*	*1.07*

THE CONTRIBUTION OF VERBAL THREATS

The figure of 1.1% of programme running time occupied by violence reported in the 1986 study excluded verbal threats. For strict comparability therefore it is necessary to remove the contribution of verbal threats from the current analysis. The total minutage accounted for by verbal threats on terrestrial television across the four weeks of monitoring amounted to 96.7 minutes. Taking this away from the total amount of violence in minutes on the four terrestrial channels (894.4 minutes) left a residual of 797.7 minutes (13.3 hours) of violence. As a proportion of terrestrial programme output monitored, this amounted to 0.56%, a modest reduction from the 0.61% found with verbal threats included. A similar analysis for the four satellite channels monitored in this study produced an overall reduction in the proportion of programme output occupied by violence from 1.53% to 1.35%.

THE CONTRIBUTION OF BOXING AND WRESTLING

Another significant factor found by Cumberbatch and his colleagues (1987), which inflated the overall television violence score, were boxing and wrestling broadcasts. When the violence catalogued in these broadcasts was discounted, the overall violence level, as expressed in terms of proportion of total programme running time, reduced in 1986 from 1.1% to 0.57%. Clearly, there is not much difference between the latter score and the one recorded for terrestrial channels in the current study (excluding verbal threats) of 0.56%.

Once again, in order to attain stricter comparability with the 1986 measures, a further analysis of violence levels was conducted omitting boxing and wrestling. Although a comparison with 1986 can only be made for the terrestrial channels, this analysis was also carried out for Sky One which contained a number of wrestling broadcasts during the weeks monitored.

Just three boxing matches were televised during the weeks analysed. Two of these were shown on ITV and one appeared on BBC1. This compares with 11 instances of contact sports broadcasts coded on the terrestrial channels in the 1986 study. Together, the two ITV broadcasts contained 88.4 minutes of violence, which accounted for 31.3% of violence on ITV during the two weeks in question and 20% of all violence minutage on that channel over the full four weeks of monitoring. The single BBC1 televised boxing match contained 15.5 minutes of violence, which accounted for 37.3% of violence on the channel during that particular week and 9.2% of violence minutage over the entire four-week period of monitoring.

On Sky One, there were 16 wrestling broadcasts coded, four per weekend. Together, these programmes contained 277.3 minutes of violence, representing 44.8% of all violence minutage recorded on that channel during the weeks monitored.

Table 3.3 Levels of TV violence with and without boxing and wrestling

	Percentage of programme running time occupied by violence	
	Wrestling and boxing included	Wrestling and boxing excluded
All channels	1.07	0.94
Sky One	1.74	0.96
ITV (boxing weeks)	1.41	0.97
ITV (all weeks)	1.11	0.89
BBC1 (boxing week)	0.50	0.31
BBC1 (all weeks)	0.51	0.46

Next, it is necessary to establish what difference to overall levels of violence the subtraction of the violence contained in these programmes made. This is summarized in Table 3.3 for all channels, and for those channels which featured wrestling and boxing. Over all channels, 1.07% of programme running time was occupied by violence across the four weeks. With wrestling and boxing excluded, this was reduced to 0.94%. On Sky One, exclusion of wrestling reduced violence running time by almost 45% from 1.74% to 0.96% of programme output time.

On ITV, there was a reduction of more than 30% in violence minutage when boxing was taken out for the two weeks when boxing was broadcast. Omitting these boxing broadcasts reduced the overall minutage of violence on ITV across the four weeks of monitoring by 20%. During the two boxing weeks, violence occupied 1.41% of programme output time. This reduced to 0.97% when boxing was taken out. Over the four weeks, the removal of boxing led to a reduction from 1.11% to 0.89% of programme running time occupied by violence.

On BBC1, a single boxing broadcast accounted for more than 37% of violence minutage during the week it was shown and for over 9% of violence minutage across the four weeks of monitoring. Taking the contribution made by this broadcast out of the equation reduced the percentage of programme running time occupied by violence from 0.50% during the week in question to 0.31%. Over the total monitored period, programme running time occupied by violence fell from an average of 0.51% to 0.46%.

If we add boxing to verbal threats for terrestrial channels and exclude both from the violence count, an overall reduction is achieved in the proportion of programme time filled with violence from 0.61% to 0.49%. This compares favourably with the 0.57% figure which emerged in 1986 when boxing/wrestling and verbal threats were discounted. Ultimately, there was an overall, though modest, reduction in violence on terrestrial television between the mid-1980s and mid-1990s.

NUMBERS OF VIOLENT ACTS AND VIOLENT SEQUENCES

For each programme in which some violence was found, every single violent *act* was noted, and coded in the complex set of variables listed in the appendix. There were periods in programmes when a number of violent acts occurred together and, together with isolated single acts, these were noted as individual violent *sequences*. The rates of incidence of violent acts and violent sequences constitute a further way of assessing the amount of violence on television. Table 3.4 shows, by channel, the numbers of violent acts and violent sequences, and the average numbers of violent acts and of violent sequences in those programmes which contained some violence.

Table 3.4 Numbers of violent acts and violent sequences

Channel	Violent acts		Violent sequences	
	Total Number	Number per programme	Total number	Number per programme
BBC1	1,406	5.9	759	3.3
BBC2	1,115	5.9	632	3.4
ITV	2,385	8.0	1,401	4.7
Channel 4	1,333	6.0	665	3.0
Terrestrial	*6,239*	*6.3*	*3,457*	*3.6*
Sky One	3,714	13.5	1,646	6.0
UK Gold	1,706	6.0	972	3.4
Sky Movies	4,758	18.1	2,222	8.4
Movie Channel	4,753	15.0	2,362	7.4
Satellite	*14,931*	*13.1*	*7,202*	*6.3*
All channels	*21,170*	*9.7*	*10,659*	*5.0*

Overall, a grand total of 21,170 violent acts were catalogued across the four weeks of the content analysis of which 6,239 occurred on terrestrial channels and 14,931 on satellite channels. The greatest number of violent acts occurred on the two movie channels, followed by Sky One. The greatest total number of violent acts on the terrestrial channels was on ITV.

These violent acts combined to form 10,659 violent sequences. As indicated already, violent sequences were periods within a programme when a number of different violent acts might have occurred. An individual violent sequence might thus comprise a single violent act or a succession of two or more such acts. On average, each violent sequence comprised 1.99 violent acts across the four weeks.

THE CONTRIBUTION OF VERY VIOLENT PROGRAMMES

General measures of violence on television can provide a variety of quantitative assessments which in turn can offer a range of impressions about how much violence there is on television. Under four in ten programmes (37.1%) were found to contain any violence on the eight channels monitored in this study during the four weeks that the analysis was carried out. The distribution of violence was found to vary between channels both in terms of the proportion of programmes transmitted on a channel which contained any violence and in terms of the total quantity of violence these programmes contained collectively and the rates at which violent incidents occurred within those programmes. *It is important to treat general measures of television violence with care because they may give misleading impressions of the extent to which television channels are permeated with violence. Further analysis of these general measures indicated that relatively small numbers of programmes may contribute disproportionately to the overall amount of violence registered in broad terms for a particular television channel.*

Taking this important point forward, further analyses were carried out to identify those programmes which contained especially high numbers of violent acts or exceptionally large amounts of time occupied by violence. Thresholds of 50 acts of violence or at least five minutes of running time occupied by violence per violence-containing programme were set. These analyses demonstrated that relatively small numbers of programmes could account for substantial proportions of the total violence coded on each television channel monitored.

A small percentage of programmes (1%) across the eight channels were found to contain 50 or more acts of violence. Together these 56 programmes contained 4041 or 19% of all violent acts coded. On some channels, it became clear that substantial proportions of the total violent acts recorded for them were accounted for by just a handful of programmes.

Across the four weeks of analysis, 10 movies on The Movie Channel, representing 3% of the movies shown on that channel during that period, contained 20% of all violent acts for that channel. Two movies each scored over 100 violent acts. The highest scoring movie on this channel in terms of violent acts was *Teenage Mutant Ninja Turtles*, which was broadcast twice during the period of analysis (10.00 am and 6.00 pm, Sunday, 15 January 1995). It was scored as depicting 142 violent acts on both showings. Since each showing was analysed by different coders, this result served as a useful inter-coder reliability check. The second highest scoring movie on this channel was *Double Impact* (10.00 pm Friday, 10 February 1995), starring Jean-Claude van Damme, which scored 105 violent acts.

On Sky Movies, 21 movies were found to contain 50 or more violent acts, representing 6% of all movies coded for this channel during the period of analysis. This small part of the channel's total output contained a total of 1938 violent acts, representing 41% of all the violent acts identified for this channel. Four movies achieved individual scores in excess of 100 violent acts. The highest scoring of these was *Karate Kop* (10.00 pm, Thursday, 9 February 1995) which scored 170 violent acts. This was followed by *Pray for Death* (midnight, Saturday, 8 October 1994) with 120 violent acts; *Out For Justice* (10.00 pm, Friday, 20 January 1995) with 112 violent acts; and *Braindead* (midnight, Wednesday, 18 January 1995), with 102 violent acts.

On Sky One, 14 programmes, or 2% of all coded programmes on this channel, contained 948 violent acts or 26% of the total for the channel during the period of analysis. Just one of these programmes, *DJ Kat TV* (7.00 am, Saturday, 22 October 1994) with 106 violent acts exceeded the 100 act threshold. Indeed, eight editions of this programme contributed 550 violent acts, or 15% of the total, over the period of analysis.

The terrestrial channels contained far fewer programmes with 50 violent acts or more. In fact, only four such programmes were identified. These were *Pink Cadillac* (ITV, 9.00 pm, Saturday, 4 February 1995) with 51 violent acts; *Ghayal* (ITV, 1.45 am, Monday, 6 February 1995) with 79 violent acts; *The Wild Bunch* (ITV, 2.50 am, Saturday, 8 October 1994) with 61 violent acts; and *Battle for the Planet of the Apes* (Channel 4, Sunday, 5.20 pm, 23 October 1994) with 53 violent acts. There were no programmes scoring 50 or more violent acts on either BBC1 or BBC2. It is perhaps worth noting that *Ghayal* accounted for 11% of the violent acts on ITV during the week it was shown, and *The Wild Bunch* accounted for 10% of the violent acts on ITV during the week it was broadcast. *Battle for the Planet of the Apes* accounted for 13% of the violent acts on Channel 4 during the week it was shown.

While counting violent acts can give one indication of how much violence programmes contain, it can also be a misleading measure because two violent acts may themselves display differing quantities of violence, especially if they differ in terms of their duration. Another method of establishing how much violence programmes contain is to measure the amount of time occupied by violent activity. Following the same procedure that was described for the violent acts analysis, a threshold was created so as to identify any programmes that contained 300 seconds (five minutes) or more of violence. This analysis served to illustrate that substantial proportions of the total amount of violence coded for a specific channel could be located within a handful of that channel's programmes.

During the four weeks analysed, 142 programmes, across the eight channels, were found to contain at least five minutes of violence. Together these programmes contained an aggregated total of 1,417.6 minutes of violence. Thus, 2.5% of the programmes monitored on the eight channels contained 46% of all the time occupied by violence in that output.

On BBC1, for example, five programmes contained 22% of the total time occupied by any violence during the four weeks of coding. On BBC2, five programmes contained 26% of the time occupied by violence. On ITV, 19 programmes contained 51% of all time occupied by violence. On Channel 4, just three programmes emerged which crossed the five-minute threshold, and together these programmes accounted for 13.5% of all violence-occupied time coded on that channel.

The proportions of total violence time accounted for by the most violent programmes were equally significant on the four satellite channels monitored. On UK Gold, nine programmes accounted for 27% of the total time occupied by violence. On The Movie Channel, 26 movies (7% of total coded) accounted for 39% of total amount of time occupied by violence. On Sky Movies, 47 movies (14% of total) accounted for 60% of time filled with violence. Finally, on Sky One, 28 programmes (4% of total) accounted for 60% of time occupied by violence.

Twenty-two programmes were found to contain at least 15 minutes of violence and represented the most violent programmes according to the criteria of amount of time occupied by violence. These programmes fell into two categories: cinema films and sports broadcasts. The sports broadcasts comprised entirely boxing matches and wrestling events. Nine out of 12 high-scoring sports broadcasts comprised the *World Wrestling Federation* shows transmitted on Sky One on Saturdays and Sundays. The three remaining sports programmes were *The Big Fight* on ITV (10.40 pm, 12 October 1994) with 47 minutes of violence, *Sportsnight* on BBC1 (10.25 pm, 26 October 1994) with 15.5 minutes of violence, and *The Big Fight* on ITV (11.15 pm, 4 February 1995) with 41.3 minutes of violence. The *World Wrestling Federation* broadcasts contained between 17 and 30 minutes of violence.

The most violent movies, in terms of amount of total running time occupied by violence, comprised *Karate Kop* (Sky Movies, 10.00 pm, 9 February 1995) with 19.5 minutes of violence; *The Wild Bunch* (ITV, 2.50 am, 8 October 1994) with 18 minutes of violence; *Midnite Ride* (Sky Movies, 2.45 am, 15 January 1995) with 17.6 minutes of violence; *Jersey Girl* (The Movie Channel, midnight, 23 October 1994) with 16.7 minutes of violence; and *The Bear* (Sky Movies, 8.00 pm, 23 October 1994) with 15.6 minutes of violence.

THE TV VIOLENCE LEAGUE TABLE

In addition to setting violence-level thresholds as in the foregoing analysis of the most violent programmes on television, the contribution made by the top ten and top 100 most violent programmes, in terms of violent acts and in terms of violence minutage, was also examined. The top 100 programmes across all eight TV channels, in terms of violent acts, accounted for 28.7% of all violent acts. Thus, less than one fiftieth of the programmes coded accounted for between one in four and one in three violent acts. These programmes averaged 60.7 violent acts per programme, yielding an aggregated total of 6,073 violent acts. These acts occupied 11.75 hours of programme running time, averaging just over seven minutes per programme.

The top 10 violent programmes, according to the violent act measure, contained a combined total of 1,194 acts, averaging 119.4 acts per programme (see Table 3.5). These few programmes (which represented one in

500 of all coded programmes) accounted for 5.6% (or more than one in 20) of all violent acts coded across the eight TV channels.

Table 3.5 Top ten violent programmes (violent acts)

Programme title	Channel	Acts
1 Karate Kop	Sky Movies	171
2 Teenage Mutant Turtles	Movie Channel	142
3 Teenage Mutant Turtles	Movie Channel	142
4 Pray for Death	Movie Channel	120
5 Out for Justice	Sky One	112
6 DJ Kat TV Show	Sky One	106
7 Double Impact	Sky Movies	105
8 Braindead	Movie Channel	102
9 No Retreat, No Surrender	Movie Channel	99
10 American Cyborg: Steel Warrior	Movie Channel	95

Note: *Teenage Mutant Ninja Turtles* was broadcast on two occasions

The top 100 violent programmes in terms of minutage of violence accounted for 39.5% of all programme running time occupied by violence across the eight TV channels. These programmes in total contained 20.25 hours of violence, averaging just over 12 minutes of violence per programme. These programmes contained an aggregated total of 4,424 violent acts, averaging just over 44 violent acts per programme.

The top ten violent programmes in terms of violence minutage are shown in Table 3.6. These programmes represented one five hundredth of programmes monitored and contained 9% of all violence minutage. In all, there were 4.6 hours of violence in these programmes, averaging 27.5 minutes per programme. The relatively low average of 34.6 violent acts per programme, however, was lower than the average act rate registered across the top 100 programmes indicating fewer but longer sequences of violence in the most violent programmes of all. Eight out of the top ten programmes were sports broadcasts featuring boxing or wrestling.

Certain programme genres were disproportionate contributors to the most violent programmes on television. Among the top 100 programmes in terms of violent acts, 72 were cinema films, 18 were non-cartoon children's programmes, five were children's cartoons, four were sports broadcasts, and one was a long-running UK-produced drama serial. Nine out of the top ten programmes were cinema films, with the other one being a children's programme. Among the top 100 programmes in terms of violence minutage, there was a much greater spread across genres. Once again, cinema films were the major contributing genre (67), followed by sport (18), children's programmes (five), children's cartoons, UK-produced long-running serials and non-UK-produced long-running serials (two each), and finally, documentaries, family shows and UK-produced and non-UK-produced series (one each). In an interesting anomaly, however, the top ten programmes in terms of violence minutage were mostly sports broadcasts (eight out of ten), with the remainder being cinema films. This result is not too surprising, however, considering that all the sports programmes featured here were aggressive contact sports (e.g., boxing and wrestling).

Table 3.6 Top ten violent programmes (violence minutage)

Programme title	Channel	Amount
1 *The Big Fight*	ITV	47.0
2 *The Big Fight*	ITV	41.4
3 *World Wrestling*	Sky One	30.0
4 *World Wrestling*	Sky One	28.3
5 *World Wrestling*	Sky One	27.0
6 *World Wrestling*	Sky One	26.7
7 *Karate Kop*	Movie Channel	19.5
8 *World Wrestling*	Sky One	19.2
9 *World Wrestling*	Sky One	18.4
10 *The Wild Bunch*	ITV	18.0

Note: Violence amount shown in minutes

Table 3.7 Proportion of all violence on each channel contributed by top 100 and top 10 violent programmes

| Channel | Top 100 | | Top 10 | |
	Acts/amount	% violence	Acts/ amount	% violence
BBC1	1,185 acts	84.3	395 acts	28.1
	2.6 hours	91.9	1.1 hours	37.9
BBC2	964 acts	86.5	269 acts	24.1
	2.2 hours	93.1	1.0 hours	41.8
ITV	1,890 acts	79.2	508 acts	21.3
	6.6 hours	88.8	3.0 hours	40.8
Channel 4	1,068 acts	80.2	292 acts	21.9
	2.1 hours	88.0	0.7 hours	29.5
Sky One	2,930 acts	78.9	795 acts	21.4
	9.1 hours	88.6	3.6 hours	35.2
UK Gold	1,284 acts	75.2	333 acts	19.5
	3.5 hours	85.3	1.2 hours	29.6
Sky Movies	3,796 acts	79.8	1,007 acts	21.2
	10.2 hours	84.0	2.4 hours	20.2
Movie Channel	3,405 acts	71.6	803 acts	16.9
	7.7 hours	78.2	2.0 hours	20.4

Substantial proportions of the total violent acts and total violence minutage for each television channel were located within the 100 most violent programmes for that channel. For the six non-movie channels, between 30 and 40% of all violence minutage occurred in the ten most violent programmes. This figure dropped to around 20% for the two movie channels. These findings underline, once again, the fact that much of the violence on television tends to be found in a small portion of the total programme output (see Table 3.7).

SUMMARY AND CONCLUSION

Across the four weeks of television monitoring, a grand total of 2,084 programmes (37%) were found to contain violence on the eight channels analysed. On the four terrestrial channels, 944 programmes (28% of programmes on those channels) were found to contain violence, compared to 1,140 programmes (52%) on the four satellite channels.

The numbers of programmes, over all channels, found to contain violence fluctuated to some extent from week to week (week one: 541; week two: 494; week three: 543; week four: 506). In percentage terms, this meant that between 35% and 39% of programmes coded contained violence each week.

A total of 21,170 violent acts were coded on all eight channels over the four weeks. There were 6,239 violent acts registered on terrestrial channels and 14,931 acts coded on the four satellite channels. These violent acts combined to produce a grand total of 10,659 violent sequences (3,457 on terrestrial channels; 7,202 on satellite channels). Far greater numbers of violent acts occurred on the two satellite movie channels (Sky Movies: 4,758 violent acts: The Movie Channel: 4,753 violent acts) than on any other channel.

The overall amount of time occupied by violence over the period coded was 3,075.1 minutes (51.2 hours) of which 894.4 minutes (14.9 hours) occurred on terrestrial channels and 2,180.2 minutes (36.3 hours) on the four satellite television channels.

In general, violence occupied 1.07% of programme output time on all eight channels over the four-week period coded. On terrestrial channels only, a total of 0.61% of output time was occupied by violence, whereas on the four satellite channels, 1.53% of programme output was occupied by violence. While these results indicated a substantial drop in violence on terrestrial channels compared with 1986 (1.1%), a more precise comparison was needed in which the contributions of verbal threats and boxing and wrestling matches were removed, thus more closely mirroring the television violence universe for these channels that had been examined by Cumberbatch and his colleagues ten years earlier. On doing this, violence on terrestrial channels exhibited a modest reduction from 0.57% of output time in 1986 to 0.49% in 1994/95.

There were, on average over the four weeks, around 10 violent acts per violence-containing programme and five violent sequences. Average violence rates were higher across the monitoring period on the four satellite channels (13.1 acts per violence-containing programme) than on the terrestrial channels (6.5 acts per violence-containing programme).

The general level of violence on television was disproportionately inflated by a small number of programmes which contained exceptionally large quantities of violence. Just 1% of programmes across the eight channels were found to contain 19% of all violent acts coded. Just 2% of the programmes monitored contained 46% of all the programme output time occupied by violence.

League tables were computed showing the ten most violent programmes and the 100 most violent programmes on television for the channels and period monitored, according to the numbers of violent acts found in programmes and amount of programme running time occupied by violent footage. The top 100 programmes in terms of violent acts contained between a quarter and a third of all the violent acts catalogued. The top 100 programmes in terms of violence minutage accounted for nearly four-tenths of all violence footage found. Televised films originally made for the cinema tended to contain the greatest number of violent incidents, while sports broadcasts tended to contain the greatest amount of violence in terms of programme running time filled with violence.

The current chapter has demonstrated that there are various ways in which the quantity of violence on television can be expressed. Different measures of television violence can give different impressions about how much violence television programmes contain. While a substantial minority of programmes over the channels and weeks monitored in this study were found to contain at least some violence, in terms of overall programme running time, violence is a minor aspect of television output, especially on the four terrestrial channels. What also emerged was the fact that, in addition to violence on television occurring at a low level in terms of the programme minutage it occupied, much television output contains little or no violence at all. If nearly half of all violence minutage occurred in just one in 50 of those programmes monitored, the great proportion of programmes which contain violence do not generally contain very much of it.

The quantity of television violence reveals nothing about its qualities. Yet, in the context of audience reactions which are ultimately where concern about television violence rests, it is essential to know about the character of any violence that is shown. The following chapters examine the nature of violence and the setting or context in which it was found to occur.

4   Nature of violence on television

The violence shown on television may take on many different forms and involve a variety of different instruments or techniques of aggression. In this chapter, the violence monitored on television is classified according to an extensive taxonomy of physical forms and types of weapons or instruments of aggression. The significance of any analysis of the forms of violence on television rests on their potential to elicit varying degrees of audience response – perceptual, emotional and behavioural. Research concerned with measuring the effects of television violence and audience perceptions of violence on television has occasionally examined the way in which viewers' responses can vary with the physical nature of the violence portrayed on screen.

In research concerned with establishing a behavioural impact of televised violence, some evidence has emerged that individuals can, under artificial laboratory conditions, be triggered into behaving more aggressively after viewing violence of several distinct physical varieties. No comparisons have been made of the relative impact of different physical forms of violence; instead, comparisons have tended to be made between one type of violent portrayal and a nonviolent portrayal.

Following up on a real-life incident in which two high school youths re-enacted a knife-fight scene from the film *Rebel without a Cause*, resulting in one boy being seriously injured, a group of researchers at the University of Toronto conducted a series of experimental investigations with the same knife-fight scene from the movie to test its aggression-stimulating properties further (Walters *et al.*, 1962; Walters and Thomas, 1963). They found that watching this scene increased the punitiveness of adult viewers relative to a nonviolent scene from another source.

In a subsequent experimental study, Liebert and Baron (1972) showed groups of five- to nine-year-old children either an exciting sports sequence or a short extract from the crime-drama series *The Untouchables* which contained a chase, two fist-fights, two shootings and a knifing. Each child was subsequently placed in front of a large box that had wires leading into the next room. On the box were two buttons, a green one labelled 'HELP' and a red one labelled 'HURT'. The experimenter explained that the wires were connected to a game another child was playing in the next room. The child viewer could either help or hurt the other child by pressing the appropriate buttons. Children who had been shown the episode from *The Untouchables* pressed the HURT buttons more frequently and for longer durations than those who watched the sports sequence. Whilst this study indicates different strengths of behavioural reaction of young viewers following exposure to a nonviolent sequence and a violent one containing a variety of forms of physically violent activity, it offers no indications of any different degrees of impact for different physical forms of violence depicted in the violent scene. Thus, we do not know whether the use of a knife had any more or less profound an impact on young viewers than did a gun fight or a scene featuring unarmed fighting.

These 'imitation' and 'disinhibition' effects are undoubtedly important, but another aspect of concern over the potential behavioural impact of different instrumental forms of televised aggression relates to their capacity to 'trigger' aggression among viewers. Some researchers have suggested that media portrayals can be particularly likely to evoke aggression in viewers when they contain specific features which have come to be strongly asso- ciated with violence through cultural learning processes (Berkowitz, 1970; Berkowitz and Le Page, 1967).

Among the features that are presumed to have this powerful aggression- eliciting property are weapons. Behavioural research on the so-called 'weapons effect' has indicated that the actual presence of weapons or pic- tures of weapons or instruments of violence can make an already angry person behave more violently against the source of his anger than would be the case in a weapon-free environment (Berkowitz, 1971; Berkowitz and Le Page, 1967; Leyens and Parke, 1975; Tannenbaum, 1971.) This work, how- ever, has not convincingly demonstrated whether or not certain types of instrument or techniques of violence have stronger aggression-eliciting prop- erties than others, thereby providing a measure of the relative seriousness or intensity of violence represented by different physical forms or actions.

Just one study of this kind made any attempt to vary the levels of violent content shown to individuals. Even here, the evidence is inconclusive because of questionable definition of key variables. Leyens and Parke (1975) compared viewers' behavioural aggressive reactions under a mood of anger and frustration, following exposure to photographic slides which they defined as high, moderate or low in aggressive content (depicting a revolver, a whistle and a box of chocolates respectively). Although exposure to the revolver slide elicited most aggression from viewers, the definition of a photograph of a whistle as a moderately 'aggressive' stimulus seems highly dubious.

Another point to be noted about 'weapons effect' research is that the presence of weapons or photographs of weapons usually elicited aggressive responses only amongst individuals who had previously been annoyed, whilst little impact was observed amongst non-angered respondents. From the perspective of measuring any distinctions made by viewers between different types of weapons of violence as depicted on screen, however, the 'weapons effect' research offers no useful indicators.

Although behavioural research evidence has yielded no data which can assist with a meaningful classification of television violence by, say, weapon-type, as derived from the different types of behavioural reactions that might be caused by different physical forms of violence, there is evidence that viewers do make perceptual distinctions between scenes of violence on television on the basis of weaponry. Research carried out for the Surgeon General's Scientific Advisory Committee on Television and Social Behaviour in the United States in the early 1970s examined young boys' perceptions of selected programme scenes of differing kinds and degrees of violence (Greenberg and Gordon, 1972a). Some of these scenes involved the use of weapons, others did not. Results showed that scenes of violence involving weapons such as hand-guns or rifles were rated as more violent, less real, and less acceptable than weaponless scenes depicting, for example, hand-to-hand combat. This study indicated that at the level of viewers' perceptual judgements about television violence, the physical characteristics of that violence may be an important mediator of its perceived seriousness.

Later research in the United Kingdom also found that the physical form of violence could exert a marked effect on viewers' judgements about violent scenes in programmes (Gunter, 1985). Once again, scenes which featured stabbings or shootings were perceived as far more violent and disturbing than scenes depicting fist fights. Scenes from a violent western movie featuring different kinds of weaponry were ranked as follows in terms of how violent they were perceived to be:

1 slashing with a sword;
2 knife throwing;
3 cannon fire at fortress;
4 shooting in street;
5 clubbing with a gun-butt;
6 fist fight.

The same research found that programme context could mediate audience perceptions of different physical forms of televised violence. Viewers' concerns about certain of the more serious forms of violence, particularly those involving the use of sharp instruments, became especially acute in contemporary dramatic settings (Gunter, 1985).

PREVALENCE OF DIFFERENT VIOLENT FORMS

Content analyses of television programming have indicated that the different physical forms of violence discussed above occur with varying frequencies. Even quite early American research revealed that over half the violent incidents coded in dramatic entertainment programmes on mainstream

American television involved the use of weapons and that the distribution of incidents featuring weapons varied from one type of programme to another. Weapons were generally more prevalent in cartoons (64% of all violent incidents) than in non-cartoon shows (50%) (Gerbner, 1972). Later American work indicated that the nature, levels and distribution of violence remained fairly stable over time and that a range of forms and varieties of violence still characterized television drama (Gerbner *et al.*, 1979, 1980).

Content analyses of dramatic entertainment programming on British television during the early 1970s elaborated further on the American findings in cataloguing a number of different kinds of physical violence. Researchers at the BBC found that shootings featuring hand-guns and rifles (39% of violence) and fist-fights (37%) were the most commonly occurring forms of violence. These were followed in decreasing order of prevalence by stabbing instruments (12%), domestic items such as chains or vases (8%), specialized instruments such as traps or poisons (8%), hitting or lashing instruments (7%), and finally military equipment and explosions (6%) (Shaw and Newell, 1972).

Cumberbatch *et al.* (1987) found an enormous range of violence. A total of 3,872 different violent actions comprised a variety of violent forms. Violence frequently involved shootings; used fists or hands; pushing, tripping or other kinds of physical assault; and the deployment of a wide range of more specialized forms of violence. Examining types of weapons used revealed the predominance of hand-to-hand combat in violent acts. The body was used in 934 cases (35% of total), while everyday objects such as knives and clubs added a further 12%. Thus, nearly half of all incidents involved fighting at close quarters. All shooting weapons (including bows and arrows) accounted for a further one-third (32%) of total weapons used.

NATURE OF VIOLENCE ON UK TELEVISION IN THE MID-1990s

The current research examined the nature of violence on television in three ways. First, each violent act was classified in terms of whether it represented a 'first strike', 'retaliatory action', or 'self-inflicted' action of characters or persons against themselves. Secondly, violent acts were categorized into 53 different types of activity. Thirdly, all violent acts were classified in terms of the types of weapons or instruments of aggression deployed. Here, 48 different coding categories were used. These were divided into ten superordinate categories of weapon or instruments of aggression: gun (military); gun (criminal); other shooting instruments; knife/stabbing instrument; throwing instrument; clubbing instrument; body; vehicle; animal; other instruments.

Stimulus of violence

Over the four weeks of television output analysed, a total of 14,581 violent acts (70% of all violent acts identified) represented first strike aggression, while 5,649 violent acts (27%) were retaliatory acts. Just 92 violent acts (less than half a per cent of all violent acts) were self-inflicted violence. Just over 3% of violent acts (713 acts) were uncodable in this respect.

Ten years earlier, Cumberbatch *et al.* (1987) reported that just over 60% of violent acts they coded were 'first strike' aggression, while just under 13% were retaliatory actions. The latter research was, of course, limited to the four terrestrial channels. In comparison, on terrestrial channels only in the current study, 'first strike' acts comprised 71% of total violent acts and retaliatory acts comprised 23% of all violent acts. Just 12% of violent acts were uncodable in this way on the terrestrial channels, compared with 27% of non-coded violent acts in the earlier study.

There was little difference between terrestrial channels in the proportions of violent acts designated as 'first strike' or 'retaliatory'. Levels of 'self-inflicted' violence were low across all channels, but were most likely to occur on Channel 4 (0.7% of acts) and least likely on BBC2 (0.2%).

On the satellite channels, 'first strike' violence dominated once again. This form of violence was most frequently occurring on UK Gold (74.7% of acts) and least likely to occur on Sky One (64.6%). Retaliatory violence was generally more commonplace on these channels (27% of acts on average) than on the four terrestrial channels (23%), but was easily most likely to occur on Sky One (34%). Levels of 'self-inflicted' violence were generally low across all four satellite channels (0.5% of acts).

TYPES OF VIOLENT ACT

Types of violent act were coded under 53 different categories. For the purposes of reporting, these were re-grouped under nine headings: use of body; hand held weapon; execution; injury outcomes; torture/cruelty; threat of violence; property; military/explosions; and miscellaneous. The results covering all television output coded are summarized in Table 4.1 which shows the proportional distribution of acts under each major and sub-category.

The most commonly occurring types of violence involved use of a body part (8,897 acts in total), followed by violence involving hand held weapons (6,544 acts) and incidents involving the threat of violence (2,407 acts). Less frequently occurring categories were violence involving military weapons or explosions (868 acts), violence coloured principally by injury outcomes (536 acts), property-related violence (322 acts), violence involving torture and cruelty (161 acts), and violence involving executions (137 acts).

On looking in greater detail at the nature of violent acts, the most commonly occurring types of violence occurred within the two major categories, involving use of a part of the body or use of a hand held weapon. Six out of the top ten most often occurring specific types of violence fell into these two broad categories of violent behaviour on television.

Top ten types of violence

		No. acts	% acts
1	Shoot at	4,183	19.8
2	Push/trip	3,707	17.5
3	Punch	2,314	10.9
4	Hit with object	1,868	8.8
5	Verbal threat	1,653	7.8
6	Kick	1,141	5.4
7	Attempted violence	754	3.6
8	Throwing	717	3.4
9	Explosion	499	2.4
10	Sport aggression	486	2.4

In percentage terms, forms of violence involving use of a part of the body (42.3%) or a hand held weapon (31.2%) accounted for nearly three-quarters of violence registered across all eight channels over the four weeks monitoring period (see Table 4.1). Three specific types of behaviour, shooting, pushing or tripping, and punching together accounted for nearly half of all violence coded.

Acts involving stabbing

Audience research has indicated that viewers may be especially sensitive to acts of violence involving sharp instruments in which someone gets stabbed (Gunter, 1985). The current analysis found 416 stabbing incidents across the eight channels monitored. Most of these (72%) appeared in cinema films shown on television. Others were found in children's cartoons (8%), other children's programmes (5%) and long-running drama series/serials produced outside the UK (5%). Compounded with the anxiety-invoking potential of this type of violence was the further finding that more often than not, stabbing incidents resulted in someone's death (53% of cases) or at least being seriously hurt (23%). Whereas in the case of many forms of televised violence substantial numbers of incidents resulted in no obvious physical injury to the people involved, the same could not be said of stabbings, for which no physical injury was observed in just 6% of cases. Most stabbing scenes, however, were rated as being relatively painless to victims (67%), bloodless (72%) and horror-free (67%). Nevertheless, there was a greater than average tendency for such scenes to be rated as causing victims considerable pain and suffering (10% compared with an overall violent act average of 3%), to produce lots of blood (6% versus 1%) and to be horrific (10% versus 3%).

A more detailed look was taken at particular scenes from movies which had been rated as being especially graphic in the dramatic detail of the

Table 4.1 Types of violent act

	Percentages of violent acts				
	All weeks	Week one	Week two	Week three	Week four
Use of body					
Push/trip	17.5	14.2	16.8	18.4	20.9
Punch	10.9	10.2	10.8	12.8	9.5
Kick	5.4	3.5	4.6	7.3	6.1
Throwing	3.4	3.6	3.4	3.6	2.9
Slap	2.1	2.5	2.0	2.0	1.7
Fall/throw	1.0	1.0	1.0	0.8	1.2
Strangle	0.9	1.0	0.8	1.1	0.8
Bite	0.7	0.7	0.7	0.9	0.6
Scratch	0.1	0.0	0.0	0.3	0.0
TOTAL	42.0	36.7	40.1	47.2	43.7
Hand held weapon					
Shoot at	19.8	21.7	18.3	18.8	20.2
Hit with object	8.8	8.6	9.3	8.9	8.5
Stab	2.0	2.1	2.4	1.5	1.8
Fire	0.3	0.3	0.5	0.2	0.2
Poison	0.2	0.2	0.3	0.0	0.2
Spray	0.1	0.2	0.2	0.1	0.0
TOTAL	31.2	33.1	31.0	29.5	30.9
Execution					
Electrocution	0.2	0.3	0.3	0.1	0.2
Decapitation	0.1	0.1	0.1	0.1	0.2
Lethal injection	0.1	0.0	0.1	0.1	0.2
Gassing	0.1	0.2	0.1	0.1	0.0
Hanging	*	0.1	0.0	0.0	0.0
TOTAL	0.5	0.7	0.6	0.4	0.6
Injury outcomes					
Crushed	0.8	0.8	1.3	0.5	0.5
Wounding	0.5	0.7	1.0	0.2	0.1
Cut	0.5	0.4	0.4	0.5	0.5
Burn	0.4	0.5	0.4	0.2	0.3
Self wounding	0.2	0.2	0.2	0.1	0.1
Trample	0.2	0.3	0.0	0.1	0.2
Fracture of bones	0.1	0.1	0.1	0.1	0.1
Blinding	0.1	0.1	0.0	0.0	0.1
TOTAL	2.8	3.1	3.4	1.7	1.9
Torture/cruelty					
Torture	0.2	0.3	0.2	0.1	0.3
Bullying	0.2	0.3	0.2	0.1	0.1
Cruelty	0.2	0.2	0.1	0.2	0.1
Psychol. torture	0.2	0.2	0.1	0.2	0.1
Rape	0.1	0.0	0.1	0.1	0.1
TOTAL	0.9	1.0	0.7	0.7	0.7
Threat of violence					
Verbal threat	7.8	8.3	7.7	6.9	8.4
Attempted violence	3.6	2.9	4.3	4.1	2.9
TOTAL	11.4	11.2	12.0	11.0	11.3

Property					
Damage to property	1.1	1.4	0.9	0.8	1.1
Damage to car	0.4	0.5	0.3	0.4	0.4
Car explosion	0.1	0.2	0.0	0.1	0.1
TOTAL	1.6	2.1	1.2	1.3	1.6
Military/explosions					
Explosion	2.4	2.8	2.6	1.9	2.1
Bombardment	1.5	1.5	1.4	2.1	1.0
Other disaster	0.1	0.1	0.1	0.1	0.0
Sink/scuttle	0.1	0.1	0.1	0.1	0.0
Chemical explosion	0.1	0.0	0.1	0.0	0.1
Nuclear explosion	0.0	0.0	0.0	0.0	0.0
TOTAL	4.2	4.5	4.3	4.2	3.2
Miscellaneous					
Sport aggression	2.4	2.3	2.7	1.0	3.4
Trap	0.9	0.6	0.9	1.2	0.9
Abduction	0.7	0.9	1.1	0.4	0.3
Supernatural	0.5	0.4	0.5	0.4	0.5
Sabotage	1.0	0.1	0.0	0.1	0.2
Suffocation	0.1	0.2	0.1	0.0	0.0
Drown	0.1	0.1	0.1	0.0	0.1
Cannibalism	0.1	0.0	0.1	0.0	0.2
Disease	0.0	0.0	0.0	0.0	0.0
TOTAL	5.8	4.6	5.5	3.1	5.6

Note: * Represents less than 0.05%

violence displayed. *Basic Instinct* (Carolco and Le Studio Canal + Production) shown on The Movie Channel on 25 October 1994 was preceded by a warning as follows: 'The following film contains scenes of extreme violence particularly in its first few minutes. It has been certificated 10 and is suitable only for persons of 18 years and over.' There are two stabbing scenes in *Basic Instinct*, both of which were rated at the highest level in terms of horror. The first stabbing scene occurred at the beginning of the film. The opening shot is from above a bed where a man and a woman are having sex. The scene is fairly explicit with the woman on top of the man. The woman's face is not shown. She uses a scarf to tie the man's hands to a bedstead and the sex becomes more intense. The music is loud and increases in volume. The woman reaches behind her and picks up an ice-pick and stabs the man in the neck. Blood spurts out of the wound and he screams. The woman then stabs him again through the nose and then seven more times in his upper body. Three of the stabbing motions showed the hand only, the other four showed her making contact with the body. The man screamed repeatedly throughout the scene and the music was used to reinforce the impact of each stabbing action. There was a great deal of blood and much obvious pain on the part of the victim.

The second stabbing in this movie occurred as a policeman walked out of a lift. A character wearing a mask and hood stabbed the officer in the neck with an ice pick four times in quick succession. Much blood was seen pumping out from the wound, as the officer screamed in intense pain, with discordant music once again accompanying the stabbing actions. The scene then switched to the main male protagonist in the film who was running up the stairs of the building in an attempt to reach his friend (the other police officer), before switching back to the murder scene where five more stabbing actions into the man's neck were shown. The scene was very bloody and the man, showing great pain, was still alive. This scene was also coded as being extremely horrific.

Other scenes involving stabbings which were coded as being extremely graphic in nature were found in the horror movie *Braindead* (Wingnut Films Limited, 1992) which was shown on Sky Movies at midnight on 18 January 1995. At one point, a zombie character was stabbed in the head with a kitchen utensil and in another a man, who had been stabbed with large sticks, walked into a fellow zombie., impaling her too. Although these scenes were lacking in contemporary realism and the characters themselves seemed oblivious to being stabbed, these scenes were nevertheless coded as horrific in the highest degree.

Though rare, scenes of an extremely graphic nature, sometimes containing a mixture of critical attributes, such as use of sharp instruments, repeated violent actions, the agony of the victim and generous amounts of blood, do occur on television. Such material tends to occur in movies originally made for the cinema and mostly occurs in movies shown late at night on subscription channels, with warnings about the graphic nature of the violence provided beforehand.

Strangulation scenes

Another type of close-in violence about which there has been some concern is that which involves strangulation of victims. In total 193 violent acts were found which involved an aggressor putting his or her hands around a victim's neck or using a rope, scarf or some other item to choke the victim. Half (50%) of these incidents occurred on Sky Movies and The Movie Channel, with just over one in four (27%) occurring on the four terrestrial channels.

In two-thirds (66%) of cases, strangulation involved the use of the hands and in the majority of remaining cases some other instrument such as a rope, wire or item of clothing (e.g., a scarf or tie) was used. In nearly one in ten (9%) cases, however, choking was achieved through some other part of the body than the hands, such as the arm or legs.

No physical injury followed in one in four (25%) cases of strangulation, while death followed in one in five (19%) cases. In most cases, the victim survived and suffered only minor damage. Blood was rarely seen in cases of strangulation. There were just four scenes coded which resulted in moderate or large amounts of blood. Similarly, victims were rarely depicted suffering greatly (only in five cases), while ratings of such scenes as horrific were equally rare. Eight out of ten aggressors (79%) and three out of four victims

(76%) were male, usually operating on their own. Aggressors (70%) and victims (78%) were mostly white, and for the most part young to middle-aged adults (66% and 87% respectively).

Those scenes which were coded as being potentially the most disturbing in terms of graphicness were examined more closely. *Diagnosis of Murder*, shown by BBC1 on 11 October 1994 at 2.30 pm, was coded as containing a strangulation scene with a very high horror rating. Closer analysis revealed that this scene was graphic despite the fact that it occurred within a thriller with a strong theme of humour running through it. The drama was set in a hospital where a rather eccentric doctor (played by Dick van Dyke) also pursued his hobby of solving crimes. Much of the drama was played in a humorous style with the accompanying music designed to enhance the comic effect. The strangulation scene was rather incongruous in its graphic detail, but was vital to the plot.

The scene in question occurred at night in a semi-lit office. The victim was a company director who had just fired three employees in a callous and unpleasant way. The victim was sitting at his desk talking to someone on the telephone. Only the feet and gloved hands of the perpetrator were seen by the viewer. The victim clearly recognized his murderer and turned his back on him/her to continue his telephone conversation. The next shot was of a rope fashioned into a noose which was suddenly placed over the victim's head. The strangulation lasted for 25 seconds, during which time the victim gasped for breath and struggled. His eyes and tongue protruded slightly and when finally released he had died and crashed heavily onto the desk. The strangulation was accompanied by loud discordant music which further enhanced the dramatic and violent nature of the scene.

In this scene the victim was clearly seen to be suffering and the strangulation was shown in close-up for many seconds. The scene was judged to be high in horror and moderately high in terms of pain and suffering of victim. It is possible that the coder's perception of the horrific nature of this scene could have been related to the incongruous nature of this particular depiction in the context of what was essentially a relatively light-hearted programme shown in the afternoon on terrestrial television. The same programme contained three other acts of violence, a hit and run incident with a car which did not result in the victim's death, but was intended as a warning to him, and two more acts in which no injuries to victims resulted, one of which involved verbal aggression and the other an explosion. In the end the murderer was caught and punished, and the mystery resolved.

Another strangulation scene coded as extremely horrific occurred in the film *Braindead*, to which reference has already been made. In contrast to the previous strangulation scene this particular incident occurred within the context of a very violent and unpleasant film. The victim was strangled by a tentacle (like an umbilical cord) which shot out of the body of a monster caught in a giant liquidizer. As the character disappeared, feet first, accompanied by much screaming and an enormous amount of spraying blood, the tentacle caught around the victim's neck tightened and caused death by strangulation.

Braindead is a horror film in the zombies genre where 'living dead' attack humans (and each other) at random. Any human who is attacked then becomes a monster. The zombie monsters seem to feel no pain and regularly lose limbs, are stabbed, strangled and so on. The graphic nature of the violence becomes so bizarre and unreal at times that it is almost funny.

The film becomes increasingly graphic as the plot develops and more people turn into the 'living dead'. There is a steady increase in the volume of blood, gunge, exposed viscera, gore and violence as the film progresses and the acts of violence become more revolting. One example of this is where humans discover that the living dead can be halted by the insertion of a large syringe up their nose. All acts of violence such as biting, tearing of flesh and stabbing are accompanied by loud sound effects clearly designed to enhance the graphic nature of the scene.

Hanging scenes

One particular form of strangulation about which there is particular concern are scenes of hanging. Such scenes are singled out by British broadcasters in their codes of practice relating to depictions of violence on television. The current analysis found just seven scenes involving hanging across the eight channels. A closer analysis of these scenes reveals something about their qualities.

Mississippi Burning (Frederick Zollo Production) was shown at 10.20 pm on BBC2 on 9 October 1994. The stars Gene Hackman and Willem DaFoe play FBI agents sent to investigate the disappearance of three young men in Jessup County in Mississippi in 1964. The three young men were trained human rights activists, one black and two Jews. The opening scenes showed them being followed and shot at close range. The theme of the film is racism and all the violence which occurs is within the context of racial hatred and intolerance. The majority of the violence (82.8%) was committed by white Americans on black Americans and the majority of the victims were male (86%).

The hanging scene which occurred in *Mississippi Burning* was particularly unpleasant simply because it represented a racial attack. The victim did not die whilst hanging because he was rescued by his family. The scene began with an attack on the house of a black family. The children and grandmother escaped out of the back of the house and the aggressors (Ku Klux Klan members) set fire to the house. The victim, the children's grandfather, was captured and was hoisted with a rope around his neck up a tree, to be left hanging in front of his burning farm. His hands were tied and his feet kicked several times before he hung limp. The scene was accompanied by the sounds of hymn singing and lasted about 35 seconds. Eventually, the old man was rescued by his grandchildren who cut him down. The scene was particularly disturbing given the context in which it occurred and the length of time for which the victim was focused upon by the camera.

A second hanging scene occurred in the opening sequence of a *True Stories* programme, *'The Mystery of Deadman's Hill'*, broadcast by Channel Four on 9 October 1994 at 11.20 pm. Three men were seen walking down a dimly lit corridor. The scene switched to a man sitting in a prison cell with two guards. A voice-over read out the man's last letter to his mother in which he proclaimed his innocence. The prisoner was then shown walking along the corridor with two guards. When he reached a trap door his hands were tied behind his back, a noose placed over his head and the trap door opened. The viewer then briefly saw the man's legs from below the trap door.

The hanging scene itself was very brief. Indeed, it was quite striking how quickly the prisoner was hanged. There was no ceremony and the placing of the hood over the man's head and noose around his neck, followed by the release of the trap door, took only a few seconds. Unlike the scene in *Mississippi Burning*, this scene was coded at a modest level for both pain and horror. The programme went on to use a documentary/reconstruction style to reinvestigate the case of James Hanratty who was hanged for the A6 murder 30 years earlier and claimed that a miscarriage of justice had been committed. Although the implication was that the hanged man was innocent, the scene was nevertheless classified as essentially non-horrific because the camera did not depict in graphic detail the victim's suffering or indeed any reactions to the hanging itself. Nor did the camera linger on the scene afterwards.

A further hanging scene was coded in the movie, *Karate Kop*. This film was shown on Sky Movies at midnight on 22 October 1994. The victim was a criminal who was fighting with a policeman (the hero of the film). At the end of the fight, the policeman caught hold of a heavy lifting chain attached to a crane. He wrapped the chain around the victim's neck and pushed him off a platform. The victim struggled for a split second and then went limp. The policeman walked away saying 'nice suit'. The scene was very brief, contained gallows humour and was shown in the context of a good deal of violence. In fact, *Karate Kop* was the most violent programme shown during the four weeks analysed. The victim showed no pain and did not struggle for more than a brief moment.

Hanging scenes *per se* may not be sufficient to warrant a high horror or other graphic detail rating. Other factors, such as the extent to which a victim struggles or suffers pain and agony, are important here. Lingering shots of the scene also render hangings all the more horrific, especially if the victim continues to move while being hanged. In assessing such scenes from the potential affective reaction they might invoke in members of the audience, it may be vitally important to consider the context and other dramatic features of such scenes.

Channel differences

The character of violence was compared across the different television channels included in this analysis. This comparison began by examining the differences among the terrestrial channels and then among the four satellite channels in terms of rates of occurrence of the nine broad categories of violence. These findings are summarized in Tables 4.2 (terrestrial channels) and 4.3 (satellite channels). A number of differences emerged in the extent to which different types of violence occurred on particular channels.

Table 4.2 Distribution of major types of violence on terrestrial channels

	Percentages of violent acts			
	BBC1	*BBC2*	*ITV*	*Ch 4*
Use of body	45.5	35.3	42.0	41.9
Hand held weapon	29.9	34.2	28.7	29.2
Threat of violence	7.9	6.6	12.2	10.0
Military/explosions	2.8	10.2	5.2	4.1
Injurious outcomes	2.7	3.1	2.8	2.3
Property-related	1.8	3.1	1.1	1.0
Torture/cruelty	0.5	2.0	0.8	1.3
Execution	0.6	0.7	0.3	0.8
Miscellaneous	5.6	4.5	5.7	8.1
Uncoded	2.8	0.8	0.8	1.5

Table 4.3 Distribution of major types of violence on satellite channels

	Percentages of violent acts			
	Sky One	*UK Gold*	*Sky Movies*	*Movie Channel*
Use of body	43.6	46.0	42.3	36.8
Hand held weapon	28.0	24.0	33.3	34.7
Threat of violence	9.6	15.0	11.4	13.0
Military/explosions	3.3	5.0	3.3	3.8
Injurious outcomes	1.5	1.6	3.2	3.8
Property-related	1.9	2.5	1.3	1.2
Torture/cruelty	0.5	0.7	1.0	0.7
Execution	0.6	1.1	1.0	0.9
Miscellaneous	9.4	3.3	2.3	3.4
Uncodable	1.3	1.2	1.2	1.3

While use of body parts or of hand held weapons were the most common types of violence across the four terrestrial channels, there were differences between the channels in rates of occurrence of both of these violent categories. Violence involving hands or feet, pushing, tripping, punching or kicking was least likely to occur on BBC2 and most likely to be present on BBC1. Channel 4 and ITV fell in between the two BBC channels. With respect to violence involving hand held weapons such as guns, clubs, knives and so on, the positions of the two BBC channels were reversed, with such violence being more likely to occur on BBC2 than on BBC1. This sort of violence was very slightly less likely to be found on ITV and Channel 4 than on BBC1.

Violence on BBC2 was more likely than any other terrestrial channels to involve the use of military arms and explosives of various kinds, and was also more likely to be property related. Threatened violence, involving verbally threatening behaviour or attempted physical violence, was more commonplace on the commercial terrestrial channels (ITV especially) than on the BBC channels.

The distribution of violence on the four satellite channels illustrated, once again, the predominance of violence involving use of the body (e.g., hitting, punching and kicking) and hand held weapons (most usually guns). Weapon-involving violence represented larger proportions of violence on the movie channels than on the two drama/entertainment channels. Violence involving punching or kicking occurred proportionately most often on UK Gold and least often on The Movie Channel.

Incidents involving the threat of violence most frequently represented the violence found on UK Gold and least often represented the violence shown on Sky One. The movie channels occupied the middle ground where incidents of verbal threat of violence or attempted physical violence were concerned. Violence on the movie channels, however, was likely to be characterized by the injurious outcomes for those involved compared with that found on Sky One and UK Gold.

Another way of revealing differences between channels, in terms of the nature of violence shown on them, is to examine the ten most commonly occurring types of violence on each channel. In doing this for the terrestrial channels, more similarities than differences emerged. In general, the types of violence which predominated were those incidents involving shootings with hand held weapons, pushing, tripping and punching. These forms were followed by violence which involved hitting with an object and threatening behaviour. Perhaps the most significant distinction occurred with BBC2 which was the only terrestrial channel with bombardment in its top ten types of violence, and for which violence involving explosions reached a higher rank position than for any other channel. Displaced from the top ten on BBC2 because of this was sports-related aggression. The latter category achieved a top ten position on every other terrestrial channel, being most highly placed on Channel 4.

Violence on the four satellite channels was dominated by incidents involving shootings with hand held weapons, hitting a victim with an object, or

Top ten types of violence: terrestrial channels

BBC1	%	BBC2	%
1 Push/trip	20.2	1 Shoot at	22.1
2 Shoot at	19.3	2 Push/trip	16.8
3 Punch	12.5	3 Hit with object	9.4
4 Hit with object	8.9	4 Verbal threat	4.9
5 Verbal threat	5.7	5 Bombardment	4.5
6 Throwing	4.5	6 Explosion	4.4
7 Sports aggression	3.8	7 Kick	3.3
8 Kick	3.0	8 Throwing	2.7
9 Slap	2.8	9 Slap	2.1
10 Attempted violence	2.2	10 Attempted violence	2.0

ITV	%	Channel 4	%
1 Push/trip	21.2	1 Shoot at	18.7
2 Shoot at	20.2	2 Push/trip	15.5
3 Punch	11.1	3 Punch	12.2
4 Verbal threat	8.6	4 Hit with object	9.2
5 Hit with object	6.9	5 Verbal threat	7.1
6 Kick	3.8	6 Sports aggression	6.3
7 Attempted violence	3.6	7 Kick	4.3
8 Sports aggression	3.4	8 Throwing	3.9
9 Explosion	3.3	9 Slap	3.5
10 Throwing	2.2	10 Explosion	2.4

use of body parts such as in punching, pushing or tripping someone. In addition, at the lower end of the top tens of the movie channels, violence involving stabbing also appeared. These were the only channels in which this form of violence achieved such numerical prevalence. Threatened violence in the form of verbal threat or attempted physical violence featured clearly in the top ten of all four of these channels.

TYPES OF WEAPONS

Violence was classified not only in terms of types of behaviour, but also according to the different types of weapons that were used (see Table 4.4). There were 48 basic-level weapon types applied in this classification. These were further reduced to 11 broad categories: gun (military); gun (criminal); other shooting instrument; knife/stabbing instrument; throwing instruments;

Top ten types of violence: satellite channels

Sky One	%	UK Gold	%
1 Shoot at	19.4	1 Push/trip	25.8
2 Push/trip	15.6	2 Shoot at	16.3
3 Punch	11.6	3 Verbal threat	12.8
4 Hit with object	7.4	4 Punch	9.3
5 Sports aggression	6.1	5 Hit with object	5.5
6 Throwing	6.0	6 Kick	4.1
7 Verbal threat	5.1	7 Explosion	2.9
8 Attempted		8 Throwing	2.7
violence	4.5		
9 Explosion	2.4	9 Attempted	
		violence	2.2
10 Damage to		10 Damage to	
property	1.3	property	2.0

Sky Movies	%	Movie Channel	%
1 Shoot at	20.7	1 Shoot at	19.5
2 Push/trip	16.9	2 Push/trip	12.8
3 Punch	10.5	3 Hit with object	11.6
4 Hit with object	9.1	4 Punch	10.6
5 Verbal threat	8.5	5 Verbal threat	7.9
6 Kick	6.9	6 Attempted	
		violence	5.1
7 Attempted		7 Throwing	3.1
violence	3.1		
8 Slap	3.0	8 Stab	2.9
9 Stab	2.9	9 Slap	2.1
10 Explosion	2.2	10 Crushed	1.8

clubbing instruments; body; vehicle; animal; other instruments (including chemicals, electricity, gas); and other varied instruments.

Considering first the pattern of usage of different instruments of aggression across all channels for the total period of analysis, the most commonly used weapons comprised various parts of the body. This most usually meant the use of a fist or hand. In all, 9,467 acts of violence (44.7% of all violent acts coded) involved the use of the assailant's body as a weapon. Out of these acts, 5,972 specifically involved the use of the fist or hand alone. Other sub-categories of this general category comprised karate/martial arts moves, kicking, headbutting, throwing/pushing, use of some other body part (e.g., elbow) or in a very few instances, the use of a false hand.

Table 4.4 Types of weapons used in acts of violence

	Percentages of violent acts
Body	
Fist/hand	28.3
Kick	4.4
Karate/martial arts	3.9
Throw/push	2.9
Headbutt	0.4
False hand	0.1
Other part of body	4.7
TOTAL	44.7
Gun (military)	
Machine gun	3.2
Rifle	3.1
Pistol	2.9
Explosives	1.9
Military hardware	1.8
TOTAL	12.9
Gun (criminal)	
Hand-gun	7.5
Shotgun	2.2
Sawn-off shotgun	0.3
TOTAL	10.0
Knife/stabbing instrument	
Sword	4.1
Dagger	1.3
Domestic knife	0.4
Hunting knife	0.4
Hook	0.1
Other stabbing instrument	1.0
TOTAL	7.3
Other shooting instrument	
Laser weapon	3.7
Bow and arrow	0.8
Cross-bow	0.2
Flame thrower	0.1
Tear gas	0.1
Water cannons	0.0
TOTAL	4.9
Clubbing instrument	
Stick (various)	2.6
Truncheon/baseball bat	0.7
Whip/cane	0.4
Pickaxe/axe	0.4
Hammer	0.3
Stone	0.1
TOTAL	4.5

Throwing instrument

Spear or lance	0.6
Other projectiles	1.6
TOTAL	2.2

Vehicle

Car	0.8
Lorry	0.1
Bulldozer	*
Chariot	0.0
Other vehicle	0.6
TOTAL	1.5

Animal

Trained animal	0.3

Other instruments

Chemical/drugs	0.4
Electricity	0.3
Liquid	0.2
Gas	0.1
Boiling liquid	0.1
TOTAL	1.1
Other	10.3
Multiple	0.7

The next most prevalent types of weaponry comprised some form of military hardware (machine gun, pistol, rifle, explosives, other military hardware), numbering 2,745 violent acts (12.9% of total violent acts), followed by the use of guns in non-military (usually criminal) contexts (e.g., sawn-off shotgun, hand-gun, shotgun), which numbered 2,093 acts (10% of total violent acts). Among all the sub-categories of these two major types of weapon, the most commonly occurring single type of weapon in use was the hand-gun, usually in the context of crime (1,559 acts).

In order of frequency of occurrence the remaining categories of weapons registered were knife/stabbing instruments, such as domestic and hunting knives, sword, dagger and hook (1,530 acts), other shooting instruments, such as bow and arrow, cross-bow, laser weapon, water cannons, flame throwers and tear gas (1,014 acts), clubbing instruments, such as a truncheon or baseball bat, whip/cane, pickaxe/axe, stick, hammer or stone (926 acts), throwing instruments such as a spear or lance, or other projectile (477 acts), vehicle (321 acts), other instruments such as boiling liquid, other liquid, chemicals/drugs, gas or electricity (257 acts) and animals (56 acts).

Over all channels, the single most frequently occurring instrument of violence was the fist or hand. This occurred almost four times as often as the second most frequently occurring type of weapon which was the hand-gun. Half of the remaining top ten weapon types reflected the predominance of the body as a weapon. If violence did not involve the fist or hand being used in some fashion, then it often involved some other part of the body with an assailant engaged in kicking, throwing or pushing a victim. Some unarmed combat comprised the application of martial arts movements,

Top ten weapon types	No. acts	%
1 Fist or hand	5,972	28.3
2 Hand-gun	1,559	7.5
3 Other body part	1,004	4.7
4 Kick	933	4.4
5 Sword	861	4.1
6 Karate	831	3.9
7 Laser weapon	788	3.7
8 Machine gun	675	3.2
9 Rifle	667	3.1
10 Throw/push	625	2.9

which again involved the use of hands and feet. The only instrument of violence in the overall top ten which did not involve a shooting instrument or part of the body was the sword which was used in well over 800 acts of violence portrayed during the four weeks monitoring period.

Channel differences

Channel differences in terms of the extent to which television violence was characterized by the use of different weapons are summarized in Table 4.5 (terrestrial channels) and 4.6 (satellite channels), which present results for terrestrial channels and satellite channels respectively. On all four terrestrial channels, violence was dominated by the use of the body as a weapon or by the use of guns in either military or criminal contexts. Together these instrument of violence categories accounted for around two out of three violent acts on each terrestrial channel. The distribution of each of these three weapon categories among acts of violence, however, did exhibit some degree of variation among these channels. The principal difference occurred between BBC2 and the rest, and centred on a higher rate of occurrence of violence involving military weaponry on BBC2 than on the other channels, which appeared to some extent to displace the occurrence of use of body as weapon and use of guns in criminal contexts. The extent of occurrence of use of body as weapon and of violence featuring military hardware varied relatively little among BBC1, ITV and Channel 4. However, ITV displayed a higher than average representation of crime-related use of guns among its acts of violence compared with the other three terrestrial channels. Also, BBC1 can be singled out for a higher than average representation of violence involving throwing instruments.

Table 4.5 Distribution of different types of weapons on terrestrial channels

	Percentages of violent acts			
	BBC1	*BBC2*	*ITV*	*Ch.4*
Body	45.7	36.0	42.9	46.8
Gun (military)	15.3	21.5	14.5	14.0
Gun (criminal)	8.9	6.2	13.8	7.0
Knife/stabbing instrument	3.4	7.2	4.6	4.8
Clubbing instrument	3.6	6.0	3.8	3.9
Throwing instrument	6.9	2.6	2.6	4.0
Other shooting instrument	3.3	4.9	1.7	4.7
Vehicle	1.0	1.1	2.0	0.6
Animal	0.1	0.3	0.4	0.3
Other instrument	0.5	0.9	1.3	1.1
Other/multiple weapons	11.4	12.8	12.0	13.1

Table 4.6 Distribution of different types of weapons on satellite channels

	Percentages of violent acts			
	Sky One	*UK Gold*	*Sky Movies*	*Movie Channel*
Body	53.9	48.9	43.5	39.1
Gun (military)	5.0	11.4	13.5	15.0
Gun (criminal)	4.5	9.7	14.7	8.7
Knife/stabbing instrument	3.9	4.3	8.2	12.7
Clubbing instrument	3.4	3.3	4.6	5.4
Throwing instrument	1.4	1.5	1.7	2.7
Other shooting instrument	13.2	6.8	1.4	2.6
Vehicle	2.7	1.9	1.1	1.1
Animal	0.4	0.1	0.3	0.3
Other instrument	0.9	1.6	0.9	1.1
Other/multiple weapons	10.2	10.2	9.6	10.9

Violence portrayed on the four satellite channels exhibited a similar pattern of weapon-type distribution. In general violent portrayals were dominated by the use of parts of the body as a weapon, and the use of guns in either a military or criminal context. These categories were followed by violence involving the use of stabbing instruments, other shooting instruments, or clubbing instruments. Other categories of weapons, such as throwing instruments, vehicles, animals, or use of liquids, chemicals, electricity or gas also occurred but were much rarer.

Top ten weapon types: terrestrial channels

BBC1	%	BBC2	%
1 Fist/hand	32.9	1 Fist/hand	25.4
2 Hand-gun	5.9	2 Military hardware	8.7
3 Throw/push	4.6	3 Hand-gun	5.4
4 Rifle	4.2	4= Sword	5.1
5 Machine gun	4.1	4= Rifle	5.1
6 Other body part	3.8	6 Other body part	4.3
7 Shotgun	3.7	7 Kick	3.6
8 Kick	3.6	8 Explosives	3.5
9 Other projectiles	3.2	9= Machine gun	2.5
10= Laser weapon	2.9	9= Stick	2.5
10= Pistol	2.9		

ITV	%	Channel 4	%
1 Fist/hand	28.2	1 Fist/hand	34.5
2 Hand-gun	9.7	2 Hand-gun	5.4
3 Other body part	6.1	3 Rifle	4.2
4 Machine gun	4.9	4 Kick	4.1
5 Shotgun	4.1	5 Pistol	3.9
6 Kick	3.3	6 Laser weapon	3.5
7 Karate	3.2	7 Sword	3.3
8 Rifle	3.0	8 Other projectiles	3.1
9 Explosives	2.9	9 Other body part	2.9
10 Sword	2.4	10= Explosives	2.7
		10= Throw/punch	2.7

The key division in terms of distribution of weapon forms occurred between the two movie channels and the two general drama and entertainment channels. Use of the body as a weapon, for example, represented a larger proportion of violence on Sky One and UK Gold (51.4%) than on the two movie channels (41.3%). The movie channels, however, exceeded the non-movie channels in terms of violence featuring military hardware (14.3% versus 8.2% of violent acts) and violence involving stabbing instruments (10.7% versus 4.1%). In contrast, the non-movie channels exceeded the movie channels in terms of violence involving shooting instruments other than guns deployed in military and criminal contexts (10% versus 2%).

Many of the same weapon types appeared among the top tens for the satellite channels (see below). Violent behaviour involving the fist or hand was, once again, easily the most commonly occurring instrumental form of violence. Violence involving laser weapons and martial arts on Sky One reflected the prevalence on this channel, during the period of coding, of futuristic science fiction series such as *Star Trek: The Next Generation* and

Deep Space Nine, which appeared nightly, and of imported series made for the younger audience such as *Power Rangers* and *VR Troopers*.

SUMMARY AND CONCLUSIONS

The significance of the form which violent portrayals take rests principally upon evidence that viewers exhibit different perceptual responses to different physical forms or qualities of violence (Gunter, 1985). At the same time, while not distinguishing between the potency of different instruments of aggression to elicit differential degrees of response, behavioural psychologists have argued that the presence of a weapon or picture of a weapon can provide a stimulus to aggression especially among individuals who are already angry or in a state of readiness to behave in a violent manner (Berkowitz and LePage, 1967).

Top ten weapon types: satellite channels

Sky One	%	UK Gold	%
1 Fist/hand	27.7	1 Fist/hand	37.1
2 Laser Weapon	12.4	2 Hand-gun	6.2
3 Other body part	7.5	3 Laser weapon	5.6
4 Kick	6.8	4 Kick	4.3
5 Karate	6.3	5 Other body part	4.0
6 Throw/push	5.0	6= Machine gun	2.6
7 Hand-gun	3.6	6= Rifle	2.6
8 Stick	2.4	8 Throw/push	2.3
9 Sword	2.1	9= Pistol	2.2
10 Other vehicle	1.9	9= Shotgun	2.2
		9= Military hardware	2.2

Sky Movies	%	Movie Channel	%
1 Fist/hand	25.7	1 Fist/hand	25.3
2 Hand-gun	11.4	2 Sword	8.9
3 Karate	6.7	3 Hand-gun	6.9
4 Machine gun	5.1	4 Pistol	5.3
5 Kick	4.5	5 Rifle	4.2
6 Other body part	4.1	6 Other body part	3.8
7 Sword	3.4	7 Kick	3.5
8 Shotgun	3.0	8 Stick	3.3
9= Rifle	2.8	9 Karate	3.2
9= Stick	2.8	10 Machine gun	3.1

Attempts at classifying audience perceptions of televised violence have indicated that, generally, violence involving sharp instruments such as knives are more anxiety-provoking to viewers than violence involving guns being fired. Gun-fights, in turn, are more worrying than most forms of unarmed fighting (Gunter, 1985). Though interesting, even research into audience perceptions of television violence has so far compared only a limited range of physical forms of violence.

In the current study, violent portrayals were classified under 53 different categories representing various forms of violent behaviour and according to 48 different types of weapon or instruments of violence. This comprehensive classification of violence revealed that most categories or forms of violence occurred rarely. Much of the violence depicted on television was dominated by a relatively small number of forms or weapons. The ten most frequently occurring forms of violence accounted for 82% of all violent acts. The ten most frequently occurring types of weapon accounted for 65.8% of all violent acts.

Violence on television was dominated by the use of guns and the use of various body parts, such as hands or fists, feet, head and knees or elbows. Assailants generally shot at, hit, kicked, threw or tripped their targets. Guns or shooting instruments could appear in a variety of forms, however. The most regularly appearing were the hand-gun, laser gun, machine gun and rifle. These results mirror, to some extent, the findings of recent American research which also observed that the most frequently occurring forms of violence on television involved perpetrators using their own bodies to commit violence, such as hitting, punching or kicking the target. When weapons were used, hand-held firearms were the most commonly used (Wilson *et al.*, 1996a).

These two most prevalent forms of violence are of special interest not simply because of how often they occur, but also theoretically in the context of drawing possible implications about their significance in relation to their impact upon viewers. Violence by natural means during which a perpetrator uses his or her own body as the instrument of aggression is particularly important because of research evidence indicating that such actions may be the most likely portrayals to be imitated by members of the audience. Television portrayals involving guns have significance because of the potential priming effect they may have on human aggression (Berkowitz and Le Page, 1967; Carlson *et al.*, 1990).

The form of violence about which viewers have been found to exhibit the greatest concern, at an emotional level, namely stabbing, was much less frequently occurring than either violence by natural means or violence involving guns. Two per cent of all violent acts involved stabbing. Less than 1% of violent acts involving cutting of a victim. These results were reinforced by the findings for types of weapons used. The use of a dagger, domestic knife or hunting knife in an act of violence accounted for around 2% of violent acts. The use of some other stabbing instrument accounted for a further 1% of violent incidents. Other forms of violence which have been sources of concern, such as strangulation and hanging, were even less commonplace, although in the case of strangulation there were ample opportunities for viewers to witness such incidents. The same point was also true of scenes involving violence with sharp instruments. The key factor, in the context of potential audience response, where these kinds of scenes are examined, however, is the way in which these forms of violence are depicted. A close inspection of illustrative scenes of stabbing, strangulation and hanging indicated that the style of portrayal as well as the dramatic context in which such incidents occur can vary significantly from one scene to the next. The length of time the camera lingers on the victim, the degree of pain and suffering displayed by the victim, and the situation and motivational context can all act together to render a scene of stabbing or strangulation potentially horrific or relatively innocuous, from the viewers' perspective.

Although a content analysis cannot reveal anything directly about how viewers will respond to particular violent acts, there are signs that the types of instrument of aggression that are among those known to be most likely to upset viewers are relatively rare in their occurrence on screen. This is not to say that certain of the shootings or even fights not involving weapons could not give rise to concerns among viewers. It is essential to know more about a violent act than simply its physical form in order to be able to judge its potential to upset viewers. Contextual analysis of certain scenes of violence can serve to confirm or disconfirm the likelihood that they will prove to be upsetting to the audience.

5 Setting of violence

The occurrence of violence on television can be coloured by a variety of characteristics which can have independent and inter-dependent effects on viewers' reactions to violent portrayals. One intrinsic ingredient of any violent scene is the setting in which it occurs. This variable may refer to the temporal location or historical period in which violence occurs or the physical environment and geographical location in which it occurs.

Research with viewers would lead us to expect that the temporal setting of violence could make a difference to the way the violence is perceived and to any lasting impact it might have on viewers. In particular, the relevance of recording this attribute of violent portrayals stems from the importance of time period to the perceived realism of programme settings and to the level of viewer identification one might expect to find with the events portrayed. Violence depicted in contemporary settings has a much more profound impact on audience reaction than does violence depicted in non-contemporary settings. Previous research has indicated that viewers perceived the same form of violence quite differently when it occurs in different temporal settings. Contemporary violence is regarded as most serious, followed by that depicted in historical settings, with violence in futuristic settings generally perceived in less serious terms (Gunter, 1985).

It is likely, of course, that there may be other factors related to violent portrayals which might produce uncharacteristic degrees of concern among audiences even where futuristic violence in science fiction settings is concerned. Certain forms of violence are more worrying for viewers than others, while the general impression of viewers might also be affected by the sheer quantity of violence which, in some latter-day science fiction movies, can be quite substantial. As a general rule, however, the closer to everyday life is a programme's setting, the greater the likelihood that any violence it contains will be reacted to by viewers more strongly. Establishing the rate at which violence occurs in different temporal settings is therefore important since it represents a factor known to influence audience response.

In addition to temporal setting, the current research examined the environmental and geographical settings of violence. Although there is relatively little prior evidence on how viewers' reactions to screen violence are affected by physical setting attributes, one study did show that certain aspects of the physical environmental setting could make a difference to viewers' perceptions of televised violence (Gunter, 1985). Although not as significant as genre, character-type involvement, physical form of violence, or the nature of the consequences of violence, aspects of physical setting, such as whether violence occurred during daylight or after dark, and whether indoors or outdoors, had some effect on how viewers evaluated violent portrayals. Nighttime portrayals were rated as somewhat more violent and more likely to disturb people than were daytime portrayals. Differences between perceptions of violence occurring indoors or outdoors were more pronounced, with indoor portrayals typically being perceived as more seriously violent and disturbing than outdoor portrayals when the actual form or type of violence was held constant.

The perceived seriousness of violence within a particular physical setting also varied as a function of fictional context. Differences between the rated seriousness of portrayals were more refined in realistic fictional settings than in less realistic ones. There were also differences in the kind of effect physical setting had upon ratings of portrayals in different fictional contexts. Thus, whilst nighttime portrayals were perceived to be more violent than daytime portrayals within westerns, the latter were rated as the more violent in American-produced crime-drama series. Amongst indoor and outdoor portrayals, there was consistency in the direction of rated seriousness of violence across both these genres, with outdoor portrayals regarded as the more violent and potentially disturbing to viewers. Within British-produced crime-drama series, however, indoor portrayals were rated in more serious terms than were outdoor portrayals (Gunter, 1985; Gunter and Furnham, 1982).

Although weaker in their influence on viewers' perceptions than other objective features of content, physical setting attributes did have some effect on subjective judgements of episodes within contemporary crime-drama programmes. Greatest concern emerged for indoor portrayals of violence in British-made crime-drama series, and although this feature may not be potent on its own, in association with other disturbing features such as degree of harm caused to victims, types of weapons used and types of characters involved as assailants or victims, it represents a factor which could add to the overall impact of a violent television portrayal.

In this chapter, although some attention is devoted to environmental and geographical setting of television violence, the variables examined were not the same as those referred to in the audience research reviewed above. Thus, environmental location was differentiated in terms of whether the setting was urban or rural, or somewhere in between. Violent acts were not described in terms of time of day of occurrence or whether they occurred indoors or outdoors. The relevance of the distinction used in the current study is reinforced by research of public fear of crime. Members of the public surveyed in Britain, for example, have been found to perceive less risk from violent crime in rural locations than in urban locations. This difference in their perceptions of the dangers associated with such environments occurred whether they were asked to consider the position in Britain or in the United States (Gunter, 1987; Gunter and Wakshlag, 1988). In general, then, people regard inner city areas as more dangerous places to live or to visit than rural areas.

As well as the environmental location of violence, its geographical location in terms of the country where it occurs and perhaps more specifically the proximity of the location of violence to the viewers' own place of residence represent important factors in relation to public perceptions of violence. In a fairly general sense, people's perceptions of the dangers to be faced from crime and violence in different locations may depend to a certain extent on how close those locations are to the individual's own place of residence. People in Britain, for example, have been found to perceive greater risk from violent crime for those who live in Los Angeles than for those who live in a British urban location such as Glasgow or London (Gunter, 1987). The same survey showed that individuals who lived in the London area claimed that they would be more afraid of walking alone after dark in Los Angeles than they would be of walking home alone after dark from a local public house near where they live. They were least afraid of all of being stranded in the English countryside after dark (Gunter, 1987). Fear levels, in every case, rose if they themselves had been a victim of a crime at some point in their lives.

The geography of violence has been established previously to make some difference to how viewers respond to violence on the small screen. Violent portrayals, which were otherwise of a similar nature, depicted in British or American settings did produce different reactions among viewers (Gunter, 1985; Gunter and Furnham, 1982). British viewers were found to be generally more concerned about violent portrayals located in British drama settings than about those situated in American locations. Geographical location, as such, was also found to mediate perceptions of violence performed by certain categories of aggressor. For example, scenes featuring male assailants attacking a female victim were perceived in a more serious light when situated in Britain than in the United States. In contrast, scenes depicting female assailants attacking a male victim were reacted to more strongly when situated in the United States than in Britain (Gunter, 1985). On this evidence, geographical location may be an important attribute of televised violence.

HISTORICAL SETTING OF VIOLENCE

In the current research, historical setting of violence was coded in five ways: distant past, past (1900–1980), present (1980s–1990s), realistic future (next ten years) and distant future. The distribution of violent acts across the eight channels indicated that nearly half of all violence (49.2%) was located within the present. The next most popular time-period for violence was the near past (20.5%), representing events which could be judged as occurring after 1900 and before 1980. The distant past (15%) was a more likely historical setting for violence than either the near future (3.6%) or distant future (7%).

Channel differences

The historical setting of violence varied from channel to channel. On the terrestrial channels, the pattern of distribution largely reflected the overall pattern reported above in the case of the two most watched channels, BBC1 and ITV. On both channels, more than half the violence observed was set in the present. In both cases, more violence was set in the past than in the future. On BBC2 and Channel 4, however, this pattern changed. Although a considerable proportion of violence occurred in the present, a greater proportion occurred in the near past (see Table 5.1).

Table 5.1 Historical setting of violence on different terrestrial channels

	Percentages of violent acts				
	All terrestrial	*BBC1*	*BBC2*	*ITV*	*Ch.4*
Distant past	14.4	14.3	17.9	11.4	14.0
Past (1900–1980)	27.6	20.2	35.6	18.9	35.7
Present (1980s–1990s)	44.5	53.2	31.9	60.9	32.0
Realistic future	2.8	3.0	3.6	4.3	0.1
Distant future	4.6	6.0	7.2	0.8	4.2
Uncodable	6.3	3.6	3.9	3.8	14.0

On the four satellite channels, the greatest proportion of violence occurred in the present in every case, although contemporary violence represented the majority of all violent acts over the four weeks of analysis only in the case of Sky Movies. There were channel variations of some significance. On UK Gold, if violence was not located in a contemporary setting, it was most likely to occur in the recent past. This pattern was true also of Sky Movies, although not to such a marked degree. On Sky Movies, a substantial minority of violent acts occurred in a distant past setting. On The Movie Channel, however, non-contemporary violence was somewhat more likely to be situated in the distant past than in the recent past. The most significant departure from the general pattern occurred on Sky One, where non-contemporary violence was most likely to be situated in the distant future. This reflects the prominence of futuristic science fiction series on this channel which frequently contain violence (see Table 5.2).

ENVIRONMENTAL SETTING OF VIOLENCE

Environmental setting was classified into nine categories: inner city, suburban, small town, rural, uninhabited, mobile, mixed, studio and other. Across all eight channels taken together, the most common environment for violence was an inner city setting. Just over one in five violent acts (20.3%) were situated in this type of location. If violence was not located in an urban setting, it was most likely to be situated in rural (16.1% of all acts) or small town (13% of all acts) settings. Violence in the suburbs (5.9% of all acts) or uninhabited locations (7.2% of acts) were much less frequently occurring.

Table 5.2 Historical setting of violence on different satellite channels

	Percentages of violent acts				
	All satellite	*Sky One*	*UK Gold*	*Sky Movies*	*Movie Channel*
Distant past	13.1	4.8	6.2	15.5	26.0
Past (1900–1980)	20.6	7.3	32.8	23.2	18.9
Present (1980s–1990s)	48.1	47.5	43.6	55.9	45.5
Realistic future	3.7	8.0	0.8	3.5	2.3
Distant future	10.5	25.1	14.1	1.1	1.6
Uncodable	4.2	7.4	2.6	0.9	5.8

Channel differences

The principal environmental settings of violence on the terrestrial channels matched those found for channels as a whole. Inner city, rural and small town locations predominated on BBC1, BBC2, ITV and Channel 4. The appearance of violence in what were classified as studio locations was much more commonplace on ITV, however, than on any of the other terrestrial channels (see Table 5.3). Indeed, this was the second most likely location

Table 5.3 Environmental setting of violence on terrestrial channels

	Percentages of violent acts				
	All terrestrial	*BBC1*	*BBC2*	*ITV*	*Ch.4*
Inner city	20.4	26.5	22.8	19.3	12.9
Suburban	7.2	7.8	5.4	6.5	9.0
Small town	13.9	15.0	12.9	13.3	14.5
Rural	17.6	14.7	20.0	17.8	17.8
Uninhabited	4.7	2.8	3.2	6.0	6.6
Mobile	3.0	4.0	3.8	2.8	1.2
Very mixed	0.8	1.3	1.1	0.1	0.8
Studio	10.5	6.1	8.2	18.0	9.6
Other	18.4	18.0	17.8	14.3	23.3
Uncodable	3.9	3.8	4.9	2.3	4.7

identified after inner city settings for violence on this channel. Studio settings were especially prominent on ITV during weeks two (29.6% of violent acts on that channel) and three (27.7%). The studio setting was also the most common location of all for violence on Channel 4 in week one (20.8%).

A somewhat different pattern of environmental settings emerged for the four satellite channels (Table 5.4). Across the four weeks monitored, inner city settings were the most likely venues for violence on Sky One, UK Gold and

Sky Movies, but were pushed into second place by rural locations in the case of The Movie Channel. As with the terrestrial channels, suburban violence was coded, but was much less likely to occur on satellite programmes monitored than was inner city or rural-based violence. Violence was more likely to occur in a small town environment than in suburbia on all four satellite channels. In fact, small town violence surpassed rural violence on Sky One and Sky Movies. On Sky Movies, violence was also quite likely to occur in uninhabited locations.

Table 5.4 Environmental setting of violence on satellite channels

| | Percentages of violent acts | | | | |
	All satellite	Sky One	UK Gold	Sky Movies	Movie Channel
Inner city	21.4	18.7	28.9	20.7	17.1
Suburban	5.9	5.9	7.1	6.3	4.4
Small town	11.7	11.5	7.0	13.8	14.5
Rural	15.8	9.3	17.4	13.1	23.4
Uninhabited	7.1	6.5	2.6	11.5	7.7
Mobile	5.3	3.2	5.3	6.0	6.8
Very mixed	0.3	0.8	0.0	0.1	0.2
Studio	11.4	14.1	10.3	14.6	6.7
Other	18.6	27.8	20.0	11.0	15.4
Uncodable	2.7	2.4	1.6	3.0	3.9

GEOGRAPHICAL LOCATION OF VIOLENCE

A series of codes were applied to classify television violence in terms of its geographical location. For each channel, violent acts were categorized according to the country or continent in which they could be identified as having occurred or, if they had not been located somewhere on Earth, in terms of whether they had been situated on another planet or in outer space. A separate category was also reserved for cartoon violence for which no clear geographical location could be readily identified.

Aggregating across all channels and all weeks, the greatest single proportion of violent acts was found to be situated in the United States (47.4% of all acts). The second most likely location for television violence was Great Britain (12.4% of acts). The next most popular earthly locations for violence were Europe (5.9%), somewhere in the Orient (2.8%) and Australasia (2.6%). However, following the United States and Britain, violence was most likely to be found in cartoon settings (7.3% of acts) or in some non-earthly science fiction location (3.6% of acts) (see Table 5.5).

Channel differences

There were differences between terrestrial channels in the extent to which violence occurred in specific geographical locations (see Table 5.6). On

Table 5.5 Geographical location of violence

	Percentage of violent acts
Great Britain	12.4
United States	47.4
Cartoon	7.3
Europe	5.9
Various (sci. fict.)	3.6
Oriental	2.8
Australasia	2.6
Various parts/world	1.8
India/Asia	1.7
C./S. America	1.7
Africa	1.6
Middle East	1.2
Other planet	1.1
Other N. America	0.9
Unclear/uncodable	7.6

Table 5.6 Geographical location of violence on terrestrial channels

	Percentage of violent acts					
	All terrestrial	BBC1	BBC2	ITV	Ch.4	1986
Great Britain	21.5	28.7	19.5	15.2	22.4	21.3
United States	39.2	41.4	27.9	51.3	36.3	29.6
Cartoon	9.6	5.2	10.7	5.8	16.5	6.6
Europe	7.9	8.3	10.5	7.2	5.4	14.3
Various (sci. fict.)	2.1	0.8	6.2	1.1	0.2	1.3
Oriental	1.7	0.4	3.9	1.3	1.4	1.7
Australasia	2.8	3.5	5.5	1.8	0.5	2.2
Various parts/world	1.5	1.6	0.4	2.9	1.1	—
India/Asia	1.9	0.7	1.8	4.3	0.7	0.5
C./S. America	1.2	0.8	1.2	2.1	0.6	5.3
Africa	2.2	1.7	4.9	0.1	2.2	3.6
Middle East	1.8	0.9	2.8	1.5	1.9	1.8
Other planet	0.4	0.2	0.0	0.7	0.7	0.5
Other N. America	1.1	0.1	0.0	0.7	3.4	0.3
Unclear	1.9	1.5	1.6	2.4	2.1	2.4
Uncodable	3.1	3.7	2.6	1.9	4.2	8.6

three out of four terrestrial channels, the majority of violent acts occurred in either American or British locations. The exception to this rule was BBC2, for which British and American-based violence represented just under one in two violent acts. Clearly ITV was much more dominated by violence in American settings than the other three terrestrial channels, although the greatest single proportion of violent acts on any channel occurred in American settings. This American-based dominance of settings for violence was less pronounced on

Channel 4 and BBC2, and especially so in the latter's case. Comparisons with 1986 revealed a similar percentage of violent acts located in Britain, and an increase in the proportion situated in the United States. Violent incidents in European locations, in Central and South America, and in Africa, all declined compared with 1986.

The geographical location of violence on the four satellite channels reflected the predominant sources of programming for those channels. Thus, the greatest single proportion of violent acts on Sky One, Sky Movies and The Movie Channel occurred in American locations, while on UK Gold violence occurred predominantly in British locations. Even on UK Gold, however, the second most likely country in which violence occurred was the United States. This channel, however, contained the least US-located violence of any of the eight channels monitored in this research.

It should also be noted that the extent of violence in British locations was at a low level on Sky One and the two movie channels. Cartoon violence and violence on another planet were more frequently occurring than violence in British locations on Sky One. On Sky Movies, violence located in Britain was exceeded by European-based violence and science fiction violence. Finally, on The Movie Channel, British-located violence was exceeded once again by cartoon violence, with violence located in Europe not far behind (see Table 5.7).

Table 5.7 Geographical location of violence on satellite channels

| | Percentage of violent acts | | | | |
	All satellite	Sky One	UK Gold	Sky Movies	Movie Channel
Great Britain	14.4	3.1	45.6	2.6	6.3
United States	45.5	58.9	13.3	64.4	45.5
Cartoon	6.3	14.5	2.3	0.5	7.8
Europe	5.3	0.5	8.7	5.7	6.0
Various (sci. fict.)	5.4	9.2	9.1	2.9	0.2
Oriental	3.0	0.8	0.5	2.9	7.8
Australasia	2.9	1.4	3.6	5.1	1.3
Various parts/world	1.7	0.3	2.0	1.7	2.6
India/Asia	1.0	0.0	0.1	0.9	2.6
C./S. America	1.5	0.8	0.7	2.4	2.1
Africa	1.1	0.3	0.2	0.5	3.6
Middle East	1.0	*	1.2	0.8	2.1
Other planet	2.0	3.5	4.0	0.1	0.3
Other N. America	0.8	*	0.5	1.4	1.0
Unclear/uncodable	8.0	6.6	7.3	8.1	10.9

Note: * Less than 0.05%

SUMMARY AND CONCLUSIONS

In the current research, clear evidence emerged that on the major British television channels, violent portrayals are most likely to occur in particular settings. In general across the channels analysed, violence was more likely to occur in the present day than any other time period, in inner city locations than any other environmental setting, and in the United States than in any other country. Violence in the past was generally more commonly occurring than violence set in the future. Non-inner city violence was most likely to be found in small town or rural locations, and if those locations were not in the United States, then they were more likely to be in Britain than anywhere else.

The pattern was not exactly the same across all the channels studied. Present-day violence, for example, was less frequent on BBC2 and Channel 4 than on BBC1 and ITV. Compensating for this on the two former terrestrial channels was a greater than average rate of occurrence of violence situated in the past, especially the period between 1900 and 1980. In the case of the four satellite channels monitored, present-day violence was again generally the most likely time location for violence. There was, however, far greater than the average amount of violence situated in the distant future on Sky One. This was accounted for by the prevalence on that channel of science fiction series set in the future. The Movie Channel was nearly twice as likely as the overall channel average to contain violence set in the distant past.

The environmental location of violence exhibited some degree of variation across channels. Inner city violence was less commonly occurring on Channel 4 than on the other terrestrial channels. Such violence was most likely of all to occur on UK Gold. Rural violence was relatively infrequent on Sky One, on which a considerable proportion of its violence occurred in settings which could not be allocated to one of the earthly settings. This finding again reflected the strong presence of futuristic science fiction series on that channel where much of the action takes place in outer space.

The geographical location of violence on different channels is a direct reflection of the production sources of their violence-containing programmes. While American productions contributed extensively to violence found on all terrestrial channels, its presence was most keenly felt on BBC1 and ITV. In general the proportion of violent acts situated in the United States on the terrestrial channels increased markedly on findings from ten years earlier (Cumberbatch et al., 1987), while the level of violence occurring in British settings hardly changed at all over this period.

The clearest channel differences associated with the geography of violence were found on the four satellite channels. On the two movie channels US-based violence predominated, reflecting the production source of most of the movies shown on these channels. A similar finding emerged for Sky One. In contrast, UK Gold emerged with a relatively low level of US-based violence and a much higher than average level of British-based violence. This result was accounted for by the fact that this channel broadcasts mainly re-runs of old British series which have been shown previously on the mainstream terrestrial channels.

6 Motives and consequences of violence

Among the key defining attributes of violence wherever it occurs are the reasons for its occurrence and its consequences for those involved. The motives for violence and the nature of its consequences for those who are targeted or victimized can affect the way observers respond to it. These features therefore represent important aspects of violence according to which violent behaviour can be classified. By using such classifiers within the context of a content analysis of televised violence, such on-screen behaviour can be usefully qualified in terms which are known to be relevant to audience response. But just how significant are motives and consequences of media violence to the way viewers respond to it? Once again, there is both behavioural and perceptual research evidence which can be referred to.

JUSTIFICATION OF VIOLENCE

Laboratory studies of the cause–effect relationships which might exist between exposure to media violence and aggression among people exposed to it have systematically examined the mediating influences of the justification for the violence depicted. A body of research conducted in the United States during the late 1960s and early 1970s indicated that if violence on screen was represented to viewers as justified, they were more prepared to express aggressive behaviour themselves after watching a film clip that contained violence (e.g., Berkowitz et al., 1974). Such findings were interpreted with reference to an implicit morality within films which inferred that crime does not pay and that villains will justifiably suffer for their misdeeds. According to one of the leading research figures of that research era, Leonard Berkowitz, for example, if violence against the 'bad guy' in a movie is represented as justified, the audience's inhibitions against expressing their own anger towards someone, particularly if that individual had previously annoyed them in some way, would be lowered. This claim was supported by a series of laboratory-based studies.

In one study, for instance, Hoyt (1967) found that male undergraduate college students who had watched a film fight responded more aggressively against another individual who had earlier annoyed them if the introduction to the film emphasized that the victor was avenging an unfair beating he had received at another point in the film. Students who were told a slightly different version of the story according to which the character who won the fight was defending himself in a kill or be killed situation were somewhat less aggressive afterwards than the other group, but were still noticeably more aggressive than a third group of students who received no preamble which offered justification for the film violence they were shown.

In a subsequent study, Meyer (1972) used six film clips showing different kinds of justified or non-justified violence or a nonviolent film clip, or no clip at all. There were three clips of real violence footage depicting the execution of a prisoner by Vietnamese soldiers. There were also three clips of a staged fight from the movie, *From Here to Eternity*. In the case of both clips, one version was accompanied by a justification for the violence, in a second version there was no justification, and in a third version there was no sound track at all. A third film clip showed a cowboy saddling and riding a half-wild horse. This film clip served as a control or point of comparison. It offered its viewers interesting and involving, but essentially nonviolent, footage. Post-viewing aggressive behaviour was operationalized in terms of viewers being invited to deliver electric shocks to an individual who had previously insulted them in some way. Seeing violence which had been justified was associated with the administration of more powerful electric shocks than seeing unjustified real or fictional violence.

LEGAL OR CRIMINAL VIOLENCE

Another way of considering the motives for violence is in terms of whether it has fundamentally good or evil goals or purposes. One of the most consistent themes in television drama is the conflict between good and evil, between the forces of law and order and criminal elements. Similarly, much violence which occurs in factual programmes is associated with issues of goodness versus evil, whether the violence was perpetrated by villains during the course of committing a crime or by terrorists for allegedly political motives, but with the result that innocent bystanders were hurt or killed.

The importance of these variables for inclusion as part of a comprehensive analysis of television programme content is underlined by public opinion research which has indicated that legitimized violent actions are usually not perceived as unacceptable conduct. Officially sanctioned violence, for example, as employed by the police, is justified because it is behaviour designed to protect the public, to prevent the destruction of property by rioters and looters, or to deter law breakers. Evidence of a public mandate for official 'violence' of this sort from general social surveys has indicated that the process of legitimization is so powerful that even extreme forms of violent behaviour may sometimes be regarded by large numbers of ordinary people as acceptable.

Nearly a quarter of a century ago, Gamson and McEvoy (1972) reported that an American social survey found that 57% of a national sample agreed with the statement 'Any man who insults a policeman has no complaint if he gets roughed up in return' (p. 336). At around the same time, roughly half of another national sample in the United States thought that shooting was the best way to handle student protests on campus (Kahn, 1972). This tolerance of official violence may explain the persistent public perceptions of riots and rioters as 'violent' despite the fact that the number of people killed by authorities during civil disorders has been found consistently to exceed the number killed by rioters, in one analysis by an order of ten to one (Couch, 1968).

Public support for official violence is so pervasive that the definition of violence itself is affected. In one survey, for instance, again conducted in the United States, 30% of a national sample said that 'police beating students' was not an act of violence, and an astonishing 57% said that 'police shooting looters' was not an act of violence (Blumenthal *et al.*, 1972, p. 73). The semantics of the label 'violence', therefore, clearly reflect the perceived legitimacy of the actor and not merely the nature of his or her act.

Content analysis of programmes designed to explore the goals of television characters and the methods usually deployed to attain desired ends has indicated that non-legal methods tend to be used as often as legal methods in television drama productions (Larsen *et al.*, 1963). In summing up their findings, one of the main conclusions reached by Larsen and his colleagues was that there was a strong tendency for television to project content in which socially approved as well as unapproved goals were most often achieved by methods that would not in normal everyday life be regarded as socially acceptable. This observation drew attention to the frequent and rapid deployment of violent measures, often to an extreme degree, by agencies of law enforcement in television series when tackling problems of criminality.

Later American research indicated that while bad guys exhibited the greatest amount of involvement with violence and killing, it was a common aspect of television drama on mainstream American television that both good guys and bad guys used violence. Between 1969 and 1978, for example, just over 58% of good characters and 88% of bad characters on American prime-time television were involved in some form of violence (Gerbner *et al.*, 1979).

Content analysis studies of programmes on British television during the early 1970s did not elaborate on patterns of character-involvement in violence to the extent that equivalent American investigations had done. Nevertheless, a few consistent patterns emerged which indicated that perpetrators of violence were usually portrayed as belonging to the wrong side of the law. Even so, a substantial minority of good characters also used violence. About three out of four bad or villainous characters were violent, and this was about three times as high as the proportions of good characters or heroes who were violent. Bad characters were three times as likely to kill their victims as were good characters (Shaw and Newell, 1972; Halloran and Croll, 1972).

DEGREE OF OBSERVABLE HARM

The nature of character involvement in violence either as an assailant or as a victim may have a particular effect on the way in which violence is perceived by viewers. Related to this factor, however, is another different feature of violence – the degree of harm and suffering caused to a victim by a violent attack.

Television characters deal out a lot of violence, but they also extensively suffer the punitive and injurious consequences that accompany this involvement. In the content analysis work of George Gerbner and his colleagues in the United States, the relative probabilities of being hurt or killed, as manifested in their measures of 'victimization-likelihood' were interpreted as a dramatic demonstration of the power structure of television's fictional world (Gerbner and Gross, 1976; Gerbner *et al.*, 1978, 1979). Analyses of the outcomes of violence on prime-time American drama output indicated that a substantial proportion of aggressive episodes resulted in injury or painful consequences for some of the characters involved. On American television during the 1970s, for example, nearly 40% of violent incidents were found to result in casualties, and nearly 38% of all casualties were fatal (Gerbner, 1972). On British television, at around the same time, content analysis research showed that 77% of all violent episodes resulted in some pain or suffering, and one in three of these casualties were fatal (Shaw and Newell, 1972).

Behavioural research has shown that the expression of pain by a victim can have profound effects on the subsequent behaviour of that person's attacker. When one person attacks another, a frequent consequence is an expression of discomfort or annoyance by the victim. When this expression is perceived by the aggressor, it conveys certain information to the latter about the impact of his attack (e.g., that it has achieved the desired or undesired effect) and may affect the probability of further attacks upon that victim. Two hypotheses have been proposed concerning the effects of pain on further aggression against a victim by an attacker, both of which predict the severity of violent outcomes. According to one hypothesis the suffering of the victim may lead to the vicarious arousal of similar unpleasant emotional feelings on the part of the aggressor. Such empathic arousal may then act to inhibit subsequent attacks against the suffering victim. The second hypothesis argues that the pain cues emitted by the victim may serve as reinforcing stimuli for the aggressor, and thus may facilitate attacks against this victim.

Empirical investigations of these hypotheses have produced evidence to support both the facilitating and inhibitory effects of a victim's suffering on his attacker's aggressive behaviour. However, research has also indicated that the likelihood that one of these effects will occur rather than the other depends a lot on other aspects of the context in which the aggressive display takes place and upon the mood of the aggressor. Most of the studies in this area have examined the effects of observing the suffering of a live victim on a person's aggressive behaviour, and only one or two have explored the impact of the consequential nature of filmed violence on viewers' reactions. Just as witnessing 'live' victims' pain reactions can influence the strength of an aggressor's response, so research has shown that when viewers have been made aware of the painful aftermath of an aggressive film portrayal, they are subsequently less willing to behave aggressively against another person even in contrived laboratory settings where they may be encouraged to do so.

Goranson (1969) found that the effect of unpleasant consequences for the victim of violence in a film portrayal was to reduce the level of aggressiveness in angered viewers compared to a film portrayal with a more pleasant ending. In this experimental demonstration of such an effect, Goranson showed individuals a boxing match sequence from the feature film *Champion*, in which one fighter was savagely beaten by another. After seeing this fight sequence viewers next listened to a tape-recorded synopsis of events supposedly following the fight involving the loser. In one version of the story, the loser (or victim) was described as eventually dying from his injuries, whilst in another version he went on to another successful career. Afterwards, viewers took part in another experimental task in which their propensity towards aggressiveness was assessed with the Buss-Durkee 'aggression machine' technique. Results showed that subsequent aggressiveness among viewers was stronger among those who had heard the synopsis describing pleasant consequences for the defeated fighter. Hearing that the injuries from the fight resulted in the defeated fighter's death, had the effect of inhibiting a viewer's invited aggression against another person.

Goranson's findings were reinforced by those of another study by Hartmann (1969) who showed adolescent boys three versions of a film sequence depicting two boys playing basketball. Prior to seeing the film, half of the boys were made angry and then angered and non-angered boys were each divided equally into three groups. One group saw a nonviolent version of the film sequence simply depicting two boys about their own age playing basketball. A second group saw a version in which the boys in the film played happily enough to begin with, but then quarrelled and had a fight. In this version, the camera focused on the instrumental acts of aggression of the boy who won the fight. A third group also saw the fight sequence between the two boys, but on this occasion camera shots emphasized the painful reactions of the defeated boy as he was hit. When subsequently allowed to punish an experimental accomplice for his mistakes in a learning task by administering electric shocks to him, it was found that previously angered boys who had watched the pain consequences version of the film portrayal became more aggressive than those who had watched the instrumental aggression version. Boys who had not been made angry earlier on, however, became more aggressive after watching the version focusing on the actions of the aggressive film actor than after seeing the version focusing on the painful reactions of the film victim.

Hartmann interpreted these findings as showing support for the empathy hypothesis. Under conditions of no anger arousal, intense pain reactions on the part of a victimized film actor produced powerful empathic feelings in viewers which inhibited their tendencies to behave violently themselves. Anger, however, would appear to raise the threshold beyond which disturbing film portrayals give rise to these feelings in viewers and in turn inhibit their aggression (Feshbach *et al.*, 1967; Hartmann, 1969).

In another study, children were more disturbed by violent episodes in which injured victims were seen than by episodes which featured no observable harm to any of the actors (Noble, 1975). Although focusing on behavioural responses subsequent to viewing media violence, these experiments may also indicate some degree of perceptual differentiation of violent incidents by viewers on the basis of the outcomes of violence for those who are victimized.

The mediating effect of observed consequences of violence may, of course, vary in its nature or strength from one type of programme to the next. Behavioural effects research has indeed already indicated a certain degree of interdependency between the consequences of portrayed violence and fictional context. Noble (1975) reported that whilst filmed violence with sight of the victim produced more anxiety and destructive play behaviour amongst children than did portrayals not showing the victim, the impact of sight of victim was more pronounced still in a realistic setting.

Studies of behavioural aggression have indicated that the consequences of involvement in violence for the victim affect the way viewers respond to portrayals behaviourally. This, in turn, implies some degree of differential interpretation of violent portrayals in terms of the degree of harm to victims. The significance of this attribute of violent content to audience perceptions was supported in a study by Greenberg and Gordon (1972a). They obtained young male viewers' judgements of violent scenes which differed along a number of dimensions including the degree of harm inflicted on victims. Scenes in which actors physically harmed themselves or another were perceived as more violent and less acceptable than scenes in which harm was overtly intended but unsuccessful (e.g., shooting at someone and missing). The latter portrayal in turn was rated in more serious terms than scenes depicting physical damage to an inanimate object (e.g., smashing furniture).

Gunter (1985) reported two studies which investigated viewers' perceptual reactions to televised violence which resulted either in fatal consequences for the victim, non-fatal though still injurious consequences, or no observable harm. The evaluated programme materials were obtained from American-produced crime-drama and science fiction series.

In general, any kind of observably harmful violence was perceived as more 'violent' and more 'disturbing' than violence showing no harmful consequences for intended victims. Although the difference between them was typically small, there was some tendency for non-fatally harmful scenes to be rated as more serious than the fatally harmful ones. This difference might have been a function of greater depicted pain and suffering among victims following non-fatally harmful violent incidents. In contrast, killings often resulted in what appeared to be relatively painless deaths. These perceived differences suggested that the amount of suffering endured by victims of violence, as well as the ultimate outcome, is a crucial factor influencing viewers' judgements about violent television portrayals. Reinforcing further earlier observations made about the varying strength of effects of different violent forms across different fictional contexts, it was found that the consequences of violence had a much stronger influence on viewers' perceptions of portrayals in contemporary settings than in futuristic settings.

THE ROLE OF EMPATHY

The implications of the depiction of the consequences of violence for viewers stem in part from the ability of scenes of pain and suffering to invoke feelings of empathy in the audience. Over the years, empathy has meant different things to different scholars, both in philosophy (e.g., Scheler, 1913; Smith, 1759/1971; Stein, 1970) and in psychology (e.g., Berger, 1962; Hoffman, 1977; Stotland, 1969). Different theoretical notions of empathy have been construed. Definitions of empathy have included the ability to perceive accurately the emotions of others (e.g., Borke, 1971; Tagiuri, 1969), the proficiency of putting oneself in another person's position (e.g., Dymond, 1949; Katz, 1963), the skill of understanding the emotional experiences of others (e.g., Cline and Richards, 1960; Davis *et al.*, 1987), the sharing of particular emotions with others (e.g., Aronfreed, 1968; Feshbach, 1978), the conscious or unconscious assimilation of another ego through a process called identification (e.g., Fenichel, 1954; Freud, 1950, 1964) and the instigation to act so as to relieve distress in others (e.g., Mehrabian and Epstein, 1972; Stotland *et al.*, 1978).

Certainly, if viewers witness a violent event which causes an actor on screen to appear to suffer pain, they may put themselves in that actor's position and imagine what it would be like to suffer such pain themselves. Alternatively, they may wish they could do something to prevent or to relieve the suffering. The audience's emotional reaction to scenes of violence may be invoked through the anticipation of the pain that might be caused by a particular action, however, even before the blow is struck. Such an emotional reaction may be just as powerful as when the violent action is carried through and the victim is actually harmed (Smith, 1759/1971). Psychological research evidence has corroborated the existence of such 'anticipatory empathetic reactions' (Stotland, 1969).

The degree to which viewers might feel empathy for the individual on the receiving end of violence, however, can depend upon what they know about this individual and whether they like him or not. A victim of violence may be shown to suffer pain, with his or her face contorted in agony, but whether or not viewers feel concerned about this may depend upon the circumstances surrounding the incident and whether the victim is regarded as deserving of his/her misfortune or not. Psychological research has indicated that witnessing a disliked person receiving a reward might be regarded as annoying while seeing that same person have bad luck or suffer perilous consequences may be regarded as satisfying by audiences, especially if members of the audience have come to dislike that individual. In contrast, witnessing a well-liked character fall on hard times or suffer the painful consequences of violence is likely to upset viewers by invoking feelings of empathy. How viewers will respond to the victims of violence who display clear pain and suffering will depend upon whether that individual is liked and seen to deserve their fate (Zillmann, 1980; Zillmann and Cantor, 1976).

In the current chapter, aspects of the motivational context of televised violence and of its outcomes or consequences are examined. The reasons lying behind violence were classified in terms of the general context, such as war, civil strife, crime, domestic situations, in which violent acts took place and also in terms of observed goals of aggressors. The consequences of violence were classified in terms of the pain or horror caused among victims and the amount of blood spilled. In addition, a battery of injury outcomes, ranging from less to more serious consequences, was applied as a further form of classification.

MOTIVATIONAL CONTEXT OF VIOLENCE

In the most recent prior research about violence on British television, conducted ten years before the current study, Cumberbatch *et al.*(1987) reported that the single most commonplace motive for violence was for evil or destructive purposes, followed by the need for self-preservation (see Table 6.1). Violence took place twice as often in a criminal context as in the service of upholding the law.

During the early 1970s, Shaw and Newell (1972) noted that the most common reasons for violent portrayals in television drama (e.g., films, series, serials and plays) were quarrels and rivalries between individuals followed by criminal-related behaviour (see Table 6.2). More than half of all violence found in films, series and serials could be accounted for by these two sets of motives. In single plays, violence tended to be found most often in domestic, family settings and hence involved family disputes or difficulties among individuals who knew one another intimately.

Table 6.1 Goals of the aggressor

	Total	%
Other (varied)	583	26.2
Evil/destructive	398	17.9
Self-preservation	217	9.8
Upholding the law	186	8.4
Desire for money	168	7.6
Well being of society	129	5.8
Ambition or power	113	5.1
Well being of family	113	5.1
Respect for law	31	1.4
Sexual	19	0.9
Religious	2	0.1
Cannot code	265	11.9
TOTAL	2,224	100.2

Source: Cumberbatch *et al.* (1987)

Table 6.2 Circumstances of violence

Number of violent incidents	*Films (263)* %	*Series (308)* %	*Serials (110)* %	*Plays (38)* %
Violence in the course of interpersonal quarrels, rivalries, etc.	37	31	35	18
Violence in the course of carrying out a criminal act	23	39	21	21
Violence in domestic, family settings	5	3	3	32
War, armed forces action	12	4	19	5
Accidental violence	6	4	10	13
Violence in the course of carrying out the law	11	11	3	3
Civil strife, riots	2	3	3	3
Other	4	5	6	5

Source: Shaw and Newell (1972)

MOTIVES FOR VIOLENCE ON TV IN THE MID-1990s

The analysis of the motivational context of violence on television involved the classification of the general context of violence and a further analysis of the goals of the aggressor in the case of each violent act. Eight codes were used to classify the general motivational context of violence in terms of whether a violent act represented an act of war; behaviour occurring as a result of civil strife or rioting; a criminal act; an act involved in upholding the law; an act of defending civil liberties; an act of domestic violence in the home; some other form of interpersonal violence; or some other form of motivation for violence (Table 6.3).

Table 6.3 Motivational context of television violence: all channels

	Percentage of violent acts
Criminal act	24.7
Other interpersonal	23.1
Upholding the law	7.6
Defending civil liberties	6.6
War, armed forces	6.1
Civil strife, riots	2.5
Domestic at home	2.4
Other/cannot code	27.1

In general, the greatest single proportion of violent acts was found to comprise some form of criminal action (25% of all violent acts), followed by violence involving interpersonal conflict (23%). These were followed by acts of violence in the service of upholding the law (8%), defence of civil liberties (7%), and acts of war involving the use of armed forces (6%). Domestic violence (2%) was relatively infrequent.

There were some differences between terrestrial channels in respect of how often violence was depicted in particular motivational contexts (See Table 6.4). Crime and violence occurred together most often on ITV (26% of violent acts), exceeding the average frequency of this motivational setting for violence on the other three terrestrial channels (16% of acts). Various forms of interpersonal violence were the most frequently occurring type on Channel 4 (33% of violent acts on this channel), and far exceeded the rate of occurrence of such violence on the other terrestrial channels (average 21%).

A comparison of the latest results with those from 1986 revealed a fair degree of consistency among motivational categories of violence. Interpersonal violence accounted for the greatest single proportion of violent acts on

Table 6.4 Motivational context of television violence: terrestrial channels

	Percentage of violent acts					
	BBC1	BBC2	ITV	Ch. 4	1994/95 Average	1986 Average
Criminal act	16.8	16.0	26.3	15.1	18.5	17.5
Other interpersonal	20.7	21.1	18.8	32.8	23.4	21.6
Upholding the law	7.7	4.0	10.4	7.1	7.3	7.1
Defending civil liberties	9.1	3.0	10.0	7.1	7.3	7.9
War, armed forces	7.6	21.5	6.2	5.5	10.2	9.8
Civil strife, riots	6.3	3.9	2.8	2.6	3.9	8.2
Domestic at home	4.3	4.2	1.6	2.4	3.1	3.5
Other/cannot code	27.6	26.0	23.9	27.6	26.3	8.8

Table 6.5 Motivational context of television violence: satellite channels

	Percentage of violent acts			
	Sky One	UK Gold	Sky Movies	Movie Channel
Criminal act	25.5	26.3	29.3	24.9
Other interpersonal	18.6	19.1	17.3	32.7
Upholding the law	4.9	16.5	8.8	5.5
Defending civil liberties	6.1	5.9	7.7	5.8
War, armed forces	4.0	5.5	3.9	4.9
Civil strife, riots	0.4	1.3	2.8	2.8
Domestic at home	0.5	5.1	2.1	3.1
Other/cannot code	39.8	20.4	28.0	20.2

the terrestrial channels, with criminal violence being the next most commonly occurring category in 1986 and again in 1994/95.

On the four satellite channels, violence was found mostly to have been motivated by criminal goals (27% of violent acts of these channels) (Table 6.5). Over one in five violent acts were associated with some form of interpersonal conflict (22%). The latter form of motivation for violence was especially characteristic of violent behaviour depicted on The Movie Channel (33% of violent acts on that channel). The third most common specific motivation for violence depicted on satellite channels was upholding the law (8% of violent acts). However, this figure was inflated by the exceptionally high rate of occurrence of this motivational context for violence on UK Gold (15% of violent acts on that channel).

Goals of aggressor

In a further analysis of the motivational context of television violence, a set of codes was applied to classify acts of violence in terms of the apparent goals of the perpetrators of violence. Eleven codes were used: upholding the law; protection of the family home; protection of society; respect for law; self-preservation; desire for money; desire for ambition or power; religious reasons; evil or destructive reasons; sexual motives; and other various reasons (Table 6.6). The first five motives might be conceived as representing 'positive' reasons and the second group of five motives might be seen alternatively as representing 'negative' reasons for committing violent acts. In judgemental terms though, public opinion about even allegedly 'positive' motives for behaving violently might need to be persuaded that the violence used was justified and equitable.

Violence was found to be motivated more often by negative than by positive reasons. 'Positive' motives for violence accounted for 33% of violent acts across all channels, while 'negative' motives accounted for 43% of violent acts. The specific category of aggressor goals which accounted for the largest single proportion of violent acts was violence for purely evil or destructive reasons (21% of violent acts). This was followed by violence for self-preservation and violence in the service of personal ambition or power (14% of violent acts in each case).

The other key goals of aggressors were the desire for money (7% of violent acts), protection of the family home (7%), upholding the law (7%), protection of society (4%), respect for the law (2%), and sexual motives (1%).

Table 6.6 Goals of aggressor: all channels

	Percentage of violent acts
Evil/destructive	20.7
Self-preservation	14.4
Ambition/power	14.0
Desire for money	7.4
Upholding the law	6.6
Protect family home	6.6
Protect society	3.6
Respect for law	1.8
Sexual	0.9
Religious	0.0
Other/cannot code	23.5

The pattern of aggressor goals observed over all channels was largely preserved across the four terrestrial channels, with fairly minor variations (see Table 6.7). Violence for purely evil or destructive purposes was slightly more likely to occur on ITV and Channel 4 (22% of violent acts on those channels) than on BBC1 and BBC2 (17%). Violence motivated by ambition and power seeking was more likely to occur on BBC1 (16% of violent acts) than on the other terrestrial channels (an average of 12% of violent acts).

Table 6.7 Goals of aggressor: terrestrial channels

	Percentage of violent acts					
	BBC1	*BBC2*	*ITV*	*Ch.4*	*All Terrestrial*	*1986*
Evil/destructive	16.7	17.5	23.0	21.0	19.6	17.9
Self-preservation	17.1	7.7	12.7	12.7	12.6	9.8
Ambition/power	11.7	16.2	12.8	13.3	13.5	5.1
Desire for money	8.0	6.9	6.2	5.9	6.8	7.6
Upholding the law	5.5	3.7	7.6	9.3	6.5	8.4
Protect family home	6.0	3.1	3.3	3.1	3.9	5.1
Protect society	4.6	8.1	8.2	3.4	6.1	5.8
Respect for law	3.3	2.6	0.9	2.6	2.4	1.4
Sexual	0.6	0.6	0.5	1.3	0.8	0.9
Religious	0.4	0.6	0.2	0.4	0.4	0.1
Other/cannot code	25.8	33.2	24.5	27.9	27.9	38.1

Table 6.8 Goals of aggressor: satellite channels

	Percentage of violent acts			
	Sky One	UK Gold	Sky Movies	Movie Channel
Evil/destructive	18.8	23.3	21.7	21.9
Self-preservation	13.5	13.3	16.7	15.7
Ambition/power	12.4	13.5	10.9	15.5
Desire for money	8.7	7.4	9.0	6.3
Upholding the law	5.8	9.2	6.6	5.6
Protect family home	3.7	6.8	7.0	12.0
Protect society	5.6	3.5	2.8	4.9
Respect for law	4.6	1.4	2.2	1.2
Sexual	0.4	0.9	1.1	1.1
Religious	0.0	0.0	0.1	0.0
Other/cannot code	26.6	20.7	21.8	16.1

Comparisons between 1986 and 1994/95 indicated that there were slight increases in the extent to which violent acts were motivated by evil or destructive goals, self-preservation needs, and ambition for power over the ten years. There were falls in the percentages of violent acts which were accounted for by attempts to uphold the law or protect the family home. Most significant of all, however, was the marked reduction in 1994/95 compared with 1986 in the percentage of acts for which no listed aggressor goal code could be applied.

The satellite channels exhibited a similar pattern of motives for violence (Table 6.8). The most popularly occurring category of goal of violence was evil and destruction (21% of acts on satellite channels). Self-preservation (15%) and ambition and power (13%) were the second and third most common motives for violence. The Movie Channel showed a much higher than average occurrence of violence motivated by the need to protect the family home (12% of violent acts on that channel), while on UK Gold a higher than average prevalence of violence in the service of upholding the law occurred (9%).

Sexually motivated violence

A body of research has emerged over the past 20 years to show that exposure to audio-visual material depicting portrayals of rape or blending violent with sexual behaviour can have profound effects on viewers' moods and attitudes towards women, particularly among male viewers. Films depicting sado-masochistic content and group rape have been found to produce stronger feelings of aggressiveness among male and female viewers (Schmidt, 1975). Repeated exposure to sexually violent film sequences can produce changes in male viewers' sexual responses to sexual scenes and attitudes towards victims of rape (Malamuth, 1981; Malamuth and Check, 1981). Males have also been found to retaliate more severely against a female who had previously antagonized them under laboratory conditions after viewing a sequence from a film depicting rape than after watching a film of mutually consenting sexual intercourse (Donnerstein, 1980).

One particularly important factor is whether during the course of the rape, the victim becomes sexually aroused. This type of scene has been found to have especially powerful effects on the subsequent reactions of young male viewers, causing them to develop even more relaxed attitudes about rape and about the degree to which women are deeply traumatized by the experience (Donnerstein and Berkowitz, 1981).

During the course of the current analysis, 181 violent acts were coded for which the motivational context was classified as being sexual in nature. These scenes occurred mainly in films originally produced for the cinema (75%) and to a lesser extent appeared in long-running drama series acquired from overseas (8%). Most of these scenes occurred on Sky Movies (31%) and The Movie Channel (27%), with relatively smaller percentages being found on Sky One (9%), UK Gold (8%), Channel 4 (9%) and ITV (8%).

Although violence was coded as occurring within a generally sexual context for these scenes, close inspection revealed that only one of these scenes depicted action involving an attempt to force a woman to have sex against her will. For the most part, the scenes categorized under this heading took place in a context of (usually mild) sexual intimidation or harassment, which did not produce any significant harm to victims. Two particular scenes were singled out for closer inspection given the time of day and programmes in which they occurred.

The first of these two scenes occurred in an episode of the American action television series *The Fall Guy* which was broadcast on ITV on 22 October 1994 at 1.10 pm. The scene in question involved some fairly light-hearted touching of a woman who pushed off the man responsible very easily and without the situation escalating into something more serious. The woman later became the man's girlfriend. The second scene was recorded in *Little House on the Prairie* shown by Channel Four at 11.45am on 9 October 1996. In this programme, a rape is attempted and the rapist does not succeed. The victim managed to struggle from the clutches of her attacker and ran away. Apart from holding the girl tightly, the perpetrator did not injure his victim in any way. This scene was made more serious because the girl was very young (under 16) and was clearly frightened. The perpetrator was eventually shot.

CONSEQUENCES OF VIOLENCE

Consequences of violence were classified in terms of the types of injuries caused to victims. Ten codes were applied: death, mutilation, limbs broken, serious wound, minor wound, stunning, bruising, psychological damage, other injury, no physical injury.

More than one in three acts of violence (36.3%) caused no injury to victims. When injury did result, it was more likely to take a mild form, such as stunning of the victim (15.1%), minor wound (11.1%) or bruising (8.4%) than a more serious form, such as serious wound (5.5%), mutilation (0.5%), or broken limbs (0.2%). Death resulted in 12.4% of cases of violence. Psychological damage was observed to occur only very occasionally (1.7% of violent acts).

There were few differences between television channels in the patterning of injury consequences of television violence (see Tables 6.9 and 6.10). Perhaps the most notable feature was the extent to which violence resulted in no physical injury on different channels. A higher proportion of violent acts on Channel 4 (40%) produced no injury than was the case, on average, across the other terrestrial channels (33%). On satellite television, substantially higher proportions of violent acts on Sky One (46%) and UK Gold (40%) resulted in no physical injury to victims than was true of the two movie channels (29%).

Comparisons between 1986 and 1994/95 are not straightforward because the coding categories for types of injury used in the current study and those used by Cumberbatch and his colleagues (1987) were not exactly the same. Cumberbatch used a category called 'pain' which accounted for 16% of violent events in 1986. This category was not included in the current analysis within the list of injury types. Furthermore, in the current study one category was used to cover 'serious wounds', whereas in the 1986 study three distinct categories of serious injury were employed – 'stab wound' (0.4%), 'cut severe' (1.2%) and 'bullet wound' (2.2%). These three categories were aggregated to facilitate the comparison shown in Table 6.9. Here, it can be seen that the percentage of violent acts resulting in death fell significantly in 1994/95 compared with 1986, while the percentages of acts producing minor injuries increased. The extent to which violent acts produced no observable injuries to victims was unchanged over the ten years.

Table 6.9 Distribution of injury type: terrestrial channels

	Percentage of violent acts					
	BBC1	*BBC2*	*ITV*	*Ch.4*	*All terrestrial*	*1986*
Death	10	15	12	8	11	26
Mutilation	*	*	*	*	*	1
Limbs broken	*	*	*	*	*	*
Serious wound	5	5	6	4	5	4
Minor wound	12	9	12	9	11	3
Stun	19	13	12	13	15	9
Bruise	10	7	9	11	9	*
Other injury	3	4	6	3	4	1
Psychological damage	2	1	3	1	2	*
No physical injury	32	30	36	43	35	35
Cannot code	7	16	4	8	8	6

Notes: 1. Cumberbatch also included category of 'pain' which accounted for a further 16% of violent consequences
2. * Less than 0.5%

Table 6.10 Distribution of injury type: satellite channels

	Percentage of violent acts				
	Sky One	UK Gold	Sky Movies	Movie Channel	All satellite
Death	4	13	17	15	12
Mutilation	*	*	1	*	*
Limbs broken	*	*	*	*	*
Serious wound	2	5	7	7	5
Minor wound	6	10	13	14	11
Stun	20	12	14	15	15
Bruise	10	11	8	6	9
Other injury	8	5	2	4	5
Psychological damage	1	2	2	1	2
No physical injury	46	40	29	36	38
Cannot code	2	2	5	2	3

Note: * Less than 0.5%

Qualitative assessment of violence outcomes

The final part of the assessment of the consequences of violence for victims required coders to supply ratings for each violent act in terms of the degree of pain caused to victims, the amount of blood seen and the amount of horror associated with the violence. Each violent act was rated in terms of these features along a five-point scale.

Victim pain intensity

Nearly six in ten violent acts (59%), across all eight channels and aggregating over the four weeks of this content analysis, were found to have produced no pain at all in those at whom the violence had been aimed. If any pain followed at all, it was usually only of the mildest kind (24% of violent acts). Moderate degrees of discomfort, scoring 3 or 4 out of 5, were recorded for under one in ten acts of violence (8%), while intense discomfort (scale score = 5) was coded for just 1% of all violent acts. The latter 1% amounted, in numerical terms, to 112 violent acts.

The distribution of pain intensity ratings exhibited some variation across channels. Among the terrestrial channels, ITV had a smaller percentage of violent acts classified as giving rise to no pain in victims. This result was largely accounted for by a larger than average proportion of violent acts on this channel being uncodable in terms of victim pain intensity (see Table 6.11).

A comparison can also be made with the results obtained by Cumberbatch and his colleagues (1987) for the terrestrial channels in 1986. Cumberbatch used two separate measures of pain intensity associated with violence, one of

Table 6.11 Distribution of pain intensity ratings: terrestrial channels

						All	
		BBC1	BBC2	ITV	Ch.4	terrestrial	1986
Pain							
None	1	60	60	50	62	58	40
	2	26	25	24	24	25	28
	3	4	4	7	4	5	13
	4	2	1	2	2	2	4
Intense	5	*	1	*	1	1	*
Cannot code		7	9	16	7	10	15

Note: * Less than 0.5%

which was concerned with visual displays of pain, while the other was concerned with vocal pain cues where the victims may not have been visible on screen. The current analysis dealt with observable pain only, so the comparison is made with the visible pain cues measure of the 1986 analysis.

The results in Table 6.11 show that there was an increase between 1986 and 1994/95 in the proportion of violent acts on the terrestrial channels which were associated with no observable pain cues. At the same time, there was a general decrease in the proportion of acts associated with mild to moderate pain intensity (scoring between 2 and 4 out of 5). There was an increase in the proportion of violent incidents which caused intense pain cues (scoring 5 out of 5). In terms of actual numbers of acts in which the victims of violence were seen to suffer greatly, six such acts emerged in 1986 compared with 24 in 1994/95.

Table 6.12 Distribution of pain intensity ratings: satellite channels

		Sky	UK	Sky	Movie	All
		One	Gold	Movies	Channel	satellite
Pain						
None	1	74	53	53	60	60
	2	18	28	24	26	24
	3	3	6	7	7	6
	4	1	1	2	2	2
Intense	5	*	*	1	*	*
Cannot code	5	12	13	5	9	8

Note: * Less than 0.5%

Among the satellite channels, UK Gold and Sky Movies contained smaller percentages of violent acts coded as giving rise to no victim pain than did Sky One and The Movie Channel (see Table 6.12). Although this finding is partly accounted for by inter-channel differences in uncoded items, UK Gold and Sky Movies also exhibited larger proportions of violent acts scored as giving rise to mild pain (rating = 2).

Further analysis of these subjective ratings of violent acts revealed a small number of programmes which contained violent acts with the highest poss-ible rating for pain consequences. A total of 40 programmes were found which contained at least one violent act which was rated 5 for the intensity of observable pain caused to victims. Nearly half (18) of these programmes contained just one violent act with this level of observable pain, while a further 13 programmes contained two violent acts associated with this level of pain intensity. A further seven programmes contained three or more acts of violence which were accompanied by extremely high levels of observable pain. These seven programmes are individually listed below.

Programmes featuring most violent acts with extreme pain consequences

	No. of acts	
1	24	*Braindead*, Sky Movies, 11.35 pm, 18 January/9 February 1995
2	8	*Alien 3*, Sky Movies, 10.00 pm, 14 October 1994
3	5	*Sankofa*, Channel 4, 12.35 am, 10 October 1994
4=	3	*The X Files*, BBC2, 9.00 pm, 9 February 1995
4=	3	*Devlin*, Movie Channel, 3.15 am, 13 October 1994
4=	3	*Death Ring*, Sky Movies, 10.00 pm, 11 October 1994
4=	3	*American Cyborg: Steel Warrior*, Sky Movies, 11.05 pm, 26 October 1994

Six out of the seven programmes which contained the highest number of violent incidents resulting in extremely painful consequences for victims were movies originally made for the cinema. The exception was an episode of the cult American drama series with science fiction overtones, *The X Files*, shown on BBC2 just after the 9.00pm watershed.

Amount of blood

All violent acts were rated for the amount of blood accompanying them. For a clear majority of violent acts (73%) no blood was observed. In under one in ten instances (8%) a small amount of blood was seen, while moderate amounts of blood (3%) occurred fairly seldom. It was rare for violence to give rise to substantial amounts of blood (less than 0.5% of violent acts). In total, 79 violent acts were rated as showing much blood (rating = 5).

Table 6.13 Distribution of observable blood ratings: terrestrial channels

| | | | | | | All | |
		BBC1	BBC2	ITV	Ch.4	terrestrial	1986
		Percentage of violent acts					
Blood							
None	1	77	84	53	79	73	83
	2	8	4	14	6	8	8
	3	1	1	4	1	2	3
	4	*	*	1	1	1	1
Much	5	0	*	*	0	*	*
Cannot code		14	10	28	14	17	4

Note:* Less than 0.5%

Comparisons were made of the extent to which violence gave rise to blood among the terrestrial and satellite channels. Once again, variations between channels occurred mainly with regard to whether or not acts were classified as giving rise to no blood. These variations were correlated with the extent of occurrence of uncodable acts of violence. Thus, ITV scored lowest among the terrestrial channels for acts of violence with no blood seen on screen. The same channels also exhibited the greatest proportion of violent acts which could not be clearly coded for the appearance of blood. Uncodable acts only partly accounted for the lower proportion of acts scored as showing no blood. Also ITV had the greatest percentage of acts which reportedly occurred with a small amount of blood being seen (see Table 6.13).

Comparing the results of the current study for the four terrestrial channels with those obtained nearly ten years earlier (Cumberbatch *et al.*, 1987) showed that the proportion of violent acts coded as containing no observable blood or bleeding dropped 10%. The percentages of acts classified as containing varying amounts of blood or bleeding remained largely unchanged. Four acts were found in 1986 which were rated 5 for the amount of blood depicted compared with five acts scoring at this level in 1994/5. The other significant shift was in the proportion of violent acts for which no clear rating for amount of blood could be given, which increased in the 1994/5 analysis compared with 1986.

Among the satellite channels, UK Gold and Sky Movies scored smaller percentages of violent acts coded as showing no blood than did Sky One or The Movie Channel. These channels also exhibited differences in their respective proportions of uncodable acts which partly accounted for the previous difference between them. However, Sky Movies showed a higher than average proportion of violent acts accompanied by a small amount of blood (see Table 6.14).

A total of 20 programmes emerged which contained at least one violent act which achieved the highest rating of 5 for amount of visible blood or bleeding associated directly with violence. Eight of these programmes

Table 6.14 Distribution of observable blood ratings: satellite channels

		Sky One	UK Gold	Sky Movies	Movie Channel	All satellite
		Percentage of violent acts				
Blood						
None	1	91	66	60	79	74
	2	2	8	12	8	8
	3	1	2	3	3	2
	4	0	1	2	1	1
Much	5	*	*	1	*	*
Cannot code		7	22	23	8	15

Note: * Less than 0.5%

contained just one such violent act, six contained two such acts, and six contained three or more such acts, as listed below. All but one of these broadcasts were films originally made for the cinema, and all were shown well after 9.00 pm.

Programmes featuring most violent acts with large amounts of blood

	No. of acts	
1	23	*Braindead*, Sky Movies, 11.35 pm, 18 January/9 February 1995
2	7	*Alien 3*, Sky Movies, 10.00 pm, 14 October 1994
3	5	*Colors*, Sky Movies, 10.15 pm, 14 January 1995
4=	3	*Death Ring*, Sky Movies, 10.00 pm, 19 October, 1994
4=	3	*American Cyborg: Steel Warrior*, Sky Movies, 11.05 pm, 25 October 1994
4=	3	*Hidden 2: The Spawn*, Movie Channel, 10.00 pm, 5 February 1995

All six entries were movies originally produced for the cinema which were televised on the two subscription satellite movie channels. All six movies were broadcast late at night.

Horror ratings

All violent acts were coded for the amount of horror they were thought to have caused victims. A five-point scale was applied to each violent act, labelled 'mild' and 'horrific' at each end. Six out of ten violent acts across all channels (60%) were rated as 'mild', or as being devoid of any horror.

Table 6.15 Distribution of horror ratings: terrestrial channels

		BBC1	BBC2	ITV	Ch.4	All terrestrial
		Percentage of violent acts				
Horror						
Mild	1	65	61	54	61	60
	2	23	22	28	24	24
	3	5	7	9	3	6
	4	1	1	2	1	1
Horrific	5	*	*	*	*	*
Cannot code		5	9	7	10	8

Note: * Less than 0.5%

Nearly one in four (24%) was classified as being only very slightly frightening for those victimized. Nearly one in ten (9%) of violent acts was coded as containing a moderate degree of horror, while just one act in a hundred (1%) was thought to be horrific.

In total, 108 violent acts were coded as being 'horrific' (rating = 5) across all channels over the four weeks of analysis. There were no substantial variations in horror ratings of violence among the terrestrial channels. ITV contained the smallest proportion of violent acts categorized as devoid of any horror (rating = 1), and the largest percentage of acts coded as slightly frightening (rating = 2). Also ITV contained a larger proportion of moderately horror stricken violent acts (11%) than the other terrestrial channels (6%). The small percentages disguise numerical differences between channels in terms of violent acts rated as horrific. There were seven such acts in total found on ITV, three on BBC2, two on BBC1 and just one on Channel 4 (see Table 6.15).

Table 6.16 Distribution of horror ratings: satellite channels

		Sky One	UK Gold	Sky Movies	Movie Channel	All satellite
		Percentage of violent acts				
Horror						
Mild	1	74	51	52	66	61
	2	18	30	24	21	23
	3	3	7	8	5	6
	4	*	1	3	2	2
Horrific	5	*	1	1	*	1
Cannot code		5	10	12	7	8

Note: * Less than 0.5%

Among the satellite channels, UK Gold and Sky Movies contained smaller proportions of violent acts categorized as containing no horror than did Sky One or The Movie Channel. UK Gold and The Movie Channel contained larger proportions of violent acts with a small amount of frightening material (rating = 2) compared with Sky One and Sky Movies. The two movie channels contained more moderately horrific violence than did the two non-movie channels. However, Sky Movies contained the greatest number of horrific violent acts (70 acts rated as 5). This compared with 12 acts on The Movie Channel, nine acts on UK Gold and just four acts on Sky One (see Table 6.16).

A total of 38 programmes were found to contain at least one violent act which received a 5 rating for horror. Of these, 21 programmes contained just one such violent act, eight contained two such acts, and nine contained three or more such acts. The greatest amount of horrific violence occurred in the movie, *Braindead*, which appeared twice during the period of monitoring on Sky Movies. All nine entries listed were movies originally made for the cinema and were televised, late at night, in eight instances on the two satellite movie channels and in the case of *Colors* on UK Gold.

Programmes featuring most violent acts with extreme horror ratings

	No. of acts	
1	23	*Braindead*, Sky Movies, 11.35 pm, 18 January/9 February 1995
2	8	*Alien 3*, Sky Movies, 10.00 pm, 14 October 1994
3	6	*Colors*, UK Gold, 10.15 pm, 14 January 1995
4	5	*Death Ring*, Sky Movies, 10.00 pm, 11 October 1994
5=	3	*Pray for Death*, Sky Movies, 10.00 pm, 8 October 1994
5=	3	*Operation Kid Brother*, Movie Channel, 6.00 am, 22 October 1994
5=	3	*American Cyborg: Steel Warrior*, Sky Movies, 11.05 pm, 26 October 1995
5=	3	*Men of Respect*, Sky Movies, 2.40 am, 18 January 1995
5=	3	*Hidden 2: The Spawn*, Movie Channel, 10.00 pm, 5 February 1995

Some programmes which scored high ratings in terms of blood, pain and horror were examined in more detail to assess the context in which violence was shown. The film *Braindead* has already been looked at more closely in Chapter 4. It recorded 16 violent acts which each were rated at the highest level for blood, pain and horror. The film was the eighth most violent programme coded during the four-week period with 102 violent acts, divided into 44 violent sequences. A total of 7.6 minutes of the film was devoted to violence, most of which was graphic and unpleasant in form and consequences. The film contained a wide variety of violent acts including incidents of stabbing, torture, burning, hitting, pushing, throwing, slapping, biting, decapitation and injecting of victims. Given the inherent characteristics of the 'living dead' and their ability to withstand and recover from the fiercest violent attacks, most of the injuries were categorized as either minor or mutilation. Thus, a zombie character might walk around with an axe in his head or the loss of a limb without apparent concern or impairment of functioning.

Alien 3, shown on Sky Movies on 14 October 1994 at 10.00 pm, was another movie which contained a generous allocation of violent acts coded as showing a lot of blood (47% of acts), a lot of victim suffering (53%) and as being horrific (53%). Most of the violence resulted in death or serious injury. The storyline focused on the accidental introduction of an alien onto a planet used as a penal colony and the subsequent killings which it perpetrated upon the occupants of the prison. The main protagonist was a female character played by Sigourney Weaver.

The first introduction to the alien was via its host, a dog. In a key scene, the dog began to whimper and howl and tremble, and the creature burst forth out of the animal's body, reducing it to a bloodied carcass. The alien then hunted its victims. The majority of victims were seized from above by the head and were dragged away screaming. Not all the deaths were shown explicitly. However, the alien's first victim was suddenly grabbed by the head and his blood splashed a by-stander. A second victim had a large surgical instrument thrust into his head. The rest of the film followed a similar pattern. Abduction of any victim was accompanied by high-pitched terrified screaming giving the impression that the victim was in great pain. As the film became more violent and a greater number of victims were abducted, the language also became more violent and abusive. The film relied upon suspense and special effects. The horrific nature of the violence was, in many ways, exacerbated by the use of suspense techniques, shock and graphic language. This context needs to be born in mind in assessing the potential influence of the movie.

Colors (Robert H. Solo Production) was shown on UK Gold on 14 January 1995 at 10.15 pm and contained five acts which were categorized as being extreme in terms of horror, pain and suffering of victims, and amount of blood. The film was set in Los Angeles and focused on the 'war' between different street gangs. The heroes of the movie worked for the Los Angeles Police Department's Gang Crime Division. The film centred on the violent nature of LA life. An early scene showed a casual drive-by killing of a black boy. Upon being hit he was shown flying backwards through a fence, dying instantly. His mother was then heard screaming. Several scenes showed fights between the police and gang members and the film contained a lot of violent content (37 violent acts). The film depicted killing as a way of life among LA gangs.

SUMMARY AND CONCLUSIONS

Much of the violence depicted on the eight channels monitored in this study occurred as a result of criminally motivated behaviour or disputes or arguments between individuals. Nearly half the violent acts coded occurred within these two motivational contexts. The more specific goals of aggressors were characterized by evil or destructive objectives, self-preservation and ambition or power. Monetary gain *per se* was a much less frequent reason for violence indicating that a criminal context for violence could mean much more than scenarios depicting armed robberies, muggings or other forms of behaviour designed to facilitate the financial gain of villains.

Although evidence emerged that violence was used for 'legitimate' purposes such as upholding the law, the protection of a family or of society, relatively small proportions of all violent acts occurred for these reasons. The picture painted then is one of a violent, criminally driven community of television characters who readily use violence to achieve their ends, and of a law-abiding community who may fairly reluctantly get drawn into violent conflict to defend their families, protect their interests and uphold their rights. The extent to which this impression represents an accurate interpretation of events will be explored further in the next chapter with an analysis of the types of characters who get involved in violence on television.

What also emerged, however, was the clear finding that forms of aggressive behaviour about which there is a degree of public sensitivity were rare. In particular, sexually motivated violence occurred at a very low level. Violent sexual imagery has been investigated in laboratory settings and findings indicate that it can shape viewers' attitudes about female sexuality, about rape and rape victims. There is some suggestion that such images have the power to trigger male aggression against female targets, especially under circumstances where the male viewer has previously been angered and perceives certain similarities between the female victim in a movie or programme and a real life female target (Malamuth and Donnerstein, 1984).

Repeated studies with male undergraduates in the United States have revealed that a heavy dosage of exposure to violent erotic movies can produce a shift in attitudes so that they become more relaxed about the seriousness of rape and less sympathetic towards rape victims (see Malamuth, 1984; Linz *et al.*, 1985). There is even some evidence that such material can bring about similar shifts of opinion even among female viewers (Zillmann and Bryant, 1984).

Despite the very real and understandable concerns about the impact of sexually motivated violent portrayals, the current content analysis evidence indicates that the possibility for exposure to such material on mainstream channels on British television is remote. An in-depth, qualitative analysis of scenes which had been classified as depicting sexually intimidating behaviour on programmes normally regarded as innocuous, revealed that only in one case did an incident depict an attempt at forcible sexual activity. This scene actually proceeded no further than mild physical violence, but was potentially shocking for viewers because of the programme in which it occurred and the fact that the victim was a young girl.

Further evidence emerged that much of the violence coded in this analysis of British television output exhibited few signs of being highly graphic or associated with features known to invoke extreme reactions from viewers in the analysis of the consequences of violent actions. Well over one in three acts of violence were accompanied by no observable consequences or injuries for victims. When the consequences of violence were shown, the injuries depicted were much more likely to be mild than serious. This positive view of television violence is partly offset, however, by the finding that if serious consequences did follow, they more often than not resulted in the death of the victim. Instances of serious wounding, severe anatomical damage or mutilation were much rarer than depictions of violence followed by minor wounds or injuries. In a small number of cases, violence resulted in psychological rather than physical damage.

There are different schools of thought on the implications of depicting the consequences of violence. Thus, depending upon which school one adheres to, the findings reported in this study could be regarded as either positive or negative. On the one hand, it is known from audience research, some of which was reviewed in the introduction to this chapter, that viewers react with greater emotion to media violence accompanied by depictions of pain and suffering (e.g., Goranson, 1969; Hartmann, 1969; Noble, 1975; Gunter, 1985). On the other hand, there is a belief that viewers need to be exposed to the horror of violence and to the real suffering it can cause, in order to underline its abhorrent nature. Both positions have some merit and both need to be taken into account by programme makers in considering what would be in the best interests of their audiences in particular instances. The significance of this issue applies equally to producers of drama and to editors of news.

On current evidence, evaluations of the qualities of violent portrayals in terms of degrees of associated pain, horror and bloodshed, indicated that the mainstream television channels managed to keep portrayals of an extreme and graphic nature to a minimum during the weeks of output monitored. Forty-one programmes were found which depicted at least one act of violence judged to show extreme suffering by victims. Just a handful of programmes were found to contain three or more such scenes and in all cases except one, these were transmitted late at night.

Just 22 programmes emerged which contained at least one violent act accompanied by a high degree of bloodshed. As with extreme pain and suffering, just a small number contained three or more such incidents and all were broadcast late at night. In all cases except one, the latter small group of programmes were movies originally produced for the cinema. Finally, really horrific violence occurred in 39 programmes, most of which contained only one violent act judged to fall into this category. Ten movies were identified with three or more such acts of violence and all were shown late at night. All except one of these ten appeared on the two satellite movie channels.

The latter evaluative ratings depended more than any other aspect of the content analysis coding frame on coders' subjective judgements. The degree of reliability between these judgements was weaker than for other more objective coding elements. Despite this weakness, at this point in the coding operation, these results nevertheless provide some sense of the relative rarity of occurrence of extremely graphic and horrific violent scenes. Furthermore, they indicate that the programmes containing such scenes were generally restricted to late-night viewing periods.

7   Aggressors and victims

One of the fundamental ingredients of television measurement within content analysis research is the extent of involvement in violence of different types of characters. Two of the five components of the Violence Index measure used by Gerbner and his colleagues in quantifying violence on American prime-time television drama output consisted of the extent of character involvement in violent episodes either as aggressors or victims, killers or killed. Gerbner (1972) argued that the distribution of characters in television drama programmes and the extent to which different types of characters become more involved in violence and the nature of their involvement (i.e., as aggressors or victims) carry important meanings concerning chances and risks in real life for different kinds of people. According to Gerbner (1972, pp. 44–45):

> Who commits and who suffers violence of what kind is a central and revealing fact of life in the world of television drama that viewers must grasp before they can follow, let alone interpret, the play . . . who gets (and gives) what, how and why delineates the social structure of the world of television drama. The distribution of roles related to violence, with their different risks and fates, performs the symbolic functions of violence, and conveys its basic message about people.

The types of characters who are involved in violence on television is related to the way viewers respond to that violence. Much of the evidence on this point stems from research on two particular points of comparison: (1) between violence perpetrated by good guys (usually law enforcers) and bad guys (usually criminals) and (2) between violence performed by male characters and that performed by female characters.

Perhaps the most consistent theme in serious action-drama programmes on television is the conflict between good and evil, between the forces of law and order and criminal elements. Content analysis of programming designed to explore the goals of television characters and the methods usually employed to attain desired ends has indicated that non-legal methods tend to be used as often as legal methods in television action-drama shows (Larsen *et al.*, 1963). One of the main conclusions reached by Larsen *et al.*

was that there is a strong tendency for television to project content in which socially approved as well as unapproved goals were most often achieved by methods that would not be regarded as socially acceptable in normal, every-day life. This observation drew attention to the frequent and rapid deploy-ment of violent measures, often to an extreme degree, by agencies of law enforcement in television series when tackling problems of criminal behaviour.

Subsequent television monitoring indicated that although bad characters were the most involved in violence and more especially in scenes in which someone was killed, it was a prevalent feature of television drama that both good and bad characters used violence. Gerbner *et al.* (1979) reported that between 1969 and 1978 on American prime-time television, just over 58% of good characters and 88% of bad characters were involved in some form of violence.

Content analysis of programmes on British television during the early 1970s did not elaborate on patterns of character involvement in violence to the same extent that American research had done. Nevertheless, a few consistent patterns did emerge from the relatively limited analyses in this respect of the BBC and University of Leicester research teams. Instigators of violence were usually portrayed as belonging to the wrong side of the law, although a substantial minority of good characters also used violence. About three out of four bad or villainous characters were violent, which was about three times as high as the proportions of good characters or heroes who were violent. In addition, bad characters were three times as likely to kill their victims as were good characters (Shaw and Newell, 1972; Halloran and Croll, 1972).

The significance of classifying televised violence in terms of the types of perpetrators and victims involved stems in part from the fact that audiences may discriminate between different acts of violence according to the types of characters (e.g., good or bad) who lie behind the violence. Research reviewed in the previous chapter showed that surveys of public opinion towards various kinds of violence have indicated that legitimized violent actions are usually not perceived as 'violence' in the same way as illegally perpetrated actions. Officially sanctioned 'violence' which is deployed to protect mem-bers of the public from crime, terrorism or other perpetrators of evil and destruction, may be regarded by most people as essentially 'nonviolent' or, at least, legitimate behaviour. Many people will accept violence performed by the police or other law enforcers as a legitimate use of force, even if the individual on the receiving end is harmed or injured in some way.

The extent to which police figures are perceived to utilize violence legit-imately does depend upon the context and the degree to which it is used relative to the behaviour it is used to suppress. Gunter (1985) reported that British viewers held different opinions about the use of violence by police characters in British-made and American-made crime-drama series. In an American context, viewers' perceptions of the severity of violent portrayals performed by TV police and villains reinforced the findings of US public opinion surveys. Police aggression was regarded as less violent than criminal aggression. In a British setting, however, this finding was reversed. British viewers exhibited more concern about the severity of violence performance by police characters in British crime-drama series than they did about similar forms of violence performed by criminal characters. These results underline the significance of setting and context in addition to character-types involved in on-screen violence for viewers' judgements about the seriousness of televised violence.

MALE VERSUS FEMALE VIOLENCE

The extent to which violence is employed differs more markedly for male and female television characters than it does for law enforcers and villains. In general, men are much more likely to use violence than women. The latter are much more often characterized as romantic, emotional and dependent than men, whenever there is trouble, either of a personal or professional nature (Butler and Paisley, 1980; Tuchman, 1978). Once again, the significance of gender as a classifying variable for violence on television stems partly from the suggestion that viewers' judgements about violence may vary according to the involvement of men and women.

Women are traditionally considered as being the gentler sex and violence is not an attribute normally associated with them. Involvement in criminal activity is less prevalent among women than among men in fictional television, and also in real life. Female crime rates (and murder rates) do exhibit a tendency to approach closer to those for males in countries where women have greater freedom and equality, such as Western Europe and North America (Hoffman-Bustamente, 1973; Sutherland and Cressey, 1974). The rates for crime and violence among each gender have also changed over time. Police reports in the United States have indicated that violent crime by women is increasing at a faster rate than for men.

Another aspect of the way women are customarily conceptualized is the dichotomy of the female character into 'good' versus 'bad'. Some writers have referred to a cultural polarization of women as either 'mothers' or 'whores'; the 'gentler sex' or 'the more deadly species'. According to this scheme, those who conform to the idealized conceptions of 'femininity' – gentleness, passivity, maternity – would never commit a violent crime. Any woman who turns to criminality or violence is, by definition, deviant and bad, since in so doing she has abandoned her natural feminine role. With respect to murderesses particularly, their crime is not seemingly just that of killing another human being, but more significantly of having betrayed their womanhood. Buckhart (1973) reported how this dichotomy can directly affect women who have committed a crime. At first the femininity of a woman may prejudice police, judges and jurors in favour of leniency toward her, because she is considered less dangerous and less evil than a male counterpart. However, a woman who has stepped far enough out of line to be convicted can no longer expect the protection of her femininity which she has, by virtue of her criminal guilt, discarded. Such women may often receive harsh judgement.

The observations ensuing from these analyses of women, criminality and legal judgements are reinforced by data on individuals' perceptions of violent crimes committed by men and women. McGlynn *et al.* (1976) read college students a summary of a violent murder case in which an insanity plea was entered. In one version the hypothetical defendant was a male and in the other female. Respondents rated the female accused of the violent crime as more 'sick' than an equivalent male person, though all other details about the case were exactly the same in both versions.

To what extent is violence perceived as a salient or typical attribute of different television characters? Content analysis has shown that a large proportion of major fictional television characters get involved in violence at some time during a television series. Some authors have contended that the violent roles they play and the outcomes of involvement in violence for different types of characters represent a symbolic demonstration of the sources of power and vulnerability in the television world. Through a process of generalization, this symbolism can, in turn, influence public perceptions of the real world as well as of the television world (Gerbner *et al.*, 1977, 1978, 1979; Tuchman, 1978). The differential prevalence of involvement in violence of different characters might condition viewers to expect to see certain character types get involved in violent incidents more often than others, and also to be more accepting of violence. However, although violence may be *prevalent* amongst major fictional television characters, analyses of audience perceptions have not indicated 'aggressiveness' to be a *salient* defining attribute of characters for viewers.

Reeves and Greenberg (1977) asked groups of 8- to 12-year-old children to say to what extent and in what ways 14 prime-time and weekend daytime characters from television drama shows differed from each other using whichever descriptive terms they liked. In order of importance, four main attributes emerged: humour, strength, attractiveness and activity. Using a different sample of children and different television characters, Reeves and Lometti (1978) carried out a replication study. Among the new characters in the television sample were three additional women to balance more evenly the ratio of male to female characters. Essentially the same four discriminative dimensions emerged again. The one important difference was that the second dimension from the original study – physical strength – more clearly differentiated television characters of different gender. It was the only attribute which clearly separated male and female television characters in the sample.

The most interesting aspect of this set of findings was that violence did not emerge among the most salient discriminating features of television characters for young viewers of different age-bands, even though they were permitted to choose their own descriptive or evaluative terms. Indeed, even when additional female television characters were supplied in the second study, to reflect the increased presence of leading female actors on American television series during this period, there was no tendency to distinguish them spontaneously as less violent than male leads.

THE CHARACTER PROFILE OF TELEVISION

From the perspective of viewers' attitudes towards and perceptions of television violence, audience research has indicated that the kinds of television characters who are involved in violence, either as aggressors or victims, can make a difference to the way violent portrayals are evaluated. Classifying televised violence in terms of the types of people involved is therefore a relevant form of analysis in the context of establishing links between objectively quantified content data and public opinion. Simply knowing that one type of violence perpetrator is more prevalent than another yields fairly limited information about the potential impact of that material. In contrast, establishing the prevalence of portrayals which are known also to contain characteristics of significance to viewers is much more informative.

The American content analysis research which spanned a period from the late 1960s to early 1980s placed considerable emphasis on the demography of television violence portrayals (Gerbner *et al.*, 1977, 1978, 1979). Although this aspect of television violence has been examined in Britain too, researchers on this side of the Atlantic have not gone as far as producing indices of television violence built on the frequencies of involvement of different character types. Nevertheless, even British content analyses have produced descriptions of the demographics of television.

Gerbner and his colleagues reported that 68% of leading male characters were involved in violence compared with only 46% of female characters during the 1970s and early 1980s, but this did not fully reflect figures reported elsewhere which indicated a more pronounced dominance of males on television (Signorielli, 1984). In the mid-1980s on television in Britain, Cumberbatch *et al.* (1987) reported that of the people involved in violence on television, 75% of aggressors were male and only 10.2% were female (the remainder were mixed groups or could not be coded because the aggressors were off camera). Similarly, the victims of violence were overwhelmingly male (77%) whereas only around one in ten again (10.6%) was female.

Similar observations may be made regarding the age distribution of television characters involved in violence. Gerbner's work indicated that 61% of children and adolescents were involved in violence compared with 65% of young adults, 60% of settled adults, and 47% of elderly characters. Cumberbatch and his colleagues broke down those involved in violence to reveal more dramatic differences. Only 1.6% of violence perpetrators were under 16 years old, compared with 15% from the 17 to 28 years age-bracket, 24% aged between 29 and 35, 25% aged between 36 and 50, and 4.2% aged over 50 years. In this instance, age could not be unambiguously coded for three out of ten dramatic characters, however. Thus, ten years ago on British television, television aggressors were principally young or middle-aged adults, who were more likely to be male than female. The following sections will reveal the extent to which the character profile of violence perpetrators on television has changed.

AGGRESSOR DEMOGRAPHY

There were 21,104 aggressors catalogued across the four weeks of coding, the majority (62%) of whom were males operating alone. Just under one in ten violent acts (9.5%) were perpetrated by solus females. One in seven (15%) violent acts were perpetrated by males in a group context. Aggressors were most likely to be young adults aged between 20 and 35 years (51%) with around one in five being somewhat older than this – between 36 and 65 years. There were few child (less than 2%) or teenage (less than 6%) aggressors. Exact comparisons with the 1986 study are not possible because of differences in age groupings. Cumberbatch *et al.* (1987), however, reported that 39% of violent acts were perpetrated by characters aged 17 to 35 years, which is lower than the figure reported for characters estimated to be 20 to 35 years old in the current study.

In terms of ethnic origin, aggressors were more likely to be white than any other colour, and were most likely to be white Americans (40%). This compares with a figure of 28% for 1986 (Cumberbatch *et al.*, 1987). Around one in eight aggressors were white and from the UK (12%), which is less than the percentage reported in 1986 (20%). The striking presence of American aggressors stems from the significant contribution of US-made programmes to overall levels of violence on British television (see Table 7.1).

Channel comparisons yielded a number of significant differences in the demography of aggressors, once again reflecting the predominance of certain types of programming on particular channels. Among the terrestrial channels, aggressor demography differences were found in respect of gender, age and ethnic origin of aggressors. Solus male aggressors were more prevalent on BBC1 than on any other terrestrial channel. Group male aggression was particularly prominent on BBC2, probably reflecting the relatively high rate of violence on this channel which was linked to military or wartime settings. Young adult (20–35 years) aggressors featured less often on ITV than on the other three channels, but this was counter-balanced by the greater prevalence of child aggressors on ITV.

The incidence of violence perpetrated by white American aggressors was lower than the overall average across channels, underlining the strong prevalence of this category of aggressor on the two satellite movie channels and Sky One. Nevertheless, white Americans were the most prevalent category of

Table 7.1 Aggressor demography: all channels

	Percentage of violent acts
Gender	
One male	62.2
One female	9.5
Group male	14.5
Group female	*
Group mixed	3.1
Other	0.9
Cannot code	9.3
Age	
Child (up to 12)	1.5
Teenage (13–19)	5.6
Young adult (20–35)	51.3
Middle age (36–64)	20.1
65 plus	0.6
Mixed age	3.1
Cannot code	17.8
Ethnic origin	
White UK	11.8
White US	39.9
White other	14.0
Black UK	0.4
Black US	3.9
Black other	1.1
Asian	1.4
Oriental	3.3
Mixed group	4.2
Other human	2.2
Animal	4.1
Cannot code	13.8

Note: * Less than 0.5%

aggressor even on the terrestrial channels. White aggressors, generally, were much more commonplace on terrestrial television channels than were black aggressors, regardless of country of origin (see Table 7.2).

On the four satellite channels monitored in this study, aggressor demography was dominated by males, young and middle-aged adults and white Americans. At least seven out of ten perpetrators of violence on these channels were males either acting alone or in a group. Aggressors were most likely to be aged between 20 and 35 or, alternatively, were between 36 and 65 years old. The age profile of aggressors was somewhat younger on Sky One than on the remaining three satellite channels, with a relatively high proportion of teenage aggressors. This demographic pattern reflects the significant contribution to the overall level of violence on this channel made by programmes such as *Mighty Morphin Power*

Table 7.2 Aggressor demography: terrestrial channels

	Percentage of violent acts				
	All terrestrial	BBC1	BBC2	ITV	Ch.4
Gender					
One male	58.8	67.4	54.3	54.4	59.2
One female	8.0	8.6	6.6	8.1	8.6
Group male	17.4	14.5	23.3	17.7	13.9
Group female	0.2	0.0	0.3	0.5	0.1
Group mixed	3.7	3.1	1.6	5.1	5.0
Other	0.9	0.2	1.0	1.6	0.8
Cannot code	10.9	5.9	12.8	12.5	12.4
Age					
Child (up to 12)	1.0	1.2	0.7	1.1	1.1
Teenage (13–19)	3.6	2.4	4.3	4.7	3.0
Young adult (20–35)	49.4	53.2	49.2	44.9	50.1
Middle age (36–64)	18.2	24.0	13.0	19.9	15.8
65 plus	0.6	1.4	0.7	0.2	0.0
Mixed age	4.1	3.8	3.6	6.1	2.8
Cannot code	23.0	13.9	28.2	22.9	27.0
Ethnic origin					
White UK	17.8	21.9	16.0	13.3	20.0
White US	29.2	34.3	25.7	26.7	30.2
White other	15.6	19.2	20.8	12.4	10.1
Black UK	0.7	1.6	0.0	1.1	0.0
Black US	2.9	2.5	0.9	4.1	4.1
Black other	1.0	0.3	1.4	0.4	2.0
Asian	2.3	0.6	3.3	3.8	1.3
Oriental	1.9	0.2	1.8	3.8	1.8
Mixed group	5.8	6.3	2.1	9.4	5.5
Other human	2.2	1.4	4.6	1.7	0.9
Animal	3.7	3.2	3.6	2.1	5.9
Cannot code	16.8	8.5	19.8	21.2	17.7

Note: * Less than 0.05%

Rangers, in which the principal characters were coded as being in their late teens.

White American aggressors dominated three out of the four satellite channels. The exception was UK Gold, on which the greatest single proportion of aggressors fell into the white UK category, reflecting the predominance of British-made programmes on this channel (see Table 7.3).

TYPE OF AGGRESSOR

In addition to demography, aggressors were classified according to 57 further categories which identified the sort of character role they played or

Table 7.3 Aggressor demography: satellite channels

	Percentage of violent acts				
	All satellite	*Sky One*	*UK Gold*	*Sky Movies*	*Movie Channel*
Gender					
One male	64.3	60.0	68.4	66.9	62.0
One female	9.8	7.7	8.1	11.2	12.1
Group male	13.6	10.1	14.4	13.7	16.0
Group female	0.3	0.4	0.2	0.3	0.2
Group mixed	2.7	4.8	2.3	1.3	2.3
Other	1.0	1.7	1.0	0.5	0.8
Cannot code	8.3	15.1	5.3	6.3	6.4
Age					
Child (up to 12)	1.5	0.7	0.5	2.3	2.4
Teenage (13–19)	5.6	11.2	1.2	3.7	6.2
Young adult (20–35)	52.7	47.9	55.1	57.2	50.6
Middle age (36–64)	20.8	10.4	24.9	24.1	23.9
65 plus	0.7	0.0	1.6	0.7	0.6
Mixed age	2.7	1.6	3.4	1.9	3.9
Cannot code	15.9	27.8	13.3	10.2	12.2
Ethnic origin					
White UK	15.8	2.7	48.1	4.4	8.1
White US	39.0	45.1	10.7	56.3	44.0
White other	13.5	8.9	14.8	15.2	15.1
Black UK	0.5	0.0	2.0	0.0	0.0
Black US	3.7	2.8	1.9	4.4	5.5
Black other	0.7	0.0	0.7	0.9	1.8
Asian	0.7	0.0	0.9	0.9	1.0
Oriental	3.3	1.3	1.9	4.2	5.7
Mixed group	2.9	3.5	1.9	2.9	3.3
Other human	2.3	3.2	3.1	1.7	1.2
Animal	3.9	5.5	1.0	1.3	7.7
Cannot code	13.4	26.3	13.0	7.7	6.5

particular occupational group to which they belonged. These categories were grouped under nine superordinate headings: General; Law Enforcer; Criminal; Futuristic/Supernatural; Period; Occupation/Profession; Entertainment; Cartoon; and Miscellaneous.

The greatest single proportion of aggressors (17%) comprised one or other of a number of criminal-type categories. The second most significant category of aggressor was the general category comprising 'situation characters', 'members of the public', or 'domestic persons'. Situation characters comprised characters playing general roles in a variety of dramatic settings, but who could not be placed in terms of a more specific occupational or dramatic category. A domestic person comprised a character whose major role revolved around playing the part of a husband, wife or other close family member (see Table 7.4).

Table 7.4 Type of aggressor: all channels

	Percentage of violent acts
General categories	
Situation character	12.0
Member of public	2.6
Domestic person	2.1
TOTAL	16.7
Law enforcer	
Police – plain clothes	3.9
Fantasy legitimate	2.5
Police – uniformed	2.2
Special law enforcer	1.2
Quasi-law enforcer	0.6
Private eye	0.2
Executioner	*
TOTAL	10.6
Criminal	
Criminal – serious	8.8
Criminal – petty	3.3
Outlaw/pirate	2.5
Terrorist/guerrilla	0.8
Rioter	0.6
Political activist	0.4
Psychopath	0.3
Football hooligan	0.3
TOTAL	17.0
Futuristic/supernatural	
Alien	1.7
Robot	1.4
Monster	1.3
Spaceman	0.6
Supernatural power	0.5
Dracula/vampire	0.4
TOTAL	5.9
Period	
Cowboy	3.3
Indian	0.5
Nobility/royalty	0.4
Knight	0.3
TOTAL	4.5
Occupation/profession	
Professional person	2.2
Seaman	1.1
Uniformed official	0.3

Table 7.4 Contd...

	Percentage of violent acts
Inventor/scientist	0.3
Clergy	0.2
Servant	0.2
Journalist	0.1
Publican	0.1
Prostitute	0.1
Trades unionist	*
TOTAL	4.6
Entertainment	
Sports person	5.2
Entertainer	0.5
Presenter – serious	0.1
Presenter – light	0.1
Comedian	0.1
Sports commentator	*
TOTAL	6.0
Cartoon	
Cartoon – human	5.5
Cartoon – animal	4.8
Cartoon – other	2.1
TOTAL	12.4
Miscellaneous	
Armed forces	5.4
School children	2.4
Martial artist	1.4
Tribal people	0.8
Animal	0.7
Assassin	0.6
Vigilante	0.5
Inanimate object	0.3
Other	2.5
TOTAL	14.6
Aggressor not shown	1.5
Cannot code	2.2

Note: * Less than 0.05%

Criminal perpetrators of violence outnumbered law enforcer aggressors. Even so, one in ten violent acts were performed by law enforcers. One in two violent acts by criminals were perpetrated by serious criminal-types, while around the same proportion of law enforcer violence was perpetrated by a police officer (either plain clothes or uniformed).

Excluding the general category of situation character, the group most often involved in violence was the serious criminal-type (8.8% of violent acts). This type was followed respectively by human cartoon characters

(5.5%), armed forces personnel (5.4%), sports persons (5.2%), cartoon animal characters (4.8%) and plain clothes police officers (3.9%). The top ten aggressor types across all channels are shown below:

Top ten aggressor types: all channels		
		%
1	Situation character	12.0
2	Criminal – serious	8.8
3	Cartoon – human	5.5
4	Armed forces	5.4
5	Sports person	5.2
6	Cartoon – animal	4.8
7	Police – plain clothes	3.9
8	Criminal – petty	3.3
9	Cowboy	3.3
10	Member of public	2.6

Channel differences

Violence on the terrestrial channels was dominated by general character categories, cartoon characters, and characters in criminal or law enforcer roles. Cartoon characters were especially prominent on Channel 4, while criminal and law enforcer aggressors were more commonplace on BBC1 and ITV than on BBC2 or Channel 4. Aggressors from entertainment categories were especially prominent on Channel 4 (see Table 7.5).

Table 7.5 Distribution of aggressor types across terrestrial channels

	Percentage of violent acts				
	All terrestrial	*BBC1*	*BBC2*	*ITV*	*Ch.4*
General categories	20.0	24.6	15.8	20.3	19.3
Cartoon	14.9	12.8	14.8	10.0	22.0
Criminal	14.3	16.3	12.6	19.4	9.0
Law enforcer	10.3	15.6	8.0	10.5	7.0
Period	6.1	3.0	7.6	3.3	9.5
Entertainment	6.1	8.4	3.7	10.3	12.0
Futuristic/supernatural	3.7	1.4	4.7	6.0	2.7
Occupation/profession	3.3	5.3	1.7	3.1	2.9
Miscellaneous	15.6	10.8	24.6	12.1	9.8
Aggressor not shown	2.2	1.6	2.3	2.5	2.2
Cannot code	2.3	1.4	3.9	2.1	1.6

Perpetrators of violence on the four satellite channels were dominated by the same four categories – general, criminal, law enforcer and cartoon – as

Table 7.6 Distribution of aggressor types across satellite channels

	Percentage of violent acts				
	All satellite	Sky One	UK Gold	Sky Movies	Movie Channel
General categories	22.8	8.3	32.2	28.0	22.7
Criminal	18.5	9.4	22.6	20.6	21.4
Law enforcer	11.2	14.2	11.2	11.3	7.8
Cartoon	10.9	20.7	3.1	0.7	18.6
Futuristic/supernatural	7.2	14.0	7.7	3.7	3.5
Occupation/profession	4.8	2.4	4.3	6.7	4.8
Entertainment	4.7	14.8	1.5	1.6	0.7
Period	4.2	2.0	2.2	6.6	5.9
Miscellaneous	12.9	11.6	12.3	16.0	12.6
Aggressor not shown	1.4	0.7	2.2	1.6	0.7
Cannot code	2.0	1.8	1.2	3.7	1.2

the terrestrial channels. Criminal aggressors were more prevalent on the satellite channels and cartoon aggressors less so compared with the terrestrial channels. There were, however, some significant disparities between satellite channels. General categories and criminal types were perpetrators of violence much less often on Sky One than on any of the other three channels. Cartoon aggressors were much more prevalent on Sky One and The Movie Channel than on UK Gold and Sky Movies. On Sky One also, perpetrators of violence were a great deal more likely to emerge from futuristic/supernatural categories and entertainment categories than on any other channel (see Table 7.6).

The terrestrial and satellite channels can be compared further in terms of the ten most commonly occurring types of aggressors in each case. Apart from the general situation character type which was the most frequent category of aggressor to appear on three out of four terrestrial channels, the top ten positions in each case were dominated by cartoon characters, criminal and law enforcer types. Armed forces aggressors also featured prominently on every channel, and most especially on BBC2. On Channel 4, sport provided another major source of violence.

A closer examination of the distribution of the most commonly occurring aggressor types on satellite channels revealed that, in addition to the general category of situation character, which was the most frequent aggressor type of all on the two movie channels and UK Gold, the most prominent aggressor types were a mixture of cartoon characters, criminal characters and television law enforcers. While cartoon aggressors were prevalent on Sky One and The Movie Channel, however, they made no top ten appearances on Sky Movies or UK Gold. On Sky One, the most frequently occurring aggressor type of all was sports persons. This finding was mainly the result of Sky One's weekend coverage of American wrestling.

Top ten aggressor types: terrestrial channels

BBC1	%	ITV	%
1 Situation character	19.9	1 Situation character	16.7
2 Sports person	7.3	2 Criminal – serious	7.9
3= Criminal – serious	6.6	3 Armed forces	6.8
3= Armed forces	6.6	4 Cartoon – animal	6.4
5 Cartoon – human	6.1	5 Outlaw/pirate	5.2
6 Cartoon – animal	5.1	6 Police – uniformed	4.0
7 Police – uniformed	4.8	7 Criminal – petty	3.6
8 Criminal – petty	3.7	8 Police – plain clothes	2.9
9 Professional person	2.6	9 Member of public	2.5
10 Domestic person	2.4	10 Monster	2.1

BBC2	%	Channel 4	%
1 Armed forces	17.0	1 Situation character	14.3
2 Situation character	11.1	2= Cartoon – animal	8.8
3 Cartoon – human	6.7	2= Cowboy	8.8
4= Criminal – serious	5.7	4 Cartoon – human	8.7
4= Cowboy	5.7	5 Sports person	8.6
6 Cartoon – animal	5.0	6 Armed forces	7.5
7= Police – uniformed	3.1	7 Cartoon – other	4.5
7= School children	3.1	8 Criminal – serious	4.1
7= Cartoon – other	3.1	9= Police – uniformed	2.8
10 Political activist	3.0	9= Member of public	2.8

VICTIM DEMOGRAPHY

There were 21,106 acts of violence in which victims were clearly shown across all eight channels in total for the four weeks of television output analysed in this study. The demographic distribution of these characters is shown in Table 7.7. Victims of violence on television tended predominantly to be male, young adults aged between 20 and 35, and Caucasian, most probably of US origin.

Victims tended mostly to be solus males and, next most often, groups of males. If victims were not young adults, they were most probably middle aged adults aged 36 to 65 years. Relatively few victims were female, elderly or children. There were far fewer black victims of violence in programmes generally on British television than there were white victims.

Patterns of victim demography did not vary greatly from channel to channel (see Tables 7.8 and 7.9). Indeed, none of the eight channels studied here exhibited a victim demography profile which departed significantly from the overall pattern for television in general. The most significant point of note is the relatively younger profile of victims on Sky One, which matches the demography of aggressors and reflects the contribution of programmes made for younger audiences to the overall levels of violence on this channel. A second observation worth noting is the difference between the country of origin profiles for victims between Sky One and UK Gold shown under ethnic origin. UK Gold was characterized by a high proportion of UK victims (whether white or black) and a relatively low proportion of US victims. Sky One exhibited the opposite pattern. These findings reflect the programme profiles of these two channels. Sky One is dominated by imported programmes from the United States, while UK Gold broadcasts mostly British-made programmes.

Top ten aggressor types: satellite channels

Sky One	%	**Sky Movies**	%
1 Sports person	14.4	1 Situation character	22.3
2 Cartoon – human	9.5	2 Criminal – serious	13.5
3 Fantasy law enforcer	9.1	3 Police – plain clothes	6.2
4 Situation character	7.0	4 Armed forces	5.0
5 Cartoon – other	6.5	5 Cowboy	4.3
6= Criminal – serious	4.7	6 Professional person	3.7
6= Cartoon – animal	4.7	7 Criminal – petty	3.6
6= Robot	4.7	8 Member of public	3.3
9 Alien	4.1	9 School children	2.7
10 School children	3.6	10 Domestic person	2.4

UK Gold	%	**The Movie Channel**	%
1 Situation character	24.6	1 Situation character	17.3
2 Criminal – serious	10.2	2 Criminal – serious	9.8
3 Criminal – petty	7.9	3 Cartoon – human	9.2
4 Armed forces	7.2	4 Cartoon – animal	8.7
5 Police – plain clothes	6.0	5= Outlaw/pirate	4.8
6 Alien	4.6	5= Cowboy	4.8
7 Member of public	4.3	5= Criminal – petty	4.8
8 Police – uniformed	3.9	8 Police – plain clothes	4.4
9 Domestic person	3.3	9= Tribal people	4.3
10 Outlaw/pirate	2.4	9= Armed forces	4.3

TYPES OF VICTIM

Victims types were classified in the same way as aggressors using 57 basic categories representing occupation, profession or other character role identifiers, which were grouped according to nine superordinate categories. The general results for the 57 categories and major groups are summarized for the four weeks of coding in Table 7.10. Victims fell most often into the general category ('situation character', 'member of public' or 'domestic person'), criminal characters, or cartoon characters. Together these three broad categories accounted for half of all victims on violence shown in the programmes monitored.

Of the specific categories of victim, the most frequently occurring types were situation character, serious criminal, human cartoon, sports person and animal cartoon. Together these five types of character accounted for around four out of ten victims of violence visible on screen. The top ten victim types for all the channels monitored taken together are shown on page 152.

Table 7.7 Victim demography: all channels

	Percentage of violent acts
Gender	
One male	60.2
One female	9.0
Group male	11.9
Group female	0.0
Group mixed	6.1
Other	0.8
Cannot code	11.6
Age	
Child (up to 12)	1.8
Teenage (13–19)	4.8
Young adult (20–35)	47.7
Middle age (36–64)	19.7
65 plus	0.7
Mixed age	6.9
Cannot code	18.5
Ethnic origin	
White UK	11.5
White US	38.9
White other	12.8
Black UK	0.5
Black US	3.6
Black other	1.0
Asian	1.4
Oriental	3.4
Mixed group	5.1
Other human	1.7
Animal	4.1
Cannot code	16.0

Table 7.8 Victim demography: terrestrial channels

	Percentage of violent acts				
	All terrestrial	BBC1	BBC2	ITV	Ch.4
Gender					
One male	55.3	60.9	49.6	51.5	59.0
One female	8.6	9.4	9.2	8.5	7.3
Group male	14.2	12.0	16.9	14.8	13.1
Group female	0.3	0.8	0.0	0.3	0.0
Group mixed	6.9	6.2	7.2	7.8	6.3
Other	0.8	0.3	0.8	1.5	0.7
Cannot code	14.0	10.3	16.3	15.5	13.7
Age					
Child (up to 12)	1.2	1.1	2.1	1.1	0.4
Teenage (13–19)	3.6	2.5	4.8	4.2	2.9
Young adult (20–35)	46.1	49.8	45.8	41.7	47.2
Middle age (36–64)	17.4	20.8	11.5	21.4	15.9
65 plus	1.9	1.8	5.0	0.3	0.4
Mixed age	7.1	6.7	5.0	9.1	7.7
Cannot code	22.6	17.1	26.0	21.9	25.5
Ethnic origin					
White UK	16.4	18.3	16.6	12.4	18.4
White US	28.6	33.3	25.4	26.7	29.1
White other	13.7	17.6	16.0	11.4	9.7
Black UK	0.9	1.4	0.3	1.3	0.4
Black US	2.8	1.7	1.6	3.6	4.4
Black other	0.9	0.5	1.0	0.4	1.7
Asian	2.8	0.9	3.4	4.0	1.6
Oriental	2.0	0.0	2.1	4.5	1.2
Mixed group	5.7	7.4	4.9	9.5	5.9
Other human	1.9	1.1	3.1	2.0	1.2
Animal	3.6	3.6	2.7	1.8	6.1
Cannot code	19.7	13.4	22.8	22.3	20.3

Channel differences

Comparisons across channels in regard to victim-type distribution were made in the same way as for aggressor type distribution. First, the general distribution of the nine broad victim types exhibited a consistent pattern from channel to channel, with few inter-channel differences emerging (see Tables 7.11 and 7.12). Second, a list of the top ten victim types again underlines the considerable level of consistency between channels.

On the terrestrial channels, cartoon victims were more prevalent than average on Channel 4. Victims from the criminal and entertainment categories were rather more prevalent than the terrestrial average on ITV. Law enforcer victims appeared proportionately more often on BBC1 than on BBC2, while BBC2 and Channel 4 depicted more period victims than did BBC1 or ITV.

Table 7.9 Victim demography: satellite channels

	Percentage of violent acts				
	All satellite	Sky One	UK Gold	Sky Movies	Movie Channel
Gender					
One male	62.5	56.3	65.7	65.7	62.4
One female	9.4	6.3	11.3	10.5	9.5
Group male	10.7	9.9	9.0	10.9	11.9
Group female	0.2	0.6	0.0	0.0	0.0
Group mixed	5.7	7.8	4.6	4.8	5.4
Other	1.4	1.0	1.2	0.0	3.3
Cannot code	10.6	18.5	8.0	7.5	8.4
Age					
Child (up to 12)	1.7	1.1	0.5	2.9	2.4
Teenage (13–19)	4.6	9.6	1.9	1.9	4.9
Young adult (20–35)	48.9	44.7	50.6	53.7	46.8
Middle age (36–64)	20.9	10.6	26.4	23.8	22.9
65 plus	0.7	0.3	1.1	0.5	0.7
Mixed age	5.9	3.6	5.5	6.4	8.3
Cannot code	16.9	30.0	13.7	10.3	13.9
Ethnic origin					
White UK	16.2	3.0	50.0	4.0	7.8
White US	38.0	43.0	11.2	54.7	43.1
White other	12.4	8.7	12.7	14.6	13.5
Black UK	0.9	0.2	2.0	0.0	1.5
Black US	3.3	2.6	2.1	4.5	3.9
Black other	0.7	0.4	0.9	0.7	0.8
Asian	1.0	0.0	0.9	2.4	0.6
Oriental	3.0	1.0	0.7	3.5	6.7
Mixed group	3.7	4.4	2.1	4.0	4.4
Other human	1.7	2.2	2.2	1.2	1.0
Animal	3.9	4.9	1.4	1.5	7.9
Cannot code	15.2	29.4	14.4	8.5	8.5

Top ten victim types: all channels	%
1 Situation character	18.0
2 Criminal – serious	6.7
3 Cartoon – human	5.3
4 Sports persons	5.1
5 Cartoon – animal	4.8
6 Member of public	4.5
7 Armed forces	4.3
8 Criminal – petty	3.5
9 Professional person	2.9
10 Police – plain clothes	2.7

Table 7.10 Type of victim

	Percentage of violent acts
General categories	
Situation character	18.0
Member of public	4.5
Domestic person	2.1
TOTAL	24.6
Law enforcer	
Police – plain clothes	2.7
Fantasy legitimate	2.6
Police – uniformed	1.6
Special law enforcer	1.2
Quasi-law enforcer	0.4
Private eye	0.4
Executioner	*
TOTAL	8.9
Criminal	
Criminal – serious	6.7
Criminal – petty	3.5
Outlaw/pirate	2.3
Terrorist/guerrilla	0.7
Rioter	0.4
Political activist	0.4
Psychopath	0.1
Football hooligan	0.1
TOTAL	14.2
Futuristic/supernatural	
Monster	1.4
Robot	1.4
Alien	1.3
Spaceman	0.6
Supernatural power	0.4
Dracula/vampire	0.3
TOTAL	5.4
Period	
Cowboy	3.0
Indian	0.5
Nobility/royalty	0.5
Knight	0.4
TOTAL	4.4
Occupation/profession	
Professional person	2.9
Seaman	1.0
Uniformed official	0.5
Inventor/scientist	0.5
Servant	0.3
Journalist	0.2
Prostitute	0.2

Table 7.10 Contd...

	Percentage of violent acts
Clergy	0.2
Publican	0.1
Trades unionist	*
TOTAL	5.9
Entertainment	
Sports person	5.1
Entertainer	0.4
Comedian	0.1
Presenter – serious	*
Presenter – light	*
Sports commentator	*
TOTAL	5.6
Cartoon	
Cartoon – human	5.3
Cartoon – animal	4.8
Cartoon – other	1.9
TOTAL	12.0
Miscellaneous	
Armed forces	4.3
Inanimate object	2.7
School children	2.2
Martial artist	1.1
Animal	1.1
Tribal people	0.6
Assassin	0.6
Spy	0.4
Vigilante	0.3
Other	1.9
TOTAL	15.2
Victim not shown	*
Cannot code	3.7

Note: * Less than 0.05%

On the satellite channels, Sky One exhibited far lower than average rates of occurrence of victims from the general categories, criminal category and cartoon category, but a greater than average rate of victimization among the law enforcer, futuristic/supernatural-type and entertainment categories. General category victims were especially likely to occur on UK Gold and also exceeded the satellite channel average rate on Sky Movies. Criminal victims of violence were most likely to be found on Sky Movies, and cartoon victims of violence on The Movie Channel.

Turning to the top ten victim types, on the terrestrial channels the single most prominent category was that of situation character, representing regular character-types in drama situations for whom no other special occupation or role classifier was appropriate. On BBC1 and ITV, the appearance of sports persons in second place probably reflects the contribution of televised boxing matches on these two channels. Cartoon characters, whether human or animal, feature prominently on all four channels, while on BBC1 and ITV the prominence of violence in the good guy versus bad guy context is illustrated by the presence of criminal types and law enforcers as victims of violence.

Table 7.11 Distribution of victim types across terrestrial channels

	Percentage of violent acts				
	All terrestrial	BBC1	BBC2	ITV	Ch.4
General categories	23.3	24.3	20.8	24.7	23.2
Cartoon	14.9	12.5	14.6	9.9	22.4
Criminal	11.0	11.4	10.2	15.5	7.0
Entertainment	8.1	8.5	3.8	10.1	9.8
Law enforcer	8.0	11.3	5.3	8.4	6.8
Period	6.0	3.7	7.6	3.2	9.5
Occupation/profession	4.7	7.2	3.4	4.1	3.9
Futuristic/supernatural	3.3	0.6	3.8	5.6	3.0
Miscellaneous	16.8	16.9	24.7	14.6	10.9
Victim not shown	0.1	0.0	0.1	0.1	0.0
Cannot code	4.1	3.9	6.1	3.9	2.6

Table 7.12 Distribution of victim types across satellite channels

	Percentage of violent acts				
	All satellite	Sky One	UK Gold	Sky Movies	Movie Channel
General categories	26.5	8.2	40.3	32.1	25.5
Criminal	13.9	8.4	14.3	18.6	14.4
Cartoon	11.1	18.6	7.6	0.6	17.8
Law enforcer	9.6	13.5	9.7	7.7	6.7
Futuristic/supernatural	6.6	15.0	5.9	3.0	2.6
Occupation/profession	6.1	3.8	6.0	8.0	6.7
Entertainment	4.6	14.5	1.7	1.5	0.8
Period	3.3	1.9	0.7	4.9	5.6
Miscellaneous	14.4	11.9	12.4	17.9	14.4
Victim not shown	*	*	0.0	*	0.1
Cannot code	3.4	3.8	2.3	5.1	2.4

Note: * Less than 0.05%

On the satellite channels, the top ten victim-type listings underline the regularity of law enforcer versus criminal violence and violence in a cartoon setting. These two sets of victim types feature prominently after the most frequently occurring category of situation character. The latter, however, did not even make the top ten on Sky One, where violence was dominated by the contribution of American wrestling. The firm presence of science fiction series on Sky One is underlined by the appearance of alien, robot and fantasy law enforcer victims of violence. Westerns and war movies on Sky Movies and The Movie Channel resulted in the presence of armed forces and cowboys as victims of violence among the top tens for both of these channels.

Top ten victim types: terrestrial channels

BBC1	%	ITV	%
1 Situation character	18.6	1 Situation character	19.1
2 Sports person	7.4	2 Sports person	9.5
3 Cartoon – human	5.8	3 Cartoon – animal	6.5
4 Armed forces	5.4	4 Criminal – serious	6.0
5= Police – uniformed	5.2	5 Armed forces	5.6
5= Cartoon – animal	5.2	6 Member of public	4.8
7 Criminal – serious	4.3	7 Outlaw/pirate	4.4
8 Inanimate object	4.1	8 Criminal – petty	3.8
9= Member of public	3.8	9 Police – uniformed	3.5
9= Criminal – petty	3.8	10 Inanimate object	3.2

BBC2	%	Channel 4	%
1= Situation character	11.5	1 Situation character	16.0
1= Armed forces	11.5	2 Cartoon – animal	9.5
3 Cartoon – human	7.3	3 Cartoon – human	8.9
4= Cowboy	6.1	4 Sports person	8.6
4= Member of public	6.1	5 Cowboy	8.1
6 Cartoon – animal	4.8	6 Member of public	4.9
7 School children	4.4	7= Cartoon – other	4.0
8 Inanimate object	4.0	7= Fantasy law enforcer	4.0
9 Criminal – serious	3.9	9 Criminal – serious	3.7
10 Domestic person	3.2	10 Armed forces	3.2

SUMMARY AND CONCLUSIONS

Most of the television violence monitored in this study was perpetrated by characters who were white, young or middle-aged adults and male. Male aggressors generally perpetrated violence on their own, but on some occasions violence was perpetrated by groups of males. Around three quarters of all violent acts were performed by males compared with about one in ten that were perpetrated by females. Two-thirds of all violent acts were perpetrated by white characters compared with just over one in twenty by black characters. Over half of all violent acts were the behaviour of young adults, aged between 20 and 35 years, with around one in five being performed by middle-aged characters of 36 to 65 years.

Types of aggressor and victim were classified in terms of 57 additional categories representing different occupational or professional groups and character-role types. These divisions revealed that a wide variety of different types of television character were involved in violence during the weeks monitored. General characters occupying regular roles in drama series and serials represented the largest single group of perpetrators and victims of violence. After this group, results indicated that violent acts were dominated by criminal-types, law enforcers and cartoon characters. The prominence of sports competitors largely reflected the significant contribution made by a few contact sports broadcasts.

Top ten victim types: satellite channels

Sky One	**%**	**Sky Movies**	**%**
1 Sports person	14.0	1 Situation character	23.8
2 Cartoon – human	9.2	2 Criminal – serious	11.4
3 Fantasy law enforcer	9.0	3 Member of public	6.1
4 Robot	5.3	4 Armed forces	4.5
5= Cartoon – animal	4.6	5 Professional person	4.4
5= Cartoon – other	4.6	6 Criminal – petty	4.2
7 Criminal – serious	3.7	7 Police – plain clothes	3.6
8 Alien	3.6	8 Cowboy	3.1
9 Criminal – petty	3.4	9 School children	2.9
10 Martial artist	2.7	10 Domestic person	2.2

UK Gold	**%**	**The Movie Channel**	**%**
1 Situation character	30.0	1 Situation character	17.9
2 Criminal – petty	6.4	2 Cartoon – human	8.6
3 Member of public	6.2	3 Cartoon – animal	8.4
4 Criminal – serious	5.4	4 Criminal – serious	7.3
5 Police – plain clothes	5.2	5 Outlaw/pirate	4.6
6= Domestic person	4.7	6 Member of public	4.5
6= Inanimate object	4.7	7 Armed forces	4.2
8 Armed forces	4.5	8 Cowboy	4.1
9 Domestic person	4.1	9 Police – plain clothes	3.7
10 Alien	3.0	10 Domestic person	3.1

The same principal categories of violence perpetrator and victim surfaced for all eight channels. The main departures from the overall pattern featured the presence on Sky One of character-types from science fiction settings, such as fantasy law enforcer, robot and alien being. Meanwhile on BBC2 armed forces personnel featured more prominently than on any other channel among characters involved in violence as aggressors and victims, reflecting the relatively greater than average prevalence of war-time movies and programmes on this channel during the period monitored.

Victimization likelihood

Only slight evidence emerged that any particular demographic groups were being disproportionately victimized on television. This finding was calculated by dividing the percentage of violent acts in which a particular group was involved in violence as a perpetrator by the percentage of times they were involved as victims.

Among demographic groups although age group differences emerged, neither gender nor ethnic origin were found to yield any differences in victimization ratios. Male characters, for example, were slightly more likely to be aggressors than victims of violence by a narrow ratio of 1.03:1.00. This means that males were 1.03 times as likely to be aggressors as victims. Female characters generally had a much lower level of involvement in violence as both aggressors and victims. There was no indication, however, that females were any more likely to be victimized than males after controlling for their different respective overall levels of involvement. Females were 1.05 times as likely to be aggressors as victims of violence. Turning to ethnic differences in ratio of involvement as aggressors or victims, white characters were found to be 1.04 times as likely to feature as aggressors as victims, compared with a figure of 1.06 for black characters.

There were differences between age groups in the extent to which they featured as aggressors or victims. Teenagers (1.17:1.00), young adults (1.08:1.00) and middle-aged adults (1.02:1.00) exhibited ratios which indicated a greater likelihood of appearing as perpetrators of violence than as victims. In contrast, children up to age 12 (0.83:1.00) and people aged 65 and over (0.86:1.00) exhibited greater tendencies to be victims than aggressors. Thus, the very young and the elderly have a greater likelihood than teenagers, young adults and middle-aged adults to be victims of violence on television.

Among the more detailed categories of character involved in violence further analyses were computed in respect of law enforcers and criminal-types. Over the aggregation of law enforcer and criminal sub-types these analyses revealed little difference in their respective probabilities of being victims once involved in violence, in spite of the greater overall likelihood of involvement in violence on the part of criminal-types. The aggressor:victim ratio for law enforcers was 1.19:1.00 and for criminal-types it was 1.20:1.00. Among the more specific types of law enforcer and criminal, however, there was some degree of variation in the ratio of perpetration to victimization.

For plain clothes police officers (1.44:1.00) and uniformed police officers (1.38:1.00) involvement in violence meant that they were more likely to be perpetrators than victims. The same result was true also of serious criminal types (1.31:1.00). For petty criminal types, however, the pattern was reversed (0.94:1.00) with victimization being more likely.

The significance of these results stems from the argument that the extent of involvement in violence on television of particular demographic or occupational groups conveys messages to audiences about the division of power among these groups. Powerful groups feature more prevalently as perpetrators of violence, while weaker groups are the ones most often victimized (Gerbner, 1972; Gerbner and Gross, 1976; Gerbner *et al.,* 1978, 1979, 1980). Although this hypothesis about television impact on social beliefs has been challenged for Britain by earlier research (Gunter, 1988; Wober and Gunter, 1988), on the basis of research with television audiences which failed to replicate American results indicating the existence of statistically significant relationships between reported television watching and perceptions of social violence, the current research indicates limited scope for such effects on the basis of an analysis of television content alone. This is because few differences emerged in the victimization likelihoods between major demographic and other groupings of television characters.

Some support did emerge for the concern raised by other researchers (e.g., Signorielli, 1981, 1984) that television, through its portrayals of violence, may present different impressions about the relative power or weakness of certain age groups. In the current study, there was evidence that the elderly and children are victimized to a greater extent than other age groups on mainstream television channels. However, given the generally low level at which children and the elderly feature in violent scenes, the opportunities for such 'messages' to be absorbed by audiences were relatively limited.

What the current findings may well reflect as much as anything else is the relative extent to which individuals from different demographic groups appear on television in a wider sense. Television remains a medium dominated by particular demographic groups, notably males, young adults and those of Caucasian origin. In addition to this, the prevalence of particular character-types as assailants or victims reflects in turn the fact that a relatively small range and number of programmes contribute disproportionately to the overall violence count.

8   Programme genre and TV violence

THE CONCEPT OF GENRE

The concept of 'genre' as explored in film theory initially conveyed a pejorative connotation associated with formula movies and mass produced entertainment devoid of personality (Willeman, 1985). Turning to the function of genre in the context of television, one claim is that genre acts as a process of expectation on the part of the audience and this becomes a source of both meaning and pleasure (Neale, 1983). The systematic repetition and difference that is part of genre provides the basis upon which viewers derive pleasure. While individual episodes may keep viewers tuned by introducing fresh plot developments, there is a regularity to the form and content of different episodes in terms of certain key attributes which serve to identify the 'type' of programme the audience is watching. Viewers derive sets of expectations from these rules of conduct and styles of presentation which define for them the 'genre' of which the episode they are watching is a recognizable exemplar. Ryall (1979) described genres as sets of rules for the production of meaning. Such rules govern the combination of signs into specific patterns which regulate the production of texts by authors and the reading of texts by audiences.

This critical analytical perspective has received some empirical corroboration from research conducted with audiences which has attempted to define the attributes of programme quality. This work has shown that viewers can identify key attributes of genres and that these attributes emerge consistently across different programmes within a particular genre as central ingredients underpinning whether the programme is perceived to be a good example of its type (Gunter, 1995, 1997).

Another view about genres on television is that they form the basis of audience pleasure or appreciation because they allow audiences to view programmes more effortlessly by cultivating knowledge of what to expect from a particular programme type (Morley, 1981). As viewers become accustomed to certain conventions or routines being displayed within programmes it helps them to deal more effectively with whatever is new in the programme by rendering much of what is routine redundant and therefore drawing less upon their attention. Programmes which contain much that is familiar to viewers in terms of characterizations, settings, relationships, plot-lines and styles of presentation can be more readily followed, and when some new development or turn of events occurs, this has more significance for viewers because it is contrasted with a background of familiarity.

In the context of television, genre also serves an important economic function as a means of producing profit. This exerts a powerful influence upon the changing format of programmes and is the binding force behind new programme types. Genres do evolve on television, but this progression which sometimes takes the form of hybridization generally consists of de-velopments of existing successful formulas. Economic pressures also operate to perpetuate those genres which are already financially successful. Indeed, the genesis of television genres has been traced to a transference of already proven formulas in radio and film. According to Rose (1985, p. 5):

> The medium's visual possibilities and limitations clearly influenced televi-sion's reworking of traditional genres (and its eventual creation of new genres), but there was a much more important factor affecting basic program structure and formatting – the economics of broadcasting. TV genres, like radio genres, movie genres, or the genres of popular literature, are essentia'ly commodities, manufactured for, and utterly dependent on, public consump-tion and support. While popular culture theorists may argue about the hidden needs and desires genres reflect and fulfil, the formulas that have endured are those which manage to yield a regular profit for their producers.

There is therefore a close connection between the concept of 'genre' and the assumptions that are made about the potential popularity of programmes. This notion is in turn tied to an assumption that genre attributes play a central role in assisting audiences with their interpretation and understanding of programmes, a factor that is envisaged as being linked to audience apprecia-tion. On the basis of an empirical analysis of the significance of genre attri-butes originally identified by viewers themselves as linked to programme popularity, indications have begun to emerge that such attributes may not only serve to define a genre for viewers, but also underpin their loyalty to it (Gunter, 1995).

Another important aspect of programme genre is that it represents one of the key discriminating features of television output. The news, the soap opera, the quiz show, the talk show, the documentary all represent recogniz-able genres with distinctive formats, subject matter, and sets of codes and conventions which lead audiences to expect different things from them. Broadcasters define the shape and content of their schedules in terms of genres, and audiences' expectations of programmes are frequently genre-linked. One of the dynamic features of genre which affects the way audiences react to programmes is the degree of realism associated with a programme. In the broadest sense, viewers distinguish between factual programmes and fictional programmes. Even among drama output, however, there may be varying degrees of realism in that in some television dramas the story may be set in a contemporary setting not unlike everyday reality in many respects, while in others, the action may take place in settings which are totally divorced from normal, everyday life.

Where violent portrayals are concerned, viewers react differently to violence in a real life setting, a realistic fictional setting and a fantasy fictional setting. Violence depicted in realistic settings tends to give rise to more profound emotional and behavioural reactions among viewers, young and old (Berkowitz and Alioto, 1973; Feshbach, 1972; Noble, 1975; Reeves, 1978). Audiences perceive violent portrayals differently depending on the type of programme in which they occur. In this respect, viewers have been observed to judge violence as more serious and more disturbing to the degree that the programmes in which it occurred were perceived as realistic as opposed to fantasy or fiction (Gunter, 1985).

Research has shown, for instance, that young viewers shown film footage depicting violence labelled as real life action, exhibited significantly more aggressive behaviour subsequent to exposure than did similar young people for whom the same footage was labelled a pure fiction (Feshbach, 1972). Realism in drama can be an attractive feature to viewers. In the United Kingdom, for example, Greenberg (1974) reported that the extent to which teenagers perceived programmes to be realistic was related to their tendencies to watch such programmes. In particular, those young viewers who watched a great deal of violent programming and believed that it was realistic were also more likely to believe that violence was the most effective way to resolve arguments and disputes with other people.

A limitation of many studies in this area has been that the realism of television content has often been defined only very simplistically and therefore has often failed to reflect the complex nature of viewers' judgements about programmes. Whether or not a programme is perceived by viewers as realistic depends not just on labels such as 'factual' or 'drama', but instead often derives from a sophisticated critical analysis of a programme's contents which takes numerous variables into account. The realism of a programme can depend critically on the viewer's own perspective and social knowledge and environment. Whether the actions and conversations of fictional characters on television, and the relationships which exist between them, the problems they experience and the ways they deal with those problems are seen as realistic depends on the extent to which viewers identify with those things and compare them with similar aspects of their own lives (Lindlof, 1988).

Some writers have observed that when considering such programmes as crime-drama series, child and adult viewers alike often discount the 'realism' of how the police are depicted and of the work they are seen to do because these portrayals are recognized purely and simply as being 'fictional'. On this basis alone, such portrayals may be regarded as failing to hold any direct correspondence with the way things are in real life (Dominick, 1973). However, the distinctions between reality and fiction may become less clear-cut at different levels of content abstraction and also as a function of viewers' real life knowledge and experiences.

Comparisons of what people think about television police and the police in real life have shown that the two versions are not generally perceived the same way. Rarick *et al.* (1973), for example, examined non-delinquent and delinquent adolescents' images of real life and television police. Respondents indicated the extent to which they felt that each of 36 statements accurately described the way television or real life police are or operate. Six distinct patterns of perceptions emerged: three of actual and three of television police. Perceptions of actual police were diverse, ranging from highly favourable to openly hostile, with some mixed feelings in between. Perceptions of television police were relatively homogeneous and positive. Among both the delinquent and non-delinquent adolescents there was widespread belief that television police were idealized dramatizations different from the real thing. Those young people who had favourable impressions of actual police tended to see greater similarity between actual and television counterparts than did those who held unfavourable impressions of actual police. Delinquents did not, on the whole, see greater differences between actual and television police than did non-delinquents, despite their greater contact with the police in actuality.

Judgements about the realism of television can become blurred as the frame of reference under which those judgements are made is narrowed. One study found that when youngsters were asked whether or not the events shown on television drama series were like events that happened in real life, most denied there was any similarity between the two. When questions focused upon specific series or upon particular aspects of those series, however, reality–fantasy distinctions became less clear (Greenberg and Reeves, 1976).

There is little doubt that most viewers can and do make broad distinctions between the nature of television portrayals on the basis of the programme context or setting. At a fairly generalized level, distinctions between fictional settings and real life are usually quite unambiguous, and are learned by viewers by middle childhood (see Gunter *et al.*, 1991). Typically, portrayals that are perceived to be fictional have a less profound impact on viewers than do realistic portrayals. As the level of perceptual analysis or interpretation of programme content becomes more specific, even so far as focusing on particular characters or events in programmes, increasing numbers of viewers appear to find the reality–fiction distinction less easy to make. This is an important point which needs to be borne in mind especially in relation to the judged seriousness of different types of televised depiction of violence.

GENRE AND THE DISTRIBUTION OF VIOLENCE ON TV

The distribution of violence on television was assessed in terms of the types of programmes in which it occurred. The occurrence of violence in different programme genres can be examined in several different ways: the distribution of violent acts by genre; the distribution of violent sequences by genre; the distribution of amount of violence (in minutes) by genre; the rate of occurrence of violent acts and violent sequences by genre; and the average amount of violence (in minutes) in programmes with violence for different genres.

As we saw in Chapter 2, programmes were initially classified into 32 genres. To facilitate more manageable genre comparisons, in this chapter reference will be made to seven superordinate genres, representing a condensed form of the original 32-genre typology. These seven genres are: cinema films, other drama, entertainment, factual, sport, children's programmes and music/arts/religion. Separate chapters, following this one, will present more detailed findings for fictional drama, factual programmes, entertainment programmes and children's programmes, with reference made to violence levels in the genres of which each superordinate genre is comprised.

The greatest proportion of violent acts (70%) overall occurred in drama programmes. Over the four weeks of analysis, 14,683 violent acts were coded in drama programmes. More detail about how the violence was distributed among different types of drama programme is presented in Chapter 9. It is worth noting at this point, however, that most drama violence occurred in films originally made for the cinema, and not in programmes produced specifically for television. A total of 11,263 violent acts were catalogued in cinema films, representing 53% of all violent acts (see Table 8.1).

This pattern of violence distribution was further reflected in the count of violent sequences (see Table 8.1). Over half of all violent sequences monitored were found in cinema films. Movies also exhibited the highest rate of violence, in terms of average numbers of violent acts (16.1 per violence-containing programme) and violent sequences (7.7 per violent programme), of any genre.

Table 8.1 Distribution of violent acts and sequences by programme genre

	Percentage of violent acts	
	Violent acts	*Violent sequences*
Cinema films	53	51
Children's programmes	19	18
Other drama	16	18
Factual	5	6
Sport	3	3
Entertainment	2	3
Music/arts/religion	*	*

Note: * Less than 0.5%

The second highest violent act count was found in children's programmes, with 4,008 separate violent acts, representing nearly one in five (19%) of all violent acts. Over half (56%) of violent acts in children's programmes were found in non-animated children's programmes. Just over four in ten (43%) of violent acts in children's programmes occurred in children's cartoons. The analysis revealed an average of 13.2 violent acts per programme in non-cartoon children's programmes, compared with 9.1 acts per violence-containing programme in children's cartoons. To put these results into perspective, however, the apparently high rate of occurrence of violent acts within non-cartoon children's programmes is significantly inflated by the rates of violence in programmes within this category appearing on Sky One. More than seven in ten (71%) of violent acts in non-cartoon children's programmes occurred on Sky One, exhibiting an average rate of violence per programme on that channel of 16.3. The major contributors here were cartoons on the *DJ Kat TV Show* and *The Mighty Morphin Power Rangers*.

Just one in 20 acts of violence occurred collectively in factual programmes (8% of all acts of violence), entertainment programmes (2%) and music/arts and religious programmes (less than 0.5%). The total figure for factual programmes was 1,013 acts of violence over all channels during the four week monitoring period. A further 728 acts of violence occurred in sports programmes. Out of all violent acts catalogued in sports programmes, over seven in ten (71%) occurred on Sky One, almost wholly within the *World Wrestling Federation* broadcasts on Saturdays and Sundays. The average rate of violence in violence-containing sports programmes was 14.3 acts per broadcast.

Over four in ten violent acts (43%) in factual programmes occurred in national news broadcasts. These were wholly contained within the four terrestrial channels. Violent factual programmes contained an average of 4.1 acts of violence each. Out of a total of 436 acts of violence catalogued in national news programmes, 155 (36%) occurred on BBC1 and 154 (36%) occurred on ITV. However, given that 474 news programmes were coded, the overall rate of violence in national news broadcasts was less than one act per programme.

In general then, violent acts and violent sequences occurred with the greatest frequency in cinema films, sports programmes and children's programmes. Whenever programmes in any of these three genres contained violence, there were generally at least ten separate violent acts and at least five violent sequences.

Relatively few violent acts or violent sequences occurred in music, arts or religious programmes. Indeed, no violence was registered at all in religious programmes. When violence did occur in such programmes, there tended to be fewer incidents on average than in violence-containing programmes from other genres. On average, any violent music, arts and religious programmes considered together, contained fewer than four violent acts and two and a half violent sequences (see Table 8.2).

Channel comparisons

There were clear differences between channels in terms of which genres carried the greatest proportion of violent acts (see Tables 8.3 and 8.4). In the case of all

Table 8.2 Average frequency of violent acts and sequences in violent programmes by genre

	Violent acts	Violent sequences
Cinema films	16.1	7.7
Children's programmes	10.1	5.1
Other drama	5.2	3.2
Sport	5.0	1.8
Factual	4.4	2.8
Entertainment	4.4	2.9
Music/arts/religion	3.8	2.4

Table 8.3 Distribution of violent acts by genre and channel

	Percentage of violent acts						
	All	BBC1	BBC2	ITV	Ch.4	Sky 1	UK Gold
Cinema films	24	40	28	40	33	5	19
Other drama	29	20	19	22	10	27	71
Children's	28	20	23	18	26	50	5
Factual	8	14	19	11	16	2	0
Sport	6	3	1	4	6	4	–
Entertainment	4	3	8	3	7	2	4
Music/arts/religion	1	1	3	3	*	*	1

Notes: 1. '*All*' data based on average of four terrestrial and two satellite non-movie channels
2. * Less than 0.5%

Table 8.4 Distribution of violent sequences by genre and channel

	Percentage of violent sequences						
	All	BBC1	BBC2	ITV	Ch.4	Sky 1	UK Gold
Other drama	30	19	16	24	11	29	71
Cinema films	23	33	27	33	31	7	17
Children's	26	22	22	20	25	48	6
Factual	10	19	24	12	19	3	0
Sport	4	3	1	4	6	9	–
Entertainment	5	4	8	3	8	3	6
Music/arts/religion	2	1	3	4	*	*	1

Notes: 1. '*All*' data based on average of four terrestrial and two satellite non-movie channels
2. * Less than 0.5%

four terrestrial channels, the greatest single percentages of violent acts and violent sequences were found in cinema films. However, this genre made a more significant contribution towards levels of violence, expressed in terms of numbers of violent incidents, on BBC1 and ITV than on BBC2 and Channel 4. Other major contributing genres were other forms of drama, children's programmes and factual programmes. Drama, other than cinema films, made a much less pronounced contribution towards the total violence incident level on Channel 4 than on the other three terrestrial channels.

Children's programmes made a bigger contribution towards violence on Channel 4 and BBC2 than on BBC1 and ITV. Factual programmes made the most significant contribution towards violent acts on BBC2. Sports programmes made their biggest contribution by far in respect of violence found on Sky One. This was mainly accounted for by the regular World Wrestling Federation broadcasts.

Cinema films made a relatively modest contribution towards violent act and violent sequence levels on Sky One and UK Gold, reflecting the lesser prominence of this genre on these two channels. Violence on UK Gold was found principally in drama that was made for television (rather than the cinema). On Sky One, the major contributing genre, in terms of the violent act count, was children's programmes. The exceptionally high violence figure for this genre on this channel, however, was inflated by the disproportionately high rate of violent acts recorded on the *DJ Kat TV Show* and *Mighty Morphin Power Rangers*.

Turning to the amount of time occupied by violence, the analysis revealed that the greatest proportion of all violence on the channels monitored (68%) occurred in drama programmes. Over half of all violence (53%) occurred in cinema films shown on television. Nearly 27 hours of violence was catalogued in 883 cinema films in this analysis, giving an average of 1.8 minutes of violence per movie. In comparison, there was an average of 0.36 minutes (22 seconds) of violence in television drama programmes other than cinema films (15% of all violence minutage).

A total of 7.2 hours of violent activity was found in children's programmes (14% of violence minutage), of which 4.1 hours (57%) occurred in non-cartoon children's programmes and 3.1 hours (42%) occurred in children's cartoons. Thus, the average amount of violence in children's programmes was 0.46 minutes (28 seconds) per programme. Nearly 40% of violence in all children's programmes, however, occurred in non-cartoon programmes for children on Sky One (1.72 minutes of violence per programme).

A further 6.7 hours (13%) of violence occurred in sports programmes. Factual programmes contained around 1.4 hours of violence (3% of all violence minutage) with 46 minutes of violence occurring in national news programmes, giving an average rate of occurrence of around 6 seconds per bulletin.

Less than one hour of violent material (2% of violence minutage) was found in 909 entertainment programmes (51 minutes) and only a quarter of this amount (13 minutes) occurred in 184 music/arts and religious programmes (less than 0.5% of violence minutage).

Channel differences were examined to reveal how the distribution of time occupied by violence varied among programme genres on different channels. As before, these comparisons were made for six superordinate genres in respect of the four terrestrial channels and two satellite non-movie channels (see Table 8.5).

Table 8.5 Distribution of amount of violence by genre and channel (percentages)

	All	*BBC1*	*BBC2*	*ITV*	*Ch.4*	*Sky 1*	*UK Gold*
Other dramas	25	23	12	19	10	19	68
Cinema films	23	35	40	39	40	1	24
Sport	23	10	*	22	4	45	–
Children's	20	20	19	10	24	31	4
Factual	6	10	22	6	18	1	0
Entertainment	3	2	5	2	5	2	4
Music/arts/religion	1	*	3	2	*	*	*

Notes: 1. 'All' data based on average of four terrestrial and two satellite non-movie channels
2. * Less than 0.5%

On all four terrestrial channels, the greatest proportion of time occupied by violence occurred in cinema films shown on those channels. Other major contributing genres in each case were drama other than cinema films, children's programmes, sports programmes and factual programmes. Only small amounts of violence were found in entertainment programmes and music/arts/religious programmes. Non-cinema drama was the second most prominent contributor to amount of time filled by violence on BBC1. This position was occupied by sports and factual programmes in the case of BBC2, by sports programmes on ITV and by children's programmes on Channel 4.

Nearly all time occupied by violence on UK Gold occurred in drama programmes. On Sky One, however, most violence time occurred in sports programmes and children's programmes, with non-cinema drama providing most of the remainder.

SUMMARY AND CONCLUSIONS

This chapter has presented findings based on the core quantitative measures of television violence with special reference to the distribution of violence among the major programme genres. As such it provides a broad overview of where violence was located within the variety of different programme types which characterize the schedules of some of Britain's leading television channels. These figures on their own, however, have limited value in connection with identifying any possible implications of the violence catalogued in this study for indicating likely audience reactions. To achieve this particular objective, it is important to know more about the qualities of violent portrayals which derive from information about the attributes of violent acts and the specific programmes in which they occurred.

Violence, on the eight channels covered by the current study, emerged as a phenomenon primarily located in drama programming. Television's factual and entertainment programmes contributed only lesser amounts to the whole. The most significant single contributor among the major programme genres used to classify programmes here was a type of production which was not even made for television in its original form, namely cinema films. More than half of all television violence, during the weeks monitored in this study, occurred in cinema films. However, this general picture is distorted to some extent by the fact that two channels were movie channels and thus inflated the overall amount of movie material monitored and the overall amount of movie-based violence on television.

Films contained a greater number of violent incidents on average than other categories of programming, which is not too surprising given that they tend to be twice the duration of other types of programmes. In spite of criticisms about violence in such programmes made for the medium, television drama's contribution to the overall amount of violence on television was not significantly greater than the contribution made by children's programmes and sport. What is perhaps more important, of course, is whether the nature of violence shown in these programmes differs along significant dimensions. Later chapters will explore the qualities of violence shown in these different genres in more detail.

As a general observation, the finding that most of television's violence tended to be found in fictional rather than factual programming is reassuring given the evidence from audience research that viewers, young and old, usually react more strongly to depictions of real-life violence than to fictional portrayals of violence (Berkowitz and Alioto, 1973; Feshbach, 1972; Geen and Rakosky, 1973; Osborn and Endsley, 1971). Even amongst fictional drama portrayals, however, there can be significant degrees of variance in perceptions of how close they are to real life (Gunter, 1985).

The way violence was distributed among the major genres differed between the channels which were monitored. Dropping the movie channels to focus attention upon the six channels which offer a mixed range of programming puts the contribution made to overall violence levels by cinema films in a different perspective. While cinema films still represented important contributors across all six non-movie channels, they were less significant than sports programmes and children's programmes on Sky One, and fell far behind made-for-TV drama on UK Gold. In general, across these six channels just under a third of violence occurred in cinema films, which indicates how the overall figure of more than half across all eight channels was inflated by the output of the two satellite movie channels.

The four terrestrial channels exhibited a pattern of distribution of violence across genres which indicated significant contributions by children's programmes, factual programmes on BBC2 and Channel 4, sport on ITV, and made-for-TV drama (most especially in the case of BBC1) as well as by cinema films. The impact of programme diversity on the four terrestrial channels upon the distribution of violence among different programme genres was clearly apparent from these findings.

The relative prominence of sports programmes and children's programmes on some channels as sources of violence may seem a worrying finding at first glance. These bald figures on their own, however, do not reveal a great deal. It is important to establish details about the character of the violence shown in these programme genres for the channels in question. If, for instance, much of the violence occurring in children's programmes comprises cartoon portrayals or action sequences from fantastic, 'superhero' series whose characterizations, settings and events are divorced from everyday reality, such evidence would place a different complexion on the basic quantitative data from an alternative picture indicating a significant contribution from more realistic, contemporary drama series featuring characters and settings which are closer to the everyday reality of viewers. The sports contribution, as has already been firmly established, derived from a few contact sports (e.g., boxing and wrestling) broadcasts. In the chapters that follow, this sort of detail is explored for several specific programme genres and their sub-genres.

9 Violence in dramatic fiction

Dramatic fiction represents a number of the most prominent programme genres on television. Nearly four out of ten programmes coded on the four terrestrial channels and two non-movie satellite channels comprised one form of drama or another. On the movie channels, of course, most of the output comprised drama in the form of films originally made for the cinema. This chapter extends the results presented in Chapter 8, which reported general levels of violence registered across cinema films and other forms of made-for-television drama. Further results are presented to reveal how violence was distributed across different types of drama programming and across the drama shown on different television channels. In addition to cinema films, six other drama genres were distinguished: non-UK long-running serials; UK-produced long-running serials; other non-UK series or serials; other UK-produced series or serials; made-for-TV films; and single plays.

The descriptive analysis reported in this monograph cannot reveal anything directly about how audiences might react to television violence. It is possible, nevertheless, to interpret some of the findings of this content analysis in terms of what is known about how viewers respond to different types of violence in fictional drama settings on television. One particular reference point would be to identify specific attributes of violent portrayals and their settings which can influence audiences' subjective reactions. If it is known that there are particular forms of violence which are especially likely to upset viewers or certain kinds of setting or context in which the emotional impact of violence may be enhanced or alleviated, this information could be relevant to current data interpretation. If it can be demonstrated, for example, that the most troublesome forms of violence for viewers are rare occurrences on mainstream television, this will add an important perspective to this assessment of violence on television.

AUDIENCE PERSPECTIVES ON TV VIOLENCE

One aspect of the significance of violence depicted in television drama programmes stems from a commonly voiced belief that violence plays a key part in dramatic fictional storytelling. In drama therefore the entertainment value of a programme might be enhanced by the presence of violence (Eisenstein, 1949; Berlyne, 1960). Attempts, empirically, to demonstrate that violence does affect entertainment value have so far failed to demonstrate that it makes much difference to audience enjoyment or viewing loyalty. One American study on this subject has indicated that the audience sizes and subjective evaluations of mainstream drama series on network television were not predicted by the level of violence they contained (Diener and De Four, 1978). Later research in which different versions of the same programme were shown to groups of viewers, either with the original violence left in or edited out, found that the degree of violence in the programme made no difference to how much viewers enjoyed it (Diener and Woody, 1981).

If violence does not necessarily enhance audience appreciation of television drama programmes, does it instead cause them undue offence or concern while they are watching such programmes? Despite the oft-heard protestations in the press that most people believe there is too much violence on television, research into public opinion about specific drama series or episodes from those series has failed to corroborate the suggestion that people do have widespread concerns.

As the last chapter indicated, drama is a key contributor to overall levels of violence on television. Cinema films especially contained more violence than other genres, although their overall contribution to violence on the eight channels monitored in this research was inflated by the presence of two thematic movie channels. The significance of movie violence found here, however, reinforces the perceptions of viewers who have been found to regard films as one of the principal sources of violence on television, and especially of strong violence (Morrisson, 1993b). Despite this impression, viewers were concerned about cuts that were often made in films before being broadcast on television. It was not simply a concern about the implications of such editing for the integrity of the original, but annoyance at feeling they were being cheated and patronized.

The portrayal of violence in television drama programmes can vary widely in terms of the form it takes, but also more importantly, from the point of view of audience reaction, in terms of the context or setting in which it occurs. Television drama programmes can vary greatly with respect to their degree of realism. They also vary with respect to their degree of continuity from one week to the next. Serialized dramas with continuing storylines which unfold over many episodes can involve audiences more deeply than drama series composed of self-contained episodes in which a story is resolved within a single edition of the series.

The perceived realism of dramatic fiction can affect the nature and strength of viewers' reactions to any portrayed violence. In a study of adult viewers, Gunter (1985) reported that as drama settings became more like everyday life, any violence seen in them came to be rated as progressively more seriously violent and potentially or actually upsetting. Children also have been found to differentiate between more and less realistic fictional drama settings on television, and to view realistic programmes with more involvement, more emotion and less detachment. Violence depicted in realistic fictional settings is perceived by young viewers in a more serious light (van der Voort, 1986). According to Gunter (1985, pp. 97–98):

In general, shootings and physical violence occurring in contemporary settings such as those found in British and American crime-drama series were perceived in somewhat more serious terms than similar forms of violence occurring in western settings and in substantially more serious terms than similar incidents depicted in futuristic science fiction or in animated cartoon settings. Put more explicitly, violence in contemporary crime-drama settings was rated as more violent, more realistic, more frightening, more personally disturbing, more likely to disturb people in general, and less humorous and less suitable for children than violence in settings more distanced from everyday life.

A series of surveys conducted during the mid-1980s, for example, in which opinions were obtained on a number of British and American-produced crime-drama series, indicated that viewers of these programmes did not perceive them as overly violent and more often felt that any violence that was shown was necessary to the storyline (Gunter and Wober, 1988).

The same series of surveys found that viewers were more likely than not to agree with the view that violence perpetrated by fictional police characters in these dramas was nearly always justified. There were, however, differences between series in the extent to which this opinion was voiced. This suggested that viewers discriminated between the degree of justification for violence by fictional law enforcers found in different television crime series. Even so, relatively few respondents in these surveys believed that fictional police were often far more violent than they needed to be. Despite the finding that the use of violence by British fictional police was more often felt to be fully justified than that used by American fictional police, there was no overriding perception in either case that the amount of violence in these series was excessive.

An important ingredient known to affect viewers' perceptions of televised violence, as noted in the previous chapter, is its degree of realism. What emerged from the surveys of public opinion about crime series in the mid-1980s was that audiences did not perceive all crime-dramas to give an equally realistic portrayal of the police. British series such as *The Bill* and *Juliet Bravo* were regarded as offering the most realistic portrayals of the police, whereas other series such as *Bergerac, Cats' Eyes* and *Dempsey and Make-peace* were seen as rather less so, especially the latter series. On average, the fictional police in American crime-series were regarded as less realistic than their British counterparts, with the exception of Dempsey.

The significance of the realism of drama stems from the part it can play in establishing the degree of audience involvement in a programme. The more realistic the drama, the more critical it is that any violence portrayed in it is dealt with responsibly. One particularly important factor is that the use of the violence itself can be justified. As we saw above, the general opinion about many popular crime-drama series in the mid-1980s was that the violence in them was not over-played, but rather was regarded as justifiable in the context of the story. This finding has been corroborated by more recent qualitative research carried out among British viewers (Morrisson, 1993b). This work also found that adult viewers also express concerns about the possibly upsetting effects graphic portrayals of violence in realistic dramas might have upon their children. While there was no accompanying rallying cry for the abolition of such programmes, there was clear support for the related issue of adequate and properly implemented scheduling controls over such programmes.

In the context of realistic drama, Morrisson's respondents frequently illustrated their concerns with reference to one particular television series, *Casualty*. Although this is a medical drama, many of its major plots and sub-plots involve acts of violence and depict, sometimes quite graphically, their aftermath and consequences for victims. Viewers are not, it seems, generally critical of this. The depiction of violence or violence-related injuries can be justified to an extent by the fact that the setting of this series is a hospital in which one would expect to find people suffering severe as well as mild injuries being treated. In this setting, even quite graphic portrayals are regarded as acceptable by viewers.

According to Morrisson (1993b) public opinion about television violence is shaped by and cannot be considered divorced from the wider conceptions people hold about society. The vivid detail of human suffering portrayed in series such as *Casualty* is acceptable because society is viewed as having become a more violent place. In Morrisson's own words (1993b, p. 59):

> The acceptance of detailed injuries is due to the view that society has become more violent, and therefore a hospital drama that failed to show the horrifics of injuries would, if it made any claim to be a realistic portrayal of a casualty hospital, be failing in dramatic intent, and possibly even duty. The benefit of having documented viewers' experience of violence, of understanding how viewers perceive the 'real' world as violent, and their perception that it is worse now than five years ago, is that one has little difficulty in accounting for this acceptance of the visual imagery given to the injuries shown in *Casualty* – and little difficulty in seeing why such a programme is accepted as suitable for viewing before the nine o'clock watershed.

Other aspects of violence than its realism, however, are known to affect viewers' reactions to it when seen on the small screen. The nature of the setting in terms of the motivational context and the physical form that the violence takes on are also important. Morrisson's focus groups expressed concern about domestic violence and about violence that was sexually motivated. Audience sensitivities to violence in these contexts has been noted in previous chapters. Violence in a domestic setting is understandably potentially anxiety-invoking for some viewers if the setting reminds them of their own home circumstances. Once again, viewers can reveal a degree of tolerance even for those portrayals which may be distressing for them, provided there is a justifiable purpose behind their inclusion in the programme (Morrisson, 1993b).

Rape is a particularly distressing crime for its victims. It can invoke considerable distress among those who witness rape scenes, even when they are mediated by television. Rape is a form of violence that is found particularly abhorrent by women. This point was illustrated by Morrisson (1993b). As with domestic violence, rape depictions were rated as acceptable, even by women viewers, if they were justified within the framework of the story being told.

The geographical location of violence in fictional programmes plays a significant part in mediating how it is perceived by television audiences. Violence appearing in American drama series tends to be regarded as more violent than similar kinds of portrayal in British-made dramas (Gunter, 1985). Furthermore, geographical location interacted with character-type to influence how violent portrayals were evaluated. Violence perpetrated by criminals was rated as more 'violent' than that perpetrated by law enforcers in American dramas, whereas these ratings were reversed for violent portrayals situated in British dramas.

The physical form of violence was examined in Chapter 4. It was observed at that point that viewers have been found to exhibit particular sensitivities to violent scenes which involve sharp stabbing instruments. Within the context of drama programming, audience research has shown that audience sensitivities to the form of violence become particularly acute in more realistic types of televised drama. Knife scenes are generally more upsetting to viewers than gun-fights or stylized fist-fights; they become even more so in contemporary fictional drama programmes (Gunter, 1985).

Morrisson's analysis provided yet another source of evidence about viewers' sensitivity to violence involving sharp instruments. The source of concern and the perspective from which anxieties about television scenes featuring such instruments of violence stemmed varied across viewers depending upon their own social environment. Morrisson illustrated this point by quoting one woman who expressed concerns about the lessons her grandchildren might learn from such violent portrayals as she saw on an episode of *Casualty*, but grudgingly accepted that there was a socially positive function in depicting the dangers a world full of sharp instruments posed to children. In contrast to this view, an Edinburgh man interviewed by Morrisson felt that in a world full of sharp instruments, the individuals who wield them should be shown the full effects on human flesh of stabbings and knifings. As Morrisson (1993b, p. 59) comments: 'it was the understanding of the world, through experience, that shaped the attitudes to violence on television'.

Before considering the implications of what is known about viewers' concerns and opinions, we should establish the profile of violent portrayals in television drama programmes and the characteristic forms it takes.

CHANNEL COMPARISONS: GENERAL VIOLENCE MEASURES

The analysis begins by examining general measures of television violence for drama programmes shown on different channels. No differentiation is made between different drama genres at this stage. The comparisons, in the next section of this chapter, which deal with levels of violence in different drama sub-genres, focus upon the terrestrial and non-movie satellite channels which are all characterized by broadcasting a range of different types of drama programme. The two satellite movie channels are excluded from the results because they showed primarily movies.

Across the four weeks of the analysis, nearly two-thirds of drama programmes containing violence were broadcast on the two satellite non-movie channels, Sky One and UK Gold. The single greatest contribution to violence-containing drama was made by UK Gold during the period covered by this study. On the terrestrial channels, violence was more likely to be found on ITV drama than anywhere else (see Table 9.1).

Having established the extent to which different channels transmitted violence-containing drama programmes, the next question is how much violence did these programmes contain. As before, violence levels can be expressed in terms of total numbers of violent acts and violent sequences carried by these programmes, average rates of occurrence of violent acts and sequences in the programmes, and the amount of programme time occupied by violence.

Table 9.1 Distribution of violence-containing drama programmes across channels

	n	%
BBC1	88	7.0
BBC2	64	5.1
ITV	138	10.9
Channel 4	81	6.4
Terrestrial	*371*	*29.4*
Sky One	142	11.2
UK Gold	237	18.8
Movie Channel	268	21.2
Sky Movies	246	19.5
Satellite	*893*	*70.6*
All channels	*1,264*	*100.0*

Note: Data aggregated over four weeks

There were 14,700 acts of violence coded in drama programmes on the eight channels being examined here, which together yielded over 7,300 violent sequences. Around three-quarters of this violence occurred on the four satellite channels, with slightly under one quarter occurring on the four terrestrial channels. The two movie channels contributed much of this violence, together containing over half of all violent acts and violent sequences. Among the terrestrial channels, ITV contained the greatest number of violent incidents (see Table 9.2).

Table 9.2 Total number of violent acts and violent sequences in programmes with violence

	Violent acts		Violent sequences	
	n	%	*n*	%
BBC1	836	5.7	390	5.3
BBC2	522	3.6	270	3.7
ITV	1,463	10.0	810	11.1
Channel 4	564	3.8	269	3.7
Terrestrial	*3,385*	*23.1*	*1,739*	*23.8*
Sky One	1,184	8.1	602	8.2
UK Gold	1,523	10.4	846	11.6
Movie Channel	4,011	27.3	2,000	27.3
Sky Movies	4,597	31.3	2,127	29.1
Satellite	*11,315*	*77.1*	*5,575*	*76.2*
All channels	*14,700*	*100.0*	*7,314*	*100.0*

Note: Data aggregated over four weeks

The markedly greater total number of violent acts and sequences in fictional drama programmes on the satellite channels than on the terrestrial channels, was further reflected in the margin of difference between these two sets of channels in terms of average numbers of separate incidents of violence in violence-containing programmes. The two satellite movie channels broadcast the most violent programmes in terms of average numbers of acts and sequences of violence per violence-containing programme. This is not too surprising, however, given that the average length of broadcasts on these two channels was greater than on the non-movie channels (see Table 9.3). The most violent drama, in terms of numbers of incidents, was found on Sky Movies (see Table 9.3).

Another indicator of the amount of violence contained by programmes is the volume of time occupied by violence. This can be expressed in terms of minutage and as a percentage of total programme running duration. Before turning to these figures, Table 9.4. indicates the average length of violent acts and violent sequences in drama programmes on different channels. Single acts of violence tended to last just over eight seconds in drama programmes across the eight channels. The average duration of violent acts was marginally greater in drama on the terrestrial channels than on the satellite

Table 9.3 Average number of violent acts and violent sequences in programmes with violence

	Violent acts	Violent sequences
BBC1	9.5	4.4
BBC2	8.2	4.2
ITV	10.6	5.9
Channel 4	7.0	3.3
Terrestrial	*8.8*	*4.5*
Sky One	8.3	4.2
UK Gold	6.4	3.6
Movie Channel	14.9	7.5
Sky Movies	18.6	8.6
Satellite	*12.1*	*6.0*
All channels	*10.5*	*5.2*

Note: Data aggregated over four weeks

Table 9.4 Duration of violent acts and violent sequences in programmes with violence

	Violent acts	Violent sequences
BBC1	7.0	14.9
BBC2	8.6	16.5
ITV	10.6	19.1
Channel 4	7.1	14.8
Terrestrial	*8.3*	*16.3*
Sky One	6.3	12.4
UK Gold	8.8	15.8
Movie Channel	7.5	15.0
Sky Movies	9.4	20.3
Satellite	*8.0*	*15.9*
All channels	*8.2*	*16.1*

Notes: 1 Data aggregated over four weeks
        2 Durations in seconds

channels. The longest acts of violence of all tended to occur on ITV drama, averaging just over ten seconds.

Violent sequences comprised either a single act of violence or two or more violent acts occurring in quick succession. On average, these tended to last for just over 16 seconds. The longest violent sequences were found to occur in movies shown on Sky Movies, with those occurring in the variety of fictional drama offerings on ITV in second place, averaging about one second per sequence less.

Turning to the amount of time that violent portrayals filled in drama programmes, over the four weeks of television broadcasts covered by this study, a total of 2,064.6 minutes of violence (34.4 hours) of violence were found in fictional drama programming. Over three-quarters of this (76%) occurred on the four satellite channels, with around one quarter (24%) occurring on the four terrestrial channels. The two movie channels contributed nearly six-tenths (59%).

Considered as a proportion of total drama programme output time, the amount of violence-occupied time is put into perspective. Violence occupied just over one and a half per cent of total fictional programme output time on these channels. The average proportion of drama output time filled with violence, however, was marginally greater on the satellite channels (1.4%) than on the four terrestrial channels (1.2%). The greatest proportion of total output time occupied by violence on drama among the terrestrials was found on ITV, and the smallest proportion occurred for Channel 4 (see Table 9.5). Over all channels, Sky Movies exhibited the largest amount of violence in terms of proportion of total fictional drama programme running time occupied by violence.

Table 9.5 Distribution of time occupied by violence in drama across channels

	Violence (minutes)	Violence as % of total output
BBC1	97.1	1.1
BBC2	74.5	1.2
ITV	258.2	1.8
Channel 4	66.3	0.7
Terrestrial	*496.1*	*1.2*
Sky One	124.8	0.9
UK Gold	223.4	0.9
Movie Channel	500.7	1.6
Sky Movies	719.6	2.2
Satellite	*1,568.5*	*1.4*
All channels	*2,064.6*	*1.3*

Note: Data aggregated over four weeks

LEVELS OF VIOLENCE IN DIFFERENT DRAMA GENRES

The general genre of 'drama' which has been referred to in this chapter actually comprised seven distinct categories of programming including cinema films, long-running and limited run drama series and serials and one-off dramas. Drama made in the UK was distinguished from that made abroad.

Turning first to the distribution of violent incidents across these genres, most of the violence ocurring in drama programmes was found in cinema films, which contained 70% of violent acts and 74% of violent sequences. Between one in four and one in three violent acts (29%) and violent sequences (26%) in televised drama actually occurred in drama that had been made for television. The major contributors to drama violence after cinema films were drama series and serials made outside the United Kingdom. Non-UK drama (14% of violent acts and sequences in televised drama) contained more violent incidents than did UK-made drama (9%). Made-for-TV films contributed just 1% of violent acts and violent sequences, while single plays contained a negligible amount.

Seventy-eight per cent of the time occupied by violence in televised drama occurred in cinema films. Across the remaining drama genres, non-UK series and serials contributed a larger proportion of violence-occupied time than did UK-made drama (13% versus 8%). One-off made-for-TV dramas, whether movies or plays, contributed a negligible amount of violence.

Cinema films, not surprisingly, averaged more violent acts and violent sequences than did other drama categories whenever they contained any violence. On average, cinema films with any violence contained 16.1 acts and 7.8 sequences of violence. Drama that had been made for television contained far fewer violent incidents in programmes which contained any violence at all. Non-UK drama and UK-made long-running serials which depicted any violence averaged between six and eight acts and between three and four sequences of violence. Made-for-TV movies (4.4 acts/2.4 sequences) and single plays (4.0 acts/3.7 sequences) exhibited somewhat lower average frequencies of violent acts and sequences.

There was some degree of variation in average rates of occurrence of violent incidents from one week to the next. Violent films contained more violent acts in week three (17.8) than in any other week. Non-UK long-running serials with violence contained more violent acts in weeks one (7.0) and three (6.2) than in weeks two (4.9) and four (5.2). Other non-UK series and serials with violence contained the greatest frequency violent acts during weeks two and three (9.0). The average violent acts tally for UK long-running serials with violence was lower in week four (4.8) than in the earlier three weeks analysed (6.3). Made-for-TV films scored a particularly high violent act average in week four (7.9), while single plays scored highest in week one (7.0).

The average violent cinema film contained two minutes and 18 seconds of violence. Limited run television series from overseas contained an average of one minute and six seconds of violence. All the remaining drama categories averaged less than one minute of violence in those programmes which contained any violence at all.

Channel differences in levels of violence in drama genres

To what extent did violence levels for different categories of drama vary across channels? Table 9.6 shows the distribution of violent acts and violent sequences by drama genres for six of the eight channels being compared in this chapter. The channels in focus here are those which offered a mixed array of sub-genres of fictional programming. The movie channels comprised only feature films among their drama programme offerings.

Table 9.6 Distribution of violent acts and violent sequences by drama genre and channel

	All %	BBC1 %	BBC2 %	ITV %	Ch.4 %	Sky One %	UK Gold %
Violent acts							
Cinema films	50	63	57	65	77	15	21
Non-UK long-run serials	19	12	19	9	10	49	13
Other non-UK series/ials	13	10	16	14	5	32	4
UK long-run serials	11	10	2	3	3	3	43
Other UK series/ials	7	4	5	8	1	1	20
Made-for-TV films	1	1	1	2	1	1	0
Single plays	*	*	*	0	2	0	0
Violent sequences							
Cinema films	46	54	59	58	75	20	19
Non-UK long-run serials	18	8	18	11	10	47	14
UK long-run serials	12	20	2	4	4	3	41
Other non-UK series/ials	8	6	7	10	1	1	20
Other UK series/ials	14	12	14	15	5	28	6
Made-for-TV films	*	*	*	2	1	1	0
Single plays	1	*	*	0	*	0	0

Note: * Less than 0.5%

Channel differences were apparent with respect to certain genres, which largely reflected differences between channels in programme composition. More than half of the violent acts in violent drama programmes on all terrestrial channels were found to occur in cinema films shown by these channels. More than half of all violent sequences on the terrestrial channels also occurred in cinema films, with the exception of BBC1. Two-thirds of violent acts on ITV drama and three-quarters on Channel 4 drama occurred in cinema films.

Table 9.7 Distribution of amount of time occupied by violence in different drama genres by channel

	All %	BBC1 %	BBC2 %	ITV %	Ch.4 %	Sky One %	UK Gold %
Cinema films	52	56	76	67	80	5	26
Non-UK long-run serials	19	17	12	9	6	55	13
UK long-run serials	8	5	1	1	2	2	35
Other non-UK series/ials	14	16	7	12	5	35	8
Other UK series/ials	7	5	4	11	4	2	18
Made-for-TV films	*	*	0	0	2	0	0
Single plays	*	*	*	0	*	0	0

Note: * Less than 0.5%

The two non-movie satellite channels exhibited a marked departure from the terrestrial channels in that most incidents of violence in violent programmes occurred in made-for-television drama series and serials rather than in cinema films. On Sky One, around eight out of ten violent acts and violent sequences occurred in non-UK series and serials. On UK Gold, UK-made series and serials accounted for more than six out of ten violent acts and violent sequences.

Cinema films contributed the greatest proportion of overall violence-occupied time in violence-containing drama programmes on every terrestrial channel. On UK Gold, cinema films contained less violence than UK-produced long-running series. On Sky One, movies were not a major genre. Most violence on this channel occurred in non-UK television series and serials (see Table 9.7).

Table 9.8 Average amount of violence (in minutes) in violence-containing programmes for different drama genres and channels

	All	BBC1	BBC2	ITV	Ch.4	Sky One	UK Gold
Cinema films	0.1	0.1	0.1	0.3	0.1	*	0.1
Non-UK long-run serials	0.2	0.1	0.1	0.1	*	0.4	0.2
UK long-run serials	0.1	*	0.0	0.1	*	*	0.6
Other non-UK series/ials	0.5	2.1	0.1	0.3	*	*	0.4
Other UK series/ials	0.1	0.1	*	0.2	*	0.1	0.0
Made-for-TV films	0.1	*	0.0	0.0	0.4	0.0	0.0
Single plays	*	*	*	0.0	*	0.0	0.0

Note: * Less than 0.05 minutes

In spite of the impression given by the violent act counts, on average violence-containing drama programmes contained relatively small amounts of violence. If violence occurred at all in most drama genres, including cinema films, it only filled around six to 12 seconds of time. The greatest amount of violence, in terms of time occupied, occurred in non-UK drama series or serials, for which violence-containing programmes average around 30 seconds of violence (see Table 9.8).

THE NATURE OF VIOLENCE

The nature of violence was examined in terms of its setting, the form it took, the motives or goals underlying it, its consequences for victims and the kinds of characters involved as either aggressors or victims. Identifying these features of violent acts is important in so far as it helps to define the 'quality' as well as the 'quantity' of violence analysed.

The setting of violence

Around half of all violent acts (50.3%) in dramatic fiction occurred in contemporary settings, during the 1980s or 1990s. One in four violent acts (25%) occurred in the fairly recent past (1900–1980). Relatively little violence was situated in the distant past (16.1%). One in 20 acts (5/1%), however, were located in the distant future. The latter setting was particularly prevalent for violence in dramatic fiction on Sky One (33.1% of violent acts in dramatic fiction on that channel), UK Gold (19.8%) and BBC2 (25.4%). Indeed, the latter channel exhibited the greatest variety of period settings for violence, with just one in four violent acts occurring in the present day (25.3%), and one third (33.3%) occurring in the recent past. This finding reflects the higher than average frequency of wartime dramas and science fiction dramas on BBC2, especially compared with other terrestrial channels.

The physical setting of violence was also examined in terms of the environment in which violence occurred and its geographical location. More than one in five (22.3%) of violent acts occurred in an inner city location. The next most likely locations after this were in either a rural setting (16.8%) or small town location (13.7%). Inner city violence was least likely to be depicted in dramatic fiction on BBC1 (9.5% of violent acts in dramatic fiction on that channel). The same channel, however, had a relatively high frequency of violent acts in a small town location (32.2%). Rural locations for violence in dramatic fiction were more frequently observed on Channel 4 (31.8%) and ITV (24.6%).

The geography of violence was dominated by the two principal sources of programmes, namely the United States and United Kingdom. More than one in two (52.7%) violent acts in dramatic fiction were set in a US location, compared with just under one in ten (9.9%) in a UK location. Violence in a US location was particularly prevalent on Channel 4 (69.8% of violent acts in dramatic fiction), Sky One (52.9%) and ITV (51.9%). Violence situated in the UK was more commonly found on UK Gold (50.6%) which specializes in re-runs of old British series. The third most popular earthly location for violence was Australia (6.6% of violent acts in dramatic fiction). Such violence was particularly prevalent on BBC2 (17.5%) and ITV (11.3%).

The fourth most likely location for violence after the USA, the UK and Australia was Europe (6.1%). Violence in some extra-terrestrial place in outer space was particularly commonplace on BBC2 (25.3%) and Sky One (22.3%). This finding reflects the greater than average frequency of science fiction series on these two channels.

The form of violence

Violent acts were classified according to the form they took and the types of weapons which were used. Fifty-three different categories were used to classify the physical form of violent acts and 48 different weapon categories were applied to provide a separate form classification. The ten most frequently occurring types of violent act in dramatic fiction programmes are listed below. This shows that six out of ten of all violent acts in dramatic fiction programmes were accounted for by just four types of violence: a character pushing or tripping another character, incidents involving shootings, scenes depicting punches being thrown, and verbal threats levelled by one character against another.

Top ten types of violence	Number of acts	Percentage of acts
1 Shootings	2,978	20.7
2 Push/trip	2,642	18.3
3 Punching	1,742	12.1
4 Verbal threat	1,371	9.5
5 Hit with object	1,181	8.2
6 Kick	749	5.2
7 Attempted violence	490	3.4
8 Slap	359	2.5
9 Stabbing	345	2.4
10 Throwing	309	2.1

The major categories of weaponry used in violence in many ways reflected the most prevalent forms of violence on dramatic fiction programmes. Around one in three violent acts involved the use of the hand or fist, which was easily the most frequently occurring type of 'weapon' of violence deployed in fictional drama. This was followed by the use of contemporary types of gun. In general, the most prevalent instruments of aggression on television drama were various parts of the body or different types of hand held guns.

Top ten types of weapons

		Number of acts	Percentage of acts
1	Fist/hand	4,356	30.2
2	Hand-gun	1,362	9.4
3	Sword	588	4.1
4	Various body parts	577	4.0
5	Machine gun	566	3.9
6	Kick with foot	562	3.9
7	Pistol	560	3.9
8	Rifle	540	3.7
9	Karate/martial arts	537	3.7
10	Throw/push	361	2.5

Scenes featuring sharp instruments

Scenes of violence featuring sharp instruments are known to cause many viewers particular concern (Gunter, 1985). Such incidents often bring the perpetrator and victim into close proximity opening the possibility of a stronger or more graphic focus on the victim's agony or distress in being threatened or actually harmed. A special analysis was carried out upon instances of violence in fictional drama programmes to examine not just the extent but perhaps more importantly the nature of violent scenes which featured the use of sharp instruments and victims being cut, slashed or stabbed. This analysis examined televised films and television drama productions as two separate sub-categories of dramatic fiction on television. It began by looking at the nature of scenes which featured knives or other sharp instruments of violence and then moved on to examine those scenes in which someone was stabbed.

A total of 1,145 violent acts were coded which involved the use of sharp instruments such as various kinds of knife, swords and hooks, of which 90% occurred in cinema films shown on television. In films, the major weapon forms were swords (55%), daggers (20%) and then various other forms of knife. In television drama productions, there were far fewer occurrences of swords (22%); most incidents involved various kinds of knife (76%).

The presence of a sharp instrument during an act of violence, however, did not necessarily mean that someone ended up being stabbed. In films, one in four scenes featuring a knife involved stabbings (25%). In many such scenes, though, the violence took on a different form with victims being shot (17%), punched (17%) or verbally abused in some way (17%). Even so, there were 255 acts of stabbing recorded in total in televised movies. In drama productions, 43 out of 120 violent acts (36%) which featured a sharp instrument resulted in someone being stabbed.

The extent of injuries caused by these violent acts varied. Under the general category of violent acts featuring a sharp instrument as a weapon, death occurred in 23% of cases in films and in 25% of cases in television dramas. It was much more likely in both types of broadcast that no one was hurt at all (45% in films and 41% in dramas). Throughout, minor injuries tended to outnumber serious injuries, although more markedly in dramas (18% against 9%) than in films (14% against 12%).

A further analysis focused on violent acts which comprised stabbing incidents. There were 298 of these incidents in films and 47 incidents in television dramas. These figures differ from the numbers of stabbings reported above under scenes which featured sharp instruments such as knives, swords and hooks. The reason for this is that some stabbing incidents did not involve any of the group of instruments subsumed under the aforementioned weapons category, such as sharp sticks, stakes, spears and lances. When an actual stabbing occurred, the outcome was much more likely to be serious for the victim. Death followed stabbings in the majority of cases (58% in films and 57% in dramas). Serious injuries outnumbered minor injuries in films (27% versus 11%) while serious and minor injuries were equally likely to occur following stabbings in television dramas (15% of instances in each case). It was quite rare for stabbing incidents to be shown with no physical injuries in either films (3%) or dramas (6%).

In films, stabbing incidents involved daggers (32%), hunting knives (11%) and swords (16%), but there were a variety of other sharp instruments involved as well. In television drama productions, the weapons which featured most prominently in stabbing incidents were daggers (40%) and swords (19%). Domestic knives were used in a few cases (6%). These scenes often occurred in contemporary settings. The single largest percentage of stabbing incidents occurred in contemporary settings in films (45%) and dramas (32%). Just over one in five stabbing incidents in films and dramas (21%) occurred in the recent past. Hence many of these violent events took place in settings with which viewers were most likely to identify. Otherwise in films such incidents were most likely to occur in the distant past (29%) with few occurring in the distant future (2%). In dramas, however, stabbing incidents were more commonplace in distant future settings (23%) than distant past settings (15%).

While many of these acts of violence were temporally proximal to viewers' everyday reality, they were much less often geographically proximal, with one in 20 such scenes ocurring in British locations in films and under one in ten (9%) in television dramas. These incidents were more likely to be situated in the United States (47% of cases in films and 30% of cases in dramas).

Most incidents of stabbing in movies (82%) occurred on the two satellite movie channels, Sky Movies and The Movie Channel. Just 13% of these incidents were found on the four terrestrial channels. With television drama productions, most stabbing incidents occurred on three channels, Sky One

(43%), ITV (26%) and UK Gold (23%). Few were found on BBC2 (6%) and Channel 4 (2%), and none at all on BBC1.

Motivational context of violence

Violent acts were classified in terms of their general motivational context and according to the specific goals of aggressors, where these features could be clearly identified. The general context in which violence occurred was labelled according to whether it represented an aspect of wartime conflict, civil strife or rioting, a criminal act, an act of law enforcement, an act of domestic violence, behaviour related to the defence of civil liberties, or other forms of interpersonal aggression.

In general across the television channels monitored, violence in dramatic fiction most frequently occurred in a criminally motivated context (28.0% of acts). This type of violence was especially prevalent in dramatic fiction on Sky One (33.3%) and ITV (32.9%) and was relatively infrequent on Channel 4 (6.8%) and BBC1 (15.5%). The second most likely context for violence involved some form of interpersonal aggression (24.9% of violent acts in dramatic fiction), other than criminal, law enforcement, military, public disturbance-related or domestic. General interpersonal violence which could not be more specifically classified in terms of the other codes was most prevalent on Channel 4 (46.3% of dramatic fiction violent acts). Together, criminal violence and general interpersonal aggression accounted for around one in two violent acts on dramatic fiction programmes. The line-up of motivational contexts was as follows:

Criminal act	28.0%
General interpersonal	24.9%
Upholding the law	9.4%
Defence civil liberties	6.7%
War, armed forces	5.1%
Domestic violence	2.5%
Civil strife, riots	2.3%
Other forms	18.4%
Cannot code	2.8%

Violence was less likely to be perpetrated by law enforcers (9.4% of violent acts) in dramatic fiction than by criminals. Violence used to uphold the law was especially likely to occur on Channel 4 (19.8% of acts) and UK Gold (16.7% of acts). Domestic violence was relatively infrequent in dramatic fiction contexts (2.5% of violent acts), but was much more likely than average to occur on BBC1 (8.6% of acts).

Aggressors' goals were classified into 11 types. The figure below shows how often each goal accounted for violence in dramatic fiction on television. Fictional violence was most often motivated by evil or purely destructive objectives (21.0% of acts), or by needs for self-preservation (16.5%) or personal ambition and power seeking (12.3%). Together these motives accounted for four and a half out of every ten acts of violence on dramatic fiction programmes. Violence linked to more positive motives such as upholding or defending the law (7.9%) or protecting society (4.0%) or the family home (8.0%) were less frequent. Special concern has been reserved for violence with sexual motives. This type of violence was found to occur in dramatic fiction on television at a very low level (around 1% of violent acts). The breakdown of aggressor goals in televised drama was as follows:

Evil/destructive	21.0%
Self-preservation	16.5%
Ambition/power	12.3%
Desire for money	8.1%
Protect family home	8.0%
Upholding the law	7.9%
Protect society	4.0%
Respect for law	1.9%
Sexual motives	1.1%
Religious motives	0.2%
Other motives	14.8%
Cannot code	4.1%

Sexually motivated violence

One area of special concern in terms of the nature of violence on television is where violence and sexual behaviour become intermingled. Violent forms of sexual conduct, most especially incidents of rape, represent a sensitive topic when portrayed on television both because they may be upsetting to women and because of their possible influences upon men's attitudes towards women (Linz *et al.*, 1987, 1988). Scenes of sexual violence in which women are depicted as victims can be a source of arousal to some men at the same time as being a source of disgust to women. Repeated exposure to such depictions among young men, for example, may produce shifts in attitudes towards alleged rapists and rape victims, with greater sympathy for the former and reduced sympathy for the latter being a typical result (Linz *et al.*, 1984). Much of the research has focused upon some of the most extreme forms of erotica and pornography, which is unlike material normally found on mainstream broadcast television. Nevertheless, scenes involving male violence against female victims which occur within a sexual context might be found in certain cinema films which are televised as well as some made-for-television dramas. Even in their milder forms, it is important to address the question of how often such scenes occur on television.

The current content analysis made a special point of including a number of codes for classifying the motivational context of violence on television. One of these codes referred to any incidents of violence which took place within a sexual context regardless of the gender of the perpetrator or victim in such incidents. A total of 164 violent acts were found in televised dramatic fiction which fell into this category, of which 136 (83%) occurred in films originally made for the cinema and 28 (17%) occurred in drama programmes (chiefly series or serials) made especially for television.

Contrary to what one might have expected, it was by no means the case that all perpetrators in such scenes were male or that all victims were female. Two-thirds of these violent acts in cinema films (66%) had a single male perpetrator, while in nearly three in ten cases (29%) the perpetrator of violence was a female. More than four in ten (43%) of victims were female, but a greater proportion (57%) were male. In drama series and serials, more than half (57%) of the perpetrators of violence classified as occurring within a sexual context were male, while nearly four in ten perpetrators (39%) were female. The characters involved in these scenes were generally young adults aged between 20 and 35 years or middle-aged adults aged between 36 and 65 years. Few of those involved in such incidents fell outside these age groups.

The gender involvement pattern is intriguing. It is important to look even more closely at the nature of the violence occurring in a sexual context to understand more about what was actually going on. In cinema films, for instance, more than three-quarters of these incidents (77%) either involved an interpersonal dispute or a domestic dispute of some kind. A minority (13%) took place within what was classified as a crime context. The incidents themselves appeared to cause only minor injuries to victims (45% of cases) rather than serious injuries (3%) or death (4%). Very often (40%) no physical injuries were apparent at all, while psychological scars (5%) were surprisingly rare. A similar pattern throughout occurred amongst the much smaller overall number of such incidents in drama programmes made especially for television.

Although the implied seriousness of 'sexually motivated' violence might lead one to believe that the nature of consequences of such incidents ought to be more severe, what becomes clear from an analysis of the types of violence represented by this category of incidents is that few of them involved actual depictions of rape. There were eight rape scenes catalogued in the coded cinema films (6% of sexually motivated violent scenes) and two rapes coded in drama programmes (7%). Other scenes within this general category were coded as involving pushing or tripping, slapping and verbal aggression, with some punches also being thrown on occasions. The picture which emerges therefore is that whilst some sexual abuse is depicted on mainstream television, it is a relative rarity for such scenes to portray violence which is carried through to its most terrible extremes.

Violence in a domestic context

Viewers' reactions to violence on television can be shaped significantly by the context in which violent portrayals occur. As a general rule the closer to everyday reality the setting of an on-screen violent incident, the more seriously it is likely to be perceived by members of the audience (Gunter, 1985). This is one of the reasons why any violence in popular soap operas is capable of producing a powerful audience response. It is not simply the contemporary setting of such programmes which may be important in this connection, but also the fact that much of the action takes place in domestic situations involving characters who may often be portrayed as closely involved with one another as well as being well known to the television audience. The real-life lessons which might be learned from portrayals which take place in fictional situations which bear a striking resemblance to actual situations in which members of the audience have, at some time, found themselves, may cause viewers to pay especially close attention to the action on screen. This may be as true among children as among adults (Gunter *et al.*, 1991). It is important therefore that any such portrayals are handled in a responsible fashion and are neither purely gratuitous nor play unnecessarily on viewers' anxieties or sensitivities.

The current content analysis coded television violence according to the context in which it occurred. Among the different context classifications applied was whether violent acts occurred in a domestic situation. In fictional drama programming, a total of 359 such acts of violence were catalogued, of which 280 (78%) occurred in cinema films shown on television. The remainder occurred in television drama productions. 'Domestic' violence can potentially occur in a number of settings. The most significant incidents for viewers, given the importance of the perceived reality of television portrayals in shaping viewers' reactions to television (Condry, 1989), are likely to be those which occur in contemporary settings. For cinema films, more than four in ten (45%) recorded incidents of domestic violence were set in the present day, with nearly one in four further incidents (24%) set in the recent past, which meant any time between 1900 and 1980. In television drama productions, there was a much stronger contemporary flavour to these portrayals, with three out of four (75%) being set in the present day.

Portrayals of domestic violence occurred across a number of different types of environment, both in cinema films and television dramas, including small towns (30% of film portrayals and 18% of drama portrayals), suburbia (19% and 25%), inner city settings (15% and 24%) and rural settings (14% and 10%). Geographically, however, American locations were predominant in movies (71% of cases), with a few also occurring in British locations (14%). In television drama productions, domestic violence was spread fairly evenly across American (34%), Australian (30%) and British (29%) locations. Many of these incidents occurred in contemporary soaps from overseas (49%) and the United Kingdom (17%). In terms of setting, therefore, incidents of domestic violence occurred across a variety of physical locations which could this have facilitated identification among many sectors of the audience. The geographical distribution of these incidents, however, indicated that they were more likely to be depicted in foreign locations than ones close to home.

Quite apart from where incidents of violence in a domestic context were shown to occur, other factors which may be important to the way audiences will react include the types of characters involved, the nature of the violence, and the seriousness of its outcomes for those involved. In cinema films, male characters were somewhat more likely to be aggressors (69% of cases) than victims (62%), while female characters were slightly more likely to be victims (33%) than aggressors (28%). Even so, males were generally much more likely to be involved in domestic violence than women. The pattern of violence located in domestic settings therefore is not one dominated by the victimization of women. The latter pattern, when it occurs, is often associated with sexually motivated overtones. An analysis of aggressors' motives, however, indicated that sexual motives were by no means the major factor underlying many of these incidents. In cinema films, just one in ten incidents of domestic violence (10%) were classified as being associated with sexual motives. Other motives included purely evil or destructive objectives (18%), protection of the family (15%) and self-preservation (10%). Within television drama productions, the major occurring objectives which characterized aggressors' actions were protection of the family (23%), self-preservation (13%), money (13%), and evil (13%). There were just two instances recorded of violence in a domestic setting which was apparently motivated by sexual objectives (3%).

The form which violence takes is known to influence viewers' perceptions of its seriousness (Gunter, 1985). Scenes which depict close-in violence, particularly where sharp instruments are involved, together with scenes which clearly cause the victim visible distress, are especially likely to worry viewers. Within cinema films, scenes of domestic violence comprised mainly instances of one character pushing (26%), punching (15%), or slapping (11%) another, or hitting them with an object (11%). In television drama productions, pushing (37%) was an even more prominent manifestation of violence, with many more of these scenes comprising only verbal aggression (24%). There were far fewer instances of punching (5%) in a domestic setting in television drama productions than were noted in televised movies.

Manifestations of violence in domestic settings which might potentially cause audiences more serious concern were rare. In televised movies, for instance, there were four incidents which involved one character trying to strangle another, three which involved stabbings and one scene which depicted rape. In television drama serials and series, there were two instances of strangulation and one which involved a stabbing. In most cases in film portrayals of domestic violence, there was either no injury caused to victims (40%) or only minor injuries occurred (40%). In television drama productions, more than half the scenes of domestic violence resulted in no visible injury to any character (53%), while in most other incidents in which an outcome could be clearly recognized, the consequences tended to be mild (28%). In the movies that were coded, 28 incidents (9%) of domestic violence resulted in the death of a character, while in television drama productions, there were just two instances of someone dying in this context.

Consequences of violence

An analysis of the consequences of violence examined the extent to which violent acts resulted in visible harm to victims and the degree of harm caused. Thus, the consequences of violence were classified in terms of the most extreme or dire outcome for victims, such as death, mutilation, broken bones or serious wounds, to less severe outcomes such as minor wounds, being stunned or bruised. Evidence of psychological damage to victims was also logged.

Violence was more likely to result in mild physical consequences (34.9% of acts) than severe physical injuries (22.9%). Among the mild injury categories, violence was much more likely to result in victims being stunned or bruised rather than ending up with cuts or wounds. Among the severe consequences of violence, the most likely outcome for victims of violence was their death. More than one in ten acts of violence featured in fictional drama programmes produced the victim's death.

Psychological damage to victims of violence was depicted fairly rarely in fictional drama programmes (2% of acts). In around one in three acts, however, there were no observable harmful consequences to victims of violence.

Injury consequences of violence on dramatic fiction programmes	Percentage of acts
Severe physical injuries	
Death	15.5
Serious wound	6.6
Mutilation	0.5
Broken limbs	0.3
Mild physical injuries	
Being stunned	14.4
Bruises	8.3
Minor wound	12.2
Psychological	2.0
Other injuries	3.3
No injury	34.4
Not codable	2.4

Not all channels exhibited the same pattern of injury consequences to victims of violence in dramatic fiction. Death was more likely than average to follow violent acts on ITV (12.3%) and UK Gold (11.4%), and less likely than average to follow violence shown on Channel 4 (5.6%), BBC2 (6.1%) and Sky One (8.9%). On average, mild forms of injury outcome such as being stunned, bruised or slightly wounded accounted for 36.6% of violent act outcomes. Mild injuries were, however, far more prevalent on BBC2 than anywhere else (51.8% of violent acts on dramatic fiction on that channel). This was somewhat counterbalanced by the fact that BBC2 was the channel least likely to show violence with no injury outcomes (27.8% of acts).

A more subjective classification of violence in terms of its outcomes was based upon ratings of how much blood, pain and horror resulted from violent acts. Each violent act was rated on a five-point scale on each of these three attributes, where a score of 1 represented negligible amounts of blood, pain or horror and a score of 5 represented extreme degrees of bleeding, pain and horror. On dramatic fiction programmes in general, nearly three out of four violent acts (73.7%) were found to depict no bleeding, while well over half depicted no pain consequences (57.3%) or horror (58.6%). At the other end of the scale, no violent acts emerged with a rating of '5' for blood, while fewer than half a per cent of acts were rated as depicting the most extreme degree of pain (0.4%) and horror (0.1%).

Violence featuring extreme degrees of pain and suffering on the part of victims was found on three channels in particular: BBC2 (2.4% of acts), ITV (0.2%) and Sky One (0.6%). Extreme degrees of horror with violence were restricted to the satellite channels, Sky One (0.2%) and UK Gold (0.1%).

Aggressors and victims

The characters involved in violence as aggressors or victims were classified according to their demography and an extensive typology which focused upon their occupational or professional group or dramatic role. Most aggressors on fictional drama were males, acting either on their own or in a group, young adults or middle-aged adults and of white US or UK origin. As Table 9.9 shows, only around one in ten violent acts were perpetrated by female characters. Violence was rarely perpetrated by children or teenagers, and black aggressors were also a rarity compared with white aggressors.

Turning to the demography of victims of violence, the character types who featured most often as aggressors tended also to figure most commonly as victims. Thus, it was certainly not the case that females, young people or the elderly, or non-whites were being singled out for disproportionate victimization.

Character profiles in dramatic fiction were classified further in terms of 57 different categories of character type. The top ten aggressor types and victim types are shown below.

Outside of the general, catch-all category of 'situation character', which refers to regularly occurring characters or featured characters not otherwise defined or definable in terms of occupation or other specific role-type, the perpetrators of violence in dramatic fiction were dominated by agents of law enforcement or criminals, and the miltary. Period aggressors who also figured quite prominently were cowboys and outlaws or pirates. This pattern underlines the prominence of the good-guy versus bad-guy scenario, together with roles that are clearly defined in terms of whether they are on the side of right or wrong.

Table 9.9 Character demography of aggressors and victims

| | 1994/95 | | | | 1986 | | | |
| | Aggressors | | Victims | | Aggressors | | Victims | |
	n	%	n	%	n	%	n	%
Gender								
One male	9,534	76.3	9,365	65.2	702	53.1	776	58.7
One female	1,561	12.5	1,507	10.5	91	6.9	132	10.0
Group male	218	1.7	1,680	11.7	291	22.0	343	18.4
Group female	39	0.3	33	0.2	5	0.4	8	0.6
Group mixed	318	2.5	774	5.4	43	3.3	72	5.4
Other	46	0.4	49	0.3	14	1.1	15	1.1
Cannot code	784	6.3	957	6.7	177	13.4	67	5.1
Age								
Child (up to 12)	238	1.7	246	1.7	8	0.6	13	1.0
Teenager (13–19)	536	3.7	458	3.2	13	1.0[a]	25	1.9[a]
Young adult (20–35)	8,141	56.6	7,606	52.9	514	38.9[a]	605	45.7[a]
Middle-aged (36–65)	3,567	24.8	3,572	24.9	384	29.0	391	29.6
65 plus	108	0.8	103	0.7	4	0.3	6	0.5
Mixed age group	440	3.1	1,042	7.3	—	—	—	—
Cannot code	1,358	9.4	1,341	9.3	400	30.2	283	21.4
Ethnic origin								
White UK	1,575	10.9	1,539	10.7	274	20.7	304	23.0
White US	6,825	47.3	6,679	46.5	472	35.7	513	38.8
White other	2,218	15.4	2,044	14.2	282	21.3	319	24.1
Black UK	34	0.2	39	0.3	2	0.2	—	—
Black US	624	4.3	593	4.1	23	1.7	19	1.4
Black other	150	1.0	147	1.0	8	0.6	11	0.8
Asian	209	1.5	221	1.5	1	0.1	1	0.1
Oriental	578	4.0	629	4.4	18	1.4	15	1.1
Mixed group	549	3.8	712	5.0	23	1.7	28	2.1
Other human	286	2.0	238	1.7	25	1.9	27	2.0
Animal	242	1.7	254	1.8	16	1.2	11	0.8
Cannot code	1,104	7.7	1,279	8.9	179	13.5	16	1.2

Note: [a] Age groups were different in 1986 from those used in 1994/95: 13–19s were compared with 13–16s in 1986; 20–35s compared with aggregated 17–28 and 26–35 age groups from 1986.

Turning to the victims of violence, criminal types featured prominently again. Although plain-clothes police officers made an appearance among the top ten victim types, there were in fact far fewer police victims than aggressors. The opposite was true for criminals. This signals a general theme of justice prevailing in televised drama. Although criminals tend to be the bad

Top ten aggressor types

		Number of acts	Percentage of acts
1	Situation character	2,983	20.7
2	Criminal – serious	1,731	12.0
3	Police – plain clothes	818	5.7
4	Armed forces	781	5.4
5	Cowboy	654	4.5
6	Criminal – petty	625	4.3
7	Outlaw – pirate	497	3.4
8	Professional person	437	3.0
9	Domestic character	392	2.7
10	Police – uniformed	341	2.4

Top ten victim types

		Number of acts	Percentage of acts
1	Situation character	3,245	22.5
2	Criminal – serious	1,360	9.4
3	General public	777	5.4
4	Criminal – petty	696	4.8
5	Armed forces	646	4.5
6	Cowboy	593	4.1
7	Professional person	567	3.9
8	Police – plain clothes	551	3.8
9	Domestic character	392	2.7
10	Inanimate object	349	2.4

guys and will use violence if necessary to achieve their ends, ultimately or at some point, they are likely to be on the receiving end.

The general pattern to emerge from among the top ten aggressor and victim types analysis was that character-types who featured prominently as aggressors also featured prominently as victims of violence. In other words, many of those who get involved in violence are likely, in the world of televised fiction, to feel the effects of violence as well as being the ones to dish it out.

THE MOST VIOLENT FILMS AND DRAMAS ON TV

Using the criteria of numbers of violent acts and programme running time (in minutes) occupied by violence, the 20 most violent cinema films shown on television and the 20 most violent made-for-TV dramas broadcast during the period of monitoring were identified. These top 20 listings are shown in Tables 9.10 to 9.13. These two measurement criteria yielded two quite different top 20 listings. Just five movies appeared in both top 20 cinema film lists and seven TV drama programmes appeared in both top 20 drama lists.

For both movie lists, however, entries were comprised mainly of movies broadcast on the two satellite movie channels, Sky One and The Movie Channel. Seventeen out of the top 20 movies on each list had appeared on these two channels. The rest of each list was made up of movies shown on ITV and Sky One.

In spite of the different entries on each list, both lists were headed by the same movie, *Karate Kop*, which was shown on The Movie Channel. This film contained 171 acts of violence covering 19.5 minutes of programme running time. The cut-off point for entry into the top 20 listings was 60 violent acts and 10.5 minutes of violence. In the case of the TV drama programmes listings, however, each list was headed by a different programme. An episode of *Dr Who* headed the violent acts list, while an episode of *Highlander*,

Table 9.10 The 20 most violent cinema films in terms of violent acts

Film	Channel	Violent acts	Violence minutage	Violent sequences
Karate Kop	Movie Channel	171	19.5	16
Teenage Ninja Turtles	Movie Channel	142	9.8	69
Teenage Ninja Turtles	Movie Channel	142	9.8	69
Pray for Death	Sky Movies	120	6.3	30
Out for Justice	Sky One	112	3.4	65
Double Impact	Sky Movies	105	8.9	40
Braindead	Movie Channel	102	15.2	17
No Retreat, No Surrender	Movie Channel	99	14.1	35
American Cyborg Steel Warrior	Movie Channel	95	10.4	36
At the Earth's Core	Movie Channel	93	8.9	47
Ghayal	ITV	88	12.8	16
Timebomb	Movie Channel	84	4.5	20
Hard to Kill	Movie Channel	78	6.4	13
The King's Whore	Movie Channel	63	2.9	3
Hidden 2: The Spawn	Sky Movies	63	10.0	30
Kickboxer	Movie Channel	62	11.4	20
The Wild Bunch	ITV	61	18.0	36
Hook	Movie Channel	60	11.9	28
Trespass	Movie Channel	60	13.6	33
Operation Kid Brother	Movie Channel	60	6.2	25

Table 9.11 The 20 most violent cinema films in terms of violence minutage

Movie	Channel	Violence minutage	Violent acts	Violent sequences
Karate Kop	Movie Channel	19.5	171	16
The Wild Bunch	ITV	18.0	61	36
Midnight Ride	Movie Channel	17.6	51	25
Jersey Girl	Sky Movies	16.7	39	18
Rollerball	ITV	16.0	44	22
The Bear	Movie Channel	15.6	34	23
Braindead	Movie Channel	15.2	102	17
No Retreat, No Surrender	Movie Channel	14.1	99	35
Trespass	Sky Movies	13.6	60	33
The Pirates of Blood	Sky Movies	13.6	21	14
Toys	Movie Channel	13.5	13	9
Live and Let Die	Movie Channel	13.3	55	27
Ghayal	ITV	12.8	88	16
The 7th Voyage of Sinbad	Sky Movies	12.5	46	46
Hook	Sky Movies	11.9	60	28
Article 99	Movie Channel	11.6	6	6
Kickboxer	Movie Channel	11.4	62	20
Rage and Honour	Sky Movies	11.3	56	26
The King's Pirate	Sky Movies	10.8	20	11
Star Wars	Sky Movies	10.5	39	25

Table 9.12 The 20 most violent TV dramas in terms of violent acts

Programme	Channel	Violent acts	Violence minutage	Violent sequences
Dr Who	UK Gold	45	7.8	30
Blake 7	UK Gold	40	7.8	23
Micky Spillane's Mike Hammer	Sky One	38	3.3	22
Young Indiana Jones	BBC1	35	5.2	10
The Man From Uncle	BBC1	34	8.5	14
Buck Rogers	BBC2	33	2.0	12
The Wanderer	Sky One	32	2.2	14
Bandolen	ITV	31	8.9	12
Dr Who	UK Gold	30	5.8	5
Casualty	BBC1	29	0.6	20
Star Trek	Sky One	29	1.2	13
Star Trek	Sky One	29	1.2	13
Bergerac	UK Gold	28	1.7	8
Kung Fu	Sky One	27	1.4	12
The Man From Uncle	BBC1	27	5.3	14
Miami Vice	UK Gold	27	6.6	17
B L Stryker	ITV	26	2.1	10
Rowen	Sky One	24	1.8	3
The Little Picture	ITV	24	2.7	16
The Man From Uncle	BBC1	23	0.9	13

Table 9.13 The 20 most violent TV dramas in terms of violence minutage

Programme	Channel	Violence minutage	Violent acts	Violent sequences
Highlander	Sky One	9.4	12	1
Bandolen	ITV	8.9	31	12
The Man From Uncle	BBC1	8.5	34	14
Blake 7	UK Gold	7.8	40	23
Dr Who	UK Gold	7.8	45	30
Miami Vice	UK Gold	6.6	27	17
Barney Miller	Sky One	6.5	2	1
A Country Practice	ITV	6.1	4	2
Tour of Duty	ITV	5.9	17	11
Dr Who	UK Gold	5.8	30	5
The Fall Guy	ITV	5.7	19	9
Dr Who	UK Gold	5.5	9	4
The Man From Uncle	BBC1	5.3	27	14
Young Indiana Jones	BBC1	5.2	35	10
Bergerac	UK Gold	4.4	18	8
Dr Who	UK Gold	3.9	16	13
The Rockford Files	BBC1	3.9	4	2
Star Trek	Sky One	3.8	19	12
Mike Hammer	Sky One	3.3	38	22
The Little Picture	ITV	2.7	24	16

the American series, headed the violence minutage list. The *Dr Who* episode was placed in sixth position in terms of violence minutage and the *Highlander* episode did not feature in the top 20 violent acts listing because its violence was concentrated in fewer but longer violent incidents.

A closer examination of both these listings confirms, once again, that different quantitative measures of violence may reflect quite distinct patterns of violence within a specific movie or television programme. In particular, the top 20 listings by violence amount for cinema films and TV dramas both illustrate that programmes with similar amounts of violence in terms of programme running time occupied by violent action may exhibit significant degrees of variation in terms of how many separate violent incidents were contained within them. In the cinema films list, for instance, the amount of violence varied between 19.5 minutes and 10.5 minutes for entries in first and twentieth position. These same 20 movies exhibited a range of between six and 171 violent acts. In the TV drama listing, the range in terms of minutage of violence was 9.4 minutes for the first placed programme to 2.7 minutes for the last placed programme in the list. In terms of violent acts count, these programmes exhibited a range of variation from a low of two acts to a high of 45 acts of violence. Indeed, the twentieth placed programme contained more violent acts than the first placed programme.

Together the programmes in each top 20 listing accounted for a marked proportion of all the violent acts and violence minutage in televised cinema films and drama programmes. The top 20 cinema films in terms of violent acts count contained a total of 1,912 violent acts, averaging 95.6 acts per programme. These movies accounted for 16.9% of all the violent acts in coded cinema films. The top 20 listing for cinema films by violence minutage contained a total of 4.75 hours of violence between them, averaging 14.3 minutes of violence per movie. Together these 20 movies accounted for 17.6% of all the violence minutage across coded cinema films.

The top 20 listed drama programmes in terms of violent acts contained a total of 628 acts of violence, averaging 31.4 acts per programme. These programmes accounted for 18.6% of all violent acts coded in drama programmes. The top 20 listing of drama programmes in terms of violence minutage contained a total of 2.1 hours of violence, averaging 6.4 minutes per programme. These programmes accounted for 28.8% of all violence minutage coded in drama programmes.

Most violent programmes – programme context

Some of the most violent programmes analysed in this study were singled out for a more detailed assessment of the overall context in which violence occurred. In Chapter 1, for example, it was noted that the amount of violence a programme contains tells only part of the story. From the perspective of how viewers respond to violence on television, it is important to look at the context in which it occurs and the style in which it is presented.

The most violent programme shown during the four weeks coded, in terms of number of violent acts, was *Karate Kop* which contained 171 acts of violence divided into 16 sequences, which in total occupied 19.5 minutes of programme running time. This film was shown on Sky Movies at midnight on 22 October 1994. The majority of the violence in the film was related to karate-style fighting with the body used as a weapon. The types of violence comprised kicking (12.5% of acts), punching (15.3%), pushing or tripping (19.4%), slapping (1.4%) and throwing (6.9%). Shooting accounted for 13.9% of all the violent acts. Thus, the fist or hand, the foot or other body part accounted for around two-thirds (65.4%) of all 'weapons' used, with guns accounting for just under one in four acts (23.6%).

In keeping with the type of weapons used and the type of violent acts enacted, the film was mainly comprised of highly stylized choreographed karate-style fighting. Many acts of violence would occur within the same sequence which accounts for the high violent acts count, but relatively low number of sequences coded. Although deaths occurred in the film (13.9% of acts), the majority of injuries were mild, comprising either bruising (47.2%) or no physical injury (19.4%). The majority of the acts of violence were coded as being very mild in terms of the amount of blood shown (91.7% coded with no blood; 88.9% coded with no pain or only mild reactions; and 86.1% coded as innocuous in terms of horror). Although this film was the most violent in terms of numbers of violent acts and contained nearly 20 minutes of violence, it did not contain violence which could be categorized as serious in terms of known problematic attributes.

Out for Justice, a film shown on Sky Movies at 10.00 pm on 20 January 1995, was coded as the fifth most violent programme shown during the four weeks analysed. It contained 106 violent acts, divided into 65 sequences, but accounting for only 3.4 minutes of violence. In contrast to *Karate Kop* the violent acts in this film occurred in short sequences, with the violence therefore permeating the entire film. The hero, played by Steven Seagal, is depicted wishing to avenge the death of his fellow police officer and best friend. He begins a campaign against the perpetrator, who has taken so many drugs that he has ceased to be rational. The viewer is witness immediately to several random killings by this individual.

The violence in *Out for Justice* is often extremely graphic. In one scene the hero pins a man up against a wall using a meat cleaver which he sticks into his hand. The victim is left screaming and impaled throughout the whole of the next scene, during which the hero violently dispatches several more men.

The fight scenes in this film were therefore very violent, often destroying the environment in which they took place. Shootings were accompanied by large volumes of blood, either spurting from the victims or splashed on walls or car windows. Some of the scenes in the film might be judged to have contained gratuitous displays of violence, for example in the climactic scene which involved a fight between the hero and the main villain in a kitchen. The hero hit the villain many times with his fists, kicked him, threw him violently around the room smashing furniture, pushed him head first through a window, retrieved him, hit him hard over the head with a frying pan and violently stuck a sharp kitchen utensil in the villain's forehead finally killing him. He then shot him three times in the chest. The final shooting was an act of disdain and anger, which was also somewhat pointless given that the villain was already dead.

American Cyborg: Steel Warrior (Global Pictures Production) was shown on Sky Movies at 11.05 pm on 25 October 1994 and was ranked as the tenth most violent programme over the four weeks analysed. The film was set in Charleston, South Carolina in the future, 17 years after a nuclear war. People had been herded into cities which were run like prisons by a computer. The infertile population were left to live and die in these cities where humanoid computers called Cyborgs worked for the system as enforcers of order. The Cyborgs were invincible killing machines, very strong, leatherclad and immune to bullets and weapons. The main focus of the film was on a young woman who, unlike the rest of the population, had the ability to bear children. She had to smuggle her foetus (contained in a bell jar) to Europe where it would be taken care of. A Cyborg has been assigned to destroy them both.

Generally, encounters with a Cyborg resulted in death and there were many human casualties in this film. Throughout the film, killing was casual and unemotional. The young woman was befriended by a man who unbeknown to her or to himself, is also a Cyborg. The majority of the fight scenes were between the hero and the Cyborg. As both were strong and invincible the majority of the violent scenes were improbable and bizarre. On one occasion, for example, a heavy weight was dropped onto the Cyborg which recovered immediately. When the Cyborg was shot or stabbed, it emitted a white fluid and was immediately healed.

A violent incident which was coded as extreme in terms of its horror value and pain value occurred during a fight between the hero (not known to be a Cyborg at this stage of the film) and the Cyborg pursuer. The Cyborg ripped the hero's arm off. Initially the viewers (and the hero) were unaware that he was not human. He bled a little and his flesh was shown red and torn. After several seconds, the hero discovered a wire protruding from his arm and realized that he was a machine. At that point, the scene lost much of its original horror value. For those fight scenes involving machines therefore the horror was diminished by knowing that they were incapable of being harmed. In contrast, a scene in which a Cyborg used a knife to pin a human to a wall by his hand leaving him screaming in pain, was potentially more likely to invoke a stronger affective reaction from viewers.

SUMMARY AND CONCLUSIONS

Violence in television drama was more prevalent and greater in quantity than for other major television genres. More than 3,300 separate acts of violence were catalogued in drama programmes, occupying over seven hours (or just over 3%) of drama programming running time over the four terrestrial and two satellite non-movie channels.

This violence was more likely to be situated in the present day than any other time period. Violence in the past was more likely than violence in the future. Thus, violence was most likely to occur in a temporal setting which audience research has shown to induce the greatest degree of audience involvement (Gunter, 1985). Environmentally and geographically, violence was found mainly in inner city and American locations. Alternatively, it was likely to occur in rural or small town settings, geographically located in Britain if not in the United States. Thus, violence in drama programmes tends to be most often located in the kind of environment, namely inner cities, where viewers have the greatest fears about real life violence and perceive the greatest risk (Gunter, 1988).

The finding that violence in American settings was more prevalent than that in British settings is probably a more positive result, given the kinds of differences which normally emerge in viewers' perceptions of violence in these two locations. British viewers tend to regard American crime drama series as more violent though as less realistic in certain respects than violence in genre equivalents made in Britain (Gunter and Wober, 1988). Thus, the predominant geographical setting for violence on television drama is not the one about which viewers generally show the greatest concern. This is not to say, however, that viewers never find violence in American settings offensive or distressing; clearly there are certain types of portrayal (e.g., stabbings) which they are concerned about wherever they might occur.

The major physical forms of violence did not include ones which are known to cause viewers greatest anxiety. The most commonly occurring physical forms of violence involved someone pushing or tripping somebody else, a protagonist punching a victim, verbal threats and various kinds of shooting involving the use of guns. There were 46 instances of stabbing, accounting for a little over 1% of all violent acts in drama programmes, and 23 instances of strangulation (less than 1% of all acts).

The motivational context of violence in television drama most often comprised criminal activity or arguments between two individuals. Domestic violence, of the sort that viewers, and especially women, are concerned about (Morrisson, 1993b), was rare, amounting to just over 2% of violent acts. Sexually motivated violence was even rarer. Here there were just 26 incidents classified as sexually motivated violence, or less than 1% of violent acts in drama programmes during the weeks monitored.

The degree of injury, pain and suffering caused to victims has an important influence on how viewers respond to television violence. Violent scenes featuring greater amounts of victim suffering are found more disturbing (Gunter, 1985). In the present analysis, mild injuries outweighed serious injuries. If serious consequences did follow from dramatic violence, however, it was more likely to result in death than severe wounding or mutilation of victims.

The character profile of those involved in violent scenes, either as aggressors or victims, indicated that both perpetrators and victims of violence were most likely to be young adults, white and male. Children and the elderly were rarely involved in violence. Females appeared as aggressors in around one in ten violent acts, but were slightly more likely to be victims. The ratio of being a perpetrator to being a victim for different demographic and occupational groups of characters, revealed that some groups were more likely to be victimized than others, despite any differences in their overall frequency of involvement in violence.

Although involved in violence far more frequently than females, whether as perpetrators or victims, once they are involved, males are less likely to be victims (aggressor:victim ratio = 1.06) than females (aggressor:victim ratio = 0.89). Similarly, although rarely involved overall, once they were involved, teenagers had a higher probability of being victims than aggressors (0.89) compared with young adults (1.05). Ethnic origin of characters in television drama was linked to likelihood of victimization. Whites were generally far more likely to appear in violent scenes, whether as aggressors or victims, than were blacks. Yet, once involved, their respective aggressor to victim ratios indicated a higher probability of blacks being victimized (0.89) than of whites being victimized (1.01).

Similar comparisons were made between police involvement and criminal involvement in violence either as aggressors or victims. In the case of uniformed police (1.82), plain clothes police (1.31), serious criminals (1.43) and petty criminals (1.07), all were more likely to feature as aggressors than as victims of violence. Uniformed police, overall, fared better than plain clothes police, and serious criminals fared better than petty criminals.

In terms of the sheer volume of violence, as quantified by violent acts and violence minutage, the most violent cinema films on television occurred almost entirely on the subscription movie channels broadcast by satellite. Eighteen out of the 20 most violent films in terms of numbers of violent acts and 17 out of 20 of the most violent films in terms of violence minutage, were on the two movie channels. The exceptions were films shown on ITV. On the movie channels, the most violent cinema films tended mainly to fall into the martial arts and horror genres. The remainder were made up of films from the futuristic, Bond and fantasy genres. A similar analysis among dramas made for television revealed that the most violent programmes derived principally from such fictional sub-genres as contemporary crime-drama and science fiction.

It is not simply the sheer amount of violence that is significant, of course, particularly if one's ultimate concern is with the reactions of viewers. The audience's sensitivities might be aroused by a single act of violence, depending upon the nature and form it takes, and the context in which it occurs. Contextually, the motives and setting of violence can be highly significant mediators of audience reaction (Gunter, 1985; Kunkel *et al.*, 1996). Among the types of violence about which there has been particular concern are those which occur in domestic settings, which are sexually motivated, and which involve the use of sharp instruments, such as knives. In the current analysis, sexually-motivated violence was quite rare, though more likely to be found in feature films than in dramas made for television. Among scenes of sexually motivated violence, just ten scenes (eight in feature films and two in televised drama programmes) were classified as depicting rape. Other scenes did not go as far as actual rape, although they might have involved some form of physical aggression between male and female actors in which one character, usually the female, was punched, slapped or pushed around. In a smaller number of instances of sexually motivated violence (4%) the victim was killed, though very often (40% of cases) the victim appeared to survive unhurt.

Media researchers have argued about the merits or de-merits of depicting the full consequences of violence on television. The depiction of painful consequences of televised violence can result in viewers perceiving the violence in more serious terms, as being more violent and more upsetting (Gunter, 1985). Media effects research has indicated that displaying painful consequences of violence and the victim's suffering may dampen the enthusiasm of observers to behave aggressively themselves, even when provoked (Baron, 1971a, b; Goranson, 1969; Schmutte and Taylor, 1980). Although not wanting to upset viewers unduly, the effects evidence suggests that it may be better to show the full consequences of violence if it puts people off behaving more violently themselves.

It is known that violence close to home may worry viewers more than other kinds (Gunter, 1985). There is therefore special reason to be concerned about any violence that occurs in a dramatized domestic setting, particularly when it features the kind of home environment with which many viewers could identify. A total of 359 violent acts were coded as occurring in a domestic setting, most of which occurred in cinema films. Of the 89 incidents which occurred in made-for-television productions, 25 were found in UK series and serials. Thus, while some domestic violence was portrayed in British settings, most of it was not.

Violence manifested itself in the domestic context in a variety of forms, but tended most often to involve one character pushing, slapping or punching another. The victims in these incidents were proportionately more likely to be female, while the aggressors were most likely to be male. Incidents of more serious forms of violence in domestic settings, such as strangulation (four incidents), stabbings (three incidents), and rape (one incident) were fairly rare.

The form of violence is important in its own right, regardless of the setting or context in which it occurs. Viewers have been found to reserve special concern for any violence featuring a sharp instrument. While 1,145 violent acts were catalogued which involved sharp instruments, which seems like a large number, it is important to break down this figure in terms of types of instruments actually deployed. First of all, the great majority of such incidents (90%) occurred in cinema films. The major weapon types here were swords and daggers, with the setting being historical rather than contemporary. In programmes made originally for television, occurrences of sword fights were much less common, while many more incidents, proportionally, involved the use of a knife. The knife appears to be the form of violence which bothers viewers most of all. While it could be said that there is room for a reduction in scenes involving use of a knife, it was relatively rare for such scenes to be compounded with other attributes of violence known to be problematic in terms of audience reaction. The use of knives was rare in domestic settings, and, although many were contemporary, they were more likely to be situated in geographically remote rather than proximal locations. In conclusion, violence in fictional drama on television in Britain occurs in many different forms and situations. The types of violence known to be most problematic in the context of invoking undesirable and unwelcome audience reactions, tended to be relatively rare.

10 Violence in light entertainment

One of the key functions of television is to provide its audiences with entertainment. Among British viewers, being entertained is one of the main reasons given for watching (Gunter *et al.*, 1994). While entertainment is a gratification which can be obtained from drama and factual programmes, it is a feature associated in its purest form with that category of television output called light entertainment. This category includes situation comedies, quiz and game shows, variety and music shows and talk or chat shows. Other special events, family or people shows and cartoons made for adults can also be included.

Light entertainment programmes do not represent a section of television's output normally associated with the portrayal of violence. Indeed, some media researchers have questioned whether the concept of violence strictly applies in the context of television comedy or light entertainment portrayals (Morrisson, 1993a). Nevertheless, violence, in one form or another, can occur in comedy contexts as in the case of slapstick humour typified best by programmes such as *The Benny Hill Show, Blackadder, Fawlty Towers* or *Mr Bean*. While audiences may not take such portrayals seriously, taken within the frame of reference adopted by the current content analysis study, any such incidents would be counted as 'violence'. In a cartoon context, violent portrayals falling within the same frame of reference would also be included. In addition, rare and unusual incidents might occur in other forms of light entertainment programme such as, for example, one talk show guest physically or verbally attacking another.

The dispassionate approach in which violent acts are treated as the same wherever they occur is the one which typifies most objective content assessment studies. Indeed, some of the leading protagonists of this approach have argued that it is essential not to allow subjective perceptive elements to cloud the definitions that are applied in conducting objective content analysis if it is to yield reliable and accurate descriptive accounts of what actually happens on screen (e.g., Eleey *et al.,* 1972a, b). While acknowledging that viewers might, for the most part, regard aggressive behaviours in a comedy situation differently from similarly styled behaviours in a serious dramatic context, researchers studying violence on television in New Zealand argued that the precise nature of the audience's response would depend upon the context and specific nature of the behaviour involved even in a comedy programme. 'Basil Fawlty hitting Manuel over the head with a soup dish is no less a violent act because we laugh at it, though the degree to which it might be regarded as "serious" or not may differ' (Watson *et al.,* 1991, p. 66).

Setting the descriptive analysis and quantification of violence in light entertainment programmes in a wider context of potential audience reaction to certain types of content, there is relatively little prior research evidence to call upon, as compared, say, with the amount of research that has been carried out on audience reactions to drama or even to factual programmes. A small number of studies have examined why comedy programmes and quiz or game shows appeal to viewers, and in relation to audience arousal and aggression, whether such programmes can reduce aggressive arousal or add to it.

THEORIES OF VIOLENCE AND HUMOUR

Early theories of humour regarded it as a hostile response which aimed to demean certain groups while making others feel superior (see Zillmann and Bryant, 1991). A mirthful response has also been observed to occur when an audience's initial expectations are converted into a psychologically incongruous resolution which was unanticipated or meant that a stressful situation was reduced to a trivial outcome. For some theorists, humour can provide physical relief to a tense situation (Zillmann, 1983; Zillmann and Bryant, 1983).

The enjoyment of situation comedies on television has been explained in terms of the disposition theory of humour (Zillmann, 1983). Such situation comedies feature sequences of actions and transactions between characters which tend to place certain parties at a disadvantage, while at the same time yielding benefits or a position of superiority to others. Given such circumstances, comedy on television can thus give rise to hostile exchanges between the featured characters (Stocking *et al.*, 1977). Much comedy can therefore be construed as an aggregation of miniature plots in which some individuals triumph over others and in which these others are debased, demeaned, disparaged, ridiculed, humiliated, or otherwise subjected to undesirable experiences which may finish just short of grievous bodily harm.

For comedy to be effective, it is essential that its featured characters generate powerful emotional responses in members of the audience. Characters must either be loved or hated so that whatever happens to them in the programme carries significance. Decent, kind and virtuous characters must eventually triumph over the unsavoury behaviour of hatable characters, after initially having been frustrated or humiliated by them. While comedy may not be typically overtly violent in nature, it is nevertheless often characterized by distinctly hostile overtones.

Research on how viewers might use television to alter their mood states has indicated that individuals who are angry or aggressively inclined have a tendency to avoid comedy and seek exposure to more serious types of content. According to some theorists, viewing comedy material may be deemed an inappropriate experience among acutely angered people, who would rather watch serious material either involving violence or people suffering sadness or grief (Zillmann *et al.*, 1980). In contrast, there is evidence that light entertainment programmes, including situation comedies and quiz shows, attract viewers who need cheering up because of their moderately arousing qualities (Zillmann and Bryant, 1985).

Quiz shows have the potential to engage audiences provided they have the right blend of essential ingredients, such as interesting contestants, an entertaining presenter who gets on with the show, prizes which are attractive but not too easy to win, and a game in which viewers at home can join (Gunter, 1995). Engaging quiz shows have been found to have the ability to involve viewers to the extent that any anger or frustration they may have felt at the beginning of the show has dissipated by the end (Bryant and Zillmann, 1977).

As indicated earlier, comedy often contains hostile overtones. However, this may not be true of all comedy programmes. Psychologists have found that viewers' prior mood states can affect the way they react to different types of comedy. Angered or annoyed individuals were made even more angry after viewing hostile forms of comedy, while no such effect occurred after they had watched non-hostile comedy (Berkowitz, 1970).

Later research found that prior mood state was linked to programme choices and preferences. Viewers in a bad mood were more likely than those in a good mood to choose to watch a quiz show, but were less likely to choose to watch a situation comedy or a drama. Viewers in a good mood were more likely to choose a situation comedy or drama (Zillmann *et al.*, 1980). According to these researchers, the format of quiz shows, comprising as they did many short segments, was more conducive to allowing stressed viewers to become involved. Such individuals may have been too stressed to have the patience to follow through a drama storyline. Viewers who had been made annoyed by someone eschewed situation comedy because they had no wish to sit through a programme in which certain characters suffered belittlement or annoyance, thus reminding the viewers of their own recent experiences.

Zillmann and his colleagues also reported gender differences in viewers' genre preferences. Female respondents exhibited a general preference for non-hostile forms of comedy. Hostile comedy was also avoided by female viewers who had been insulted or annoyed by someone shortly before viewing. Annoyed men tended to avoid comedy altogether, whether it was hostile or non-hostile. It appears that both men and women, when extremely angry, will avoid comedy of any kind because they cannot conceive of how it may improve the way they feel. Mildly agitated women may choose to watch non-hostile comedy, however. This finding was consistent with research reported elsewhere which indicated that women exhibit less liking for violent entertainment (Gunter, 1983).

Humour can diffuse anger in viewers and turn a bad mood into a good mood or, at least, make the bad mood seem less significant. Involving, light-hearted entertainment can provide a distraction from problems and hence invoke positive feelings in viewers. Light entertainment, however, is not devoid of hostile or violent imagery or content. Viewers' particular content preferences may be guided by the way they feel at the time. The level of hostility in light entertainment programmes, most especially in comedies, will play a part in determining whether viewers choose to watch them. Whether or not this factor is likely to be a significant determinant of programme choice will depend in part also on whether and to what extent light entertainment programmes on the mainstream television channels currently feature the sort of content which will make a difference to such decisions.

VIOLENCE IN TV LIGHT ENTERTAINMENT IN THE MID-1990s

Light entertainment programming comprised eight genres: quiz and game shows; situation comedy; chat shows; family/people shows; other comedy; variety shows; cartoons; and special events. Over the four weeks of monitoring, 909 light entertainment programmes were coded across the channels monitored. This category was dominated by two genres. More than one in two light entertainment programmes comprised either quiz and game shows (28%) or situation comedies (26%). Nearly four out of ten light entertainment programmes were chat shows (15%), family/people shows (14%) or other (non-situation) comedy (12%). There were relatively few variety shows (2%), cartoons for the adult audience (2%), or special events (1%).

Sky One and ITV were especially likely to have quiz and game shows. Situation comedies were most likely to be found on UK Gold and Channel 4. Sky One contained the greatest number of chat shows. Family and people shows were most likely to be found on BBC1, ITV and Sky One. Other comedy most commonly occurred on UK Gold and Channel 4.

Channel comparisons: general violence measures

Around one in eight light entertainment programmes (13%) were found to contain any violence at all. Out of these 115 programmes, more than six in ten (64%) were broadcast on the terrestrial channels, and slightly over a third (36%) appeared on satellite channels (see Table 10.1). Violence in light entertainment was most likely to be found on UK Gold and BBC2 and least likely to occur on the two movie channels.

Table 10.1 Distribution of violence-containing light
entertainment programmes across channels

	n	%
BBC1	18	16.0
BBC2	22	19.7
ITV	17	14.7
Channel 4	15	13.2
Terrestrial	*72*	*63.6*
Sky One	13	11.2
UK Gold	24	20.4
Sky Movies	5	4.1
Movie Channel	1	1.0
Satellite	*43*	*36.7*
All channels	*115*	*100.0*

Note: Data aggregated over four weeks

The basic measure of violence was the violent act. Violent acts could also
occur in quick, uninterrupted succession, giving rise to violent sequences
within programmes. The current analysis found 508 violent acts and 347
violent sequences in light entertainment programmes. The greater proportion
of these occurred in programmes on terrestrial channels (see Table 10.2).
There was a fairly even distribution of violent acts and sequences across
BBC2, ITV and Channel 4 among the terrestrial channels, with BBC1
light entertainment programmes containing only about half as many violent

Table 10.2 Total number of violent acts and violent sequences in
programmes with violence

	Violent acts		*Violent sequences*	
	n	%	n	%
BBC1	43	8.5	31	8.9
BBC2	82	16.1	52	15.0
ITV	84	16.5	57	16.4
Channel 4	83	16.3	51	14.7
Terrestrial	*292*	*57.4*	*191*	*55.0*
Sky One	66	13.0	44	12.7
UK Gold	68	13.4	51	14.7
Sky Movies	65	12.8	46	13.3
Movie Channel	17	3.3	15	4.3
Satellite	*216*	*42.5*	*156*	*45.0*
All channels	*508*	*100.0*	*347*	*100.0*

Note: Data aggregated over four weeks

acts as each of the other three channels. A similar pattern occurred among the satellite channels where violent acts were evenly spread among Sky One, UK Gold and Sky Movies, with The Movie Channel containing fewer than one-third as many violent acts as any one of the other three satellite channels.

The rate of occurrence of violent acts and violent sequences in light entertainment programmes was also found to vary by channel. Although some channels contained many more violence-containing light entertainment programmes than others, it did not always follow that channels with the greatest number of these programmes broadcast the most violent light entertainment. Indeed, the pattern of results which emerged from the current analysis suggested that the opposite was true. The most violent light entertainment programmes occurred on those channels with relatively few violent programmes in this category. Thus, the greatest average numbers of violent acts or violent sequences were found in light entertainment on Sky Movies, a channel which broadcast very few light entertainment programmes. While UK Gold contained more violence-containing light entertainment programmes than any other channel, these programmes were among the least violent in this category in terms of average numbers of violent incidents (see Table 10.3).

Another important measure of television violence, quite apart from how many violent acts a programme contains, is the amount of time occupied by violence. Measures of violence based solely on counts of separate violent incidents can be misleading because they do not indicate how much of a programme was filled with violence. Violent acts and sequences can vary in

Table 10.3 Average number of violent acts and violent sequences in programmes with violence

	Violent acts	Violent sequences
BBC1	2.5	1.9
BBC2	3.4	2.2
ITV	5.9	4.2
Channel 4	5.0	3.0
Terrestrial	*4.2*	*2.8*
Sky One	6.4	4.0
UK Gold	2.9	2.1
Sky Movies	9.1	6.1
Movie Channel	4.3	3.8
Satellite	*5.7*	*4.0*
All channels	*5.0*	*3.4*

Note: Data aggregated over four weeks

Table 10.4 Duration of violent acts and violent sequences in programmes with violence

	Violent acts	Violent sequences
BBC1	7.2	21.0
BBC2	6.6	17.4
ITV	9.6	25.2
Channel 4	9.0	13.2
Terrestrial	*8.1*	*19.2*
Sky One	12.0	31.8
UK Gold	8.4	24.6
Sky Movies	3.6	8.4
Movie Channel	1.0	1.8
Satellite	*6.3*	*18.0*
All channels	*7.2*	*16.7*

Notes: 1 Data aggregated over four weeks
2 Durations in seconds

length from just a second or two to a minute or more. As Table 10.4 shows for light entertainment programmes, the average violent act lasted around seven seconds and the average violent sequence lasted for nearly 18 seconds. The average durations of violent acts and sequences were longer on terrestrial channels than on satellite channels, although the longest violent incidents of all occurred on Sky One. Among the terrestrial channels, violent

Table 10.5 Distribution of time occupied by violence in light entertainment programmes across channels

	Violence (minutes)	Violence as % of total output
BBC1	4.2	0.2
BBC2	6.5	0.2
ITV	10.2	0.4
Channel 4	6.0	0.2
Terrestrial	*26.9*	*0.3*
Sky One	12.2	0.4
UK Gold	7.9	0.3
Sky Movies	3.3	0.1
Movie Channel	0.6	*
Satellite	*24.0*	*0.2*
All channels	*50.9*	*0.3*

Note: Data aggregated over four weeks

incidents lasted longest on ITV. Channel 4 was found to have violent acts in light entertainment which lasted almost as long as those on ITV, but violent sequences on this channel were on average shorter than those on any other terrestrial channel. Violent incidents in light entertainment on the two satellite movie channels had the shortest average durations of any channels.

Cumulatively, nearly 51 minutes of violence occurred in light entertainment programmes over the period monitored. This amounted to 0.3% of the total duration of light entertainment output across the eight channels. The largest total amounts of violence occurred on Sky One and ITV. The smallest amounts occurred on Sky Movies and The Movie Channel. It is clear from these results that violent content represented only a tiny part of light entertainment output (see Table 10.5).

LEVELS OF VIOLENCE IN DIFFERENT LIGHT ENTERTAINMENT GENRES

Violent acts and violent sequences were most likely to occur in comedy programmes. Situation comedy (31%) and other comedy (30%) together contributed well over half the violent incidents found in light entertainment (see Table 10.6). More than one in ten light entertainment violent acts occurred in family/people shows (13%). This is quite a significant result given the fact that these shows accounted for only 2% of the light entertainment programmes monitored. Animated cartoons (10%) together with chat shows (7%) and quiz/game shows (6%) contributed more than one in five of the violent acts in light entertainment output. Further small percentages of violent acts were found in variety shows (3%) and special events (1%).

There were some marked week-on-week variations in the location of violence. During week one, for example, the amount of violence in 'other comedy' was significantly lower than the average level found in other weeks (9% versus 32%), while the contribution of variety shows during that week (37%) was at a much higher level than the other three weeks (11%). During week three, the greatest single proportions of violent acts and sequences occurred in cartoon shows (24%).

The rank order of genres changed when considering the average rates of occurrence of violent acts and violent sequences within violence-containing light entertainment programmes. Variety shows were found to contain the greatest average count of acts or sequences of violence of all light entertainment genres (8.2), ahead of other comedy (4.3) in second place and cartoons (4.1) in third place. Fewer than four acts of violence occurred in the average violence-containing situation comedy (3.9) or chat show (3.8), and fewer than three acts of violence occurred in the average violence-containing quiz/game shows (2.8) or family/people show (2.6). Special events contained violence only in week one (average of 2.0 acts for that week only).

Turning to another indicator of amount of violence on television, the amount of time occupied by violence in light entertainment programmes was largely taken up by violence in other comedy (32%), situation comedy (24%) and family/people shows (14%). Cartoon shows (12%) and quiz and game shows (9%) between them contributed more than one fifth of violence minutage. Further small proportions of violence minutage occurred in chat shows (6%) and variety shows (3%).

Across the four weeks monitored half of all the time occupied by violence in light entertainment programmes occurred in other comedy and family or people shows. There were significant week-on-week fluc- tuations, however, in the distribution of violence among these genres. There was little violence in other comedy shows during the first week of analysis (5% of all violence) compared with the second, third and fourth weeks (average of 39% of all violence). The overall average position of family and people shows was pushed up by an exceptionally high score during the fourth week (42% of all violence). Situation comedy shows made a significantly greater contribution to the amount of violence catalogued during week two (31%) than that coded during any other week (average of 16%). Cartoon shows made a significant contribution to light entertainment violence during week three (22%), but contained little or no violence during weeks one and two (less than 1%). Thus, a picture of inconsistency emerges in terms of where light entertainment violence occurs.

The average amount of violence in violence-containing programmes varied from one light entertainment genre to the next. Across all the weeks monitored, family and people shows averaged the greatest amount of time occupied by violence for those programmes which contained any violence at all (36 seconds). On average, if any violence occurred at all in other comedy or quiz and game shows, it tended to fill around 30 seconds of time. Violence-containing cartoons, variety shows and chat shows each contained an average of 24 seconds of violence. When violence occurred in situation comedies it filled around 18 seconds of time.

Channel differences in levels of violence for light entertainment genres

Channel comparisons focus on the four terrestrial channels and two non- movie satellite channels. There were too few light entertainment programmes on the movie channels to enable meaningful comparisons to be made with the other channels at the light entertainment genre level.

Across the six channels which could be compared, however, violent acts and violent sequences were most likely to occur in other comedy and situ- ation comedy programmes. The only other notable contributors were family and people shows and cartoon shows. More than six in ten violent acts and violent sequences occurred in comedy programmes (see Table 10.6). There were some significant channel differences.

Table 10.6 Distribution of violent acts and violent sequences by light entertainment genre and channel

	All %	BBC1 %	BBC2 %	ITV %	Ch.4 %	Sky One %	UK Gold %
Violent acts							
Other comedy	31	24	37	11	34	38	40
Situation comedy	30	29	45	12	48	3	44
Family/people shows	13	13	0	18	0	47	0
Cartoon/animation	10	0	7	31	7	2	15
Chat shows	7	13	9	15	0	5	0
Quiz/game shows	6	16	2	12	0	3	1
Variety	3	0	0	1	11	3	0
Special events	1	4	0	0	0	0	0
Violent sequences							
Other comedy	37	26	44	16	48	43	44
Situation comedy	27	13	38	18	47	5	40
Cartoon/animation	11	10	8	30	2	2	15
Family/people shows	10	5	0	18	0	34	0
Quiz/game shows	6	13	4	12	0	5	2
Chat shows	5	10	6	7	0	7	0
Special events	4	23	0	0	0	0	0
Variety	2	0	0	0	4	5	0

Violence in comedy programmes, other than situation comedy, was most likely to occur on UK Gold, Sky One and BBC2. It was least likely to occur in this sort of programme on ITV. Situation comedy violence most commonly occurred on Channel 4, BBC2 and UK Gold, but was a relative rarity on ITV and Sky One. Violence in family or people shows was predominantly coded for Sky One, although there were some instances on ITV and BBC1. The most likely channel on which cartoon violence could be found was ITV. Any violence in quiz shows or chat shows tended to be found on ITV and BBC1.

Turning to the amount of time occupied by violence in different light entertainment genres, comedy programmes dominated. More than half of all the violence-occupied time in light entertainment programmes on the four terrestrial channels and two non-movie satellite channels occurred in other comedy and situation comedy shows (see Table 10.7). Most of the remaining violent content occurred on family or people shows and cartoons.

There were channel differences. Other comedy violence occupied a greater proportion of the time filled by violence on UK Gold, BBC1 and BBC2 than on other channels. Situation comedy violence occupied most time on Channel 4. There was little violence-occupied time in comedy programmes on ITV. In contrast, ITV contributed more significantly to the amount of quiz and game show violence and the amount of cartoon violence. The most significant contributor to family and people show violence was Sky One.

Table 10.7 Distribution of amount of time occupied by violence in different light entertainment genres by channel

	All %	BBC1 %	BBC2 %	ITV %	Ch.4 %	Sky One %	UK Gold %
Other comedy	32	50	42	2	26	18	61
Situation comedy	24	16	36	3	61	5	23
Family/people shows	14	12	0	19	0	52	0
Cartoon/animation	12	0	7	25	6	10	15
Quiz/game shows	9	11	3	34	0	4	1
Chat shows	6	7	12	17	0	1	0
Variety	3	0	0	1	8	10	0
Special events	1	4	0	0	0	0	0

On average, light entertainment programmes contained only tiny amounts of violence. These programmes contained around six seconds or less violent content. The main exceptions to this result were family and people shows on Sky One and quiz and game shows on ITV which averaged over 20 seconds of violent content whenever violence occurred in these programmes (see Table 10.8).

Table 10.8 Average amount of violence (in minutes) in violence-containing programmes for different light entertainment genres and channels

	All	BBC1	BBC2	ITV	Ch.4	Sky One	UK Gold
Family/people shows	0.1	*	0.0	0.1	0.0	0.5	0.0
Chat shows	0.1	*	0.2	0.2	0.0	*	0.0
Quiz/game shows	0.1	0.1	*	0.4	0.0	*	*
Situation comedy	0.1	*	0.1	0.0	0.1	*	0.1
Other comedy	0.1	0.1	0.1	*	0.1	0.1	0.2
Variety	*	0.0	0.0	*	*	*	0.0
Cartoon/animation	*	0.0	*	0.2	*	*	0.1
Special events	*	0.1	0.0	0.0	0.0	0.0	0.0

Note: * Less than 0.05 minutes

The most violent light entertainment programmes

The above analyses show the way violence was distributed across different sub-genres of light entertainment programming on television. It is clear from these results that, as one might expect, violence levels were low among light entertainment programmes. Even so, they were not non-existent. Among the light entertainment programmes judged to contain any violence, which were the most violent and how much violence did they contain?

To answer this question, two sets of further analyses were computed on light entertainment data to generate two different top 20 programme listings. The first of these lists ranked light entertainment programmes according to

Table 10.9 The 20 most violent light entertainment programmes in terms of violent acts

Programme	Channel	Violent acts	Violence minutage	Violent sequences
OK For Sound	Channel 4	22	1.3	18
UK Top 10	Sky One	17	0.6	15
Bottom	BBC2	17	1.4	8
Monty Python	BBC2	16	1.7	10
The Goodies	UK Gold	14	0.5	9
Harold Lloyd	Channel 4	14	2.1	8
Nightingales	Channel 4	10	0.4	4
Strike It Lucky	ITV	10	3.4	7
The Three Stooges	Sky One	10	0.7	9
Pink Panther	UK Gold	10	1.2	8
Hale and Pace	ITV	9	0.2	9
Russ Abbott Show	ITV	8	0.1	8
The Young Ones	UK Gold	8	0.7	8
US Top 10	Sky Movies	8	0.4	3
The James Whale Show	ITV	7	0.3	2
The Word	Channel 4	7	0.2	1
Sunday Comics	Sky One	7	0.4	3
US Top 10	Sky Movies	7	0.12	7
The Danny Baker Show	BBC1	6	0.73	2
Favourite films	BBC2	6	0.65	2

the number of violent acts they contained. The second ranked programmes in terms of minutage of violence.

In terms of violent acts, the most violent light entertainment shows were *OK For Sound* on Channel 4 with 22 acts of violence, *UK Top 10* on Sky One with 17 acts, and *Bottom* on BBC2, also with 17 acts (see Table 10.9). Although the two top ranked programmes were music shows, the violent acts top 20 was dominated by comedy shows, with 35% of violent acts occurring in zany comedy shows and 30% in situation comedy shows. Music and variety shows accounted for 20%, chat shows for 10% and cartoons for 5% of violent acts among these programmes.

The top 20 programmes contained a total of 213 violent acts, with an average of 10.7 per programme. These aggregated into 141 violent sequences, averaging 7.1 per programme. The violence in these 20 programmes totalled 17.2 minutes of programme running time, with an average of 41 seconds of violent activity per programme. Thus, these 20 programmes, or 2.2% of all light entertainment programmes monitored, accounted for 41% of all the violent acts and violent sequences in light entertainment programmes.

The top 20 listing by violence minutage saw Michael Palin's *Ripping Yarns* in top spot, with 3.2 minutes of violence (see Table 10.10). This spoof episode depicting Victorian India, titled 'Roger of the Raj', depicted scenes of fighting in a comic context. In second place was an episode from Channel 4's *Harold*

Lloyd series. Once again, the 'violence' was slapstick rather than real. In all, comedy shows, whether zany comedy or situation comedy, accounted for two-thirds of the violence (65% of violence minutage) catalogued in these 20 programmes.

Table 10.10 The 20 most violent light entertainment programmes in terms of violence minutage

Programme	Channel	Violence minutage	Violent acts	Violent sequences
Ripping Yarns	UK Gold	3.2	6	4
Harold Lloyd	Channel 4	2.1	14	8
Monty Python	BBC2	1.7	16	10
Bottom	BBC2	1.4	17	8
OK For Sound	Channel 4	1.3	22	18
Pink Panther	UK Gold	1.2	10	8
This Morning	ITV	1.1	3	3
Whale On	ITV	1.0	1	1
Ripping Yarns	UK Gold	0.8	4	2
The Three Stooges	Sky One	0.8	5	4
Let the Blood Run Free	Channel 4	0.7	6	2
Pebble Mill Encore	BBC1	0.7	4	3
The Three Stooges	Sky One	0.7	10	9
The Young Ones	UK Gold	0.7	8	8
Favourite Films	BBC2	0.7	6	2
UK Top 10	Sky Movies	0.6	17	15
The Movie Show	Sky One	0.5	5	5
The Goodies	UK Gold	0.5	14	9
Night Court	Sky One	0.5	1	1
Sunday Comics	Sky One	0.5	7	3

In all, there was a total of 20.7 minutes of violence coded in this top 20 listing, with an average of 61 seconds of violence per programme. These programmes accounted for 40% of all violence minutage on light entertainment programmes. These programmes contained a total of 176 violent acts (mean = 8.8) and 123 violent sequences (mean = 6.2).

What these top 20 listings demonstrate, yet again, is the fact that considerable proportions of violence on television tended to be situated in relatively small numbers of programmes. This pattern was consistently found across the different major genres of programming monitored in this study.

THE NATURE OF VIOLENCE

There was, in general, relatively little violence in light entertainment programmes. Where violence did occur, however, it can be examined further, in terms of setting, physical form, motivational context, consequences for victims, and aggressor and victim demographics.

Setting of violence

Most violence in light entertainment programmes was situated either in the present day (53.5%) or recent past (36.6%). Only small numbers of incidents were located in the distant past, prior to the present century (6.7%) or in the future (1.4%). In terms of the environmental setting of violence, incidents tended to be spread across a variety of physical locations. The single most common 'location', however, was a studio set (25.7 of violent acts). Other than that, small town (14.3%), inner city (12.8%) and rural (8.9%) locations were the most prevalent settings for violence in light entertainment programmes.

The geography of light entertainment violence centred on the United Kingdom and United States, which were also the two major sources of production for programmes within this genre. The greatest single proportion of violent acts were found in UK locations (39.9%), with the USA (24.9%) some distance behind. Only two other geographical regions really featured to any real degree apart from the UK and USA. These were Europe (9.2% of violent acts) and Central and South America (6.5%).

The form of violence

The type of violence was differentiated in terms of its physical form and according to the kinds of weapons or instruments of aggression being used. The ten most frequently occurring forms of violence are listed below. The top ten types of violent acts accounted for over eight in ten violent acts on light entertainment programmes (82.2%). The top five types of violence alone accounted for well over six in ten violent acts in this genre (63.9%). Most of the violence in light entertainment involved the use of the body rather than of armed weapons. Thus, aggressive behaviour was more likely to involve hitting, kicking, slapping, pushing or tripping than shooting or blowing up.

Top ten types of violent act

	n	%
1 Push/trip	65	14.8
2 Hit with object	62	14.1
3 Shooting	60	13.6
4 Sport	47	10.7
5 Punch	46	10.7
6 Explosion	20	4.5
7 Throwing	18	4.1
8 Slap	17	3.8
9 Kick	14	3.2
10 Damage to property	12	2.7

The top ten weapon types used in violent acts shown on light entertainment programmes together accounted for more than six in ten (61.9%) violent acts in this genre. Easily the most used 'weapon' was the fist or hand, which accounted for half of all the cumulative violent acts among the top ten instruments of aggression.

Top ten weapon types		
	n	%
1 Fist or hand	139	31.0
2 Stick	24	5.5
3 Hand-gun	22	5.0
4 Machine gun	17	3.8
5 = Pistol	14	3.2
5 = Explosives	14	3.2
7 = Rifle	12	2.7
7 = Sword	12	2.7
9 Kick	11	2.5
10 Throw/push	10	2.3

Motives for violence

The motives for violence were classified in terms of the general motivational context of the violence and the identifiable goals of aggressors. The general context might have involved violence perpetrated for criminal motives, to uphold the law, as an aspect of war, civil strife or defence of civil liberties, or as part of a domestic dispute or some other form of dispute among individuals. In light entertainment programmes, violent behaviour was, more often than anything else, likely to be an aspect of some dispute between two individuals. Interpersonal conflicts accounted for more than one in four violent acts (25.2%) on light entertainment programmes. The next most likely reason for violence was a criminal motive (11.2% of violent acts). Acts of war (7.3%) were, surprisingly perhaps, in third place. Law enforcement violence (3.4%) was far less frequent than criminal violence. Indeed, violence in a domestic situation (5.7%) was more frequently occurring than violence in upholding the law. Civil disturbances (2.3%) and conflict related to the defence of civil liberties (2.7%) were infrequent.

Aggressors were more likely to have negative than positive goals. More than one in three (35.6%) of violent acts in light entertainment programmes were motivated by self-centred or evil goals. Less than half that number (15.9%) were motivated by positive or altruistic goals. Among the non-negative goals, the most common reason for violence was self-defence or self-preservation. The most usual reasons for violence of all, however, were to achieve purely evil or destructive aims, or to gain power or money.

Goals of aggressors	
	%
Self-preservation	5.9
Upholding the law	3.8
Protect family home	2.9
Respect for law	2.3
Protect society	1.1
Evil/destructive	13.1
Ambition/power	11.4
Desire for money	9.8
Sexual	1.3
Religious	0.0
Other	37.8
Uncodable	10.1

Consequences of violence

The observable consequences of violence to victims were classified according to a range of serious and mild forms of injury. Mild forms of injury were far more likely than serious injuries. Serious injuries coded within light entertainment included death (9.9% of acts), serious wounds (2.7%) and mutilation (1.1%). Mild forms of injury included victims being stunned (14.0%), and suffering bruises (9.0%) or minor wounds (7.8%). Violence resulting in psychological damage (0.4%) was rare. In a substantial number of cases, however, violence resulted in no injury at all (40.1%).

More subjective evaluations of the dramatic detail of violent acts were supplied by coders which included ratings of the amount of blood, pain and horror associated with individual violent acts. Ratings were provided along a five-point scale where a score of 1 represented a negligible level and a score of 5 meant an extreme level of blood, pain and horror. The great majority of violent acts in light entertainment programmes resulted in no blood (86%). Minor amounts of bleeding, obtaining ratings of 2 or 3 out of 5 were found in a small number of cases (5.7%). Most violence (69% of acts) resulted in no visible pain or suffering for the victim. Mild amounts of pain were found for over one in five acts (22.6%), and more extreme levels of pain, scoring 4 or 5, were found in a tiny number of instances (0.8%). Nearly three out of four violent acts were horror-free (73.7%). More than one in five (22.5%) contained mild levels of horror, and few contained more extreme levels (0.5%).

Aggressors and victims

Character types were examined in terms of aggressor and victim demography and according to a more extensive typology of aggressor and victim types. Most aggressors were male, white, of American or British origin, and young or middle-aged adults. The demographic pattern for victims was very consistent with that for aggressors. Few aggressors or victims were female, black and either children or teenagers or elderly. There was no evidence that particular demographic groups were disproportionately victimized (see Table 10.11).

Table 10.11 Demography of aggressors and victims

	Aggressors		Victims	
	n	%	n	%
Gender				
One male	248	18.8	273	20.8
One female	69	5.2	36	2.7
Group male	77	5.8	50	3.8
Group female	3	0.2	6	0.5
Group mixed	7	0.5	18	1.4
Other	1	0.1	0	0
Cannot code	30	2.2	53	4.0
Age				
Child (up to 12)	1	0.1	3	0.2
Teenager (13–19)	12	0.9	5	0.4
Young adult (20–35)	252	19.1	208	15.9
Middle age (36–65)	93	7.1	116	8.8
65 plus	8	0.6	9	0.7
Mixed age group	17	1.3	29	2.2
Cannot code	54	4.1	67	5.1
Ethnic origin				
White UK	150	11.4	144	10.9
White US	124	9.4	121	9.2
White other	59	4.4	58	4.4
Black UK	5	0.4	5	0.4
Black US	8	0.6	8	0.6
Black other	5	0.4	4	0.3
Asian	0	0.0	0	0.0
Oriental	8	0.6	0	0.0
Mixed group	30	2.3	25	1.9
Other human	0	0.0	0	0.0
Animal	7	0.5	5	0.4
Cannot code	48	3.6	67	5.1

Aggressors and victims in light entertainment programmes were most likely to be classified as 'situation characters' who predominantly represented the regular or guest characters found in situation comedy series. This category accounted for nearly four in ten (38.4%) aggressors and more than one in three (35.2%) victims. In second place were armed forces personnel,

(8.7% of aggressors and 9% of victims). While this may seem incongruous, such characters derived from military-based situation comedies such as *M.A.S.H.* The third most likely type of aggressor (7.1%) and victim (6.9%) fell into the category of sports person. The top ten aggressor-types and victim-types in light entertainment programmes are listed here.

Top ten types of aggressor

	n	%
1 Situation character	168	38.4
2 Armed forces	38	8.7
3 Sports person	31	7.1
4 Cartoon – human	25	5.7
5 Member of public	12	2.7
6 Police – uniformed	9	2.1
7= Outlaws/pirates	8	1.8
7= Criminal – serious	8	1.8
9= Domestic person	7	1.6
9= Entertainer	7	1.6
9= Comedian	7	1.6

Top ten types of victim

	n	%
1 Situation character	148	35.2
2 Armed forces	38	9.0
3 Sports person	29	6.9
4 Inanimate object	20	4.8
5 Cartoon – human	14	3.3
6 Comedian	13	3.1
7= Member of public	12	2.8
7= Domestic person	12	2.8
9 Seaman	9	2.1
10 Police – uniformed	8	2.1

SUMMARY AND CONCLUSIONS

Media researchers are divided in their opinion about whether hostile behaviour is 'violence' when it occurs in a light-hearted or humorous context. For some, slapstick, knock-about behaviour in a comedy programme cannot really be considered as violent (Morrisson, 1993a). For others, in contrast, if one comedy character hits another, such behaviour can be construed as violent because if such behaviour was to be enacted in real life it might be expected that the person on the receiving end would be hurt or feel pain (see Watson *et al.*, 1991).

A great deal of comedy on television is based on conflictual or hostile behaviour. The appeal of humour which centres on one character putting down or embarrassing another derives from stimulating a feeling of superiority among viewers, according to some theorists (Zillmann and Bryant, 1991). Witnessing the misfortunes of other ordinary human beings may make viewers feel better about themselves or appreciate their own situation more than they did before.

The idea that people watch television comedy and light entertainment to be cheered up has received mixed empirical support. Whether or not television comedy, for example, can serve this function depends on the kind of mood viewers are in to start with. Thus, the last thing angry viewers who are in a bad mood may want to watch is a trite sit-com; instead they may prefer something more serious (Zillmann *et al.*, 1980). On the other hand, whether or not viewers react this way depends on how bad their current mood is. Further evidence has indicated that light entertainment programmes can cheer people up and are watched for that reason (Zillmann and Bryant, 1985). To what extent violence in a comedy context specifically is an important ingredient underlying viewers' appreciation of the humour has not been clearly established. If it does represent an effective light entertainment programme among British viewers, it must presumably work in light doses because violence, although present in light entertainment output, was far from being a prominent ingredient.

Violence levels on light entertainment programmes on the channels and during the weeks monitored were generally low. Light entertainment-based violence was more likely to be found on the terrestrial channels than on the four satellite channels that were monitored, although this had much to do with the fact that most light entertainment programming was broadcast by the BBC and commercial terrestrial channels. In total, there were just 72 violence-containing light entertainment programmes on BBC1, BBC2, ITV and Channel 4 and just 43 on Sky One, UK Gold, Sky Movies and The Movie Channel. The violence in these programmes occupied 51 minutes of programme running time, or 0.3% of the total duration of light entertainment programmes monitored.

It is clear then that violence was not a prominent feature of television's light entertainment broadcasts. Most of the violence occurred in comedy programmes or in family/people shows. The average amount of violence in these shows only reached around 20–30 seconds per violence-containing programme. There were, however, significant shifts from one week to another in terms of which kinds of light entertainment programmes were the major contributors to violence levels. One week situation comedy was a major contributor, then another week family shows, and another cartoons or quiz shows. There was no consistent pattern from one week to the next. Thus, it is not just the case that levels of violence are modest on light entertainment programmes, but also the settings in which much of that violence occurs shift significantly from week to week.

When violence did occur it was generally situated in the present or recent past and was mostly located in the United Kingdom or United States. The violence itself mostly involved one person tripping, pushing or punching another, or hitting them with an object, or shooting at them. The most frequently occurring motivational contexts for violence involved either an argument or dispute between two or more individuals or criminal behaviour. Domestic-based hostilities, although numerically few, were relatively high compared with other major programme genres, and probably reflect the kinds of hostile behaviour found in situation comedies which are often based in domestic settings.

Many acts of violence in light entertainment programmes depicted no observable injuries to victims, but around one in ten were followed by death. Where injuries were shown, however, they were much more likely to be mild than severe. Only tiny numbers of incidents occurred which coders rated as extreme in terms of horror, pain or bloodiness. Thus, even when violence did occur in light entertainment programmes, it was generally very mild in nature.

The character profile differed little from that observed in other genres in terms of demography. Most aggressors and victims were male; few were female. Aggressors and victims were also much more likely to be young or middle-aged adults than to belong to any other age group. White characters were involved in violent acts far more often than were blacks. More specifically, the characters involved in violence were most likely to be classified as 'situation characters' of the sort typically involved in comedy series. The most commonly occurring character types after these were armed forces personnel and sports persons among both aggressors and victims, and human cartoon characters among aggressors only and inanimate objects among targets of violence.

Violence can certainly be detected in light entertainment programmes, but it is not a significant feature either in terms of the extent to which it occurs or in terms of the form it generally takes on. Humour is not usually a characteristic viewers associate with violent portrayals. With regard to violent portrayals in serious drama contexts, for example, the degree to which such a portrayal is rated by viewers as 'violent' and 'disturbing' tends to be inversely correlated with how humorous that same portrayal is judged to be (Gunter, 1985). Conversely, more 'humour' in a portrayal is associated with it being judged as less 'violent'. This sort of evidence, of course, does not preclude the possibility that a hurtful behaviour in a comedy context is classified as a type of violence. As a general rule, however, such portrayals are interpreted according to the context in which they occur. While comedy material has been found to have a general arousing quality which could potentially serve to energize a whole range of different kinds of behaviour in the viewer (see Zillmann, 1983), the instrumental function of engaging light entertainment material is to distract viewers from their bad moods and any ill feelings towards others they might harbour (Bryant and Zillmann, 1977).

11 Violence in news and factual programmes

Much of the news featured on television revolves around issues of conflict. Frequently this takes the form of political conflicts, industrial disputes, or arguments about the economy. From time to time, the news may be dominated by more emotionally arousing items, such as crime, violent civil disturbances, terrorism or war. Surveys of public opinion about the news have indicated that people often claim to want more of certain kinds of news and less of others (Wober, 1978). One issue which members of the public have been exercised about is the coverage given by news broadcasts to real life violent incidents. Opinions about whether and how the news on television should cover violent events vary with the type of story, the nature of the treatment it gives to the events concerned, and the types of people who are involved.

Viewers in Britain have been found to state a preference for less news about violent incidents, but this is often associated with long-running conflicts for which no clear resolution can be envisaged. One audience survey in the late 1970s found that British viewers had already grown tired of the coverage given to the troubles in Northern Ireland (Wober, 1978). With shorter-term conflicts such as the Falklands dispute and the Gulf War, in both of which British forces were involved, there was an initial public appetite for information about the latest events, which was fed by television. The public's interest in such events can, however, quickly wane, especially if it appears that nothing really dramatic is happening in the conflict. During the Gulf War, broadcast news gave extensive coverage to events, even when there was little to report. Initial public interest in the war declined until the land offensive was launched. A series of tracking surveys during this war among British viewers revealed that many felt television should relax its Gulf coverage after the first week (Gunter and Wober, 1993).

There seems to be an inherent contradiction here in that viewers' continuing interest in a conflict was dependent upon dramatic new developments which, for many, would have included violent developments, and yet elsewhere viewers have expressed concern about the depiction of violence or the reporting in detail of violent incidents in the news. As with public opinion about violence in drama on television, opinions about violence in the news are mediated by contextual and stylistic factors relating to the way violent incidents are treated. Public anxieties about violence in the news are especially likely to be aroused in connection with stories which involve ordinary people and in relation to the depiction of certain graphic images of real life violence which may be distressing to people in general or more especially to the victims or victims' families (see Shearer, 1991; Morrisson, 1993b).

VIOLENCE INVOLVING PRIVATE CITIZENS

Violent events involving private individuals, such as the victims of murder, rape, or other crimes, or the cases of individuals involved in violent disasters, can cause deep concern among many people. Although the public may show a degree of sympathy for news editors and reporters who wish to include violent incidents among their reports, sympathy for the needs of victims and their families tends to be greater. Reporting of violence involving ordinary citizens may be regarded as acceptable if it can be justified in terms, for example, of being for the greater good of people in general. Where such a justification does not exist, most people express a natural sympathy for the victims and a concern about the trauma which further reminders of critical incidents might cause to them (see Shearer, 1991; Morrisson, 1993b). Women may be especially sensitive to certain kinds of violence, such as rape, particularly where it is covered on regional news, thus bringing it closer to home. Such stories may, of course, perform a constructive function in informing women that there is a rapist at large and may also, on some occasions, play a part in aiding the apprehension of the assailant (see Morrisson, 1993b).

Tolerance for potentially distressing images involving private citizens can vary with the purpose of showing them in the news as well as with the time when they are included in bulletins. Shearer (1991) found that the degree of detail included in pictures of distressing events was also a powerfully determining factor underpinning viewers' willingness to accept particular kinds of news coverage. An overwhelming proportion of viewers (78%) surveyed across Britain felt that it was unacceptable for television news broadcasts to include scenes from a major incident which showed the dead or seriously injured in such a way that they were recognizable. However, pictures from the same scene after the bodies had been removed or where the camera was placed at such a distance that the bodies or injured were not recognizable were both generally regarded as acceptable (by 87% and 76% respectively).

When live pictures from an incident are not available because the cameras were not present when the incident happened, some television producers may decide to visualize the event anyway through a dramatic reconstruction. Such reconstructions are frequently used in programmes such as the BBC's *Crimewatch* and ITV's *Crimestoppers* where audience research has indicated that they are regarded as acceptable by most viewers provided there is a legitimate purpose behind their use. Gratuitous use of such production techniques tends to be rejected by viewers on the basis that they may engender unnecessary fear and anxiety among sensitive groups in the audience, without having the positive function of providing useful assistance to the police in the apprehension of the perpetrators (Wober and Gunter, 1990).

Shearer (1991) found that respondents to a large national survey generally felt that reconstructions of violent crimes in the news were either completely (59%) or fairly (29%) acceptable. People who had themselves been victims of violent crime were even more emphatic with two out of three (66%) finding such reconstructions 'completely' acceptable. By comparison, nearly two out of three viewers in general (64%) felt that dramatic reconstructions of natural disasters were either completely or fairly unacceptable, while nearly one in five (18%) felt they were not acceptable at all. The lower level of endorsement of the latter scenes stemmed from a concern that they served no useful purpose.

News editors often face difficult choices when deciding whether or not to use reconstructions of potentially distressing events. They not only have to consider the range of possible reactions of the general audience to such scenes but also the degree of distress they might cause to the survivors of such events or their families. Among the latter group, reactions can in turn vary with oppositional points of view taken up by different individuals. Shearer (1991) found that some rape victims endorsed the use of reconstruction techniques, while others could not tolerate them. There was general recognition of the rights of the individual to decide whether or not such techniques should be used. For some the need to obtain help in apprehending their assailant outweighed the pain of living through the event again, while for others that pain was just too great to experience once more.

CONFLICT IN THE NEWS

Acts of violence covered by television news, whether they involve military conflict, organized criminal activity, civil disturbances or domestic disputes, may have causes which vary in complexity. According to some writers, however, television news often tends to simplify such events (Murdock, 1973). Television news is event oriented and focuses on overt actions, especially ones for which film coverage is available, but seldom goes into detail about why events occurred (Findahl and Hoijer, 1976). According to some observers of news coverage, television news tends to emphasize the more intense moments of conflicts because these events make for good film items (Hall, 1973). American media scholar, Gaye Tuchman (1978), noted that whereas riots in actuality seldom feature continuous intense, violent activity, being characterized rather by sporadic outbursts and periods of calm, 'news reports usually ignore this, collapsing the course of riots into continuous intense activity' (pp. 190-191).

Some researchers have accused television news of bias in the presentation of conflicts. According to this line of argument, intensive, often violent or disruptive activity tends to be associated with particular groups who are not representatives of the political and economic power centres of society. The Glasgow University Media Group (1976) found in their extensive content analysis of British network television news that coverage of industrial disputes tended to depict management in calm office settings and as sources of authority, reason and responsibility, whereas strikers were shown in noisier locations at mass meetings or picket lines.

In an international study of television news, Cohen and Bantz (1984) reported on the frequency with which television news in five countries – the United States, West Germany, Britain, South Africa and Israel – reported social conflicts on domestic and foreign news fronts during December 1980. In general, three-quarters of all items were devoted to politics, economics, and law enforcement matters. More coverage was given to the reporting of disasters than to all the problems under such headings as environment, health, education, housing and immigration. There were few human interest or cultural stories. Much of television news was therefore depicted as having a serious tone.

The distribution of conflict items in the news revealed differences between the five countries. South African news appeared least conflictual (34% of items), followed by the United States (35%), and West Germany (38%), while Israel and Britain carried the highest proportion of items on social conflicts (60% each).

Cohen and Bantz also examined the characteristics of the way news stories involving conflicts of one sort or another were reported. Looking further at the number of items on American and British television news that contained aggression, for example, they found that 37% of US conflict items featured verbally reported physical aggression, 17% had visually shown physical aggression, 9% had verbally reported verbal aggression, 4% had shown verbal aggression, 2% had verbally reported emotional display, and 9% had visually shown emotional display. Of British conflict items, 52% had verbally reported physical aggression, 22% had visually shown physical aggression, 33% had verbally reported verbal aggression, 14% had visually shown verbal aggression, 5% had verbally reported emotional display, and 22% had visually shown emotional display. On a further point, physical aggression was more likely to be verbally reported and visually shown with foreign items than with domestic ones. Thus, violent news tended to be emphasized more in geographically remote rather than geographically proximal locations.

The significance of proximity of violence was noted in earlier chapters, especially in relation to fictional portrayals of violence. In the news and factual programmes, proximity can be defined in a psychological sense as well as in a purely geographical one. Violent conflict which occurs thousands of miles away may have little impact on viewers if it occurs between foreign parties and where the outcome is perceived to have no bearing on the future of Britain. In contrast, a conflict such as the hostilities between Britain and Argentina over the Falkland Islands in 1982 occurred at the other end of the world, but was of considerable interest to the British public because it involved their own country. Despite this interest, however, public opinion surveys at the time showed that clear majorities of people in Britain did not want television to show the carnage of war and indeed felt that television should be restrained about showing the victims and the bereaved. This opinion applied almost as strongly to Argentine as to British casualties (Wober, 1982).

Research carried out during the Gulf War in 1991 found that viewers were prepared to tolerate certain images of war and not others (Morrisson, 1992). In a nationwide public opinion survey, respondents were asked for their views about four specific events from the war which were shown on the television news coverage: (1) the bombing of a bunker/shelter in Baghdad that resulted in heavy civilian casualties; (2) coalition pilots captured by Iraq and displayed on Iraqi television broadcasts; (3) the filming of Iraqi troops surrendering; and (4) the aftermath of coalition air attacks on Iraqi forces as they were withdrawing from Kuwait in the final days of the conflict.

For three out of the four items listed here, most respondents thought it had been right to show pictures on television. In the case of the transmission of Iraqi film showing captured coalition pilots – including two Britons – the majority view was that this should not have been shown. Viewers' main reasons for believing it was right to show these events included the view that it was important to show what war was really like; it could serve to remind people that war causes casualties; and the opinion that there is a need to provide a view of the war from both sides. Reasons given for believing it was wrong to show such events rested primarily on concerns about upsetting people in general, and children or the families of war victims in particular, together with a concern about the propaganda application of footage depicting allied or enemy casualties and its impact on public morale.

Morrisson found, in addition, that despite a certain degree of tolerance among many members of the public for scenes showing the outcomes of war, few people were willing to accept close-up shots of the dead or dying. This was true with respect to both British and Iraqi casualties. Although it was felt by many people that television had an important duty to inform the public accurately and truthfully about the horrors of war, this opinion was outweighed by concerns about being taken by surprise by the sudden appearance on screen of detailed shots of injury. It was felt that such coverage might be more appropriately placed in current affairs programmes or documentaries where the build-up could give advance warning of what was to come, allowing viewers sufficient opportunity to decide whether or not they wished to continue watching (Morrisson, 1992).

CIVIL DISTURBANCES

Apart from wars and military conflicts, civil disturbances and attacks on private citizens provide other sources of real life violent injury and death which may be covered in the news. The 1980s, for example, witnessed a number of urban riots in Britain's inner city areas, such as Handsworth, Brixton and Toxteth, which were vividly reported by television news bulletins. Through this reporting, fire and fighting became familiar sights leading some commentators to allege that this coverage may have led sections of the disaffected population to be more ready to take part in such incidents. A debate thus was fuelled about television's role on such occasions. One school of thought was that television had a duty to report the facts and to do so by showing what really happened. This responsibility needed, however, to be weighed against the possibility that reports of civil disturbances could produce imitation elsewhere or alternatively might serve to limit any further spreading of such events by causing an informed public to prompt its politicians to take remedial action.

Public opinion in the mid-1980s revealed that an overwhelming majority of people (83%) felt that there was never any excuse for such civil disturbances, whatever the social conditions of the people involved. Equally, there was widespread opinion (80%) that news reporters should try harder to make sure that all sides had an opportunity to put their views across. Many people (68%) were worried to see on television the apparent inability of the police to control the riots. Relatively few (26%), however, felt that television had made people realize that there were often good reasons for these disturbances. Many (61%) were concerned though about possible copy-cat effects of news coverage of such incidents (Gunter and Wober, 1988).

There are clearly many different considerations which must be borne in mind by news editors when deciding how to cover violent events in the news. Many similar considerations are relevant also to the producers of other types of factual programming. Television audiences comprise a variety of types of people whose personalities, values and opinions vary widely. In turn, these psychological aspects of their make-up play an important part in determining what kinds of factual violence they will find acceptable or unacceptable, and how strongly they will react to different types of violence in the news or other factual programmes. Audience research has begun to provide some insights into these matters. It is important, however, to establish just what appears on screen. The analysis which follows attempts to provide further evidence on this issue.

VIOLENCE ON NEWS AND FACTUAL PROGRAMMES IN THE MID-1990s

The news and factual category comprised seven programme genres: national news; regional news; current affairs (political/social/economic); current affairs (consumer affairs); current affairs (special events); documentaries;

and hobbies and leisure. The biggest single programme type was national news, which comprised more than one in three (35%) of all news and factual programmes coded. In all, 474 national news programmes were content analysed over the four weeks of monitoring. The next biggest programme genre was documentaries, of which 304 were coded (23% of all news and factual programmes monitored). The study covered 164 current affairs programmes, 156 regional news programmes, and 102 hobbies and leisure programmes.

All coded national news programmes were broadcast on the terrestrial channels, and all regional news programmes were broadcast only on BBC1 and ITV. During the period monitored BBC2 was the biggest current affairs provider.

General measures of violence: channel differences

Twenty-one per cent of all news and factual programmes monitored contained any violence. Among these violent programmes, nine out of ten (90%) occurred on terrestrial channels (see Table 11.1). Just 23 factual programmes were found to contain any violence on the satellite television channels monitored in this study. Most of these programmes (15) occurred on Sky One. Given the small base size, the data concerning violence in factual programmes on the satellite channels should be treated with caution.

Table 11.1 Distribution of violence-containing news and factual programmes across channels

	n	%
BBC1	70	27.6
BBC2	39	15.9
ITV	72	28.8
Channel 4	43	18.1
Terrestrial	*224*	*90.4*
Sky One	15	6.4
UK Gold	—	—
Sky Movies	5	2.1
Movie Channel	3	1.1
Satellite	*23*	*9.6*
All channels	*247*	*100.0*

Note: Data aggregated over four weeks

More than 1,000 acts of violence were found in news and factual programmes which combined to form more than 650 sequences of violence. Nearly nine out of ten violent incidents (87% of acts and 90% of sequences) occurred on terrestrial channels. Among the terrestrial channels, however, the incidence of violence in news and factual programmes was fairly evenly

Table 11.2 Total number of violent acts and violent sequences in programmes with violence

| | Violent acts | | Violent sequences | |
	n	%	n	%
BBC1	198	19.5	141	21.6
BBC2	206	20.4	152	23.3
ITV	273	26.9	174	26.6
Channel 4	206	20.4	120	18.4
Terrestrial	*883*	*87.2*	*587*	*89.9*
Sky One	56	5.5	39	6.0
UK Gold	0	0.0	0	0.0
Sky Movies	53	5.2	13	2.0
Movie Channel	21	2.1	14	2.1
Satellite	*130*	*12.8*	*66*	*10.1*
All channels	*1013*	*100.0*	*653*	*100.0*

Note: Data aggregated over four weeks

distributed. News and factual programmes on ITV contained somewhat more violent incidents than did the other three channels (see Table 11.2).

When violence occurred in news and factual programmes there were, on average, just over four acts of violence. While ITV contained more violent news and factual programmes than any other channel, its programmes were among the least violent in terms of average numbers of violent acts and violent sequences. There were relatively few violent news and factual programmes on the satellite channels, but levels of violence in these programmes when violence did occur, was higher, especially for the two movie channels (see Table 11.3).

Table 11.3 Average number of violent acts and violent sequences in programmes with violence

	Violent acts	Violent sequences
BBC1	2.9	2.0
BBC2	5.2	3.9
ITV	3.5	2.4
Channel 4	4.8	2.8
Terrestrial	*4.1*	*2.8*
Sky One	4.5	3.0
UK Gold	0.0	0.0
Sky Movies	8.9	2.6
Movie Channel	6.8	2.5
Satellite	*5.1*	*2.0*
All channels	*4.6*	*2.4*

Note: Data aggregated over four weeks

Table 11.4 Duration of violent acts and violent sequences in programmes with violence

	Violent acts	Violent sequences
BBC1	5.4	7.8
BBC2	7.8	11.4
ITV	5.4	8.4
Channel 4	7.2	12.0
Terrestrial	*6.5*	*9.9*
Sky One	7.8	9.0
UK Gold	0.0	0.0
Sky Movies	6.0	19.8
Movie Channel	5.4	6.6
Satellite	*4.8*	*8.9*
All channels	*5.7*	*9.4*

Notes: 1 Data aggregated over four weeks
2 Durations in seconds

The average durations of violent acts and violent sequences varied across channels. Once again, ITV, despite its relatively high total violent act count, tended to have among the shortest duration violent acts in news and factual programmes of any channel. Violent acts in news and factual programmes on ITV, BBC1, and The Movie Channel tended to be just over five seconds in length on average. Violent acts on Sky Movies were six seconds long on

Table 11.5 Distribution of time occupied by violence in news and factual programmes across channels

	Violence (minutes)	Violence as % of total output
BBC1	17.4	0.3
BBC2	30.8	0.4
ITV	26.5	0.3
Channel 4	24.1	0.3
Terrestrial	*98.8*	*0.3*
Sky One	5.4	0.2
UK Gold	0.0	0.0
Sky Movies	2.9	0.1
Movie Channel	2.7	0.1
Satellite	*11.0*	*0.1*
All channels	*109.8*	*0.2*

Note: Data aggregated over four weeks

average, and violent acts on Channel 4, BBC2 and Sky One averaged over seven seconds in length (see Table 11.4).

In total, nearly 110 minutes of violence was coded in news and factual programmes over the four weeks of monitoring. This was equivalent to half of one per cent of total programme output time within this category of programming. All but 1% of time occupied by violence in news and factual programmes occurred on terrestrial channels (see Table 11.5).

LEVELS OF VIOLENCE IN DIFFERENT NEWS AND FACTUAL GENRES

National news broadcasts and documentaries supplied most of the violent incidents in news and factual programmes. Each of these genres contained 43% of the violent acts in factual programmes. Few violent incidents were detected in current affairs programmes (6%), hobbies and leisure programmes (5%) or regional news programmes (3%).

When looking at the average rates of occurrence of violent incidents in programmes containing violence, documentaries were recorded as having the highest rates of violent acts among factual programmes. There were around six acts of violence (6.2) on average in documentaries which contained any violence, compared with four acts per violence-containing hobbies and leisure programme and three acts of violence per news broadcast with violence.

Lower rates still were found in current affairs programmes dealing with consumer issues (2.6), current affairs programmes concerned with politics and economics (2.3), regional news programmes (2.0) and special current affairs programmes (0.9).

There were some fluctuations in these violence figures from one week to the next. Documentaries scored a relatively low rate of violence in week four (3.8), while hobbies and leisure programmes with violence exhibited an exceptionally high rate of violent acts during that week (10.3).

The significant contribution of national news and documentaries to the overall level of violence recorded in news and factual programmes was further illustrated by the violence minutage results. Here it was found that 90% of all the time filled by violence in factual programmes occurred in these two genres. More than half the violence minutage in factual programmes occurred in national news broadcasts (53%) and nearly four-tenths (37%) occurred in documentaries. Just one-tenth of the time occupied by violence in factual programmes occurred in other factual sub-genres. Current affairs programmes (5%), regional news (3%), and hobbies and leisure programmes (3%) contributed only small amounts of the total amount of time containing violence in factual programmes generally.

When violence did occur in factual programmes, it occupied far more time in documentary programmes than in any other type of factual programmame. When violence occurred in a documentary, on average the programme contained around 48 seconds of violence, compared with an average of 18 seconds of violence in any national news programmes containing violence. Hobbies and leisure programmes and political/economic current affairs programmes contained an average of 12 seconds of violence whenever violence did occur in these programmes, while violence-containing regional news and consumer-oriented current affairs programmes contained around six seconds of violence.

Channel differences in levels of violence for different news and factual genres

Channel comparisons will focus on just the four terrestrial channels and Sky One. There were no qualifying programmes with violence on UK Gold and too few on the two movie channels to facilitate proper comparisons at the genre level. Among these five channels, the major contributing genres to violent acts and violent sequences were national news and documentaries. Violent incidents in factual programmes on Sky One and BBC2 were especially likely to occur in documentaries, while on BBC1 and ITV, the national news was a much more significant contributor (see Table 11.6).

There were marked variations between television channels in the way violence was distributed among different factual genres. As Table 11.7 shows, national news broadcasts accounted for most of the violence on BBC1 and ITV, whereas documentaries accounted for most of the violence appearing in

Table 11.6 Distribution of violent acts and violent sequences by news and factual genre and channel

	All %	BBC1 %	BBC2 %	ITV %	Ch.4 %	Sky One %
Violent acts						
Documentaries	46	12	78	12	49	80
News – national	39	78	18	56	41	0
Current affairs (PSE)	6	1	3	6	1	18
Hobbies/leisure	4	0	*	17	1	2
News – regional	3	6	0	8	0	0
Current affairs (CA)	1	3	0	0	0	0
Current affairs (SE)	1	0	0	0	7	0
Violent sequences						
Documentaries	45	8	84	10	44	80
News – national	42	78	11	72	48	0
Current affairs (PSE)	6	3	4	2	2	19
News – regional	3	10	0	7	0	0
Hobbies/leisure	3	0	1	9	3	0
Current affairs (SE)	1	0	0	0	3	0
Current affairs (CA)	*	1	0	0	0	0

Note: * Less than 0.5%

Table 11.7 Distribution of amount of time occupied by violence in different news and factual genres by channel

	All %	BBC1 %	BBC2 %	ITV %	Ch.4 %	Sky One %
Documentaries	51	13	85	7	62	86
News – national	40	82	12	72	35	0
Current affairs (PSE)	4	*	1	8	1	12
Hobbies/leisure	2	0	1	8	*	1
News – regional	2	4	0	6	0	0
Current affairs (CA)	1	1	0	0	2	0
Current affairs (SE)	0	0	0	0	0	0

Note: 1 * Less than 0.5%
2 PSE = political, social and economic affairs; CA = consumer affairs;
   SE = special events

factual programmes on BBC2, Channel 4 and Sky One. Relatively small proportions of the time occupied by violence occurred on the other factual programme types.

The average amounts of violence, in terms of minutage, were generally small across all factual genres and channels (see Table 11.8). Even in documentaries and national news programmes, which together accounted for the overwhelming majority of violent incidents in factual programmes, the amounts of violence which occurred were generally at a very low level. In the average violence-containing documentary, the violence would last for around 12 seconds, while on the national news it was only half that level.

Table 11.8 Average amount of violence (in minutes) in violence-containing programmes for different news and factual genres and channels

	All	BBC1	BBC2	ITV	Ch.4	Sky One
Documentaries	0.1	*	0.4	*	0.2	0.1
News – national	0.1	0.1	*	0.1	0.1	0.0
Hobbies/leisure	*	*	*	0.2	*	*
Current affairs (PSE)	*	*	*	0.1	0.1	*
News – regional	*	*	0.0	0.1	0.0	0.0
Currant affairs (CA)	*	*	0.0	0.0	0.1	0.0
Current affairs (SE)	0.0	0.0	0.0	0.0	0.0	0.0

Note: 1 * Less than 0.05 minutes
2 PSE = political, social and economic affairs; CA = consumer affairs;
   SE = special events

The most violent factual programmes

Levels of violence in factual programmes were generally low, with national news bulletins and documentaries representing the major contributors. A closer look was taken at which were the most violent factual programmes among those monitored by computing top 20 listings in terms of those which contained the greatest number of violent acts and those with the greatest minutage of violence.

These analyses confirm, once again, that national news broadcasts and documentaries contained most of the factual programme violence (see Table 11.9). In a reversal of their overall position, however, among the top 20 listed programmes only, documentaries accounted for a greater proportion of violence minutage (70%) than national news programmes (25%).

The violent acts top 20 shows the first six positions occupied by documentaries. The total of 326 violent acts found in these programmes (mean = 16.3) represented just over 32% of all violent acts found in factual programmes. The 192 violent sequences in these programmes (mean = 9.6) accounted for 29% of all violent sequences found in factual programmes.

Among the top 20 factual programmes in terms of violence minutage, the top five were all documentaries (Table 11.10). These 20 programmes contained 23.4 minutes of violence (average of 1.2 minutes each), which represented 21% of all violence minutage in factual programmes. Thus, 1.7% of all factual programmes contained more than one-fifth of all violence minutage in the genre.

Table 11.9 The 20 most violent factual programmes in terms of violent acts

Programme	Channel	Violent acts	Violence minutage	Violent sequences
World at War	BBC2	30	2.0	29
Movies, Games, Videos	ITV	27	0.9	5
Gamesmaster: Gore Special	Channel 4	26	6.3	7
The World at War	BBC2	21	8.7	12
Sumodo	Channel 4	18	2.4	9
The World at War	BBC2	17	3.5	14
GMTV	ITV	16	0.8	16
GMTV	ITV	15	2.2	10
White Heat	BBC2	13	5.6	11
GMTV	ITV	13	1.6	13
Those Fabulous Clowns	BBC2	12	1.4	12
Right to Reply	Channel 4	12	0.2	3
UN Blues	Channel 4	12	1.0	7
10 by 10	BBC2	11	1.0	10
Cinema, Cinema, Cinema	ITV	10	0.8	6
This is David Harper	Channel 4	10	1.4	4
Movies, Games, Videos	ITV	10	0.4	8
News	BBC1	10	0.7	6
The Little Picture	ITV	10	0.8	2
White Heat	BBC2	9	0.3	8

Table 11.10 The 20 most violent factual programmes in terms of violence minutage

Programme	Channel	Violence minutage	Violent acts	Violent sequences
The World at War	BBC2	8.7	21	12
Gamesmaster:				
Gore Special	Channel 4	6.3	26	7
White Heat	BBC2	5.6	13	11
The World at War	BBC2	3.5	17	14
Sumodo	Channel 4	2.4	18	9
GMTV	ITV	2.2	15	19
The World at War	BBC2	2.0	30	29
Big Breakfast News	Channel 4	1.9	9	6
GMTV	ITV	1.6	13	13
This is David Harper	Channel 4	1.4	10	4
Cops	Sky One	1.4	2	2
News	ITV	1.2	7	5
Network First	ITV	1.1	9	3
Unsolved Mysteries	Sky One	1.0	7	4
Big Breakfast News	Channel 4	1.0	5	2
10 by 10	BBC2	1.0	11	10
UN Blues	Channel 4	1.0	12	7
Chris Eubank:				
The Real Me	Sky One	0.9	11	8
The Last Machine	BBC2	0.9	5	3
The World at War	BBC2	0.9	7	7

Programme context features

The most violent factual programme, in terms of violence minutage, was *The World at War* shown at 6.50 pm on BBC2, 10 October 1994. This was a documentary about World War II. The violence was contained in short clips of black and white footage of wartime combat. This footage depicted war planes bombing a city, armed military combat on land, trench warfare, and showed pictures of prisoners of war and shell-shocked prisoners in hospital. Often the scenes of devastation were accompanied by a modern day voice-over providing analysis of the situation depicted. The scenes were frequently shown in slow motion and accompanied by music. The bombing of Hiroshima was shown in the context of a discussion of the theory of bombing in wartime.

The programme was informative and contained interesting insights into wartime planning, actions and results. It examined changes in military strategy and operational procedures and discussed issues such as the break-down of chivalry in war due to advancements in technology. The violent nature of the footage was in the context of a carefully considered analysis of war. In general, the violent scenes avoided any depiction of close-up, graphic detail of consequences, but certain scenes did show real deaths (in black and white footage and in a clearly historical context). These scenes were classified as being severe in terms of their horror value. On the basis of prior audience research, such scenes might be expected to invoke stronger emotional reactions among viewers (Gunter and Wober, 1988). At the same time, though, viewers are often prepared to accept depictions of real world horrors presented in factual and explanatory contexts in which images of violence represent an integral part of enhancing audience understanding of particular issues (Morrisson, 1992a).

THE NATURE OF VIOLENCE ON FACTUAL PROGRAMMES

Violence in factual programmes occurred at a generally low level, even compared with the rest of television. When it did occur, however, what was its character? As with the other genres, it is interesting to examine the kinds of violence that appear in factual programmes and the way in which violence is shown.

Most violence in factual programmes (67.8% of violent acts) was situated in the present day. Given the fairly prominent contribution of national news programmes, this finding is to be expected. One in five violent acts in factual programmes (19.4), however, were located in the recent past, covering the years between 1900 and 1980. A small percentage (3.8%) occurred in the distant past, and a tiny amount (2.8%) was coded as futuristic violence. Much of this material occurred in documentaries.

The greatest single proportion of violent acts (31.1%) occurring in factual programmes was situated in inner city locations. Otherwise, violence was most likely to be in rural settings (13.4%), small town settings (10.6%), or in suburbia (7.3%). Geographically, most factual programme violence was located in the United Kingdom (34.1% of violent acts). Alternatively, factual programmes featured mainly violence in the United States (18.8%), Europe (10.6%) or Africa (6.2%).

Much of the violence in factual programmes comprised shootings, people being pushed or tripped or punched, and bombardment. Other most commonly occurring forms of violence involved people being hit with an object, people throwing things, people getting kicked, explosions and aggression in a sports context. The top ten types of violent acts in factual programmes are listed below.

The types of weapons of violence featured mirrored the forms of violent acts. Shootings involved the use of a rifle (5.3% of acts), machine gun (4.1%) or hand-gun (4.1%). The use of military hardware occurred in 11% of acts, with explosives accounting for 4.1%. One in four acts of violence (25%) involved the use of a fist or hand, which was presumably deployed in hitting someone, pushing them or possibly throwing something at them.

Analysis of the motivational context of violence in factual programmes revealed that it occurred primarily either in the context of war or conflicts between armed forces (25% of acts) or in the context of civil strife and rioting (19.9%). A certain proportion of violent acts in factual programmes occurred either in a law breaking or criminal context (10.8%) or law enforcing context (7.9%). There was relatively little domestic violence (2.5% of violent acts) on factual programmes.

Ten types of violent act		
	n	%
1 Shootings	233	22.5
2 Pushing/tripping	163	16.2
3 Punching	102	10.1
4 Bombardment	88	8.7
5 Hitting with object	71	6.7
6 People throwing things	59	5.6
7 Aggression in sport	49	5.5
8 Explosion	48	4.9
9 Verbal threat	44	4.3
10 People kicking others	26	3.0

Injuries caused by violence shown in factual programmes tended to be mild, involving minor wounds (9.4%), bruising (7.8%) or stunning of victims (6.1%). More serious wounding (4.2%) was less common and broken limbs depicted on screen were very rare (less than 1% of acts). There were no instances of mutilation. However, death was the next most likely outcome (8.7%) after minor wounding. More than one in four violent acts (27.7%) in factual programmes produced no visible signs of injury. Ratings of dramatic detail indicated the extent to which violent incidents were thought to be bloody, painful and horrific. Ratings were given along a five-point scale where 1 meant no blood, pain or horror and 5 meant an extreme degree of pain and horror and lots of blood. More than seven in ten acts of violence (72.4%) on factual programmes were rated 1 for blood, with most acts being rated similarly for pain (58.7%) and horror (51.3%). Copious amounts of blood, with scenes rated as 4 or 5 amounted to 1% of violent acts. The same ratings were given to under 1% of violent acts for pain and to 1.8% of acts for horror.

The aggressors and victims of violence in factual programmes were mainly males, operating either on their own or in a group, aged between 20 and 35 years, and white. Violence perpetrated by female assailants was rare in factual programmes. If young adults were not responsible for the violence in this category of programming, the next most likely age group to be involved was the middle-aged adult group. Few children or elderly people were involved in reported real-life violence. Likewise, black aggressors and victims of violence were relatively rare. Indeed, perpetrators and victims of violence were more likely to be of Asian or Oriental origin in factual programmes (see Table 11.11).

The most commonly occurring specific categories of aggressor in factual programmes were armed forces (22.1%), sports participants (9.2%), uniformed police (8.5%) and football hooligans (5.2%). Victims of violence in factual programmes were principally members of armed forces (13.5%), uniformed police (9.2%), sports participants (8.8%) and members of the public (8.1%). Inanimate objects (6.4%) were also among the most often featured targets of violence.

Table 11.11 Demography of aggressors and victims

	Aggressor %	Victim %
Gender		
Solus male	41.7	35.6
Solus female	3.6	6.5
Group male	33.5	22.8
Group female	0.2	0.0
Group mixed	7.5	12.2
Other	0.2	0.4
Cannot code	13.4	22.5
Age		
Child (up to 12)	1.9	1.5
Teenager (13-19)	3.7	1.1
Young adult (20-35)	45.2	40.1
Middle-age adult (36-65)	9.5	7.6
65 plus	0.1	0.3
Mixed age	11.1	15.8
Cannot code	28.6	33.6
Ethnic origin		
White UK	21.3	19.5
White US	15.4	13.2
White other	12.9	8.6
Black UK	1.8	2.1
Black US	1.8	0.9
Black other	2.2	1.7
Asian	3.0	2.6
Oriental	4.6	3.7
Mixed group	12.6	12.8
Other human	1.4	0.8
Animal	1.0	1.6
Cannot code	22.3	32.5

SUMMARY AND CONCLUSIONS

The net finding from the analysis of television's factual programmes was that compared with fiction output, these programmes were not very violent. In all, 247 violence-containing programmes were detected over the eight channels monitored for the four weeks period of analysis. In these programmes, over 100 separate acts of violence emerged, giving an average of around four acts per violence-containing factual programme, and occupying around 110 minutes of programme running time.

Factual programmes were divided into seven genres. Most of the violence monitored occurred either in national news bulletins or documentaries. Very little violence was found in current affairs programmes, factual magazine programmes or regional news. Not surprisingly, much of the violence was set in the present day. If this was not the case, violent events were historical rather than situated in the future. Violence occurred mostly in urban locations, although a certain amount also occurred in small town and rural locations. Geographically, the main locations for violence during the period monitored were the United Kingdom and United States. However, these two locations did not dominate the geography of violence in the same way as they did in drama programmes. Violence was more prominent in Europe and Africa in factual programmes than in other genres, reflecting the locations of the major conflicts in the world.

Top 20 listings of factual programmes in terms of violent acts and violence minutage confirmed that national news and documentaries were the major contributors to violence in this genre. The most violent factual programmes of all in terms of amount of violence were documentaries. Thus, these 1.7% of all factual programmes monitored comprised over one-fifth of violence minutage and around one-third of violent acts and sequences.

Violence in factual programmes generally comprised actions of physical force involving people pushing, tripping or punching one another, or the use of guns and military hardware. Scenes depicting bombardment were, relatively speaking, more likely in factual programmes than in drama. In terms of the motivational contexts of violence therefore events in factual programmes generally occurred in an armed conflict context or, if not, then in criminal or civil disturbances contexts. There was little domestic violence and sexually motivated violence was extremely rare. Depicted injuries to victims tended to be minor rather than serious. However, death did result in around 9% of violent incidents. More than one in four violent acts in factual programmes depicted no visible signs of injury.

The profile of people involved with violence in factual programmes revealed that aggressors and victims were most usually male, aged between 20 and 35 years, and white. These individuals were most likely to be members of the armed forces, police, sports persons or football hooligans if they were assailants, and armed forces personnel, police, sports persons, and members of the public if they were victims.

For the most part, there was little evidence to suggest that the types of violence depicted in factual programmes for the television output monitored in this study represented the kinds of scenes likely to cause undue distress to the great majority of viewers. The real-life violence presented in the news and other factual output was restricted to certain types of events and, for the most part, involved specified groups. There was some evidence that members of the public were among the most prevalent groups of victims of violence, representing just over 8% of violent acts in factual programmes. There was little evidence, however, of the more vulnerable groups, such as women, children or the elderly being widely involved in violence.

The anxieties of viewers in general and of specific victimized groups more especially about violence in certain contexts, such as domestic incidents or incidents involving rape and sexual abuse, were also rare occurrences. Audience research has confirmed repeatedly that domestic violence (Shearer, 1991; Morrisson, 1993b) and sexually motivated violence (Gunter, 1995; Shearer, 1991) are among the most disturbing to viewers. Just 17 incidents of violence linked to domestic contexts were identified and just three incidents of sexually motivated violence occurred.

Viewers are known to be concerned about the amount of pain and suffering caused to victims of violence and the more graphically such consequences are depicted, the stronger do viewers' emotional reactions become (Gunter, 1985). In the current study, most incidents of violence in which injuries were shown depicted only minor amounts of suffering. There were no cases of victims having been mutilated and just one case where a victim had suffered broken bones. There were 42 cases in which serious wounding had occurred, which amounted to 4% of all violent acts in factual programmes. Only tiny numbers of incidents were identified as depicting victims suffering an extreme degree of pain, or as being extremely horrific or bloody.

12 Violence in children's programmes

Programmes made for children represent an area of television output of special concern because of who their target audience is. While the occurrence of violence in programmes produced for the general audience, or for adults in particular, has generated some degree of concern, not least because of the fact that children may also watch these programmes, broadcasters' programme policies adopt a gradually more relaxed attitude towards the depiction of violence in programmes as the temporal distance from peak children's viewing times becomes greater. Indeed, there is a degree of acceptance of the view that violence may represent a vital ingredient in the telling of stories, whether in drama or in the news. It is generally hoped, however, that those parts of the transmission schedule which are reserved especially for children's programmes will be spared violence or, at least, violence in its more graphic forms.

ARE CHILDREN'S PROGRAMMES VIOLENT?

The answer to this question according to much content analysis research appears to be 'yes'. In the United States, children's cartoons and other child-oriented action programmes televised during designated children's viewing time on Saturday mornings were found to contain among the highest rates of violent incidents of any programme genre (Gerbner *et al.*, 1978, 1979, 1980).

In the United Kingdom, Cumberbatch *et al.*(1987) reported that around one in six (16.1%) of the programmes they analysed on the four terrestrial channels were classified as children's programmes. A distinction was made between cartoons and 'children's television', however, which proved to be highly significant in terms of locating where on children's programming most violence occurred. Cartoons (54%) were found far more often to contain violence than children's programmes (13.8%). When violence did occur on children's television, it was most likely to be found in newer magazine shows such as *The Wide Awake Club, Get Fresh,* and *Number 73,* which also contained cartoons. When cartoon violence was excluded from these programmes, fewer than 5% of children's television programmes were found to portray any violence. Indeed, excluding cartoons Cumberbatch and his colleagues reported that there were just ten acts of violence in 195 children's television programmes. These incidents were largely slapstick or innocuous.

Cartoon 'violence' contributed more than one-tenth (11.3%) of all violent acts catalogued on the terrestrial channels in 1986. On BBC1, cartoons averaged 8.2 acts per hour, while on ITV, the average rate of violence was 6.5 acts per hour. As Cumberbatch and his colleagues noted, however, there is a question-mark hanging over whether this cartoon material can truly be regarded as 'violence'. It is certainly the case that adult viewers dismiss hostilities between cartoon characters as essentially 'nonviolent' (Gunter, 1985; Howitt and Cumberbatch, 1974). Even children draw distinctions between the high fantastic contexts of cartoons and reality (Hodge and Tripp, 1986). Children's programme tastes and character preferences, however, change as they grow older. Among very young children, up to eight years of age, cartoon characters predominate as their TV favourites. As they get older, between the ages of nine and 12 years, their preferences shift towards the personalities they see in more serious drama productions (Hodge and Tripp, 1976).

Cartoons have been the centre of criticism nevertheless because of the unreality and mindlessness of the violence they portray, whether it is perceived by young audiences as real or not. What cannot be seriously doubted is that they represent a significant aspect of the viewing diet of children at a stage of development when the adoption of salient role models from the media in pretend or imaginative play is a prominent activity. It is natural therefore that parents and teachers might exhibit some degree of concern about the kinds of examples current media role models provide to young children. This concern extends not only to animated cartoon heroes but also to the human or human-like characters now featuring in children's action-drama series such as *The Teenage Mutant Ninja Turtles* and *The Mighty Morphin Power Rangers*.

Observations of preschool children's play have indicated an increase in the adoption of superhero themes (French *et al.*, 1987; Jennings and Gillis-Olion, 1980; Kostelnik *et al.*, 1986; Paley, 1984; Singer and Singer, 1981). Television programmes featuring superhero cartoons have been observed to have increased significantly following marketing and promotional developments between the toy industry and broadcast organizations from the mid-1970s. Concern has grown that such programmes, along with the reinforcement of toy action figures, may be contributing to the increase of children's adoption of superhero themes in their imaginative play behaviour (see French and Pena, 1991).

More especially, concerns have been expressed about the social values conveyed to young children through the new style of 'superhero'. Questions have been raised about the amount of aggression associated with these fictional characters, their use of weapons, and the frightening nature of the characterizations contained in these programmes. One of the questions being asked is what are the benefits versus the drawbacks of children playing games in which they pretend to be one of their favourite superheroes, particularly when such role models are often associated with largely violent themes?

The issues surrounding children's television superhero-related play are numerous and complex. They are embedded in the contexts of the known benefits of fantasy play, the importance of heroes and the historical aspect of adults' memories of their own childhood heroes, and the recent influences of television on children's play and hero types.

The significance of pretend play

Fantasy play is generally acknowledged by child development experts to be beneficial and even essential to healthy psychological growth. Pretend play can enhance a child's creativity, ability to think in a more flexible way, and social skills when dealing with other people, whether peers or adults (Athey, 1984; Bretherton, 1984; Fein, 1981; Rogers and Sawyers, 1988). Children's tendency to engage in imaginative play has been shown to correlate positively with their ability to make friends and to control any hostile impulses they might have towards others (Fein, 1981). There is also evidence that fantasy play experiences in which children imagine they are characters from fairy tale themes may lead to more complex forms of play, more complex modes of thinking, and to greater ability to see other points of view than their own (Saltz *et al.*, 1977).

Role of the hero

Heroes exert profound influences on individuals and even upon entire civilizations. For children, heroes, with their accompanying myths and legends, represent material which feeds their dreams and imaginations. Playing out these hero themes is one of the ways in which children come to understand their society and their own role within that society (Erikson, 1977)

Heroes are the source of many qualities which children select and incorporate into their pretend play. Prestige is one particular quality that attracts children to a hero model (Bandura and Walters, 1963). Power is another important quality which renders a hero an attractive role model (Elkind, 1981; Sousa and Schneiderman, 1986). One view is that children may play at being superheroes in order to understand their own place in the hierarchy of power (Elkind, 1981). Children may be attracted to superheroes because they are characters who demonstrate control over a hostile environment (Sousa and Schneiderman, 1986). Children may wish to acquire this quality for themselves.

In the debate about the possible antisocial effects of television's violent superheroes upon children, a distinction is seldom clearly drawn between real aggression and pretend play. When children play at being Power

Rangers does this represent real aggression? This distinction may be very important because, according to some child psychologists, these activities represent distinct classes of behaviour (Smith, 1994).

Pretend play represents a natural aspect of a child's psychological development. It evolves in form as the child progresses through successive stages of psychological development, with children engaging in different types of imaginative role playing and identifying with different role models as they pass from one stage of cognitive and emotional maturity to the next. While television does not cause children to engage in pretend play, because this is something they do quite naturally, it may nevertheless provide some influence over the way such behaviour is manifested. If the dominant themes associated with heroes in today's media are different from those of the pre-television era, does this also mean that the nature of children's pretend play has changed as well?

Some observers claim that styles of pretend play have changed and that the mass media hero themes can be held accountable. Brown (1985) reported that most middle-aged adults recalled traditional images of heroes when they were children whose conduct was based on standards of altruism, patriotism and unselfish behaviour. Tucker (1985) argued that, in the past, children admired people who possessed honour, truth and bravery because parents and teachers saw to it that information about those who had done admirable deeds was passed on to them.

Studies of superhero changes in comic books from the 1940s to the 1970s found that the more modern superheroes suffered from confusion about their roles and fought on the same level as villains (Perigard, 1985; Lanyi, 1984). The lines between good and evil had become blurred, both the hero and the villain were more omnipotent, and the weapons they wielded were more destructive. An increase in acts of aggression was also observed alongside a decrease in acts of punishment (Yarian, 1974).

Further evidence stems from research into whether children's play themes have changed over time. Studies of the play themes of schoolchildren in the United States more than 60 years ago showed that themes of cops and robbers and cowboys and Indians were popular for seven- to 11-year-olds, while playing house, school, nurse and shopkeeper were popular pastimes for girls (Lehman and Witty, 1927; Foster, 1930). Certain themes were found to persist over many years. Sutton-Smith and Rosenberg (1961) compared the results of four studies of school-age children's play preferences in the years 1896, 1898, 1921 and 1959. Fantasy play behaviour for boys throughout this period was dominated by cowboys and Indians themes.

Recent studies of play styles and characters indicate that television represents a source of information and ideas for children in their play (Guddemi, 1986; Jennings and Gillis-Olion, 1980; Kostelnik *et al.*, 1986; Singer and Singer, 1981). In a study of the play of three- and four-year-olds, Singer and Singer (1981) found frequent references to characters and adventures which were drawn from television shows, cartoons and fantasy-action shows. Play themes associated with heroic adventure play showed a steady increase over a one-year period. Almost all the children studied exhibited some evidence of television themes in play. Girls as well as boys engaged in superhero play. Inherent in many adventure and fantasy situations were the underlying themes of power and danger.

Recently, French and Pena (1991) reported evidence that young children's play themes, heroes and sources of information about play have changed since the advent of television. Historically, preschool-age children were noted playing dramatic roles of people they were close to and wished to model. Most often, these models were family members and other real people of the community – teachers, shopkeepers, firemen, nurses and doctors (Caplan and Caplan, 1973; Hartley *et al.*, 1952). By middle childhood, between the ages of seven and 11 years, children were observed to have moved from pretending to be these real life characters to playing out adventure themes with more distant fantasy characters – cowboys, armed forces, cops and robbers and so on (Caplan and Caplan, 1973; Foster, 1930; Sutton-Smith and Rosenberg, 1961). This same progression in preferences for play themes and favourite character types was found among present-day adults who represented pre-television era children (French and Pena, 1991). Present-day preschoolers, however, reported pretend play themes which reflected more heroic adventure play with fantasy heroes as their favoured role models. The shift away from modelling pretend play behaviour on the activities of family or local community members to television fantasy heroes was regarded by these researchers as a worrying development because television's heroes lack the range and depth of qualities to be found among real people. 'Thus young children may not be working on the full range of human qualities that help create well-rounded emotionally healthy people' (French and Pena, 1991, p. 92).

VIOLENCE IN CHILDREN'S PROGRAMMES

As part of the series of special analyses carried out by this research into the depiction of violence in specific programme genres, a closer look was taken at violence as portrayed in children's programmes. These programmes were mainly broadcast during late weekday afternoons and Saturday and Sunday mornings on the terrestrial channels and Saturdays and Sundays during the day on Sky One. During the four-week monitoring period, 943 children's programmes were identified and coded for violence. More than four out of ten (43%) of these programmes were cartoons, and over half (55%) comprised a range of other non-cartoon children's programming (e.g., children's drama, children's information and children's entertainment). A small proportion (2%) of this output comprised pop music videos. These programmes were analysed in terms of their violent content in the same way as all other programme genres.

General measures of violence: channel differences

A total of 368 children's programmes were found to contain at least some violence, representing 39% of all coded children's programmes. Among those programmes containing any violence, more than half (57.5%) occurred on the four terrestrial channels (see Table 12.1). The greatest number of violent children's programmes occurred on Sky One which accounted for nearly one in four of all the violent acts coded for children's programmes in this research. Among the four terrestrial channels, Channel 4 contained the greatest number of children's programmes with violence. There was little difference between BBC1, BBC2 and ITV on this measure.

More than 4,000 violent acts and well over 1,900 violent sequences were recorded for children's programmes over the full analysis period. While there were more violence-containing programmes on the terrestrial channels than on the satellite channels, the latter contained many more violent incidents. Around two-thirds of all violent acts occurred on satellite channels. Nearly 47% of all violent acts in children's programmes occurred on Sky One alone (see Table 12.2).

These channel differences are confirmed further by an analysis of the average numbers of violent acts and violent sequences in violence-containing children's programmes. As Table 12.3 shows, children's programmes with violence contained many more distinct incidents of violence on satellite channels than on terrestrial channels. Particularly high average violent act rate averages were recorded for violent children's programmes on Sky One and The Movie Channel. Violent children's programmes on Sky One contained at least three times as many violent acts as the average violent children's programme on the terrestrial channels.

Table 12.1 Distribution of violence-containing children's programmes across channels

	n	%
BBC1	50	13.6
BBC2	50	13.6
ITV	51	14.0
Channel 4	62	16.8
Terrestrial	*213*	*58.0*
Sky One	83	23.0
UK Gold	21	5.6
Sky Movies	4	1.1
Movie Channel	47	12.5
Satellite	*155*	*42.2*
All channels	*368*	*100.0*

Note: Data aggregated over four weeks

Table 12.2 Total number of violent acts and violent sequences in programmes with violence

| | Violent acts | | Violent sequences | |
	n	%	*n*	%
BBC1	287	7.2	168	8.7
BBC2	275	6.8	147	7.6
ITV	399	10.0	256	13.2
Channel 4	348	8.6	163	8.4
Terrestrial	*1,309*	*32.6*	*734*	*37.9*
Sky One	1,870	46.7	787	40.6
UK Gold	97	2.3	64	3.3
Sky Movies	28	0.6	21	1.1
Movie Channel	704	17.4	333	17.2
Satellite	*2,699*	*67.4*	*1,205*	*62.1*
All channels	*4,008*	*100.0*	*1,939*	*100.0*

Note: Data aggregated over four weeks

Table 12.3 Average number of violent acts and violent sequences in programmes with violence

	Violent acts	Violent sequences
BBC1	6.0	3.5
BBC2	5.5	3.3
ITV	8.0	5.1
Channel 4	5.4	2.5
Terrestrial	*6.2*	*3.6*
Sky One	22.5	9.5
UK Gold	5.2	3.3
Sky Movies	5.3	3.6
Movie Channel	15.3	7.4
Satellite	*12.1*	*6.0*
All channels	*9.2*	*4.8*

Note: Data aggregated over four weeks

On average violent acts in children's programmes lasted for between six and seven seconds, while violent sequences were a little under 12 seconds in duration. Violent acts were longest of all on BBC1, UK Gold and The Movie Channel. Violent sequences were longest on average on Sky One and The Movie Channel (see Table 12.4).

The amount of time occupied by violence in children's programmes over all channels during the entire period monitored totalled more than 433 minutes (7.2 hours). More than two-thirds (68%) of this time occupied by

Table 12.4 Duration of violent acts and violent sequences in programmes with violence

	Violent acts	Violent sequences
BBC1	7.2	12.6
BBC2	6.0	10.8
ITV	6.6	10.2
Channel 4	6.0	13.2
Terrestrial	*6.5*	*11.7*
Sky One	6.6	15.6
UK Gold	7.2	10.8
Sky Movies	6.0	6.6
Movie Channel	7.2	15.0
Satellite	*6.8*	*12.0*
All channels	*6.7*	*11.9*

Notes: 1 Data aggregated over four weeks
2 Durations in seconds

violence occurred on the satellite channels monitored in this study. The results shown in Table 12.5 indicate the significant contribution of Sky One to the total figure. In fact 45% of all the time occupied by violence in children's programmes occurred on Sky One. This amounted to nearly 7% of total children's programme output time transmitted on Sky One during the period of monitoring. It can be clearly seen that no other channel comes close to this

Table 12.5 Distribution of time occupied by violence in children's programmes across channels

	Violence (minutes)	Violence as % of total output
BBC1	33.8	1.2
BBC2	29.4	1.0
ITV	43.5	1.5
Channel 4	32.3	1.2
Terrestrial	*139.0*	*1.2*
Sky One	194.7	6.9
UK Gold	11.9	*
Sky Movies	2.0	*
Movie Channel	85.9	0.3
Satellite	*294.5*	*1.8*
All channels	*433.5*	*1.5*

Notes: 1 Data aggregated over four weeks
2 * Less than 0.05%

level of violence in children's programmes. This finding, however, needs to be put into further context. Around 15% of all the violent acts of Sky One consisted of incidents in cartoons shown in the *DJ Kat TV Show* (see Chapter 3). This material, in turn, represented more than 29% of the violent acts in children's programmes on Sky One during the period monitored.

During the fourth week of coding, single episodes of two American children's adventure series featuring 'superhero' characters, *VR Troopers* and *The Mighty Morphin Power Rangers*, together accounted for 30% of all the violent acts in children's programmes on Sky One during that week. In each case, the episode was shown twice on the same day. The episode of *VR Troopers* was coded as containing 41 violent acts and the episode of *The Mighty Morphin Power Rangers* was coded as containing 49 violent acts. (*DJ Kat TV's* cartoons contributed 9% of the violent acts on Sky One's children's programmes during that same week.)

On the terrestrial channels considered together violence in children's programme accounted for just over 1% of total running for these programmes. Despite the relatively high violence minutage for Sky One, the overall average for the four satellite channels monitored is not that much greater than for the terrestrial channels because of the very low levels of violence, in terms of running time occupied by violent material, on UK Gold, Sky Movies and The Movie Channel.

LEVELS OF VIOLENCE IN DIFFERENT CHILDREN'S GENRES

Violent acts and violent sequences were most likely to occur in general children's programming. More than half of all acts of violence (56%) and all violent sequences (52%) in children's programmes were coded in general children's drama/entertainment/information programmes. Over four out of ten violent acts (43%) and sequences (47%) occurred in children's cartoons. Only a tiny fraction of all recorded violence in children's programmes occurred in pop music videos.

The pattern of violent incident distribution did vary to some degree from one week to the next. During the first week of coding, for example, more violent acts and sequences were found to occur in cartoons (54%) than in other children's programmes (43%).

Violent acts had a higher rate of occurrence in general children's programmes that were violent than in children's cartoons that were violent. The average violent non-cartoon children's programmes contained 13.2 acts of violence compared with an average of 9.1 acts of violence for violent children's cartoons. Of all the time occupied by violence in children's programmes, more than half (57%) occurred in general children's programmes, while just over four-tenths (42%) occurred in cartoons. Just 1% occurred in pop music videos.

On average, 1.4 minutes of programme running time was occupied by violence in violent general children's programmes compared with an average of one minute's running time for violent cartoons. In pop music videos which contained violence there was an average of 12 seconds of violence.

Channel differences in levels of violence for different children's genres

More than half the violent acts and violent sequences in children's programmes were found in cartoons, with just under half occurring in general children's programmes. This pattern was not observed consistently across all channels. On ITV and Sky One, for instance, cartoons accounted for a far greater proportion of violent acts and sequences on those two channels. In contrast, on BBC2 and most especially on Channel 4, cartoons accounted for relatively small proportions of all violent acts and sequences (see Table 12.6).

Table 12.6 Distribution of violent acts and violent sequences by children's programme genre and channel

	All %	BBC1 %	BBC2 %	ITV %	Ch.4 %	Sky One %
Violent acts						
General children's	48	44	64	19	86	25
Cartoons	52	56	35	79	13	75
Pop videos	1	0	1	2	1	0
Violent sequences						
General children's	47	51	57	17	84	25
Cartoons	53	49	42	82	15	75
Pop videos	1	0	1	1	1	0

Despite the greater total number of violent acts and sequences on cartoons, the average rate of occurrence of violent incidents was greater on general children's programmes (see Table 12.7). This difference may seem somewhat surprising, but is largely accounted for by the excessively high rate of occurrence of violent acts in general children's programmes on Sky One,

Table 12.7 Average number of violent acts and violent sequences per violence-containing programme by genre and channel

	All	BBC1	BBC2	ITV	Ch.4	Sky One	UK Gold
Violent acts							
General children's	2.2	1.0	0.7	1.5	0.4	9.5	0.1
Cartoons	0.9	0.6	0.8	0.7	1.4	1.5	0.4
Pop videos	0.2	0.0	0.0	0.2	0.8	0.4	0.0
Violent sequences							
General children's	1.0	0.5	0.5	0.9	0.2	3.9	0.1
Cartoons	0.5	0.4	0.4	0.4	0.7	0.7	0.3
Pop videos	0.1	0.0	0.0	0.2	0.3	0.3	0.0

where programmes such as *The Mighty Morphin Power Rangers* and *VR Troopers* made a disproportionate contribution to the overall level of violence in children's programmes during those weeks when they occurred.

The distribution of amount of time occupied by violence in children's programmes revealed that there was more violence in general children's programmes than in cartoons. Across all the channels, more than half of the minutage occupied by violence in children's programmes occurred in non-cartoon programmes. The distribution of violence between cartoons and other types of children's programmes varied from channel to channel. As Table 12.8 shows, significant amounts of violence occurred in general children's programmes on Sky One and BBC1, while the reverse pattern occurred on Channel 4 and UK Gold.

Table 12.8 Distribution of amount of time occupied by violence in different children's programme genres by channel

	All %	BBC1 %	BBC2 %	ITV %	Ch.4 %	Sky One %	UK Gold %
General children's	54	78	53	60	16	88	28
Cartoons	45	22	47	39	81	11	72
Pop videos	1	0	0	1	3	1	0

The most violent children's programmes

Relatively large numbers of violent acts and sequences were found in children's programmes. Together these incidents totalled over 433 minutes (over seven hours) of programme running time in the programmes monitored. Analysis of the distribution of this violent content, however, revealed that it was not evenly spread over the eight channels. Some channels contained more violent content in children's programming than did others. A sub-genre analysis also revealed certain variations in the distribution of violence among different categories of children's programming. Which particular programmes, though, contained the greatest amount of violence?

This question was addressed as with other genres by computing top 20 programme listings within the genre in terms of numbers of violent acts and violence minutage (Tables 12.9 and 12.10). The top 20 programme listing in each case was dominated by the *DJ Kat Show*, which contained a great deal of cartoon violence. Other prominent entrants were episodes of *The Mighty Morphin Power Rangers* and *VR Troopers*.

The top 20 programmes in terms of violent acts contained a total of 1,096 acts (mean = 54.8) and 410 sequences of violence (mean = 20.5). The mean scores indicate large numbers of separate violent incidents occurring in each of these programmes. Indeed, the programmes in this listing contained just under six minutes of violent action each on average.

Table 12.9 The 20 most violent children's programmes in terms of violent acts

Programme	Channel	Violent acts	Violence minutage	Violent sequences
DJ Kat Show	Sky One	106	16.1	30
DJ Kat Show	Sky One	87	6.9	41
DJ Kat Show	Sky One	69	11.5	35
DJ Kat Show	Sky One	61	8.7	29
DJ Kat Show	Sky One	60	5.6	22
DJ Kat Show	Sky One	60	5.6	22
DJ Kat Show	Sky One	56	9.6	11
Bugs Bunny Superstar	Sky Movies	55	6.4	12
DJ Kat Show	Sky One	51	3.6	31
Mighty Morphin Power Rangers	Sky One	49	4.6	22
Mighty Morphin Power Rangers	Sky One	49	4.6	22
Black Arrow	Sky Movies	45	1.8	25
VR Troopers	Sky One	44	4.0	6
VR Troopers	Sky One	44	4.0	6
VR Troopers	Sky One	44	4.8	6
Mighty Morphin Power Rangers	Sky One	44	2.4	17
Mighty Morphin power Rangers	Sky One	44	2.4	17
Live and Kicking	BBC1	43	4.2	8
DJ Kat Show	Sky One	43	6.3	25
DJ Kat Show	Sky One	42	4.4	23

Table 12.10 The 20 most violent children's programmes in terms of violence minutage

Programme	Channel	Violent acts	Violence minutage	Violent sequences
DJ Kat Show	Sky One	106	16.1	30
DJ Kat Show	Sky One	23	12.3	12
DJ Kat Show	Sky One	69	11.5	35
DJ Kat Show	Sky One	56	9.6	11
DJ Kat Show	Sky One	61	8.7	29
Young Mr Lincoln	Sky Movies	23	7.3	12
DJ Kat Show	Sky One	87	6.9	41
DJ Kat Show	Sky One	39	6.5	24
Bugs Bunny Superstar	Sky Movies	55	6.4	12
DJ Kat Show	Sky One	43	6.3	25
DJ Kat Show	Sky One	60	5.6	22
DJ Kat Show	Sky One	60	5.6	22
Mighty Morphin Power Rangers	Sky One	10	5.5	3
Sinbad	Sky Movies	11	4.7	4
Sinbad	Sky Movies	11	4.7	4
Pied Piper of Hamlin	Sky Movies	12	4.7	10
Mighty Morphin Power Rangers	Sky One	49	4.6	22
Mighty Morphin Power Rangers	Sky One	49	4.6	22
Hunchback of Notre Dame	Sky Movies	20	4.6	11
Hunchback of Notre Dame	Sky Movies	20	4.6	11

The programme entrants in the top 20 listing in terms of violence minutage contained a total of 140.8 minutes of violence (an average of just over seven minutes each), representing 32% of all violence minutage found in children's programmes. These programmes comprised just 2% of all children's programmes monitored in this study.

THE NATURE OF VIOLENCE IN CHILDREN'S PROGRAMMES

The foregoing findings indicate the levels of violence in children's programmes but what about its character? In what kinds of settings did violence in children's programmes occur? What physical forms did it take? Were there certain predominant motivational themes underlying the violence shown? Did violence in children's programmes prove to be particularly harmful and injurious to its victims? Who were the aggressors and victims? As with the other major programme genres, this study examined the nature of violence in children's programmes in terms of a variety of setting, contextual and character role attributes.

The setting of violence

There were three key setting variables: historical setting, environmental setting and geographical location. The historical settings of violence in children's programmes exhibited a wider dispersion than other major programme genres. While it was found that the greatest single proportion of violent acts occurred in present-day settings (30.2%), there were also greater than average proportions of violent incidents situated in the past (23.5%) and future (24.3%). In particular there were relatively high percentages of violent acts set in the distant past (17.8%) and distant future (15.1%).

There were some interesting channel differences. On ITV, most violence in children's programmes (64.5% of acts) occurred in the present day. Futuristic violence was especially likely to occur on Sky One (31.1% of violent acts in this genre on that channel) and BBC1 (21.8%). Historical violence was more likely than average to occur on BBC2 (37.4%) and Channel 4 (36.7%).

The environmental setting of violence in children's programmes in general was dominated by rural locations (19.1%), inner city locations (14.3%) and small town locations (13.1%). Violence occurred less often in uninhabited locations (9.3%), suburban locations (5.4%) and in a recognizably studio setting (4.2%). Rural violence was especially likely to occur on UK Gold (42.3%), The Movie Channel (33.2%), BBC2 (29.9%) and Channel 4 (28.9%). Inner city violence occurred most frequently on BBC1 (25.3%) and BBC2 (24.4%). Small town violence was especially likely on The Movie Channel (21.9%).

The most frequent geographical location for violence in children's programmes was the United States (33.9% of acts). This was especially true for Sky One (48.5%). British locations were the next most likely location (9.8%).

Both of these two locations were surpassed by cartoon settings (34.2%) which dominated violence locations on Channel 4 (53.9%), BBC2 (46.1%), and UK Gold (42.9%).

The form of violence

Violent acts were classified according to their physical form and the types of weapons they utilized. The top ten ranked types of violence in children's programmes, over all channels, are listed below. Together these ten types of violence accounted for more than eight in ten violent acts (80.7%) on children's programmes. The most likely form of violence involved shootings, and

Top ten types of violence		
	n	%
1 Shootings	775	18.9
2 Push/trip	549	13.6
3 Hit with object	515	12.8
4 Punch	301	7.3
5 Kick	266	6.4
6 Throwing	248	6.2
7 Attempted violence	232	5.6
8 Verbal threat	174	4.3
9 Explosion	138	3.5
10 Use of trap	88	2.1

Top ten types of weapons		
	n	%
1 Fist/hand	741	18.3
2 Laser weapon	454	11.2
3 Body part[1]	275	6.7
4 Karate/martial arts	247	6.1
5 Sword	244	6.0
6 Kick	238	5.8
7 Stick	122	3.0
8 Explosives	105	2.6
9 Various projectiles	94	2.3
10 Vehicle[2]	81	2.0

1 Part of body other than hand, head or foot
2 Vehicle other than car, lorry, chariot or bulldozer

this was followed by actions involving a person pushing or tripping someone else, and then by someone hitting someone else with an object. More than 400 acts of violence on children's programmes involved attempted or verbally threatening behaviour rather than actual physically violent behaviour.

The ten top weapon types accounted for almost two-thirds (64%) of all violent acts in children's programmes. Violence involving the fist or hand, futuristic hand held weapons and martial arts dominated in children's programmes. The use of laser weapons was most especially prominent on Sky One (18.6% of acts on that channel). Martial arts violence in children's programmes was somewhat more likely than average to be found on ITV and Sky One (9.3% of violent acts on each channel).

Motives for violence

Goals of aggressor	
Self-preservation	13.2
Protect society	9.8
Protect family home	4.6
Uphold the law	2.9
Respect for law	1.7
Evil/destructive	24.5
Ambition/power	18.4
Desire for money	3.9
Sexual	0.1
Religious	*
Other	15.9
Uncodable	4.5
Note: * Less than 0.5%	

The reasons underlying violence were classified in terms of a number of broad motivational contexts which included violence as an aspect of war or armed forces conflict, that associated with civil strife or defending civil liberties, criminal behaviour, law enforcement, domestic conflicts and other interpersonal disputes. Violence in children's programmes was most frequently either motivated by criminal goals (21.6%) or resulted from an argument or dispute between two or more people (21.3%). No other reasons really matched these two motivational contexts for violence. Violence used in defence of civil liberties (7.8%), in war (6.2%), for law enforcement (3.5%) or as a consequence of domestic disputes (1.9%) were all less frequently occurring. Interpersonal violence was much more likely than average to occur on BBC2 (34.4% of violent acts in children's programmes), Channel 4 (32.3%) and The Movie Channel (31.1%). Criminal violence was most prevalent on Sky One (28.8%) and war-time violence on BBC2 (16.3%).

The ten principal categories of aggressor goals were broadly divisible into two general classes of activity: violence in the service of positive or constructive goals and violence in the service of negative or destructive objectives. The latter outnumbered the former (46.9% versus 32.2% of violent acts) in children's programmes. The most common goal of violence was evil and destruction, followed by ambition and power seeking. On a less negative note, violence was quite commonly used as a means of self-defence or self-preservation. The other main positive reason was to protect society. There were few differences between channels. Violence for purely evil or destructive reasons in children's programmes was most often catalogued on ITV (36.4%), though so too was violence in the service of protecting society (15.6%).

Consequences of violence

Types of injuries caused by violence	
	%
Death	4.2
Serious wound	3.1
Mutilation	0.5
Limbs breaking	0.1
Stun	16.9
Minor wound	8.8
Bruises	7.8
Psychological	1.2
Other	7.6
No injury	45.7
Uncodable	3.9

The outcomes of violence were classified in terms of a series of objectively identifiable, visible injury outcomes and also in more subjective terms according to the amount of blood, pain and horror accompanying particular violent acts. Injury outcomes could be serious or mild. Relatively few violent acts (7.9%) in children's programmes caused serious outcomes for victims. The most likely serious outcome following violence in this genre was death. Around one in three violent acts (33.5%), however, caused mild injuries to victims. Around half of the latter, mild outcomes entailed victims being stunned, rather than cut and bruised. Psychological damage following violence in children's programmes was a rarity. Well over four out of ten violent acts on children's programmes depicted no injury consequences for victims. There were few differences between television channels in the patterns of injury consequences displayed following violence in children's programmes. Death, as an outcome, was slightly more likely than average to occur in programmes on The Movie Channel (9.2%) and BBC2 (7.8%). Serious injuries were also more frequently occurring than average on these two channels (8.1% and 5.2% respectively). No observable injury to victims following violence was most likely to be found on ITV (52.7%) and least likely to occur on BBC1 (27.6%).

Subjective assessments of violent acts were employed in an attempt to obtain further insights into the seriousness of violence depicted in children's programmes. Coders were asked to evaluate individual violent acts in terms of the amount of blood, pain and horror accompanying them. In each case, a violent act was rated along a five-point scale, with a score of 1 signifying a negligible degree of each quality and a score of 5 signifying an extreme degree of each quality. On this basis, a score of up to 3 would indicate a modest amount of blood and a mild amount of pain and horror. Scores which were higher than that indicated more worrying levels of such attributes.

More than eight out of ten violent acts (82.7%) contained no blood, while a tiny proportion (1.5%) contained very small amounts. Just a tiny fragment of the total (0.1%) was scored as containing a large amount of blood. This occurred on Sky One.

Around seven in ten violent acts (69.3%) depicted no pain or suffering by victims, while one in five (20%) depicted mild amounts of pain for victims. Less than one act in one hundred on children's programmes (0.7%) depicted severe pain and suffering of victims. Once again, this occurred on Sky One.

Extreme horror was a rarity in violence in children's programmes. More than seven in ten violent acts were accompanied by no horror at all (72.8%), while less than one in five (17.2%) were judged to depict mild levels of horror. Just a tiny proportion of acts (0.2%) were found to be characterized by extreme degrees of horror. These acts occurred in programmes broadcast on Sky One and UK Gold.

Aggressors and victims

Finally, violent acts were examined in terms of the types of characters who featured as aggressors and victims in children's programmes. Characters were classified according to their demography, which centred on their gender, age and ethnicity, and in terms of a range of character roles or occupational/professional roles (see Table 12.11). The demography of characters involved in violence on children's programmes revealed that aggressors and victims, for whom such characteristics could be identified, were most likely to be male, white and young adults (20-35 years) or teenagers. There were more American aggressors and victims than any other nationality, whether white or black. Female aggressors and victims of violence were far less numerous than males. There was no tendency for any demography group to be disproportionately victimized.

The demography of aggressors and victims of violence did not differ significantly from that found in other major programme genres. There were two exceptional points about the characters involved in violence in children's programmes however. First, teenage characters were more prominently involved on both the giving and receiving side of violence. They were the age group most likely to be involved in violence after young adults. In all other major programme genres, violence was more likely to be perpetrated and suffered by middle age range characters. A second important distinction is the large proportion of characters involved in violence who could not be clearly coded in terms of demography. The reason for this probably has

Table 12.11 Demography of aggressors and victims

	Aggressors		Victims	
	n	%	n	%
Gender				
One male	2,017	49.9	1,777	44.0
One female	268	6.6	204	5.1
Group male	415	10.3	455	11.2
Group female	23	0.6	19	0.5
Group mixed	228	5.6	339	8.4
Other	152	3.8	120	3.0
Cannot code	939	23.2	1,125	27.9
Age				
Child (up to 12)	64	1.6	102	2.5
Teenager (13–19)	571	14.1	504	12.5
Young adult (20–35)	999	24.7	909	22.5
Middle age (36–65)	326	8.1	271	6.7
65 plus	26	0.6	26	0.6
Mixed age group	68	1.7	177	4.4
Cannot code	1,994	49.2	2,051	50.8
Ethnic origin				
White UK	380	9.3	367	9.1
White US	758	18.5	674	16.7
White other	415	10.1	382	9.5
Black UK	5	0.1	10	0.2
Black US	97	2.4	82	2.0
Black other	51	1.2	41	1.0
Asian	19	0.5	7	0.2
Oriental	64	1.6	34	0.8
Mixed group	157	3.8	186	4.6
Other human	198	4.8	82	2.0
Animal	500	12.2	571	14.1
Cannot code	1,446	35.5	1,604	39.7

much to do with the fact that a great deal of the violence in children's programmes features either animated characters or supernatural/futuristic characters from other worlds for whom no clear demographic labelling can be made. This last point is reinforced by listings of the top ten character types involved in violence as aggressors or victims on children's programmes, as shown below.

The top ten aggressor types represented the great majority of violent acts (86.3%) on children's programmes, as did the top ten victim types (85.6%). The difficulty of assigning demographic characteristics to aggressors and victims of violence in this genre is underlined by the prevalence of such characters as cartoon animals, other non-human cartoon characters, robots, monsters and alien beings. The two top ten listings further underline the significance of cartoon characters as perpetrators (56.3% of violent acts) and

Top ten types of aggressor

		n	%
1	Cartoon – human	1,023	25.2
2	Cartoon – animal	825	20.9
3	Cartoon – other	416	10.2
4	Fantasy – law enforcer	392	9.6
5	Robot	201	4.8
6	Schoolchildren	192	4.6
7	Situation character	155	3.8
8	Monster	113	2.8
9	Martial artist	99	2.2
10	Alien	97	2.2

Top ten types of victim

		n	%
1	Cartoon – human	988	24.2
2	Cartoon – animal	847	21.4
3	Fantasy law enforcer	397	9.7
4	Cartoon – other	384	9.4
5	Robot	231	5.5
6	Situation character	156	3.9
7	Monster	139	3.6
8	Schoolchildren	136	3.4
9	Inanimate object	107	2.7
10	Martial artist	83	1.8

victims of violence (55% of violent acts) in children's programmes. Violence in this genre was characterized by its extensive involvement of animated or fantasy characters, as distinct from real human beings. Schoolchildren and situation characters, for instance, accounted for just 8.4% of aggressors and 7.3% of victims.

The most violent programmes – contextual features

It is important to examine in greater detail the contextual features relating to violence that were found in some of the most 'violent' children's pro-grammes. The most violent children's programme was the American series, *The Mighty Morphin Power Rangers*, which was shown on ITV and Channel Four during the four weeks of analysis. The programme shown on 25 October has been taken as an illustration. This programme is representative of the type of depictions shown on this series, but is of particular interest for two reasons. First, it was one of the most violent programmes on terrestrial television, in terms of number of violent acts, with an act count of 36. Second, it contained an incident coded as 'stabbing', which has previously been identified as a potentially problematic form of violence from the perspective of the affective reactions of viewers.

The high number of violent acts was accounted for by the Power Rangers' activities, much of which involved violent conflict. All this violent activity was categorized as 'defending civil liberties', a socially positive motivation. For the most part (in 89% of cases), they only used violence as retaliatory or defensive action. Thus, the overriding rationale for violence in the case of the Power Rangers themselves was presented as being legitimate, designed to defend themselves or protect the victimized. Such violence was also por-trayed as an extension of the political order, in that the Power Rangers' actions were concerned with maintaining the status quo. A normative judge-ment is made here which implies that certain types of violence are politically acceptable. The question is whether this motivational context renders the violence suitable for a children's programme. The reinforcement of this political and cultural message about violence via the use of iconography as well as dialogue among the characters is a prevailing theme throughout this particular fantasy children's series.

The violence shown in *The Mighty Morphin Power Rangers* is highly stylized with the majority of acts taking the form of martial arts style kicking (33%) and punching (17%). No physical injury occurs in 95% of the violent acts. There is no blood shown and the acts were generally categorized as mild in terms of horror value. An interesting feature of this particular episode was that one violent act was coded as "high" in terms of pain experienced by a victim. A closer analysis revealed that this incident involved the killing of a monster bee which had been attacking the Power Rangers. The bee was catapulted backwards and landed on the ground and did not recover. The death of this bee was over very quickly, however, and there were few signs of prolonged agony.

The monsters and evil characters in *The Mighty Morphin Power Rangers* tend to be anthropomorphized animals or are presented as other non-human creatures, thus underlining the fantasy theme of the show. In addition to martial arts style fighting, nearly one in five incidents in this episode (17%) involved a laser-type gun and the spraying of venom by the bee. The identified stabbing incident, which upon initial registration was of some concern, was found on closer inspection to comprise a relatively innocuous stabbing of a sword into the ground. Incidents involving sharp cutting instruments were rare in this programme, although a Power Ranger did use a sword to slash at the monster bee on one occasion. It was obvious, in this case, that no contact had been made.

Overall the violence in this programme was concentrated in a choreographed dance and was an acrobatic and highly stylized version of martial arts, performed in an almost balletic way. Physical contact between characters performing these movements was rare.

The *DJ Kat TV Show* was coded as the sixth most violent programme in the four weeks analysed. However, this needs to be qualified. The programme lasts for two hours and consists of a compilation of cartoons and other children's programmes. The show is presented by DJ Kat, an anthropomorphic cat. He introduces each separate programme or cartoon as well as talks to guests and other characters. On 22 October 1994, the *DJ Kat TV Show* was coded as containing 106 violent acts. On this occasion, the show contained several cartoons (all containing violence); a soap opera for children called *General Accident: Superman*, where the Superman character was a college student; a *vox populi* in a fish warehouse; and *The Mighty Morphin Power Rangers*.

Although a child watching the show for two hours would be subjected to numerous acts of violence, these varied in intensity and in the context in which they occurred. Cartoon violence accounted for two-thirds (66%) of the violence shown, much of which was set in the distant future and was surreal. Although nearly one in five (19%) of the violent acts involved shooting, the majority of these were with a laser weapon, reinforcing the unreal nature of the violence. In approaching half the cases (46%), no physical injury was inflicted upon victims of violence and in nearly one in three cases (30%), the worst damage victims suffered was to be stunned. Death following violence was rare on this programme with only three instances (3%) where a cartoon character was eliminated altogether. None of the violence was in any way graphic. No blood was recorded as being visible in any of the 106 acts of violence. Pain was non-existent in an overwhelming majority (96%) of cases, and was coded as mild in a handful (4%) of incidents. None of the acts of violence recorded in this show was classified as 'horrific'. Once again, the great majority (96%) were coded as completely devoid of horror, while a small number (4%) were categorized as mild in horror terms.

Clearly, this contextual analysis of the *DJ Kat TV Show* projects a completely different perspective in interpreting the real nature of this programme, from what might be inferred on the basis of a purely quantitative count of violent acts. The show itself is a compilation of cartoons and other programme items and the 'violence' is of the most fantastic kind in terms of style and context. Although concerns have been voiced about the potential impact of cartoon violence on young children, the evidence for significant and lasting effects of such content, over and above observations of short-term effects which occur in play settings, is not yet convincing.

SUMMARY AND CONCLUSIONS

There is particular concern about the portrayal of violence in programmes that are aimed specifically at very young viewers because they are perceived as psychologically vulnerable to the potentially harmful side effects such material is believed by some people to have. Since such programmes can be expected to attract audiences predominantly made up of these vulnerable individuals, it is important that they provide socially responsible examples of conduct and project values and norms that are likely to encourage rather than undermine acceptable forms of behaviour among children.

While it is natural that parents and teachers especially should be concerned about the possible role played by television in any destructive, anti-social or potentially harmful behaviour shown by children, it is equally important, in identifying the causes of misbehaviour, to understand and to acknowledge the varying levels of sophistication different children bring to the viewing situation. Children do not automatically accept everything and anything they see on television at face value, nor do they invariably identify with character portrayals and regard them as having some relevance to their own lives (Gunter and McAleer, 1990).

As the current research has indicated, violence does form a part of children's programming on television shown in the United Kingdom. As the top 20 programme listings indicated, though, a small proportion of all children's programmes (2%) accounted for around a third of all violence minutage found in this genre. Any statements about the quantity and distribution of violence in children's programmes, however, must be qualified by the caveat that this finding is true in the context of the frame of reference adopted by the content analysis carried out in this study. It was noted in Chapter 1 that content analysis attempts to provide a dispassionate, descriptive account of what happens on screen in terms of prescribed definitions of programme content and its attributes. As such, an analysis of this sort can reveal nothing directly about the possible impact of programmes upon viewers. What it can do, however, is catalogue the frequency with which certain types of behaviour occur on television, the shape or form such behaviour takes on, the settings in which it occurs and the nature of the actors involved.

During the period covered by this current analysis, more than 900 programmes produced for children were monitored of which a substantial minority (39%) were found to contain at least some violence. Within those programmes, violent acts occurred on average around six times per programme on terrestrial channels and around twice as often on the four satellite channels monitored. These violent incidents occupied more than seven hours of programme running time in total across the children's programmes that were monitored, which gave an average of 1.2 minutes of violence per violence-containing programme. These bald quantitative figures, on their own, disguise the often widely varying forms which the catalogued violence took on. As we have seen in earlier chapters, from the point of view of assessing the implications of the content analysis results for the way such material might be perceived or reacted to by viewers, it is essential to examine the nature of the portrayed violence.

Children's reactions to television violence vary with the form of the violence and the context in which it is shown (Noble, 1975). Another key factor is the degree to which they identify with the perpetrators of violence (Bandura and Walters, 1963). Children make distinctions between violence from realistic and fantasy settings, although the ease with which this occurs varies with the age of the child. Confusions may exist about whether the people on television are 'real' people or not, especially among very young children aged six years or less. By the age of seven or eight, however, although some confusions still persist, most children can generally discriminate between human and animated characters on screen (Dorr, 1983).

Children become more sophisticated about television programmes as they grow older. This development occurs at more than one level. Deciding about the realism of television may involve comparing television portrayals with real life. There is accumulating evidence that the knowledge that most fictional television programmes are made up develops during elementary school years. One study found that from the age of five through to 12 the knowledge that television characters are portrayed by actors (and are not real people) gradually improved. Among five- to six-year-olds, 58% did not understand this. Among eight-year-olds, 45% completely understood that characters were actors; another 26% partially understood it and 29% did not understand it. Among 11- and 12-year-olds, 65% had complete understanding (Fernie, 1981). Research elsewhere indicated that the age of eight is a crucial period when understanding about fictional television programmes and fictional television characters suddenly improves (Hawkins, 1977).

When presented with pairs of programmes and asked to say which was the more real and why, children aged over eight were found to be better able to explain the differences than children younger than eight. This difference in performance was in part due to children's varying abilities to express themselves with age, but stemmed in part also from the deeper level of understanding about television which emerged among the older children. In making reality–fantasy distinctions, it has been shown that younger children tend to focus on physical features of a programme which provide cues to its lack of reality, including the presence (or absence) of stunts, camera tricks, costumes, props and sets. Distinctions are also dependent on whether a presentation is acted, scripted, rehearsed, live or filmed (Dorr, 1983).

In the current research, much of the violence occurring in children's programmes took place in unreal settings or circumstances, involving either animated characters or fantastic superheroes who would transform from ordinary looking human beings into costumed alter egos with special, super-human powers. Much of the violence therefore had 'fairy tale' qualities about it. On the basis of media effects research with children, such content does not represent the kind of violence which young viewers would take seriously.

The most popular forms of violence involved the use of the hand or fist, futuristic hand-held weapons, or martial arts. The goals of aggressors were dominated by evil or destructive needs or the lust for power. Lined up against these antisocial goals were the needs to protect oneself or society. Such motives typified the relatively simplistic plot structures of children's fantasy action series such as the currently popular *Mighty Morphin Power Rangers* and *VR Troopers*. The outcomes of violence in these contexts, however, were frequently not shown while those that were depicted were generally minor injuries.

The setting for much of the violence in children's programmes is therefore clearly divorced from everyday reality. Concern also exists, of course, about the capacity of such programmes to provide undesirable examples to young viewers because they depict lead characters with whom children can identify. Identification can occur especially when viewers perceive some degree of similarity between themselves and characters on screen and when those characters have sufficient attractive and sought-after attributes such as having prestige, status or popularity. Identification can play an important part in rendering a media communication more likely to produce a shift in audience attitudes (Kelman, 1961) and is associated with increased like-lihood of viewers imitating an actor's behaviour (Bandura, 1973; Mischel and Liebert, 1967).

An analysis of the character-type profile of aggressors and victims in children's programmes can provide one source of evidence related to the potential for audience identification with violent action in these pro-grammes. Perhaps the most significant feature here is the age of characters involved in violence. While children's programmes reflected the general pattern of gender involvement found in other genres, with males predomin-antly featuring as aggressors and victims of violence, the age profiles of aggressors and victims differed from those of other programme types. Sub-stantial proportions of the characters involved in violence in children's programmes fell within the teenage or young adult age groups. The prevalence of young adult aggressors reflected the age profile observed in other major programme genres. The representation of teenage aggressors, however, was proportionately more prominent in children's programmes than anywhere else. At the same time, there were relatively few middle-age range aggressors, again marking a departure from the age profile observed in other programme genres. Thus, in terms of age profile, it could be argued that children's programmes provide a greater proportion of opportunities for character identification among members of their young audiences.

A further examination of the character types involved in violence in children's programmes suggests, however, that the age factor may be counterbalanced to some degree by the fact that perpetrators of violence were dominated by cartoon and fantasy human characters. There was also a more significant likelihood of prominent violence perpetrators taking on the form of robots, monsters or alien beings in children's programmes than anywhere else. One recent study has suggested that fantasy superheroes such as the currently popular *Mighty Morphin Power Rangers* can provide role models which young children in the five to seven years range may copy. In this study, groups of young American children were observed playing in a room with a range of toys before and after watching an episode of *The Mighty Morphin Power Rangers*. According to the researchers, boys (though not girls) exhibited more aggressiveness in their play after watching this programme than they had been showing before seeing it. In particular, observation was made of boys' emulation of the Power Rangers violence in performing similar karate movements (Boyatzis *et al.*, 1995). Unfortunately, this study failed to indicate whether the behaviour displayed during the post-viewing represented 'real aggression' or 'pretend play' with the children adopting characters from a recently viewed programme as role models (Smith, 1994). Since no control was used in which a different kind of programme was shown to children (either with no violence or a different kind of violence) it is difficult to know as well whether the 'effect' on observed play behaviour was caused by specific portrayals in the programme or the children being generally aroused by having just watched an exciting programme. The latter effect might have occurred even with an exciting non-violent programme and the forms of play behaviour observed after the programme had been shown may represent regular styles of play among children today.

The distinctions which children draw between different programme contexts represent the most important mediating factor in relation to their responses to television violence. Much of the violence contained in children's programmes occurs in cartoons or fantastic 'fairy tale' type action-adventure series where there are many physical cues present to indicate the unreal nature of these programmes and the characters and events they contain.

13 Scheduling and television violence

One of the key concerns about television centres on the suitability of programmes for children. Younger members of the audience are generally
regarded as lacking the psychological maturity to cope with certain types
of programming and should therefore be protected from exposure to unsuitable content as far as possible. At the same time, only around one in three
television households have children aged up to 15 years resident in them,
leaving a great majority occupied by adult viewers only. As well as the need
to protect children, there is also a need to cater for the mature tastes of the
wider adult audience. For this reason, broadcasters employ a Family Viewing Policy which aims to create a balance between these two sets of needs.
Up to 9.00 pm in the evening, no material may be shown which is unsuitable
for children. After 9.00 pm there is a gradual relaxation of that rule.

The Independent Television Commission's Programme Code requires that
'material unsuitable for children must not be broadcast at times when the
largest numbers of children are viewing' (Section 1.5(i)). Although it is
recognized that there is no part of the evening when no children at all
are watching, there is a view that in providing a diverse programme
service designed to cater for a wide array of tastes and interests, an inevitable
consequence is that some material may be broadcast which is not suitable for
children.

Public opinion research has established that the television audience in the
United Kingdom has widespread general awareness of a 'Family Viewing
Policy', with such awareness being especially well developed among parents
whose children still live at home with them (Gunter *et al.*, 1994). Almost as
widespread is the knowledge that family viewing time ends at 9.00 pm on the
terrestrial channels.

When a channel is encrypted, or only available to cable customers on
payment of a fee additional to the basic subscription to the service, its
availability to children will be more restricted and parents can, in principle,
assume a greater degree of control over whether their children will be able to
watch. Under these circumstances, the ITC's Programme Code, for example,
permits the point at which parents may be expected to share responsibility
for what is viewed to be shifted from 9.00 pm to as early as 8.00 pm,

depending on the nature of the service concerned. Similarly, the Code states that material of a more adult kind than would be acceptable at the same time on a more broadly available channel may be shown after 10.00 pm and before 5.30 am. This flexibility does not extend to basic subscription channels.

The ITC's Programme Code also applies to the contents of acquired material, including films, as well as to the production of programmes. British Board of Film Classification (BBFC) certifications of the versions of films or programmes proposed for transmission may be used as a guide to scheduling where they exist. Stricter rules apply to video classification than cinema classification since the former includes a test of suitability for viewing in the home. An even stricter classification applies to material intended for transmission on a subscription television service.

Public awareness of a scheduling policy applied to cable and satellite channels is generally much less widespread than that for the mainstream terrestrial channels. Annual public opinion surveys conducted by the ITC found, however, that there were signs of a steady improvement in awareness (Gunter *et al.*, 1994). Just 8% of a national UK survey sample were aware of such a policy for the new channels in 1992. This figure reached 15% by 1993 (19% among respondents with children).

Not surprisingly, reported awareness of a scheduling policy on cable and satellite channels was related to whether or not individuals received these channels. Over one in three respondents (39%) who could receive cable television and over one in two (58%) of those who could receive satellite channels were aware of a scheduling policy on these channels compared with just one in 15 (7%) of those individuals who could only receive terrestrial channels (Gunter *et al.*, 1994).

Amongst those who did know that there was a scheduling policy for cable and satellite channels, 41% thought that the time at which scheduling restrictions occur focused, in the case of satellite and cable movie channels, on 8.00 pm, 14% nominated 9.00 pm and 33% though the key time was 10.00 pm. One in five respondents (20%) were unable to name a time. In the case of other non-movie satellite and cable channels the stated times mentioned focused on 8.00 pm (18%), 9.00 pm (17%) and 10.00 pm (24%). More than two out of five respondents (42%) were unable to state a time, even amongst the group aware of some scheduling policy.

When the twin scheduling restrictions of 8.00 pm for 15–rated material and 10.00 pm for 18–rated material were mentioned for certain satellite and cable channels (e.g., Sky Movies, HVC and The Movie Channel) awareness rose to just over two fifths of cable viewers (42%) and to almost three-fifths of satellite viewers (59%), which represented significant increases on the previous year's figures (27% and 24% respectively), particularly for satellite dish viewers.

For the benefit of all respondents, and most especially those who were ignorant of family viewing policies, they were informed that the mainstream terrestrial channels employed a 9.00 pm scheduling time and some satellite and cable channels operated two scheduling times. One of these was at 8.00 pm for 15–rated material and the other at 10.00 pm for 18–rated material. Did they think that these times were about right, too early or too late?

The 9.00 pm watershed on ITV, BBC and Channel 4 was regarded by over seven out of ten respondents (72%) as 'about right', while one in five (20%) thought it was 'too early' and one in twenty (5%) thought it was 'too late'. Respondents with young children aged up to nine years old were more likely to agree that the 9.00 pm scheduling restriction was 'about right' (78%) than were respondents with older children aged 10 to 15 years (69%). Respondents with children aged 10 to 15 years (24%) were more likely than any others to say that 9.00 pm was 'too early'.

Opinions about the two scheduling restriction times on certain cable and satellite television channels revealed a majority of all respondent (54%) saying that 8.00 pm and 10.00 pm were 'about right', with fewer than one in ten (7%) preferring 9.00 pm. One in five (21%) thought that 8.00 pm was too early, while few (1%) thought it was too late. The watershed at 10.00 pm was seen as either too late (2%) or too early (6%) by only small proportions of respondents. Fewer than one in five (17%) had no opinion at all about these timing restrictions on identified categories of material.

VIOLENCE AND TIME OF TRANSMISSION

The general measures of violence on television were examined in terms of time of transmission in order to find out if levels of violence varied across the day. The day was divided into a number of different time-bands to represent peak-time and non-peak-time; pre- and post-watershed periods; and other time periods within these principal time-bands. Common time-bands were used to compare the four terrestrial channels and two satellite entertainment channels (Sky One and UK Gold), while different time-bands were employed for the two movie channels which represented their distinct classification periods.

Data are presented for violent acts, violent sequences, and amount of violence measured in terms of minutes filled by violent activity in violence-containing programmes. As well as presenting data on the total amount of violence coded for different channels at different times of the day, data are also shown for the average amount of violence occurring in violence-containing programmes.

Violent acts

Table 13.1 shows the total number of violent acts in violence-containing programmes on terrestrial and satellite entertainment channels aggregated over the four weeks of analysis. Looking at the day as divided into five parts: 06.00–18.00, 18.00–21.00, 21.00–22.30, 22.30–midnight and

Table 13.1 Total number of violent acts in violence-containing programmes on terrestrial and satellite entertainment channels as a function of time of transmission

	Time-bands				
	06.00– 18.00	18.00– 21.00	21.00– 22.30	22.30– 24.00	00.00– 06.00
BBC1	605	172	259	158	212
BBC2	473	272	172	80	118
ITV	931	223	227	244	760
Channel 4	735	122	103	64	307
Sky One	2,656	421	383	173	81
UK Gold	757	138	353	135	326
TOTAL	6,157	1,348	1,497	854	1,804

midnight–06.00, it is clear that the greatest number of violent acts occurred during the 06.00–18.00 period. However, this result, taken at face value, is misleading because 06.00–18.00 represents far and away the biggest time-band. As later results will demonstrate, a better indicator is the average rate at which violence occurs per programme or per hour during these time-bands. Such a comparison reveals a lower rate of occurrence of violence in programmes with violence or on an hourly basis during the early part of the day compared with later on.

Channel comparisons on the basis of total number of violent acts revealed that Sky One contained the greatest number of acts during the day (up to 6.00pm) of any of these six channels, with ITV in second place. Sky One also contained the greatest total number of violent acts during peak time (18.00–22.30). Late-night (post-10.30 pm) ITV achieved the greatest number of violent acts of any of these six channels.

Table 13.2 shows the average number of violent acts per violence-containing programme on terrestrial and satellite entertainment channels. In general, violence-containing programmes contained more violent acts when shown post-9.00 pm than when shown before 9.00 pm. Average rates of violence exhibited the biggest increase from the immediately pre-9.00 pm period to the immediately post-9.00 pm period (21.00–22.30). This pattern was generally true for all channels here, with the exception within this period of analysis of BBC2. For this channel, a higher rate of violence, in terms of violent acts, occurred during the 6.00 to 9.00 pm period than for the 9.00 to 10.30 pm period.

Channels such as BBC1 and ITV broadcast their most densely packed violent programmes after midnight, whereas on Sky One, programmes with the highest frequencies of violent acts were shown during daytime. The latter violence rates were principally contributed towards by cartoons and cartoon-like, fantasy science fiction series featuring human or humanoid characters.

Table 13.2 Average number of violent acts per violence-containing programme on terrestrial and satellite entertainment channels as a function of time of transmission

	Time-bands				
	06.00–18.00	18.00–21.00	21.00–22.30	22.30–24.00	00.00–06.00
BBC1	4.96	4.37	7.31	6.88	11.35
BBC2	5.43	8.22	5.09	5.56	7.03
ITV	6.79	6.43	8.37	8.97	11.08
Channel 4	6.01	4.77	5.57	6.50	6.98
Sky One	16.78	9.86	12.92	8.01	4.05
UK Gold	4.97	4.79	9.21	5.22	8.15
AVERAGE	7.49	6.41	8.08	6.86	8.11

Average rates of violence (in terms of violent acts) per hour are shown in Table 13.3. Average hourly rates of violence across all six channels were found to be highest during the late evening (9.00–10.30 pm) period (6.0 acts per hour). They were lowest during the late-night (post-midnight) period (1.8 per hour). A somewhat higher rate per hour occurred during the very late evening (10.30 pm–midnight) period (3.4). The hourly daytime rate of violence was a little lower than this (3.1), while in the early evening, the rate was lower still (2.7).

On all six channels, and most markedly so on Sky One, UK Gold, BBC1 and ITV, average hourly rates of violence increased dramatically during the 9.00–10.30 pm period compared with the preceding period.

Table 13.3 Average number of violent acts per hour on terrestrial and satellite entertainment channels as a function of time of transmission

	Time-bands				
	06.00–18.00	18.00–21.00	21.00–22.30	22.30–24.00	00.00–06.00
BBC1	1.8	2.0	6.2	3.8	1.3
BBC2	1.4	3.2	4.1	1.9	0.7
ITV	2.8	2.7	5.4	5.8	4.5
Channel 4	2.2	1.5	2.5	1.5	1.8
Sky One	7.9	5.0	9.1	4.1	0.5
UK Gold	2.3	1.6	8.4	3.2	1.9
AVERAGE	3.1	2.7	6.0	3.4	1.8

Violent sequences

The results for violent sequences largely mirrored those for violent acts (see Tables 13.4 and 13.5). The largest overall number of violent sequences

Table 13.4 Total number of violent sequences on terrestrial and satellite entertainment channels as a function of time of transmission

	Time-bands				
	06.00– 18.00	18.00– 21.00	21.00– 22.30	22.30– 24.00	00.00– 06.00
BBC1	355	110	130	83	81
BBC2	246	168	111	49	58
ITV	594	138	147	122	300
Channel 4	356	52	71	25	161
Sky One	1,105	192	213	91	45
UK Gold	422	94	193	89	174
TOTAL	3,078	754	865	459	819

Table 13.5 Average number of violent sequences per violence-containing programme on terrestrial and satellite channels as a function of time of transmission

	Time-bands				
	06.00– 18.00	18.00– 21.00	21.00– 22.30	22.30– 24.00	00.00– 06.00
BBC1	2.9	2.9	3.8	3.6	5.0
BBC2	3.0	5.3	3.3	2.8	3.3
ITV	4.2	4.2	5.4	4.6	5.8
Channel 4	2.9	1.2	3.5	2.8	3.7
Sky One	6.9	4.7	7.1	3.8	2.2
UK Gold	2.8	3.3	4.8	3.6	4.3
AVERAGE	3.8	3.6	4.7	3.5	4.1

occurred during the daytime. This was also the biggest time-band, spreading over 12 hours per day. The average rates of violent sequences per violence-containing programme revealed relatively small differences between time-bands, with the late-night, post-midnight period exhibiting the highest rate of violent incidents. There were some differences between channels in terms of total numbers of violent sequences and their average rate of occurrence in particular time-bands. On BBC1, for instance, violent sequences were more numerous during the day than during peak-time or late-night programmes. However, daytime programmes were individually less violent than those occurring later in the day.

On ITV, the greatest total number of violent sequences were again found during the daytime time-band. There was also a much higher total count of late-night violent sequences for this channel than was found for BBC1. Post-midnight programmes were also the most violent in terms of average number of violent sequences per violent programme. On BBC2, the most violent period in terms of density of violent sequences was the early peak-time between 6.00 pm and 9.00 pm. On Channel 4, the most violent programmes were again reserved for the post-midnight hours. On Sky One, daytime programmes contained more violent sequences in total and a higher rate of violence per violent programme than did the late evening or post-midnight periods. The most violent programmes of all on this channel, in terms of violent sequences, occurred during late peak-time. The late peak-time highest rates of violent sequences per violent programme were repeated for UK Gold.

Amount of violence

The amount of violence in minutes for different time-bands indicated, once again, that the total amount of time filled by violent acts may be a somewhat misleading measure. The greatest amounts were recorded for the pre-peak and post-peak times. However, these periods were far more extensive than peak-time (just 4.5 hours) and hence provided far more opportunity for violence to occur (see Table 13.6).

Table 13.6 Total amount of violence (in minutes) on terrestrial and satellite entertainment channels as a function of time of transmission

	Time-bands				
	06.00–18.00	18.00–21.00	21.00–22.30	22.30–24.00	00.00–06.00
BBC1	74.7	19.3	33.1	13.3	27.4
BBC2	55.7	44.3	21.4	8.4	12.9
ITV	110.2	33.6	41.8	113.9	142.0
Channel 4	71.4	11.8	10.1	5.4	42.9
Sky One	481.1	80.4	25.7	15.6	16.2
UK Gold	103.6	16.9	55.2	17.6	50.3
TOTAL	896.7	206.3	187.3	174.2	291.7

A better indicator may be the average amount of violence in violence-containing programmes, since this may reveal whether violence-containing programmes shown at different times of the day vary in terms of the quantity of violence they contain. There was some evidence that such variation does occur (see Table 13.7). In general, violence-containing programmes shown after 9.00 pm contained more violence than those shown before 9.00 pm. Programmes containing the greatest average amount of violence tended to occur during the late-night, 10.30 pm to midnight period. This pattern was most clearly the case in respect of ITV and Channel 4. There were, however, channel variations in this measure. On Sky One, for example, the most violent programmes, in terms of amount of time filled by violence, occurred

Table 13.7 Average amount of violence (in minutes) per violence-containing programme on terrestrial and satellite entertainment channels as a function of time of transmission

	Time-bands				
	06.00–18.00	18.00–21.00	21.00–22.30	22.30–24.00	00.00–06.00
BBC1	0.6	0.5	0.8	0.6	1.4
BBC2	0.8	1.4	0.7	0.5	0.7
ITV	0.8	1.0	1.6	3.8	2.2
Channel 4	2.0	0.5	0.5	1.9	1.0
Sky One	2.6	2.0	0.9	0.7	1.0
UK Gold	0.7	0.6	1.4	0.7	1.3
AVERAGE	1.3	1.0	1.0	1.4	1.3

during the daytime. On BBC2, the most violent programmes, by this measure, occurred in peak-time. On BBC1, the most violent programmes occurred after midnight.

Violence levels on the two satellite movie channels, Sky Movies and The Movie Channel, were examined for four time-bands: 06.00–20.00, 20.00–22.00, 22.00–24.00, and 00.00–06.00. The results are presented in Table 13.8.

Levels of violence in terms of violent acts were high throughout the day compared with terrestrial channels and satellite non-movie channels. There was a clear difference between pre-10.00 pm and post-10.00 pm levels, however. The latter were higher than the former. This pattern was true for the other violence measures as well.

SUMMARY AND CONCLUSIONS

In looking at the occurrence of violence on different television channels by time of day, this chapter, at initial glance, suggests that violence occurs across the day and that the daytime hours on many channels contain large numbers of violent incidents. Different quantitative measures of violence can provide varying impressions of the amount of violence that occurs in programmes as a function of when during the day they are transmitted. Quite apart from this level of interpretation, however, the current results need to be considered alongside evidence presented earlier about the different types of violence on television.

The daytime totals for violent acts, sequences and minutage can be misleading when compared directly with other periods of the broadcast day because the time-bands adopted in this analysis were not all equal in length. It is understandable that daytime programmes accumulated higher violence totals than other time-bands given that the band was at least twice as long as the next longest. A more equitable way of comparing time-bands is in terms of the average rates of occurrence figures which show for violent

Table 13.8 Levels of violence on satellite movie channels as a function of time of transmission

	Time-bands			
	06.00– *20.00*	*20.00–* *22.00*	*22.00–* *24.00*	*00.00–* *06.00*
Violent acts: total				
Sky Movies	1,735	283	982	1,758
Movie Channel	2,841	360	671	881
Both	*4,576*	*643*	*1,653*	*2,639*
Violent acts: mean				
Sky Movies	13.4	10.4	24.2	25.3
Movie Channel	14.6	14.9	15.9	14.3
Both	*14.0*	*12.7*	*20.0*	*19.8*
Violent sequences: total				
Sky Movies	924	178	377	743
Movie Channel	1,427	161	339	435
Both	*2,351*	*339*	*716*	*1,178*
Violent sequences: mean				
Sky Movies	5.2	6.4	9.6	10.7
Movie Channel	7.5	6.7	8.0	6.8
Both	*6.4*	*6.6*	*8.8*	*8.8*
Amount: total (in minutes)				
Sky Movies	273	60	136	259
Movie Channel	339	36	94	120
Both	*612*	*96*	*230*	*379*
Amount: mean (in minutes)				
Sky Movies	8.5	8.5	13.1	15.0
Movie Channel	7.1	6.0	13.1	7.5
Both	*7.8*	*7.3*	*13.1*	*11.3*

Note: Mean scores show averages for violence-containing programmes

programmes how many violent incidents they contained on average. These figures indicate that for many of the channels analysed here, late-night rates of violence were higher than those for daytime programmes. Thus, if a programme contained violence at all, it was likely to contain a greater number of separate violent acts when shown post-peak-time than when shown pre-peak-time. Sky One was an exception to this rule. On this channel the largest numbers of violent incidents occurred in violent programmes shown during the day. With this channel, though, it is important to consider what the nature of this 'violent' daytime content might be. As earlier chapters were able to show, much of the violence found on Sky One is likely to be located in cartoons, 'superhero' children's action series, and American wrestling. All of these programmes were broadcast during the day in the weeks monitored.

On the two most-watched channels, ITV and BBC1, the most violent programmes in terms of average numbers of violent acts and sequences were broadcast after midnight. Post-midnight programmes also accumulated the largest total amount (minutage) of violence of any time-band in the case of ITV, although late-evening but pre-midnight violent programmes averaged the greatest minutage of violence per programme. In terms of average minutage of violence, the most violent programmes on terrestrial channels and the two satellite entertainment channels analysed here tended to occur late at night. In general, therefore, performance was in line with the expectations of the 9.00 pm watershed policy. The latter policy, of course, is perhaps more sensitive to the nature of the violence that is shown than simply to the overall amount that is shown.

The classification periods on the movie channels differ from those used on the other channels, with movies being designated as appropriate for broadcast before 8.00 pm, between 8.00 pm and 10.00 pm, and after 10.00 pm. Once again, the largest cumulative number of violent incidents occurred during the daytime/early evening period because this was the largest single time-band. In terms of the density of violence per violent programme, however, the most violent programmes were transmitted during the post-10.00 pm period. The least violent programmes occurred during the 8.00 to 10.00 pm period when family audiences are likely to be at their peak. As before, quantitative measures alone lack the information needed to judge whether the movie channels were observing broadcasting policies for the depiction of violence. Evidence reported earlier (Chapters 3 and 6), however, indicates that the most violent movies in terms of amount of violence and amount of potentially disturbing violence tended to occur during late-night periods.

14 Violence on British television: A cause for concern or comfort?

Television violence is a perennial issue reflecting the fact that it is of enduring public concern. The debate about television and violence has been among the most vociferously contested in the social sciences and one that has been joined by a variety of interest groups including educators, politicians, morals campaigners, the press, child psychologists and media researchers from the hard empiricist to the more 'intuitive' critical schools of thought. In addition, of course, there are the broadcasters and programme makers themselves who bear a responsibility for what is presented on the small screen.

Criticisms of television violence have centred on the observation that there is too much of it, that people are generally concerned about how much there is, and that violence on the small screen can promote aggressive behaviour or cultivate unnecessary anxieties among viewers. Arguments about the amount of violence on screen often become mixed up with those about the alleged effects of television violence. Viewers' opinions about violence on television in general may be at odds with their opinions about specific programmes. Self-reported reactions to televised violence are sometimes accepted as reasonable evidence for its effects, when they usually represent little more than opinion. Thus, the debate about violence on television has often been clouded in confusion with frequent misunderstandings about the nature of different kinds of research evidence or distortions of what some studies actually show.

The study reported in this book was concerned specifically with measuring the amount of violence on television. In addition, it attempted to identify different classes and attributes of violent portrayals. This further analysis was deemed to be important if inferences were to be drawn or links were to be attempted between what is known about audience reactions to television violence and what was catalogued as occurring on screen.

This study cannot demonstrate anything about the effects of television violence or about public attitudes concerning violence in programmes. What it can attempt to achieve, however, is an analysis of the extent to which certain forms of violence occur or the extent to which violence occurs in different contexts and settings, who is involved and with what outcomes. If certain types of violent scene are known to cause viewers special concern or to give rise to particularly strong reactions, it may be useful to know how often they occur.

THE EFFECTS DEBATE

The debate about violence on television has been dominated by oppositional points of view, whether its focus at any one point in time has been upon the amount of violence shown in programmes, the degree of public concern about on-screen violence, or the impact that violence on television has on viewers. The American empirical social science school has concentrated on elaborating the extent of television's effects upon the members of its audience and the psychological mechanisms through which such effects operate. The consensus view emanating from this school and the collective body of evidence it has accumulated is that violence on television does contribute towards the development of aggressive tendencies in individual members of the audience and may therefore influence levels of violence across society (Kaplan and Singer, 1976; Friedrich-Cofer and Stein, 1986).

In the United States, the recent political debate about television violence has reached the point where public opinion, the view of government officials and also of certain parts of the media industry have come to accept that television violence contributes to violence in the real world in a significant way. The question of whether or not televised violence can have harmful effects is no longer at the centre of the debate; rather the controversy has shifted to a consideration of what can be done about such effects (Kunkel *et al.*, 1996b).

This viewpoint has not been universally accepted by members of the scholarly media research community in different countries. Critics from the same empirical school have questioned the assumptions and methodologies used in effects research (Cumberbatch and Howitt, 1989; Freedman, 1984), while other media scholars have not simply challenged the methodologies of effects research, but the ability of the empiricist paradigm to offer an appropriate mode of analysis of the issue at all (Hodge and Tripp, 1986; Gauntlett, 1995). According to Hodge and Tripp (1986, p. 201):

The inadequacies of the dominant paradigm come from its biases: towards proof rather than insight; towards pseudo-mechanical rather than semiotic causality; its concern with behaviour rather than meaning, and with short-term, small-scale explanations. It fatally lacks an explicit account of broader political and social processes in which to situate the behaviour it studies, or its own practice as a discipline. It equally lacks a powerful theory of mind and meaning, to decode meanings and to trace thought processes into the inner recesses of the mind, and study the formation of structures of thought and feeling as they evolve over a lifetime.

THE SIGNIFICANCE OF PUBLIC SENSIBILITIES

Whether or not the effects of television violence can be demonstrated will no doubt remain a vexed question presenting a source of continuing academic debate. In the meantime, however, broadcasters will remain under a degree of legislative and regulatory restraint in respect of what might permissibly be shown on television. Such regulatory frameworks and the codes of practice which flow from them reflect concerns about the offence which might be done to public sensibilities and tastes by the depiction of violence in programmes more than they represent any degree of acceptance of effects research evidence. Offence may be caused by the presentation of particular types of event, by the style or nature of such portrayals, and as a result of judgements about the overall amount of certain types of content.

While being mindful of these sorts of concerns, there is a clearly recognized need also that any rules or codes which place restrictions on programme content must be balanced against the established interests of viewers to receive a diverse range of programmes (Duval, 1995). The need for diversity, however, if met comprehensively ought to place a naturally occurring restraint on the quantity of violence, since it would result in a television schedule composed of a variety of programme types, a great many of which would be essentially nonviolent. Any claims that television is devoid of violence, or that the levels of violence have changed over time, cannot rest simply on the informal observations of broadcasters or anyone else for that matter. They must be demonstrated through some form of systematic monitoring procedure. Duval (1995, p. 21) has concisely made this point: 'If broadcasters wish to sustain an argument that violence on television is in decline, they will need to generate some hard, objective evidence of it.'

THE AMOUNT OF VIOLENCE ON TV: MEASUREMENT ISSUES

Generating acceptable hard evidence about the amount of violence on television, which can stand up to critical scrutiny, however, depends on the methodology used to measure violence and upon the way it is defined in the first place. The measurement of television violence has been approached in different ways. The standard methodology used to quantify violence on screen is content analysis. Although increasing emphasis is quite correctly being placed by content analysis researchers on elaborating the nature and context of violence, producing an acceptable and representative method of measuring the quantity of television violence remains important because it establishes the opportunity for viewer exposure to violence in general or to particular forms of violence during the natural course of viewing.

Content analysis is based on a methodology which defines, as objectively as possible, the aspects of programmes that are to be counted. With violence on television, this entails drawing up a definition of violence and devising a coding frame which comprises a set of explicit instructions which guide trained coders dispassionately to identify distinct events which match the given definition. This is the approach that has been adopted in the current study. As we saw in Chapter 2, however, this measurement perspective is fraught with difficulties. With its focus firmly fixed on reliable, descriptive cataloguing of incidents in programmes, there are question marks over whether it effectively represents the frame of reference audiences would adopt for judging whether programmes or the events shown in them are violent or not (Gunter, 1985; Howitt and Cumberbatch, 1974; Hodge and Tripp, 1986).

Even putting aside the validity issue in respect of the definition of television violence, other issues relating to measurement methodology have surfaced. These concern whether particular expressions of the quantity of violence on television give a fair or accurate impression of how violent television really is. Assuming that a particular *a priori* definition of violence is accepted as offering a reasonable starting point for classifying violent behaviour depicted on screen, there remains a question about the units of measurement that are adopted under this definitional scheme. The amount of violence on television has generally been expressed in terms of the basic unit of 'acts of violence'. Once violent acts have been identified, researchers have then tended to express the quantities of violence on television in terms of the rates at which violent acts occur per hour or percentages of programmes broadcast during the period monitored which contained any violence at all.

The two key measures of 'violent acts per hour' and 'proportion of programmes with violence' frequently give an impression that there are large amounts of violence on television. Over a 20-year period between 1967 and 1986, one research group reported that violence occurred on fictional drama programmes on American network prime-time television at an average rate of six acts per hour (Gerbner *et al.*, 1986). In the United Kingdom in 1986, the average hourly rate of violent acts in dramatic fiction across the four television channels studied was 3.6 (Cumberbatch *et al.*, 1987, 1988). One implication of an average hourly rate, however, is that, as a general rule, viewers could expect to find the reported number of violent acts every hour they view. The fact that there may be wide discrepancies between programmes from different genres or between programmes from the same genre in terms of how many violent acts they each contain, and how those acts are distributed within a programme, is ignored.

In the current study, the average rate of violent acts was used as one representation of the overall violence count, but with more emphasis being placed on the notion of violent acts per violence-containing programme than upon the average rate of violent acts per hour, for which the score across all monitored output on the terrestrial channels was 2.3. The reason for this was that, as the data were examined in detail and in terms of a number of different forms of measurement, it became clear that there were many programmes which contained no violence at all on the channels monitored, while there were a few programmes which contained large numbers of violent acts. For instance, 1% of programmes across the eight channels monitored were found to contained nearly one in five (19%) of the violent acts coded.

Another important issue relating to the measurement of violence on television when considered purely in terms of 'violent acts' is that effective comparisons across studies over time and in different countries may prove difficult because, even if the same basic definition of violence is used throughout, the way in which this definition is then applied to identify 'acts' may vary in subtle ways. A coding frame needs to explain how the boundaries of violent acts will be defined; in other words, when does one violent act end and another begin. This is seldom made clear in published content analysis studies and yet it is a key factor influencing any violent act scores that are produced. The definition of 'violence' *per se* is only one part of the standardizing process enabling accurate comparisons to be made between television violence measurement studies. The definition of a 'violent act' within the context of the general violence definition is vitally important.

A more robust measure may be the amount of running time a violent incident occupies. Two violent acts may differ in length and thus, in a quantitative sense alone, they may not represent equal amounts of violence. It also becomes clear when expressing the amount of violence on television in terms of the running time it occupied, that all the different types of violence identified filled a little over 1% (1.07%) of total monitored programme running time. This kind of figure clearly gives a totally different impression about the amount of violence than, for example, the finding that 37% of programmes contained violence. The distribution of violence on television was put in a more cautiously measured perspective again with the finding that 2.5% of programmes monitored across the eight channels contained 46% of all the time occupied by violence. This finding reflected the fact that there were a few particularly violent programmes, mostly broadcasts featuring contact sports such as boxing or wrestling, and movies originally made for the cinema.

Contact sports broadcasts could significantly inflate the overall amount of violence minutage on a channel during the weeks when such programmes were shown. For example, when televised American wrestling broadcasts were discounted, the level of violence on Sky One was found to fall by nearly one-half. On ITV the removal of the contribution of televised boxing matches reduced the violence minutage on that channel by 30% during the weeks when these bouts were shown. On BBC1, a single televised boxing match occurred during the weeks monitored, which accounted for 37% of the violence on that channel during the particular week it was shown. So it can be seen that the use of different measures for quantifying violence on television can give rise to quite different impressions about how much violence actually occurs in programmes.

The most violent channels, in terms of violent act counts and the percentages of programmes containing violence, were the two satellite movie channels, Sky Movies and The Movie Channel, on which 79% and 81% of transmissions respectively contained violence. Even so, on Sky Movies just 14% of all the movies shown during the period monitored accounted for 60% of violence minutage, while on The Movie Channel 7% of transmissions contained 39% of total violence minutage for that channel.

The general impression which derives from a closer analysis of violence minutage is that violence on television occupies a very small part of total programme running time. Furthermore, a considerable portion of the total violence minutage occurs in a relatively small number of programmes. The notion that television is permeated by violence is not supported by these findings. Instead, it is nearer the truth to say that while violent acts are distributed across a substantial minority of all programmes, and on some channels such as the two satellite movie channels monitored in this analysis across a clear majority of transmissions, much of this violence in minutage terms occurs in just a handful of broadcasts.

TYPES OF TV VIOLENCE

The quantity of violence on television is not the only matter about which concern has been expressed. Attention has also been paid to the *nature* of violence depicted in programmes. The overall amount of violence to which viewers might be exposed has implications for certain kinds of alleged effects upon audiences such as 'desensitization' or the increased tolerance for violence through excessive exposure (Drabman and Thomas, 1974; Osborn and Endsley, 1971) and the cultivation of exaggerated fear of social violence and of being personally victimized (Gerbner and Gross, 1976; Gerbner *et al.*, 1979). It is quite possible, however, that even a single violent act could make an indelible impression on viewers, if it graphically depicts a particularly horrific incident. Violent incidents which have certain qualities may be regarded by viewers as particularly offensive or distressing.

Specific portrayals of violence on television may strike a chord with some viewers who might be inclined to copy them. There has been a long-standing concern about the imitation effects of televised violence (Bandura, 1986, 1994). It has also been indicated by behavioural psychologists that the effects of television violence may be powerfully mediated by a variety of attributes relating to the form the behaviour takes, the setting in which it occurs, the motives underlying it and the consequences following from it, and the nature of the perpetrator and victim (see Gunter, 1985).

Although a content analysis study cannot offer any demonstration of the effects of violent portrayals or indicate what viewers' opinions about them might be, it can nevertheless provide a useful function by indicating the extent to which violence with certain qualities occurs. Thus, violence profiles can be particularly informative if they are combined with knowledge about how viewers respond to different types of violence. The National Television Violence Study in the United States has stressed the need to examine the nature and context of violence on television. Here, much emphasis was placed on methods of classifying violent incidents on screen in terms of attributes and features known, through the media effects literature, to represent important mediators of audience response (Potter *et al.*, 1996; Wilson *et al.*, 1996a). This approach can be particularly valuable in addressing a question such as: 'How often does violence with potentially worrying or damaging qualities for viewers occur?'

In the current study, all violent acts were attribute coded so as to identify a number of important features about them. These features included a classification of each act in terms of the form of behaviour it took and the types of weapons used, the setting in which it occurred, the motivational context of the violence, the consequences of violence for victims, and the types of characters who were involved. Each of these features has previously been investigated in relation to audience reactions to television violence, whether perceptual, attitudinal or behavioural. Certain features have been found to cause viewers more anxieties than others. To what extent then did violence occur with attributes known to cause viewers problems?

FORMS OF TV VIOLENCE

The form of violence has been found to have an effect on how portrayals are perceived by viewers. In the current study more than eight out of ten (82%) of all violent acts were accounted for by ten forms of violence. These represented a variety of different kinds of violent behaviour which generally involved the use of a part of the body (usually the hand or foot), or a hand held weapon (such as a gun or blunt hitting object). It is certainly the case that even portrayals of violence which involved no weapon could be found distressing by viewers, depending upon other features such as how much pain and suffering, blood and damage are shown. In general, however, other conditions being equal, audience research has indicated that the kind of violence viewers appear to be most distressed about is that which involves sharp, stabbing instruments and close-in contact between aggressor and victim (Gunter, 1985). In the current study, just 2% of all violent acts coded involved some form of stabbing. While it was certainly not the least likely form of violence to occur, it was nevertheless infrequent. Furthermore, just 1% of violent acts involved the cutting of a victim. An examination of the types of weapons used confirmed the relative infrequency of this type of violence, with only 2% of violent acts involving the use of a dagger or knife.

MOTIVES, CONSEQUENCES AND CHARACTERS

Other key factors which affect how seriously violent portrayals are taken by members of the television audience include the motives underlying the violence and the consequences of the violence for those who are its targets. These factors cannot be considered properly without some reference to the types of characters or people who are involved in violence either as the aggressors or victims. For many years, it has been observed by sociologists that the public are more accepting of violence when it is perpetrated in the service of goodness, or law and order (e.g., Couch, 1968; Gamson and McEvoy, 1972). This normative view may be taken to the point where even acts of open hostility are labelled as essentially nonviolent behaviour if they are performed by police officers in contexts where they are trying to quell violent civil disturbances or to combat criminal behaviour (Blumenthal *et al.*, 1972).

Perceptions of television portrayals of violence involving law enforcers and criminal characters in fictional drama settings, however, have not always been found to support the pattern whereby police violence is invariably judged to be justified, legitimate behaviour which does not therefore warrant the label 'violent'. British viewers have been found to regard violence perpetrated by fictional police characters in British crime-drama series as more worrying than similar portrayals involving fictional American police characters and even more worrying than violence exhibited by certain criminal characters (Gunter, 1985). In the latter research, violence in American crime-drama settings was consistently rated as more violent and disturbing if it was performed by a criminal. In contrast, in British crime-drama settings, violence was judged to be more serious if it was performed by a law enforcer. Such findings were explained in terms of both societal norms and television norms. The law of equity is one potentially important factor:

> Traditionally, society approves of some forms of violence under certain circumstances, and disapproves of others. Certain forms of legitimised violence are approved of. For example, violence used by police officers to uphold the law, that used by the armed forces to protect the nation against an enemy, and that used by private individuals in self defence against an attacker. Under all these circumstances, however, the employment of a violent response must not far outweigh the magnitude of the behaviour of the intimidator or attacker. Where the force used to repel an attacker is much greater than that justified by initial provocation, it will not be found so acceptable.

> (Gunter, 1985, p. 247)

At the time of that study, British viewers were not accustomed to witnessing British police behave violently. British police were generally unarmed, unlike their American counterparts, and extreme forms of violence were rarely used by the police in the normal, everyday performance of their duties. This real life image of the police was reflected in many television fictional portrayals of the police. There were some exceptions to this rule, however, which began to emerge during the 1970s and 1980s. About 20 years ago, the police drama genre began to evolve with new, more action-oriented series such as *The Sweeney*, followed in later years by such series as *The Professionals* and *Dempsey and Makepeace*, which adopted the kind of fast paced sequences normally associated with American productions. The out of the ordinary behaviour of this new style of British law enforcer was regarded as more violent than the norm either for real police or traditional television police in Britain. While surveys of British viewers during the 1980s indicated that the majority were not unduly concerned about these programmes, in some cases significant minorities did voice some worries about certain of the more extreme forms of law enforcement technique which were on occasions deployed by these British-based fictional law enforcers (Gunter and Wober, 1988).

From this audience research evidence, it became clear that the types of characters who perpetrate violence on screen and their reasons for doing so can affect audience judgements about the violence that is shown. Violence generally has a target, however. On occasions the target may escape unscathed, while on others, victims of violence may be depicted suffering pain and injury. Quite apart from why violence occurs, it has been long established that the degree of pain and suffering associated with scenes of violence can also exert a powerful influence over audience reactions. Graphic depiction of a victim's suffering can cause viewers distress (Noble, 1975). The greater the pain and injury that results from violence, the less acceptable and more violent it is perceived to be (Greenberg and Gordon, 1972a; Gunter, 1985). Viewers' reactions to a victim's pain and suffering, however, may be mediated by how much he or she is perceived to deserve the fate (Zillmann, 1980; Zillmann and Cantor, 1976).

The current content analysis of selected British television output in the mid-1990s revealed that much of the violence depicted was the result of criminally motivated behaviour or disputes or arguments between individuals. Although violence was found that was used for 'legitimate' purposes such as upholding the law and for the protection of a family or of society, this was much less commonplace than violence which had negative or antisocial motives. The general impression to emerge from this analysis was that violence was principally the behavioural domain of criminal types or of individuals driven by evil or destructive desires, who were prepared to use aggressive means to achieve their objectives regardless of the outcomes. At the same time, television was also found to be populated by a law-abiding community who might get drawn into violence, though not as readily as criminal types, and with motives that were more usually legitimate or defensive.

Some forms of violence can be found particularly distasteful by viewers. Among these are sexually motivated aggression. This type of violent imagery has been linked to the development of callous attitudes towards rape victims and greater sympathy with alleged rapists (Linz *et al.*, 1985). Such portrayals were found to be extremely rare on the television channels monitored in this study. In less than 1% of violent acts on the four terrestrial channels were the aggressor's goals sexual in nature, a level which was largely unchanged from ten years earlier (see Cumberbatch *et al.*, 1987). A marginally higher rate of occurrence of such acts was found across the four satellite channels monitored, which was largely accounted for by portrayals found in films originally made for the cinema televised on the two movie channels. On this evidence, therefore, mainstream television in Britain appears to offer few opportunities for exposure to incidents of sexually motivated violence.

The consequences of violence can significantly affect viewers' emotional reactions to portrayals. Greater depicted pain and suffering on the part of victims has been found to cause viewers greater concern (Noble, 1975; Gunter, 1985). There are mixed views about showing in graphic detail the full horror or harm that violence can cause. If this is something which causes viewers great distress, it may be argued that violent scenes should therefore be sanitized to spare viewers any upset. A different view is that it is better for viewers to be made aware of the damage that violence can inflict, so that they will continue to support sanctions against it and be less likely to become involved in violence themselves. Another view which points to a potentially undesirable side effect of regular exposure to graphic violence is that viewers eventually become habituated to such content and their initial distress reactions lessen. This desensitization hypothesis asserts that repeated exposure to violence may render viewers more callous in their attitudes and may cause them to develop a weakening concern not only about violence that occurs on screen but also about violence in actuality (Cline *et al.*, 1972; Drabman and Thomas, 1974). For the most part, however, the early empirical studies of desensitization indicated only that people exposed to televised violence increased their tolerance for further televised violence (Comstock, 1980).

Any possibility that viewers may have been rendered more callous in their opinions about televised violence or caused to develop a lessened sensitivity to it by British television, particularly to that which depicts most graphically the pain and suffering of victims, rests upon the degree of opportunity they are given to experience such scenes. Evaluations of the qualities of violent portrayals on the eight television channels monitored in this study in terms of the magnitude of pain suffered by victims, the amount of bloodshed, and the degree of horror associated with violent acts revealed that potentially really offensive or upsetting portrayals were relatively rare. Forty-one programmes were found to contain at least one violent act judged to show extreme suffering on the part of a victim, 22 programmes contained at least one act with a great deal of bloodshed, and 39 programmes occurred which had at least one act thought to be really horrific in nature. In each case, only a handful of programmes contained three or more such acts of violence and these were generally movies which were broadcast late at night.

On this evidence, it is reasonable to conclude that viewers were afforded few opportunities to witness violent acts which were characterized by extremes of pain, bloodshed and horror. The best chances of experiencing an intense dose of extremely graphic and potentially distressing violence were offered by those transmissions which contained several such acts of violence. However, very few programmes provided such repeat dosages of this sort of material. When such programmes did occur, they were broadcast on different days or different weeks.

Audience judgements about televised violence are influenced by the kinds of characters who are featured as the perpetrators and victims of violence. Character involvement is tied closely to the role of motives and consequences in determining how viewers perceive specific violent acts. The goals of aggressors can determine whether or not a violent action is regarded by viewers as justified. Physically forceful behaviour used to perpetrate a crime may be judged quite differently than when the same behaviour is used to prevent a crime. However, viewers have certain expectations of characters. Criminal behaviour performed by a bad guy is expected. Criminal behaviour performed by a character who was thought to be a good guy may be seen as much worse because his or her conduct may be seen as out of character and therefore as a disappointment through failing to meet expectations. This sort of rationale may underpin the finding that viewers may judge law enforcer violence in more critical terms than criminal violence (Gunter, 1985).

Another realm in which the expectations of audiences may play a significant part in influencing their judgements about violent scenes is where the violence involves women as perpetrators. Perceptions of female characters are often polarized; either the character is good or she is bad. This reflects a dichotomized view of women as either 'mothers' or 'whores', 'the gentler sex' or 'the more deadly of the species'. Under this value system, the essence of 'femininity' is gentleness, purity, passivity and maternity. Anyone possessing these attributes would never be expected willingly to commit a violent crime. Any woman who therefore turns to criminality or violence must by definition be evil and bad, since in doing so she has abandoned her natural feminine role. This dichotomy has been observed to affect public and legal opinion of women who commit crimes (Buckhart, 1973). One empirical test of this phenomenon found that females accused were judged to be more 'sick' than males accused who had committed the same offence (McGlynn *et al.*, 1976). Thus, women who murder or commit violent crimes are perceived as deviating from the norm more so than men who commit similar crimes.

This pattern of perceptions was partly corroborated by research which showed that British viewers exhibited greater concern about violent portrayals featuring female aggressors than about similar portrayals featuring male aggressors in American-made crime drama series. In British-made crime drama series, in contrast, female aggression was rated as less violent than equivalent male aggression (Gunter, 1985). The latter result was explained through reference to societal norms and television norms. The scenes in question feature either male aggressors attacking a female victim or female aggressors attacking a male victim. The former is endorsed by societal norms, given that men are regarded as the physically dominant and stronger sex, while women are generally regarded as physically weaker. Thus, the perceptions of these two types of violent scene in a British context might have been more influenced by the norms of conduct that prevail in British society. With American-based violence, however, the same rules might not have applied to the same extent because the settings were distanced from the everyday reality of British viewers. Instead, such factors as the frequency and familiarity of particular types of portrayal within these programmes, but not in relation to everyday life, may have been more important mediators of judgements made about them. More unusual or less familiar portrayals may have had a stronger impact than more frequently occurring portrayals, for example. In the latest British content analysis research, perpetrators of violence were predominantly male, accounting for more than three-quarters of all violent acts, while female perpetrators of violence accounted for under one in ten violent acts.

The other aspect of character involvement in television violence stems from a belief that patterns of victimization may convey 'messages' to viewers about who has power and who does not in the world of television. If certain character groups are portrayed predominantly as victims of violence, this profile may cultivate among members of the audience the belief that these groups are also more at risk in the real world (Gerbner and Gross, 1976; Gerbner *et al.*, 1977, 1978, 1979). While these so-called 'cultivation effects' have not been universally accepted to occur in the way suggested (see Wober and Gunter, 1988), there is nevertheless some evidence that viewers' perceptions of the risks to individual safety that are present in some remote and unfamiliar environments may be shaped in part by what they experience on television (Gunter and Wakshlag, 1988). American research indicated that the most at-risk groups on US network television were women, the elderly and racial minorities in that they were more likely to be victims than victors whenever involved in acts of violence on fictional television (Signorielli, 1990, 1993).

The current study found that the characters most likely to be involved in violence both as aggressors and victims were either young or middle-aged white males. No clear patterns emerged that women or ethnic minorities were victimized disproportionately compared with other demographic groups. There were some indications of age differences in victimization likelihood, with characters judged to be aged over 65 and ones under 12 more likely to be victims than aggressors whenever involved in acts of violence.

Victimization likelihood ratios were found to differ for law enforcers and criminals. Both criminals and law enforcers were found to be more often portrayed as aggressors than purely victims. This finding, however, disguised differences which were present in this respect between different categories of criminal. The greater likelihood of being an aggressor than a victim was true only of serious criminals. Petty criminals, on the other hand, were more likely to be victims than aggressors. Different 'messages' may therefore be conveyed in respect of different classes of criminal. If anything is learned from these violence profiles it might be that petty criminality is a risky business. This conclusion assumes, of course, that such messages are apprehended by audiences at all. As research with viewers has shown, any influence that television character portrayals may have on viewers can depend upon a variety of other factors, such as real life experiences with such people (Rarick *et al.*, 1973), belief in the veracity of television (Potter, 1986), and distinctions between beliefs about the incidence of crime in society at large and about personal risks of victimization (Tyler, 1980; Tyler and Rasinski, 1984).

GENRES AND TV VIOLENCE

The programme genre in which violence occurs is a key variable affecting how violence is judged by viewers. It is intimately linked to distinctions between 'real life', 'realistic' and 'fantasy' violence which represent perhaps the most fundamental dimensions along which television violence is differentiated (Gunter, 1985; Gunter and Furnham, 1984; van der Voort, 1986; Hodge and Tripp, 1986). 'Real life' violence consists of scenes of violence shown in news bulletins or other factual programmes. It might also comprise violence which occurs in sports broadcasts. 'Realistic' violence is that which occurs in fictional programme settings, but has many characteristics of reality and represents incidents which could conceivably occur in real life. 'Fantasy' violence is that which occurs in fictional settings which are divorced from the everyday, known reality of viewers and which is not regarded as the kind of incident likely to occur in real life.

Realistic portrayals of violence can cause viewers greater concern than unrealistic ones, whether audience reactions are studied at a behavioural, emotional or perceptual level. Behavioural effects research has indicated that film violence produced greater subsequent aggressive responses among male viewers when described as a documentary than as a Hollywood production (Berkowitz and Alioto, 1973). This result was confirmed by other similar pieces of research (Geen, 1975; Thomas and Tell, 1974). This mediating effect of realism on subsequent behavioural reactions of viewers has been found to occur among children as well as adults (Atkin, 1983; Hapkiewicz and Stone, 1974). One of the reasons for this effect might be that viewers identify more closely with perpetrators of screen violence when they are shown in true-to-life settings compared with fantasy situations (Jo and Berkowitz, 1994).

Quite apart from the nature of viewers' behavioural responses to realistic screen violence, what they think about it at a cognitive level may also be influenced by how close to reality it is judged to be. The nearer to real life violent episodes get, for example, the stronger are viewers' opinions about the violence likely to be (Gunter, 1985).

In the current study, violence was found to occur predominantly in fictional drama programmes which contributed nearly 70% of violent acts and violence minutage found to occur on the eight channels monitored. Factual programmes contributed just 8% of all violent acts and 16% of violence minutage. On the non-movie channels, much of the violence in drama programming occurred in films originally made for the cinema. Over 70% of violent acts and approaching 80% of the violence minutage on televised drama programmes on these channels occurred in cinema films. On factual programmes, most of the violence observed occurred in national news bulletins and documentary films. Documentaries, however, displayed a much higher rate of violence per programme than did news bulletins. Indeed, the average violence-containing news bulletin contained just six seconds of violent footage. The average violence-containing documentary contained around 12 seconds of violent footage.

These results indicate that the settings known to give rise to the most severe audience reactions tended to contain very little violence in individual programmes. Only small amounts of violence occurred in news programmes and this was generally rated modestly in terms of the degree of pain and suffering, bloodshed and horror that were depicted. The violence in the news and factual programmes tended to be linked mainly to armed conflicts and civil disturbances, with other incidents being mostly crime related. On this evidence there would appear to be little cause for concern about the current performance of the major broadcasters with regard to factual programmes.

The same cannot be said to the same extent for drama output, which contributed a more significant amount to the overall violence total. Although drama-based violence is fictional in nature, evidence did emerge that a few programmes, most notably films originally made for the cinema, contained exceptionally large numbers of violent acts, or an amount of violence which was characterized by graphic depictions of victims' pain and suffering, bloodshed and horror. Despite this finding, most of these broadcasts occurred late at night on subscription channels and represented a tiny part of the overall drama output on the channels studied.

Television in Britain offers a diverse array of programming designed to cater for a range of audience tastes and interests. In doing so, it is almost inevitable that some of these programmes will contain violence. Like it or not, violence represents a part of everyday life. Not to show any violence at all would place severe constraints on drama production, since much drama revolves around conflict, some of which will inevitably be violent in nature (Eisenstein, 1949). To ignore all violence in the news or on factual programmes would result in a sanitized view of the world which failed to reflect and therefore properly to inform the public about current events. It is difficult to imagine therefore, a television service devoid of all violence.

The question of whether there is 'too much' violence on television is a value judgement rather than a problem which can be solved by setting some absolute threshold beyond which broadcasters should not venture. A more crucial question is whether broadcasters use violence unnecessarily, whether in the news or in drama or entertainment programmes. While this is not a question addressed directly by the research reported in this book, the findings from it do serve to place the amount of violence on television in perspective. What has been indicated quite clearly is that violence does not represent a significant part of television output. Nor is it something which permeates the schedules throughout. Instead, it tends to be concentrated in relatively small numbers of programmes which contribute disproportionately to the overall violence tally. Even on those channels which contain a high percentage of programmes with violence in them, the overall amount of violence is still only a small part of the total running time of their programme output, with much of that violence still tending to be concentrated in a relatively few programmes out of the total transmitted.

Appendix

Coding schedule – Violence Content Analysis code for all programmes

1.1   Programme number (numbered and listed per day)   ☐☐☐☐   (1.4)

1.2   Channel: BBC1 = 1 ☐   BBC2 = 2   ☐   ITV = 3 ☐   (5)

       C4 = 4 ☐   The Movie Channel = 5 ☐   Sky Movies = 6 ☐

       Sky 1 = 7 ☐   UK Gold = 8 ☐

1.3   Transmission Date   ☐☐☐☐   (6–9)

1.4   Time Start   ☐☐☐☐   (10–13)

1.5   Programme Genre (from list   ☐☐   (14–15)

1.6   Length (minutes)   ☐☐☐   (16–18)

1.7   Country of production (Please tick)   (19)
       0. Cannot Code ☐   3. Acquired (USA) ☐
       1. Channel's own production ☐   4. Acquired (other) ☐
       2. Independent production ☐

1.8   Coder identification number   ☐☐   (20–21)

Coders – Please complete the following for each programme (tick the appropriate boxes)

1.9   Is there any violence in the programme (see definitions supplied)   0. Yes ☐   1. No ☐   (22)

1.10   Is there a warning about violent content?   (23)
       0. Before the programme ☐   1. During the programme ☐   2. No warning ☐

1.11   Total number of violent acts in the programme   ☐☐☐   (24–26)

(Note: Please use the grids overleaf and tick once each time there is a violent act in the programme – please remember to separate the violent sequences – the number of ticks overleaf should correspond to the number of coding sheets you have completed)

1.12   Total amount of violence (in seconds) in the programme   ☐☐☐☐   (27–30)

1.13   Total number of violent sequences in the programme   ☐☐☐   (31–33)

Definition of violence (see also separate information sheet)

- Any overt depiction of **a credible threat of physical force or the actual use of physical force**
- **With or without a weapon**
- Which is intended to **harm or intimidate an animate being or a group of animate beings or inanimate objects** (i.e. property).
- Whether **carried out** or **merely attempted**
- Whether **the action causes injury or not**
- The acts of violence may be **intentional or accidental** (in the context of an intentional violent event – e.g. a car crash during a car chase)
- **Violent accidents** and **catastrophes** (if caused by human agents – e.g. a terrorist bomb explodes on a plane causing the plane to crash)

If you have encountered any particular difficulties coding this programme please outline them below. Please include as many details as possible and indicate the violent act number.

....
....
....
....
....

VIOLENT ACT NO.	LENGTH OF ACT (SECS)	VIOLENT ACT NO.	LENGTH OF ACT (SECS)	VIOLENT ACT NO.	LENGTH OF ACT (SECS)	VIOLENT ACT NO.	LENGTH OF ACT (SECS)	VIOLENT ACT NO.	LENGTH OF ACT (SECS)	VIOLENT ACT NO.	LENGTH OF ACT (SECS)

The Violent Act (code separately for **each** act)

2.1 **Violent Act Number** ☐☐☐☐☐ (1–5)

2.2 **Programme Number** ☐☐☐☐ (6–9)

2.3 **Channel** ☐ (10)

2.4 **Time Start** ☐☐☐☐ (11–14)

2.5 **Genre** ☐ (15–16)

2.6 **Origin** ☐ (17)

2.7 **Act Number** ☐☐☐ (18–20)

2.8 **Length of Violent Act** (in seconds) ☐☐☐ (21–23)

2.9 **Historical Setting** (the time period the programme is about) (24)

    0. Cannot code ☐   2. Past (1900–1980) ☐   4. Realistic future (up to early 21st century) ☐

    1. Distant Past (pre 20th century) ☐   3. Present (1980s/90s) ☐   5. Distant future ☐

2.10 **Environment** (25)

    0. Cannot code ☐   3. Small Town ☐   6. Mobile (e.g. in a moving vehicle) ☐

    1. Inner City ☐   4. Rural ☐   7. Very mixed ☐

    2. Suburban ☐   5. Uninhabited ☐   8. Studio setting ☐   9. Other ☐

2.11 **Country where act of violence takes place** (26–27)

    00. Cannot code ☐   06. Middle East ☐   12. Other Planet ☐

    01. Great Britain ☐   07. India/Asia ☐   13. Other (Sci-Fi) ☐

    02. USA ☐   08. Oriental ☐   14. Cartoon (unclear) ☐

    03. Europe ☐   09. Australasia ☐   15. Unclear ☐

    04. Other N. American ☐   10. Central/S. America ☐

    05. Africa ☐   11. Other parts of the World ☐

2.12 **Type of violent acts by the aggressor** (see separate violent acts list) ☐☐ (28–29)

2.13 **Was the violent act** (30)

    0. Cannot code ☐   1. First strike ☐   2. Retaliatory ☐   3. Self inflicted (i.e. suicide) ☐

2.14 **Context of violence** (31)

    0. Cannot code ☐   5. Defending civil liberties (non-legitimate) ☐

    1. War, armed forces action ☐   6. Domestic (e.g. at home) ☐

    2. Civil strife, riots ☐   7. Other interpersonal setting (e.g. argument) ☐

    3. Criminal act ☐   8. Other ☐

    4. Upholding the law (legitimate) ☐

2.15 **Weapon used** (see separate list) ☐☐ (32–33)

2.16 **Types of injuries caused** (please tick appropriate box(es)) (34–35)

    00. Cannot code ☐   04. Serious Wound ☐   08. Psychological Damage ☐

    01. Death ☐   05. Minor wound ☐   09. No physical or mental injuries ☐

    02. Mutilation ☐   06. Stun ☐   10. Other ☐

    03. Limbs breaking ☐   07. Bruises ☐

2.17 **Dramatic detail** (0 cannot code) – **(score on scales below)**

No blood	1	2	3	4	5	Much blood	(36)
No pain	1	2	3	4	5	Intense pain	(37)
Mild	1	2	3	4	5	Horrific	(38)

Aggressor/Perpetrator/Violent Actor

3.1   **Aggressor Codes** (enter appropriate code numbers from actor list)

Status Number ☐ (39)

Type Number ☐☐ (40–41)

3.2   **Gender** (42)

0. Cannot code ☐	3. Group male ☐	5. Group mixed ☐
1. One male ☐	4. Group female ☐	6. Other ☐
2. One female ☐		

3.3   **Ethnic Origin etc.** (43–44)

00. Cannot code ☐	04. Black UK ☐	08. Oriental ☐
01. White UK ☐	05. Black US ☐	09. Mixed group ☐
02. White US ☐	06. Black other ☐	10. Other human ☐
03. White other ☐	07. Asian ☐	11. Animal ☐

3.4   **Age** (45)

0. Cannot code ☐	3. Young adult (20–35) ☐	6. Mixed age group ☐
1. Child (up to 12 years) ☐	4. Middle aged adult (36–65) ☐	
2. Teenager (13–19) ☐	5. 65+ ☐	

3.5   **Goals of aggressor** (46–47)

00. Cannot code	06. Desire for money/material goods ☐
01. Upholding the law	07. Ambition/will for power ☐
02. Well being of family/home aquaintances ☐	08. Religious ☐
03. Well being of society/humanity	09. Evil/destructive goals ☐
04. Respect for the law	10. Sexual ☐
05. Self preservation	11. Other ☐

Victims

4.1   **Victim Codes** (enter appropriate code numbers from actor list)

Status Number ☐ (48)

Type Number ☐☐ (49–50)

4.2   **Gender** (51)

0. Cannot code ☐	3. Group male ☐	5. Group mixed ☐
1. One male ☐	4. Group female ☐	6. Other ☐
2. One female ☐		

4.3   **Ethnic Origin** (52–53)

00. Cannot code ☐	04. Black UK ☐	08. Oriental ☐
01. White UK ☐	05. Black US ☐	09. Mixed group ☐
02. White US ☐	06. Black other ☐	10. Other human ☐
03. White other ☐	07. Asian ☐	11. Animal ☐

4.4   **Age** (54)

0. Cannot code ☐	3. Young adult (20–35) ☐	6. Mixed age group ☐
1. Child (up to 12 years) ☐	4. Middle aged adult (36–65) ☐	
2. Teenager (13–19) ☐	5. 65+ ☐	

CODE LISTS

A Programme Genre

1 Programme type

01 Music programmes – classical
02 Music programme – contemporary
03 Arts programme
04 Children's cartoons/animation
05 Pop videos
06 Other children's programmes
07 Current affairs – political/social/economic
08 Current affairs – special events
09 Current affairs – consumer affairs
10 Hobbies and leisure pursuits
11 Documentaries and features
12 Religious programmes
13 Single plays
14 Other UK series/serials
15 Other non-UK series/serials
16 UK long-running series
17 Non-UK long-running series
18 Cinema
19 Made for TV
20 Situation comedy
21 Other comedy
22 Variety
23 Chat shows
24 Quiz and panel games
25 Cartoons and animations
26 Family/people shows
27 Special events
28 News programmes – national
29 News programmes – regional
30 Sport
31 Party political broadcasts

B Actor list

1 Status

0 Cannot code
1 Real
2 Fictitious

2 Type

00 Cannot code
01 Member of general public
02 Situation character
03 Domestic person (major role revolves around being husband, wife, etc.)
04 Rioter
05 School kid
06 Football hooligan
07 Political activist
08 Presenter – serious
09 Presenter – light
10 Sports commentator
11 Publican
12 Prostitute
13 Monster
14 Sports person
15 Entertainer/pop star
16 Seaman
17 Servant
18 Clergy/religious
19 Trades union member
20 Spy
21 Nobility/royalty
22 Knight
23 Martial arts
24 Police – uniformed
25 Police – plain clothed
26 Non/quasi-police law enforcer – armed forces – sheriff
27 Legitimate – special law enforcers (professional)
28 Not legitimate – vigilante

29 Armed forces
30 Not legitimate – fantasy (e.g. Batman)
31 Not legitimate – private detective
32 Outlaws/pirates
33 Criminal – petty
34 Criminal – serious
35 Terrorist/guerrilla
36 Cowboy (or cavalry)
37 Indians
38 Cartoon characters – human
39 Cartoon characters – animal
40 Cartoon character – other
41 Supernatural power
42 Animal
43 Professional person (eg. doctor, vet, lawyer, teacher, accountant, etc.)
44 Inanimate object (eg. car/ building)
45 Tribal people
46 Assassin
47 Comedian
48 Spaceman
49 Psychopath
50 Uniformed official
51 Journalist
52 Alien
53 Executioner
54 Culler
55 Inventor/scientist
56 Robot
57 Dracula/vampire
58 Aggressor not shown
59 Other

C   Type of violent act

00 Cannot code
01 Self wounding
02 Stab
03 Torture
04 Psychological torture
05 Rape
06 Bullying
07 Cruelty
08 Blinding (e.g., chemicals thrown in face)
09 Burn
10 Drown
11 Strangle
12 Fall/throw from height
13 Fire
14 Poison
15 Trampled
16 Suffocation
17 Crushed
18 Abduction
19 Shoot at
20 Attempted violence
21 Wounding
22 Cut
23 Punch
24 Kick
25 Hit (with object)
26 Push/trip/other physical assault
27 Use of trap or other special device
28 Throwing
29 Slap
30 Bite
31 Spray
32 Sabotage
33 Fracture of bones
34 Scratch
35 Explosion
36 Chemical explosion
37 Nuclear explosion
38 Supernatural
39 Other disaster/accident
40 Disease
41 Sink/scuttle (of a boat, etc.)
42 Cannibalism
43 Verbal/threat
44 Car explosion
45 Damage to car

46 Damage to property
47 Aggression in sport
48 Gassing
49 Electrocution

50 Decapitation
51 Hanging
52 Lethal injection

D Weapons Used

GUN (MILITARY)
01 Machine gun
02 Pistol
03 Rifle
04 Military hardware (e.g., cannon, rocket, bazooka)
05 Explosives

GUN (CRIMINAL)
06 Sawn-off shotgun
07 Hand-gun
08 Shotgun

OTHER SHOOTING INSTRUMENTS
09 Bow and arrow
10 Cross-bow
11 Laser weapons
12 Water cannon
13 Tear gas
14 Flame thrower

KNIFE/STABBING INSTRUMENTS
15 Domestic
16 Hunting
17 Sword
18 Dagger
19 Hook
20 Other

THROWING INSTRUMENTS
21 Spear or lance
22 Other projectiles (stones, etc.)

CLUBBING INSTRUMENTS
23 Truncheon/baseball bat
24 Whip/cane
25 Pickaxe/axe
26 Other stick
27 Hammer
28 Stone (not as projectile)

BODY
29 Fist/hand
30 Karate/martial arts
31 Boot/kick
32 Headbutt
33 Throw/push
34 Other part of the body
35 False hand

VEHICLE
36 Car
37 Chariot
38 Lorry
39 Bulldozer
40 Other

ANIMAL
41 Trained animal (e.g., attack dog)

OTHER INSTRUMENTS
42 Boiling liquid
43 Chemicals/drugs
44 Liquid
45 Gas
46 Electricity

47 Other

References

Aronfreed, J. (1968) *Conduct and Conscience: The Socialization of Internalized Control over Behaviour.* New York: Academic Press.

Athey, I. (1984) Contributions of play to development. In T. D. Yawkey and A. D. Pelligrini (Eds), *Child's Play: Developmental and Applied* (pp. 9–28). Hillsdale, NJ: Lawrence Erlbaum Associates.

Atkin, C. (1983) Effects of realistic TV violence versus fictional violence on aggression. *Journalism Quarterly, 60,* 615–621.

Baker, R. K., and Ball, S. J. (1969) *Violence and the Media: A Staff Report to the National Commission on the Causes and Prevention of Violence.* Washington, DC: US Government Printing Office.

Bandura, A. (1973) *Aggression: A Social Learning Analysis.* Englewood Cliffs, NJ: Prentice-Hall, Inc.

Bandura, A. (1977) *Social Learning Theory.* Englewood Cliffs, NJ: Prentice-Hall.

Bandura, A. (1986) *Social Foundations of Thought and Action: A Social Cognitive Theory.* Englewood Cliffs, NJ: Prentice-Hall.

Bandura, A. (1994) Social cognitive theory of mass communication. In J. Bryant and D. Zillmann (Eds), *Media Effects* (pp. 61–90). Hillsdale, NJ: Lawrence Erlbaum Associates.

Bandura, A., and Walters, R. H. (1963) *Social Learning and Personality Development.* New York: Holt, Rinehart and Winston.

Baron, R. A. (1971a) Magnitude of victim's pain cues and level of prior anger arousal as determinants of adult aggressive behaviour. *Journal of Personality and Social Psychology, 17*(3), 236–243.

Baron, R. A. (1971b) Aggression as a function of magnitude of victim's pain cues, level of prior anger arousal, and aggressor–victim similarity. *Journal of Personality and Social Psychology, 18*(1), 48–54.

Baron, R. A. (1979) Effects of victim's pain cues, victim's race, and level of prior instigation upon physical aggression. *Journal of Applied Social Psychology, 9*(2), 103–114.

Berger, S. M. (1962) Conditioning through vicarious instigation. *Psychological Review, 29,* 450–466.

Berkowitz, L. (1970) Aggressive humour as a stimulus to aggressive responses. *Journal of Personality and Social Psychology, 16,* 710–717.

Berkowitz, L. (1971) The 'weapons effects', demand characteristics and the myth of the compliant subject. *Journal of Personality and Social Psychology, 20,* 332–338.

Berkowitz, L., and Alioto, J. (1973) The meaning of an observed event as a determinant of its aggressive consequences. *Journal of Personality and Social Psychology, 28,* 206–217.

Berkowitz, L., and LePage, A. (1967) Weapons as aggression-eliciting stimuli. *Journal of Personality and Social Psychology, 7,* 202–207.

Berkowitz, L., Parke, R. D., Leyens, J. P., and West, S. G. (1974) The effects of justified and unjustified movie violence on aggression in juvenile delinquents. *Journal of Research in Crime and Delinquency, 11*, 16–24.

Berlyne, D. E. (1960) *Conflict, Arousal and Curiosity*. New York: McGraw-Hill.

Blank, D. M. (1977a) The Gerbner violence profile. *Journal of Broadcasting, 21*(4), 273–279.

Blank, D. M. (1977b) Final comments on the violence profile. *Journal of Broadcasting, 21*(4), 287–296.

Blumenthal, R., Kahn, R., Andrews, F., and Head, K. (1972) *Justifying Violence: Attitudes of American Men*. Ann Arbor, MI: Survey Research Centre, Institute for Social Research, University of Michigan.

Boemer, M. L. (1984) An analysis of the violence content of the radio thriller dramas and some comparisons with television. *Journal of Broadcasting, 28*(3), 341–353.

Borke, H. (1971) Interpersonal perception of young children: Egocentrism or empathy? *Developmental Psychology, 5*, 263–269.

Bouwman, H. and Stappers, J. (1984) The Dutch violence profile: A replication of Gerbner's message system analysis. In G. Melischek, K. E. Rosengren and J. Stappers (Eds), *Cultural Indicators: An International Symposium*. Vienna, Austria: Austrian Academy of Sciences.

Boyatzis, C. J., Matillo, G. M., and Nesbitt, K. M. (1995) Effects of *The Mighty Morphin Power Rangers* on children's aggression with peers. *Child Study Journal, 25*(1), 45–55.

Bretherton, I. (1984) Representing the world in symbolic play: Reality and fantasy. In I. Bretherton (Ed.), *Symbolic Play: The Development of Social Understanding* (pp. 3–41). Orlando: Academic Press.

Broadcasting Standards Council (1994) *Monitoring Report II*. London: Broadcasting Standards Council.

Broadcasting Standards Council (1995) *Monitoring Report III*. London: Broadcasting Standards Council.

Brown, L. (1994) TV violence: The job of the US Congress is to make it bad business. *Intermedia, 22*(2), 34–35.

Bryant, J., and Zillmann, D. (1977) The mediating effect of the intervention potential of communications on displaced aggressiveness and retaliatory behaviour. In B. D. Ruben (Ed.) *Communication Yearbook I*, (pp. 291–306). New Brunswick, NJ: ICA-Transaction Press.

Buckhart, K. (1973) *Women in Prison*. New York: Doubleday.

Butler, M., and Paisley, W. (1980) *Women and the Mass Media*. New York: Human Sciences Press.

Caplan, F., and Caplan, T. (1973) *The Power of Play*. New York: Anchor Press.

Carlson, M., Marcus-Newhall, A., and Miller, N. (1990) Effects of situational aggression cues: A quantitative review. *Journal of Personality and Social Psychology, 58*(4), 622–633.

Caron, A. H. and Couture, M. (1977) Images of different worlds: An analysis of English- and French-language television. *Report to the Royal Commission on Violence in the Communications Industry, Vol. 3, Violence in Television, Films and News*. Toronto, Canada: The Royal Commission, pp. 220–341 (in French) and pp. 343–463 (in English).

Ceulemans, M., and Fauconnier, G. (1979) *Mass Media: The Image, Role and Social Conditions of Women*, Report No. 84. Paris: UNESCO.

Christian Science Monitor (1968) Monitor of TV Violence, July and October, 1968.

Clark, D. G., and Blankenburg, W. G. (1972) Trends in violent content in selected mass media. In G. A. Comstock and E. A. Rubinstein (Eds), *Television and Social Behaviour, Vol. 1, Media Content and Control* (pp. 188–243). Washington, DC: US Government Printing Office.

Cline, V. B., and Richards, J. M. Jr. (1960) Accuracy of interpersonal perception: A general trait? *Journal of Abnormal and Social Psychology, 60*, 20–30.

Cline, V. B., Croft, R. G., and Courrier, S. (1972) Desensitization of children to television violence. *Journal of Personality and Social Psychology, 27*, 360–365.

Coffin, T. E., and Tuchman, S. (1972a) Rating television programs for violence: A comparison of five surveys. *Journal of Broadcasting, 17*(1), 3–20.

Coffin, T. E., and Tuchman, S. (1972b) A question of validity: Some comments of 'apples, oranges, and the kitchen sink'. *Journal of Broadcasting, 17*(1), 31–33.

Cohen, A. A., and Bantz, C. (1984) *Social Conflicts in TV News: A Five-Nation Comparative Study.* Paper presented at the annual meeting of the International Communication Association, San Francisco, May.

Columbia Broadcasting System (1980) *Network Primetime Violence Tabulations for 1978–1979 Seasons.* New York: Columbia Broadcasting System.

Comstock, G. (1980) New emphases in research on the effects of television and film violence. In E. L. Plamer and A. Dorr (Eds), *Children and the Faces of Television.* New York: Academic Press.

Comstock, G. (1982) Violence in television content: An overview. In D. Pearl, L. Bouthilet, and J. Lazar (Eds), *Television and Behaviour: Ten Years of Scientific Progress and Implications for the Eighties*, (pp. 108–125). Rockville, MD: National Institute of Mental Health.

Condry, J. (1989). *The Psychology of Television.* Hilldale, NJ: Lawrence Erlbaum Associates.

Couch, C. J. (1968) Collective behaviour: An examination of some stereotypes. *Social Problems, 15*, 310–322.

Cumberbatch, G., and Howitt, D. (1989) *A Measure of Uncertainty: The Effects of the Mass Media.* London: John Libbey.

Cumberbatch, G., Jones, I., and Lee, M. (1988) Measuring violence on television. *Current Psychology; Research and Reviews, 7*(1), 10–25.

Cumberbatch, G., Lee, M., Hardy, G., and Jones, I. (1987) *The Portrayal of Violence on British Television: A Content Analysis.* Applied Psychology Division, Aston University.

Cumberbatch, G., McGregor, R., Brown, B., and Morrisson, D. (1985) *Television News and the Miners' Strike.* Unpublished report, Aston University/Broadcasting Research Unit.

Dale, E. (1935) *The Content of Motion Pictures.* New York: Macmillan.

Danielson, W., Lasorsa, D., Wartella, E., Whitney, C., Campbell, S., Hadda, S., Klijn, M., Lopez, R., and Olivarez, A. (1996) Television violence in 'reality' programming: University of Texas, Austin study, in *National Television Violence Study: 1994–95 – Executive papers*, (pp. II–1 to II–55). Los Angeles, CA: Mediascope, Inc.

Davis, M. H., Hull, J. G., Young, R. D., and Warren, G. G. (1987) Emotional reactions to dramatic film stimuli: The influence of cognitive and emotional empathy. *Journal of Personality and Social Psychology, 52*, 126–133.

Diener, E., and De Four, D. (1978) Does television violence enhance programme popularity? *Journal of Personality and Social Psychology, 36*, 333–341.

Diener, E. and Woody, L.W. (1981) TV violence and viewer liking. *Communication Research, 8*, 281–306.

Dominick, J. R. (1973) Crime and law enforcement in prime-time television. *Public Opinion Quarterly, 37*, 243–250.

Donnerstein, E. (1980) Aggressive erotica and violence against women. *Journal of Personality and Social Psychology, 39*, 269–277.

Donnerstein, E., and Berkowitz, L. (1981) Victim reactions to aggressive erotic film as a factor in violence against women. *Journal of Personality and Social Psychology, 41*, 710–724.

Dorr, A. (1983) No shortcuts to judging reality. In J. Bryant and D. R. Anderson (Eds), *Children's Understanding of Television: Research on Attention and Comprehension*. New York: Academic Press.

Drabman, R. S., and Thomas, M. H. (1974) Does media violence increase children's toleration of real-life aggression? *Developmental Psychology, 10*, 418–421.

Duval, R. (1995) Violence: The right agenda. *Spectrum*, Winter, 20–21.

Dymond, R. F. (1949) A scale for measurement of empathetic ability. *Journal of Consulting Psychology, 14*, 127–133.

Eisenstein, S. (1949) *Film Form* (trans. Jay Levda). New York: Harcourt, Brace and World.

Eleey, M. F., Gerbner, G., and Tedesco, N. (1972a) Apples, oranges, and the kitchen sink: An analysis and guide to the comparison of 'violence ratings'. *Journal of Broadcasting, 17*(1), 21–31.

Eleey, M. F., Gerbner, G., and Tedesco, N. (1972b) Validity indeed! *Journal of Broadcasting, 17*(1), 34–35.

Elkind, D. (1981) *The Hurried Child*. Menlo Park, CA: Addison-Wesley.

Erikson, E. H. (1977) *Toys and Reasons*. New York: W. W. Norton.

Fein, G. G. (1981) Pretend play: An integrative review. *Child Development, 52*, 1095–1118.

Fenichel, O. (1954) *The Psychoanalytic Theory of Neurosis*. New York: Norton.

Fernie, D. E. (1981) *Ordinary and Extraordinary People: Children's Understanding of Television and Real-Life Models*. Paper presented at the Society for Research in Child Development Biennial Meeting, Boston, MA.

Feshbach, N. D. (1978) Studies of empathetic behaviour in children. In B. Maher (Ed.), *Progress in Experimental Personality Research* (Vol. 8, pp. 1–47). New York: Academic Press.

Feshbach, S. (1972) Reality and fantasy in filmed violence. In J. P. Murray, E. A. Rubinstein and G. A. Comstock (Eds), *Television and Social Behaviour, Vol. 2., Television and Social Learning* (pp. 318–345). Washington, DC: US Government Printing Office.

Feshbach, S., Stiles, W.B., and Bitter, E. (1967) Reinforcing effect of witnessing aggression. *Journal of Research in Personality, 2*, 133–129.

Findahl, O., and Hoijer, B. (1976) *Fragments of Reality: An Experiment with News and TV Visuals*. Stockholm: Swedish Broadcasting Corporation, Audience and Programme Research Department.

Foster, J. (1930) Play activities of children in the first six grades. *Child Development, 1*(3), 248–254.

Freedman, J. L. (1984) Effect of television violence on aggressiveness. *Psychological Bulletin, 96*, (2), 227–246.

Friedrich-Cofer, L. K., and Stein, A. H. (1986) Television violence and aggression: The debate continues. *Psychological Bulletin, 100* (3), 364–371.

French, J., and Pena, S. (1991) Children's hero play of the twentieth century: Changes resulting from television's influence. *Child Study Journal, 21*, 79–94.

French, J., Pena, S., and Holmes, R. (1987) The superhero TV dilemma. *The Newsletter of Parenting, 10*(1), 8–9.

Freud, S. (1950) *Group Psychology and the Analysis of the Ego* (trans. J. Strachey). New York: Bantam Books. (Original work published 1921.)

Freud, S. (1964) New introductory lectures of psycho-analysis. In J. Strachey (Ed. and trans.) *The Standard Edition of the Complete Psychological Works of Sigmund Freud* (Vol. 22, pp. 7–182). London: Hogarth Press. (Original work published 1933.)

Galloway, S. (1993) US rating system: Sex before violence. *Hollywood Reporter*, 27 July.

Gamson, W. A., and McEvoy, J. (1972) Police violence and its public support. In J. F. Short and M. E. Wolfgang (Eds), *Collective Violence*. Chicago: Aldine.

Gauntlett, D. (1995) *Moving Experiences: Understanding Television's Influences and Effects*. London: John Libbey.

Geen, R. G. (1975) The meaning of observed violence: Real versus fictional violence and consequent effects on aggression and emotional arousal. *Journal of Research in Personality, 9*, 270–281.

Geen, R. G., and Rakosky, J.J. (1973) Interpretations of observed aggression and their effect on GSR. *Journal of Experimental Research in Personality, 6*, 289–292.

Gerbner, G. (1972) Violence in television drama: Trends and symbolic functions. In G. A. Comstock and E. A. Rubinstein (Eds), *Television and Social Behaviour, Vol. 1, Media Content and Control* (pp. 28–187). Washington, DC: US Government Printing Office.

Gerbner, G. (1988) *Violence and Terror in the Mass Media*. Reports and papers on mass communication, No. 102. Paris: UNESCO.

Gerbner, G., and Gross, L. (1976) Living with television: The violence profile. *Journal of Communication, 26*, 173–199.

Gerbner, G., Eleey, M.F., and Tedesco, N. (1972) *The Violence Index: A rating of Various Aspects of Dramatic Violence on Prime-Time Network Television, 1967 through 1970*. Philadelphia: Annenberg School of Comunications, research report.

Gerbner, G., Gross, L., Eleey, M. E., Jackson-Beeck, M., Jeffries-Fox, S., and Signorielli, N. (1977) Television violence profile No. 8: The highlights. *Journal of Communication, 27*, 171–180.

Gerbner, G., Gross, L., Jackson-Beeck, M., Jeffries-Fox, S., and Signorielli, N. (1978) Cultural indicators: Violence profile No. 9. *Journal of Communication, 28*, 176–207.

Gerbner, G., Gross, L., Signorielli, N., Morgan, M., Jackson- Beeck, M. (1979) The demonstration of power: Violence profile No. 10. *Journal of Communication, 29*, 177–196.

Gerbner, G., Gross, L., Morgan, M., and Signorielli, N. (1980) The 'mainstreaming' of America: Violence profile No. 11. *Journal of Communication, 30*, 10–29.

Gerbner, G., Gross, L., Morgan, M., and Signorielli, N. (1986) Living with television: The dynamics of the cultivation process. In J. Bryant and D. Zillmann (Eds), *Perspectives on Media Effects* (pp. 17–40). Hillsdale, NJ: Lawrence Erlbaum Associates.

Ginpil, S. (1976) Violent and dangerous acts on New Zealand television. *New Zealand Journal of Educational Studies*, 152–157.

Glasgow University Media Group (1976) *Bad News*. London: Routledge and Kegan Paul.

Goranson, R. E. (1969) A review of recent literature on psychological effects of media portrayals of violence. In R. K. Baker and S. J. Ball (Eds), *Violence and the Media: A Staff Report to the National Commission on the Causes and Prevention of Violence* (pp. 395–413). Washington, DC: US Government Printing Office.

Gordon, D. R., and Ibson, T. L. (1977) Content analysis of the news media: Radio. *Report of the Royal Commission on Violence in the Communications Industry, Vol. 3, Violence in Television, Films and News* (pp. 677–703). Toronto, Canada: The Royal Commission.

Gordon, D. R., and Singer, P. D. (1977) Content analysis of the news media: Newspapers and television. *Report of the Royal Commission on Violence in the Communications Industry, Vol. 3, Violence in Television, Films and News*. Toronto, Canada: The Royal Commission.

Greenberg, B. (1974) Gratifications of television viewing and their correlates for British children. In J. Blumler and E. Katz (Eds), *The Uses of Mass Communication. Current Perspectives on Gratifications Research*. Sage Annual Reviews of Communications Research, Vol. 3. Beverly Hills, CA: Sage.

Greenberg, B., and Gordon, T. (1972a) Perceptions of violence in television pro-
grammes: Critics and the public. In G.A. Comstock and E. A. Rubinstein (Eds),
Television and Social Behaviour, Vol. 1, Media Content and Control (pp. 244–258),
Rockville, MD: National Institute of Mental Health.

Greenberg, B., and Gordon, T. F. (1972b) Social class and racial differences in
children's perceptions of television violence. In G. A. Comstock, E. A. Rubinstein,
and J. P. Murray (Eds), *Television and Social Behaviour, Vol. 5. Television's
Effects: Further Explorations* (pp. 185–210). Rockville, MD: National Institute of
Mental Health.

Greenberg, B., and Gordon, T. F. (1972c) Children's perception of television
violence: A replication. In G. A. Comstock, E. A. Rubinstein, and J. P. Murray
(Eds), *Television and Social Behaviour, Vol. 5. Television's Effects: Further
Explorations* (pp. 211–230). Rockville, MD: National Institute of Mental
Health.

Greenberg, B. S., and Reeves, B. (1974) Children and the perceived reality of television. *Journal of Social Issues, 4*, 86–97.

Greenberg, B., Edison, R., Korzenny, F., Fernandez-Collado, C., and Atkin,
C. (1980) *Life on Television.* Norwood, NJ: Ablex.

Guddemi, M. P. (1986) The effects of television on children's play themes. Doctoral
dissertation, University of Texas, 1985. *Dissertation Abstracts International, 46*,
3243A.

Gunter, B. (1981) Measuring television violence: A review and suggestions for a new
analytical perspective. *Current Psychological Reviews, 1*, 91–112.

Gunter, B. (1983a) Personality and perceptions of harmful and harmless TV violence.
Personality and Individual Differences, 4, 665–670.

Gunter, B. (1983b) Do aggressive people prefer violent television? *Bulletin of the
British Psychological Society, 36*, 166–168.

Gunter, B. (1985) *Dimensions of Television Violence.* Aldershot, UK: Gower.

Gunter, B. (1987) *Television and the Fear of Crime.* London: John Libbey.

Gunter, B. (1995) Understanding the appeal of TV game shows. *Medien Psychologie,
7*, June, 87–106.

Gunter, B. (1997) An audience-based approach to assessing programme quality. In
P. Winterhoff-Spurk, and T. van der Voort (Eds), *New Horizons in Media Psychology* (pp. 11–34). Westdeutscher Verlag.

Gunter, B., and Furnham, A. (1984) Perceptions of television violence: Effects of
programme genre and physical form. *British Journal of Social Psychology, 23*, 155–
184.

Gunter, B., and McAleer, J. (1990) *Children and Television: The One-Eyed Monster?*
London: Routledge.

Gunter, B., and Wakshlag, J. (1986) Television viewing and perceptions of crime
among London residents. In P. Drummond and R. Paterson (Eds), *Television and
its Audience: International Research Perspectives* (pp. 191–209). London: BFI
Publishing.

Gunter, B., and Wober, M. (1988) *Violence on Television: What the Viewers Think.*
London: John Libbey.

Gunter, B., and Wober, M. (1993) The Gulf crisis and television: The Public's
response in Britain. In B. Greenberg and W. Gantz. (Eds), *Desert Storm and the
Mass Media* (pp. 281–298). Cresskill, NJ: Hampton Press.

Gunter, B., McAleer, J., and Clifford, B. (1991) *Children's Views about Television.*
Aldershot, UK: Avebury.

Gunter, B., Sancho-Aldridge, J. and Winstone, P. (1994) *Television: The Public's
View – 1993.* London: John Libbey.

Gurevitch. M. (1972) The structure and content of television broadcasting in four
countries: An overview. In G. A. Comstock and E. A. Rubinstein (Eds), *Television*

and Social Behaviour, Vol. 1, Media Content and Control (pp. 374–385). Washington, DC: US Government Printing Office.

Haines, H. (1983) *Violence on Television: A Report on the Mental Health Foundation's Media Watch Survey*. Mental Health Foundation of New Zealand, Auckland.

Hall, S. (1973) A world at one with itself. In S. Cohen and J. Young (Eds), *The Manufacture of News*. London: Constable.

Halloran, J. D., and Croll, P. (1972) Television programmes in Great Britain: Content and control. In G. A. Comstock and E. A. Rubinstein (Eds), *Television and Social Behaviour, Vol. 1, Media Content and Control* (pp. 415–492). Washington, DC: US Government Printing Office.

Hapkiewicz, W. G., and Stone, R. D. (1974) The effect of realistic versus imaginary aggressive models on children's interpersonal play. *Child Study Journal, 4*(2), 47–58.

Hartley, R., Frank, L., and Goldenson, R. (1952) *Understanding Children's Play*. London: Routledge and Kegan Paul.

Hartmann, D. P. (1969) Influence of symbolically modelled instrumental aggression and pain cues on aggressive behaviour. *Journal of Personality and Social Psychology, 11*, 280–288.

Hawkins, R. P. (1977) The dimensional structure of children's perceptions of television reality. *Communication Research, 4*(3), 299–320.

Himmelweit, H. T., Oppenheim, A. N., and Vince, P. (1958) *Television and the Child: An Empirical Study of the Effect of Television on the Young*. London: Oxford University Press.

Hodge, B., and Tripp, D. (1986) *Children and Television*, Cambridge, UK: Polity Press.

Hoffman, M. L. (1977) Empathy, its development and prosocial implications. In H.E. Howe, Jr. (Ed.), *Nebraska Symposium on Motivation* Vol. 25, pp. 169–217. Lincoln: University of Nebraska Press.

Hoffman-Bustamente, D. (1973) The nature of female criminality. *Issues in Criminology, 8*, 117–136.

Holsti, O. R. (1969) *Content Analysis for the Social Sciences and Humanities*. Reading, MA: Addison-Wesley.

Howitt, D. and Cumberbatch, G. (1974) Audience perceptions of violent television content. *Communications Research, 1*, 204–223.

Hoyt, J. (1967) *Vengeance and Self-deferral as Justification for Filmed Aggression*. Unpublished masters dissertation, Madison, WI: University of Wisconsin.

Iwao, S., de Sola Pool, I., and Hagiwara, S. (1981) Japanese and US media: Some cross-cultural insights into TV violence. *Journal of Communication, 31*(2), 28–36.

Jennings, C. M., and Gillis-Olion, M. (1980) *The Impact of Television Cartoons on Child Behaviour*. Paper presented at annual meeting of the National Association for the Education of Young Children, Atlanta, GA. (ERIC Document Reproduction Service No. 194–184.)

Jo, E., and Berkowitz, L. (1994) A priming effect analysis of media influences: An update. In J. Bryant and D. Zillmann (Eds), *Media Effects* (pp. 43–60). Hillsdale, NJ: Lawrence Erlbaum Associates.

ITC (1991) *The ITC Programme Code*. London: Independent Television Commission.

Kahn, R. L. (1972) The justification of violence: Social problems and social issues. *Journal of Social Issues, 28*, 155–172.

Kaplan, R. M., and Singer, R. D. (1976) Television violence and viewer aggression: A reexamination of the evidence. *Journal of Social Issues, 32*(4), 35–70.

Katz, R. L. (1963) *Empathy: Its Nature and Uses*. Glencoe, IL: The Free Press.

Kelman, H. C. (1961) Processes of opinion change. *Public Opinion Quarterly, 25*, 57–78.

Kostelnik, M. J., Whiren, A. P., and Stein, L. C. (1986) Living with He-Man – Managing superhero fantasy play. *Young Children, 41*(4), 3–9.

Krippendorf, K. (1980) *Content Analysis: An Introduction to its Methodology*. Beverly Hills, CA: Sage.

Kunkel, D., Wilson, B. J., Linz, D., Potter, J., Donnerstein, E., Smith, S.L., Blumenthal, E. and Gray, T. (1996a) Violence in television programming overall: University of California, Santa Barbara study, in *National Television Violence Study: 1994–95 – Executive Papers* (pp. I–1 to I–172). Los Angeles, CA: Mediascope, Inc.

Kunkel, D., Wilson, B. J., Potter, J., Linz, D., Donnerstein, E., Smith, S. L., Blumenthal, E., and Gray, T. (1996b) *Content Analysis of Entertainment Television: Implications for Public Policy*. Paper presented at the Duke University Conference on Media Violence and Public Policy in the Media in Durham, NC, 27–29 June.

Lanyi, D. L. (1984) Comic books and authority: An interview with 'Stainless Steve' Engelhart. *Journal of Popular Culture, 18*(2), 139–146.

Larsen, O. N., Gray, L. N., and Fortis, J. G. (1963) Goals and goal achievement in television content: Models for anomie. *Sociological Inquiry, 33*, 180–196.

Lehman, H. C., and Witty, P. A. (1927) *The Psychology of Play Activities*. New York: A.S. Barns.

Leyens, J. P., and Parke, R. D. (1975) Aggressive slides can induce a weapons effect. *European Journal of Social Psychology, 5*, 229–236.

Liebert, R. M, and Baron, R. A. (1972) Some immediate effects of televised violence on children's behaviour. *Developmental Psychology, 6*, 469–475.

Lindlof, T. R. (1988) Media audiences as interpretive communities. In J. A. Anderson (Ed.) *Communication Yearbook 11* (pp. 81– 107). Beverly Hills, CA: Sage.

Linton, J. M., and Jowitt, G. S. (1977) A content analysis of feature films. *Report to the Royal Commission on Violence in the Communications Industry, Vol. 3, Violence in Television, Films and News* (pp. 574–580). Toronto, Canada, The Royal Commission.

Linz, D., Donnerstein, E., and Penrod, S. (1984) The effects of multiple exposures to filmed violence against women. *Journal of Communication, 34*(3), 130–147.

Linz, D., Donnerstein, E., and Penrod, S. (1987) Sexual violence in the mass media: Social psychological implications. In P. Shower and C. Hendick (Eds), *Review of Personality and Social Psychology, Vol. 7*, pp. 95–123. Beverly Hills, CA: Sage.

Linz, D., Donnerstein, E. and Penrod, S. (1988) Effects of long-term exposure to violent and sexually degrading depictions of women. *Journal of Personality and Social Psychology, 55* (5), 758–768.

Malamuth, N. M. (1981) Rape fantasies as a function of exposure to violent sexual stimuli. *Archives of Sexual Behaviour, 10*, 33–47.

Malamuth, N. M. (1986) Aggression against women: Cultural and individual causes. In N. M. Malamuth and E. Donnerstein (Eds), *Pornography and Sexual Aggression* (pp. 19-52). Orlando, FL: Academic Press.

Malamuth, N. M., and Check, J. V. P. (1981) The effects of mass media exposure on acceptance of violence against women: A field experiment. *Journal of Research in Personality, 15*, 436–446.

Malamuth, N. M., and Donnerstein, E. (Eds) (1986) *Pornography and Sexual Aggression*. Orlando, FL: Academic Press.

McCann, T. E., and Sheehan, P. W. (1985) Violence content in Australian television. *Australian Psychologist, 20*(1), 33–42.

McGlynn, R. P., Megas, J. C., and Benson, D. H. (1976) Sex and race as factors affecting the attribution of insanity in a murder trial. *Journal of Psychology, 93*, 93–99.

Mediascope, Inc. (1996) *National Television Violence Study: Executive Summary: 1994–95*. Los Angeles, CA: Mediascope, Inc.

Mees, U. (1990) Constitutive elements of the concept of human aggression. *Aggressive Behaviour, 16*, 285–295.

Mehrabian, A., and Epstein, N. (1972) A measure of emotional empathy. *Journal of Personality, 40*, 515–543.

Menon, V. (1993) Violence on television: Asian data for an Asian standard. *Intermedia, 21*(6), 40–41.

Meyer, T. P. (1972) Effects of viewing justified and unjustified real film violence. *Journal of Personality and Social Psychology, 23*, 21–30.

Mischel, W., and Liebert, R. M. (1967) The role of power in the adoption of self-reward patterns. *Child Development, 38*, 673–683.

Morley, D. (1981) The 'Nationwide Audience': A critical postscript. *Screen Education*, No. 39.

Morrisson, D. (1992) *Television and the Gulf War*. London: John Libbey.

Morrisson, D. (1993a) The idea of violence. In A. M. Hargrave (Ed.) *Violence in Factual Television: Broadcasting Standards Council Annual Review 1993* (pp. 124–129). London: John Libbey.

Morrisson, D. (1993b) *The Viewers' View of Violence: Attitudes to Violence in Relation to Television Guidelines*. Leeds: Leeds University Institute of Communication Studies, Report to the British Broadcasting Corporation.

Murdock, G. (1973) Political deviance: The press presentation of a militant mass demonstration. In S. Cohen and J. Young (Eds), *The Manufacture of News*. London: Constable.

Mustonen, A., and Pulkkinen, L. (1993) Aggression in television programmes in Finland. *Aggressive Behaviour, 19*, 175–183.

National Association for Better Broadcasting (1969) Television for the family. *Better Radio and Television* (newsletter). Los Angeles: National Association for Better Broadcasting.

Neale, S. (1983) *Genre*. London: British Film Institute.

Noble, G. (1975) *Children in Front of the Small Screen*. London: Constable.

Osborn, D. K., and Endsley, R. C. (1971) Emotional reactions of young children to TV violence. *Child Development, 42*, 321–331.

Paley, V. G. (1984) *Boys and Girls – Superheroes in the Doll Corner*. Chicago: University of Chicago Press.

Perigard, M. A. (1985) Death of the superheroes: My turn. *Newsweek*, 6 November, p. 15.

Perloff, R., Brown, J., and Miller, M. (1982) Mass media and sex-typing: Research perspectives and policy implications. *International Journal of Women's Studies, 5*, 265–273.

Potter, W. J. (1986) Perceived reality and the cultivation hypothesis. *Journal of Broadcasting and Electronic Media, 30*, 159–174.

Potter, W. J., and Ware, W. (1987) An analysis of the contexts of antisocial acts on prime-time television. *Communication Research, 14*, 664–686.

Potter, J., Linz, D., Wilson, B. J., Kunkel, D., Donnerstein, E., Smith, S.L., Blumenthal, E., and Gray, T. (1996) *Content Analysis of Entertainment Television: New Methodological Developments*. Paper presented at the Duke University Conference on Media Violence and Public Policy in the Media, Durham, NC, 27–29 June.

Rarick, D. L., Townsend, J. E., and Boyd, D. A. (1973) Adolescent perceptions of police: Actual and as depicted in TV drama. *Journalism Quarterly, 50*, 438–446.

Reeves, B. (1978) Perceived TV reality as a predictor of children's social behaviour. *Journalism Quarterly, 55*, 682–689.

Reeves, B., and Greenberg, B. (1977) Children's perceptions of television characters. *Human Communication Research, 3*, 113–127.

Reeves, B., and Lometti, G. (1979) The dimensional structure of children's perceptions of television characters. A replication. *Human Communication Research, 5*, 247–256.

Remmers, H. H. (1954) *Four Years of New York Television: 1951–1954*. Urbana, IL: National Association of Educational Broadcasters.

Rogers, C. S., and Sawyers, J. K. (1988) *Play in the Lives of Children*. Washington, DC: NAEYC.

Rose, B. G. (1985) *TV Genres: A Handbook and Reference Guide*. Westport, CT: Greenwood Press.

Rowland, W. D. (1983) *The Politics of TV Violence: Policy Uses of Communication Research*. Beverly Hills, CA: Sage.

Ryall, T. (1979) The notion of genre. *Screen, 11* (2).

Saltz, E., Dixon, D., and Johnson, J. (1970) Training disadvantaged preschoolers on various fantasy activities: Effects on cognitive functioning and impulse control. *Child Development, 48*, 367–380.

Sanders, G. S. and Baron, R. S. (1973) Pain cues and uncertainty as determinants of aggression in a situation involving repeated instigation. *Journal of Personality and Social Psychology, 32* (3), 495–502.

Scheler, M. (1913) *Zur Phanomenologie und Theorie der Sympathiegefuhle und von Liebe und Hass*. [On the phenomenology and theory of feelings of love and hate]. Hall A. S.: Niemeyer.

Schmidt, G. (1975) Male–female differences in sexual arousal and behaviour during and after exposure to sexually explicit stimuli. In E.A. Rubinstein, R. Geen and E. Brecher (Eds), *New Directions in Sex Research*. New York: Plenum Press.

Schmutte, G. T. and Taylor, S. P. (1980) Physical aggression as a function of alcohol and pain feedback. *Journal of Social Psychology, 110*, 235–244.

Schramm, W., Lyle, J., and Parker, E. B. (1961) *Television in the Lives of Our Children*. Stanford: Stanford University Press.

Scott, W. A. (1955) Reliability of content analysis: The case of nominal scale coding. *Public Opinion Quarterly, 19*, 321–325.

Shaw, I., and Newell, D. (1972) *Violence on Television: Programme Content and Viewer Perception*. London: British Broadcasting Corporation.

Shearer, A. (1991) *Survivors and the Media*. Broadcasting Standards Council Research Monograph Series: 2. London: John Libbey.

Shinar, D., Parnes, P., and Caspi, D. (1972) Structure and content of television broadcasting in Israel. In G. A. Comstock and E. A. Rubinstein (Eds), *Television and Social Behaviour, Vol. 1, Media Content and Control*. Rockwell, MD: National Institute of Mental Health.

Signorielli, N. (1981) Content analysis: More than just counting minorities. In H. Myrick and C. Keegan (Eds), *In Search of Diversity: Symposium on Minority Audiences and Programming Research*. Washington, DC: Corporation for Public Broadcasting.

Signorielli, N. (1984) The demography of the television world. In G. Melischek, K. E. Rosengren, and J. Stappers. (Eds), *Cultural Indicators: An International Symposium*. Vienna, Austria: Austrian Academy of Sciences.

Signorielli, N. (1990) Television's mean and dangerous world: A continuation of the Cultural Indicators perspective. In N. Signorielli and M. Morgan (Eds), *Cultivation Analysis: New Directions in Media Effects Research*. Newbury Park, CA: Sage.

Signorielli, N. (1993) Television, the portrayal of women, and children's attitudes. In G. L. Berry and J. K. Asamen (Eds), *Children and Television: Images in a Changing Sociocultural World*. Newbury Park, CA: Sage.

Signorielli, N., Gross, L., and Morgan, M. (1982) Violence in television programmes: Ten years later. In D. Pearl, L. Bouthilet, and J. Lazar (Eds), *Television and Behaviour: Ten Years of Scientific Progress and Implications for the Eighties, Vol. 2* (pp. 158–173). Rockville, MD: National Institute of Mental Health.

Singer, J. L., and Singer, D. G. (1981) *Television, Imagination and Aggression: A Study of Preschoolers*. Hillsdale, NJ: Lawrence Erlbaum Associates.

Smith, A. (1971) *The Theory of Moral Sentiments*. New York: Garland. (Original work published 1759.)

Smith, P. K. (1994) The war play debate. In J. H. Goldstein (Ed.), *Toys, Play and Child Development* (pp. 67–84). Cambridge: Cambridge University Press.

Smythe, D. W. (1954) *Three Years of New York Television: 1951–1953*. Urbana, IL: National Association of Educational Broadcasters.

Sousa, C., and Schneiderman, J. (1986) Preschoolers and superheroes – A dangerous duo. *Early Years*, December, 75–77.

Stein, A. H., and Friedrich, L. K. (1975) The effects of television content on young children. In A. D. Pick (Ed.) *Minnesota Symposia on Child Psychology* (Vol. 9). Minnesota: University of Minnesota Press.

Stein, E. (1970) *On the Problem of Empathy* (2nd edn). The Hague: Nijhoff.

Stewart, D. E. (1983) *The Television Family – A Content Analysis of the Portrayal of Family Life in Prime Time Television*. Melbourne: Institute of Family Studies.

Stocking, S. H., Sapolsky, B. S., and Zillmann, D. (1977) Sex discrimination in prime time humour. *Journal of Broadcasting, 21*, 447–457.

Stotland, E. (1969) Exploratory investigations of empathy. In L. Berkowitz (Ed.), *Advances in Experimental Social Psychology* (Vol. 4, pp. 271–314). New York: Academic Press.

Stotland, E., Mathews, K. E., Jr., Sherman, S. E., Hansson, R. O., and Richardson, B. Z. (1978) *Empathy, Fantasy, and Helping*. Beverly Hills, CA: Sage.

Sutherland, E. H., and Cressey, D. R. (1974) *Principles in Criminology*. Philadelphia/New York: Lippincott.

Sutton-Smith, B., and Rosenberg, B. G. (1961) Sixty years of historical change in game preferences of American children. *The Journal of American Folklore, 74*, 17–46.

Tagiuri, R. (1969) Person perception. In G. Lindzey and E. Aronson (Eds), *The Handbook of Social Psychology: Vol. 3. The Individual in a Social Context* (2nd. edn, pp. 395–449). Reading, MA: Addison-Wesley.

Tannenbaum, P. H. (1971) Emotional arousal as a mediator of erotic communication effects. In *Technical Report of the Commission on Obscenity and Pornography*, Vol. 8. Washington, DC: US Government Printing Office.

Taylor, H., and Dozier, C. (1983) Television violence, African-Americans and social control, 1956–1976. *Journal of Black Studies, 14*(2), 107–136.

Thomas, M. H. and Tell, P. M. (1974) Effects of viewing real versus fantasy violence upon interpersonal aggression. *Journal of Research in Personality, 8*, 153–160.

Tuchman, G. (1978) *Making News: A Study in the Construction of Reality*. New York: The Free Press.

Tucker, S. (1985) Facets – Today's kids and hero worship: Who can they look up to? *English Journal, 74*, 2–23.

Tyler, T. R. (1980) The impact of directly and indirectly experienced events: The origin of crime-related judgements and behaviours. *Journal of Personality and Social Psychology, 39*, 13–28.

Tyler, T. R., and Rasinski, K. (1984) Comparing psychological images of the social perceiver: Role of perceived informativeness, memorability and effect in mediating the impact of criminal victimization. *Journal of Personality and Social Psychology, 46*, 308–329.

Van der Voort, T. H. A. (1986) *Television Violence: A Child's Eye View*. Amsterdam, Holland: Elsevier Science Publishers.

Walters, R. H., and Thomas, E. L. (1963) Enhancement of punitiveness by visual and audiovisual displays. *Canadian Journal of Psychology, 17*, 244–255.

Walters, R. H., Thomas, E. L., and Acker, C. W. (1962) Enhancement of punitive behaviour by audiovisual displays. *Science, 136*, 872–873.

Watson, C., Bassett, G., Lambourne, R., and Shuker, R. (1991) *Television Violence: An Analysis of the Portrayal of 'Violent Acts' on the Three New Zealand Broadcast Television Channels during the Week of 11th-17th February 1991*. Research project for the Broadcasting Standards Authority by the Educational Research and Development Centre, Massey University.

Wertham, F. (1954) Comic books . . . very funny! *Saturday Review of Literature*, May, p. 6.

Willeman, P. (1983) Presentation. In S. Neale (Ed.) *Genre*. London: British Film Institute.

Williams, T. M., Zabrack, M. L., and Joy, L. A. (1982) The portrayal of aggression on North American television. *Journal of Applied Social Psychology, 12*(5), 360–380.

Wilson, B. J., Donnerstein, E., Linz, D., Kunkel, D., Potter, J., Smith, S.L., Blumenthal, E., and Gray, T. (1996a) *Content Analysis of Entertainment Television: The Importance of Context*. Paper presented at the Duke University Conference on Media Violence and Public Policy in the Media, Durham, NC, 27–29 June.

Wilson, B. J., Smith, S.L., Linz, D., Potter, J., Donnerstein, E., Kunkel, D., Blumenthal, E. and Gray, T. (1996b) *Content Analysis of Entertainment Television: The 1994–95 Results*. Paper presented at the Duke University Conference on Media Violence and Public Policy in the Media, Durham, NC, 27–29 June.

Wimmer, R. D. and Dominick, J.R. (1994) *Mass Media Research: An Introduction* (4th edn). Belmont, CA: Wadsworth Publishing Company.

Wober, M. (1978) *The Need for News: Audience Attitudes towards Nine News Topics*. London: Independent Broadcasting Authority, Research Report.

Wober, M. (1982) *The Falklands: Some Systematic Data on Viewing Behaviour and Attitudes*. London: Independent Broadcasting Authority, Research Report.

Wober, M., and Gunter, B. (1988) *Television and Social Control*. Aldershot, UK: Avebury.

Wober, M. and Gunter, B. (1990) Fearstoppers. *Police Review*, 23 November, 2312–2313.

Yarian, S. (1975) The comic book hero, a cultural fantasy. Doctoral dissertation, Adelphi University, 1974. *Dissertation Abstracts International, 75*, 4144.

Zillmann, D. (1980) Anatomy of suspense. In P. H. Tannenbaum (Ed.), *The Entertainment Functions of Television* (pp. 133–163). Hillsdale, NJ: Lawrence Erlbaum Associates.

Zillmann, D. (1983) Mood management: Using entertainment to full advantage. In L. Donohew, H. E. Sypher, and E. T. Higgins (Eds), *Communication, Social Cognition and Affect* (pp. 147–171). Hillsdale, NJ: Lawrence Erlbaum Associates.

Zillmann, D., and Bryant, J. (1984) Effects of message exposure to pornography. In N. M. Malamuth and E. Donnerstein (Eds), *Pornography and Sexual Aggression* (pp. 115–138). Orlando, FL: Academic Press.

Zillmann, D., and Bryant, J. (1985) Affect, mood, and emotion as determinants of selective exposure. In D. Zillmann and J. Bryant (Eds), *Selective Exposure to Communication* (pp. 157–190). Hillsdale, NJ: Lawrence Erlbaum Associates.

Zillmann, D., and Bryant, J. (1991) Responding to comedy: The sense and nonsense in humour. In J. Bryant and D. Zillmann (Eds), *Responding to the Screen: Reception and Reaction Processes* (pp. 261–279). Hillsdale, NJ: Lawrence Erlbaum Associates.

Zillmann, D., and Cantor, J. R. (1976) A disposition theory of humour and birth. In A. J. Chapman and H. C. Foot (Eds), *Humour and Laughter: Theory, Research and Applications* (pp. 93–115). London: Wiley.

Zillmann, D., Hezel, R. T., and Medoff, N. J. (1980) The effect of affective states on selective exposure to television entertainment fare. *Journal of Applied Social Psychology, 10*, 323–339.

Author index

Subject index

accidental violence 11, 20, 22, 33, 42, 45, 53

action/adventure programmes 6, 10, 12, 15, 20, 25, 28–30, 38

acts of violence: aggressors and 141–2, 145, 291; on British television 29–31; in cartoons 246; character and audience reaction 136; in children's programmes 250–61, 263–7; consequences of 122–31, 133; as content analysis measurement 9–10, 17, 35, 205, 283–6; definition of 53; in dramatic fiction 176–81, 184–5, 187, 189, 192–3, 195–201, 203–4, 292–3; form of violence 80–90; genre and 164–7; in light entertainment 209–14, 216–18; motives and 118–22, 132; in news and factual programmes 228, 232–6, 238–9, 242–3; in other countries 19–28; quality of violence 289–90; quantity of 42–4, 46, 50, 62–5, 68–75; research and 46, 54, 57–60; scheduling 272–4, 276–9; settings 102–8; sexual 288–9; as stimulus of violence 79–82; victims and 148, 150–5

age: of aggressor 17, 140–3; of at-risk victims 291; of character 139–40, 156, 159; perceptions of violence and 36; research and 54, 59; of victim 148–52; victimization and 158; violence profile 13

age of aggressor/victim: in children's programmes 261–2, 268–9; in dramatic fiction 189, 193–4, 202; in light entertainment 221, 224; nature of violence and 85; in news and

factual programmes 241–3; in other countries 27

aggression: arousal and humour 206–7, 224; arousal and rape 188; audience levels 113–14, 121–2, 132; behavioural response 162, 292; cause–effect relationship 109–10; levels of 33–4; physical and verbal in factual programmes 229; play and 247–8, 269; superhero action-drama 246, 248; TV as trigger 76–7, 97–9, 280–1

aggressor/victim: in children's programmes 261–4, 268–9; content analysis 11, 16; in dramatic fiction 191, 193–5, 202–4; in light entertainment 221–2, 224; in news and factual programmes 243; perceptions of 6, 9; research 48, 51, 52, 54, 58–60; suffering 112–15; violence profile 13–14

aggressors: content analysis and 287; victims and 135–59, 290

Alien 3 126, 128, 130–1

alien beings 263, 269

ambition/power as motive 60, 117, 119–21, 132, 188, 219–20, 259–60, 268

American Cyborg: Steel Warrior 72, 126, 128, 130, 200

amount of violence *see* quantity of violence

animal as weapon 79, 91, 93, 95

animated characters 52–3, 263–4, 268

Annenberg School of Communication, University of Pennsylvania 7

anthropology 17

anthropomorphization 52

anticipatory empathy 115